Iliyana Krapova, Brian Joseph (Eds.)
Balkan Syntax and (Universal) Principles of Grammar

Trends in Linguistics
Studies and Monographs

Editor
Volker Gast

Editorial Board
Walter Bisang
Hans Henrich Hock
Natalia Levshina
Heiko Narrog
Matthias Schlesewsky
Amir Zeldes
Niina Ning Zhang

Editor responsible for this volume
Volker Gast

Volume 285

Balkan Syntax and (Universal) Principles of Grammar

Edited by
Iliyana Krapova
Brian Joseph

ISBN 978-3-11-070804-2
e-ISBN (PDF) 978-3-11-037593-0
e-ISBN (EPUB) 978-3-11-039337-8
ISSN 1861-4302

Library of Congress Control Number: 2018951331

Bibliographic information published by the Deutsche Nationalbibliothek
The Deutsche Nationalbibliothek lists this publication in the Deutsche Nationalbibliografie;
detailed bibliographic data are available on the Internet at http://dnb.dnb.de.

© 2020 Walter de Gruyter GmbH, Berlin/Boston
This volume is text- and page-identical with the hardback published in 2019.
Typesetting: Integra Software Services Pvt. Ltd.
Printing and binding: CPI books GmbH, Leck

www.degruyter.com

Contents

Brian D. Joseph and Iliyana Krapova
Introduction – Morpho-Syntactic Convergences and Current Linguistic Theory —— 1

Part I: Contact Phenomena, Causes and Types of Explanations

Petya Asenova
Balkan Syntax: Typological and Diachronic Aspects —— 13

Victor A. Friedman
Parallel Universes and Universal Parallels: Balkan Romani Evidential Strategies —— 37

Andrey N. Sobolev
Areal Typology and Balkan (Morpho-)Syntax —— 49

Jouko Lindstedt
Diachronic Regularities Explaining the Tendency towards Explicit Analytic Marking in Balkan Syntax —— 70

Part II: Balkan Syntax and Universal Principles of Grammar

Raúl Aranovich
Impersonal reflexives in Romance and Slavic: Contact effects in the Balkans —— 87

Andrea D. Sims and Brian D. Joseph
Morphology versus Syntax in the Balkan Verbal Complex —— 99

Iliyana Krapova and Guglielmo Cinque
Universal Constraints on Balkanisms. A Case Study: The absence of Clitic Climbing —— 151

Dalina Kallulli
Balkan Clitic Doubling Revisited: Micro-Variation, Typological Generalizations, and a True Universal —— 192

Lena Baunaz and Eric Lander
Cross-categorial Syncretism and Containment in Balkan and Slavic —— 218

Part III: Variation in the Sprachbund

Eleni Bužarovska and Liljana Mitkovska
Modal *habere*-Constructions in the Balkan Slavic Context —— 249

Gabriela Bîlbîie and Alexandru Mardale
The Romanian subjunctive from a Balkan perspective —— 278

Tomislav Sočanac
Subjunctive complements in Balkan languages: Problems of distribution —— 315

Language Index —— 337

Subject Index —— 339

Brian D. Joseph and Iliyana Krapova
Introduction – Morpho-Syntactic Convergences and Current Linguistic Theory

In this volume, which grew out of a workshop on Balkan morpho-syntax organized by the editors as part of 2013 annual meeting of Societas Linguistica Europaea, held in Split, Croatia, we reassess what is now known about balancing the effects of linguistic universals and language-particular elements of structure in various languages of the Balkans, especially in the wake of intense language contact in the region over centuries that has led to many convergent features in Balkan syntax, and in related matters of grammar, in particular with regard to morpho-syntax and the syntax-semantics interface. Such investigations shed light on the causes of Balkan convergence in these domains.

The convergent aspects of Balkan linguistic structure – known in the literature since Seliščev 1925 as 'Balkanisms' – are not just a random collection of acquired features (loan constructions, calques, syntactic borrowings, etc.) as can be the case with contact-induced innovations among two or more neighbouring dialects; rather, they are deeply integrated into the structure of some or all of the Balkan languages. Contact here has produced specific effects leading to a Sprachbund – a "language union"[1] or better understood as a "convergence zone" – which go beyond a simple areal explanation and raise a number of theoretical questions in such areas of study as diverse as contact linguistics, language variation, language change, typology, grammaticalization, and universal grammar, specifically:

a) What processes of **language contact can affect the syntax of languages?** Are they the same processes that affect other components of a language, e.g. borrowing, calquing, interference (transfer), etc., or are there syntax-specific processes, perhaps, e.g., code-switching, or processes specific to other domains of grammar?

b) **What types of linguistic structures are favored by bi- or multilingual speakers**, i.e., are they based on similarities or entirely new, or such that they can be identified more easily cross-linguistically? What are the structural

---

1 Trubetzkoy (1923) was the first to use such terminology, in his original Russian, *jazykovoj sojuz*, which translates rather literally into English as "linguistic union". However, connotations of the word *union* in English make this a less than felicitous term (e.g., a "linguistic union" like the Balkans is very different from, say, the *European Union*), so that the contributors to this volume, and most other scholars, also use the term *Sprachbund*, borrowed from the German.

conditions which facilitate innovations or retentions (the duel between innovative and the conservative tendencies)?

c) **Do usual processes of language change that affect other domains**, such as analogy or socially determined diffusion, **play a role in Balkan morpho-syntactic convergence?**

d) **Are all aspects of morpho-syntax equally prone to being affected in language contact** or do language universals "exempt" certain parts of the morphology and the syntax from contact effects? More specifically, which grammatical properties and distinctions (e.g. *pro*-drop, word order type, etc.) can be borrowed and which cannot be borrowed, if any?

Summarizing research results of the last two decades, the 12 papers in this volume, representing a variety of theoretical frameworks (contact linguistics, functional linguistics, typology, areal linguistics, and generative grammar), seek to provide a state-of-the art answer to these questions in relation to the main focus of the volume: exploring the nature and the effects of "universal" or more "deeply embedded" principles of syntax on morpho-syntactic convergences, in the formation and the diffusion of the common Balkan types, and their role in constraining the outcomes of language change in the Sprachbund situation. This issue receives multiple answers, combining insights from different frameworks and pointing towards a bridge-like understanding of language variation and language change at the crossroads between social factors underlying contact situations and the nature of possible grammars.

The empirical coverage in this volume presents varieties and phenomena that have not been considered in a broad Balkan and theoretical context before. Each section is built around a specific theoretical problem whose significance for the study of Balkan morpho-syntactic convergences and convergence in general is being evaluated by each paper.

In Part I, **Contact Phenomena, Causes and Types of Explanations**, first, **Petya Asenova** examines critically the relation between the European linguistic union and the Balkan Sprachbund, considered by some (e.g. Hock 1988, Heine and Kuteva 2006) to be a constitutive part of the former. She outlines a typology of Europeanisms vis-à-vis Balkanisms, an exercise that is methodologically particularly useful. In line with her own extensive work (cf. in particular Asenova 2002 [1989]), the author concludes that in the hierarchy of the linguistic system, primacy is given to morphology, and consequently that the characteristic features in a Sprachbund situation pertain to morphology and morpho-syntax, as the major Balkanisms do.

This part is also dedicated to the potential causes for convergences involving syntax across various Balkan languages, and specifically to those processes of language contact that affect the (morpho)-syntax of Balkan languages, as well as to the degree to which language contact interacts with parametric variation between Sprachbund languages in terms of both form and content. Different methodological solutions are proposed for the empirical phenomena under scrutiny, which for the most part constitute novel findings.

Victor Friedman's paper contributes to Bisang's (2004, 2006) argument in favor of an integrative approach to language change utilizing typology, dialectology, sociolinguistics, and contact linguistics. The author examines the use of the Slavic interrogative particle *li* in Arli Romani to mark dubitativity in declarative sentences and demonstrates how typological (universal) and areal (contact) explanations can be used together in a nuanced fashion, and without conflation, to account for language change in this case.

The next important question in this section is what can be borrowed and what cannot be borrowed in contact situations leading to convergence in syntactic properties. This issue is discussed in **Andrey Sobolev**'s paper in the light of the borrowability hierarchy and it is argued that features/functional content higher on the borrowability hierarchy should be amenable to a definition as a Balkanism, while features/functional content lower on the same hierarchy should be considered "anti-Balkanisms". The paper presents the author's views on the state of affairs in Balkan linguistics and presents theoretical, methodological and practical results he has obtained in the last decade in the field of comparative-historical and contrastive Balkan linguistics, especially with regard to (morpho-)syntax.

In a discussion of the effects of borrowing on the formation of the Balkan Sprachbund, **Jouko Lindstedt** widens the perspective of contact phenomena to diachrony and explores the relative degree of probability of two sociolinguistic scenarios, proposed by Trudgill (2011), that have arguably led to the establishment of the Balkan morpho-syntactic type, characterized by explicit analytic marking of grammatical features. Commenting on the degree of analytism of each of the Balkan language groups, and rejecting "simplification" and "complexification" as possible ways of characterizing the outcomes of language contact in the Balkans, he then goes on to propose a third kind of contact situation, namely adult-based long-term, stable, mutual and intense multilingualism, which he argues is directly related to the need for increasing 'intertranslatability' between the contact languages.

Part II, **Balkan Syntax and Universal Principles of Grammar**, is dedicated to the issue of whether syntactic convergence is a "deep" phenomenon, in which abstract elements and different levels of representation such as those posited in some syntactic theories come into play, or a strictly "surface" phenomenon, in which just overt strings of words and morphemes are involved and not any deeper apparatus underlying them. The papers in this section highlight the underlying tension between the two schools of thought: the "universal" (based on the theory of parameters and universal principles of grammar) and the "areal" (based on relative principles and contact-determined) and provide numerous insights into this complex matter.

Raúl Aranovich connects in his paper to the highly contentful proposals of this part by showing that the distribution of impersonal reflexive constructions in the Balkans represents a case in which language contact comes into (apparent) conflict with the theory of parameters. The author proposes an areal account, arguing that it provides a better explanation than Parameter Theory does for the (illusory) clustering of features found across impersonal reflexives, raising the question of how predictive formal principles of grammar are when dealing with language contact. The author's own proposal strongly favors a "compromise" solution according to which the transfer of superficial features from one language to another in situations of intense language contact can override the parameter settings of an otherwise "deep" Universal Grammar principle.

Andrea Sims and **Brian Joseph** take up the issue of the relation between syntax and morphology in accounting for the Balkan verbal complex in regard to the order of functional elements and their morphological and semantic content. Using the verbal complex as a testing ground, the authors argue for the hypothesis that morphologization processes proceed at different rates in different languages, depending on the particularities of the language or languages involved. They also discuss the ramifications of their proposal for the specific type of contact explanation that can be assumed for the formation of the verbal complex, and more broadly, for morphologization processes both specifically and generally within the boundaries of a Sprachbund.

Iliyana Krapova and **Guglielmo Cinque** address the question of why the phenomenon of clitic climbing is absent in the bona fide Balkan languages (even if present in the non-Balkan languages belonging to the same language families). In relating the issue to the absence (or reduction) of the infinitive, the authors argue that the apparently finite "subjunctive" that the Balkan languages have developed in order to replace the missing infinitive is in fact a more complex structure that covers three distinct categories: Restructuring (Raising), involving modal and aspectual verbs, Control, and Romance-like subjunctive constructions. In particular, they analyze the restructuring modal and aspectual verbs in terms of a monoclausal rather than a bi-clausal structure, arguing that monoclausality is independent of both the presence of an infinitive and clitic climbing, which is actually instantiated to a limited extent in some dialectal Balkan varieties. The authors eventually attempt an explanation for the lack of clitic climbing in standard Balkan languages in terms of a universal syntactic principle responsible for the "freezing" of the clitic in the post-particle position in which it shows up superficially.

Dalina Kallulli discusses another phenomenon, clitic doubling, that has close bearing on the issue of universal principles as driving forces behind grammaticalization. What distinguishes this paper from previous work on this much-researched topic is the proposed analogy with the phenomenon of differential object marking (DOM), which is argued to be another typological offspring of the same universal principle that guides the distribution of features relevant to both phenomena (prominence, specificity, topicality, etc.), namely the so-called D-hierarchy of Kiparsky (2008). The author also comments on some interesting consequences of this principle, such as the so-called "person case constraint" (PCC), whose effects extend beyond the Balkans and are thus to be seen as language-specific realizations of the ways in which the "universal" (in the sense of Universal Grammar) mitigates the "particular".

From a comparative perspective, finally, **Lena Baunaz** and **Eric Lander** offer a discussion of the nature of complementizers in the Balkan and Slavic languages and demonstrate points of systematic syncretisms between complementizers and demonstratives, and relative and *wh*-pronouns. The view that complementizers are internally complex items that can be decomposed into smaller units, as elements of a unique functional sequence, receives a strictly formal and novel explanation spelled out in the framework of the nanosyntax approach (developed at the University of Tromsø).

Part III, **Variation in the Sprachbund**, is dedicated to parametric and microparametric variation internal to the Sprachbund. The focus in the three papers is on the Balkan subjunctive, which is another of the most salient Balkan linguistic features and a complex area of comparative research extending over the last several decades. Parts of this chapter evaluate recent insights into the conclusions reached in the seminal work of Brian Joseph (1983)[2] and how they can be integrated into current frameworks of typology and generative linguistics. The Balkan subjunctive is more widely distributed than most of its cross-linguistic counterparts, and as a consequence is more semantically diverse. While this inevitably increases the theoretical difficulties related to reaching any type of cross-linguistic definition of the subjunctive mood as such, the area is a fruitful field of investigation since it opens a window to both the syntax-semantics as well as to the morphology-syntax interface. At the same time it raises important questions of contact and its effects on the language-particular realization of common developmental models.

Eleni Bužarovska and **Liljana Mitkovska**'s paper analyzes in great detail one type of modal construction (*habere* ('have'-based) constructions) in the

---

[2] Needless to say, this is the judgement of only one of the editors!

Balkans and focuses on its semantic variability and internal typology. In order to explain why Balkan Slavic has developed several Balkan features to a higher degree than the other Sprachbund languages, the authors conjecture that grammatical borrowing that favours change towards analytism may occur both when L1 speakers regularly use another language as well as when L2 speakers transfer features from their native languages.

Gabriela Bîlbîie and **Alexandru Mardale** discuss the Romanian subjunctive and its mixed Balkan-Romance character, drawing a distinction between, and studying the details of, main and embedded clause occurrences. They pay particular attention to the use of the subjunctive in main interrogative clauses, where there are cross-Balkan parallels, and also tackle the thorny question of whether the subjunctive marker in Romanian and other Balkan languages is a true complementizer or not.

Finally, **Tomislav Sočanac** seeks to explain the distribution of the Balkan subjunctive and the semantic diversity underlying some peculiar patterns not represented in apparently analogous structures outside of the Balkans. The analysis put forward in the paper develops out of the assumption of a unitary clause-type structure at the deeper level enriched, however, with a syntactic mechanism (structural truncation) to which the differences in pattern realization are attributed. At the same time, the importance of the syntax-semantics interface is highlighted whereby different complements are allowed to send different "chunks" of the basic subjunctive CP clause structure to the interface with semantics.

These studies, individually and collectively, make for a compelling view of morpho-syntax, syntactic change, and the languages of the Balkans, leaving little to say beyond what is included in the chapters that follow. Still, by way of concluding, it is fair to ask: Why the Balkans? Why should the focus of these studies of the interplay of universals and the particular in morpho-syntactic change take as its backdrop the peninsula that is southeastern Europe and is home to so many languages and now, so many nations? Is there something about the Balkans that makes this region a particularly useful venue for the languages that serve as the basis for this sort of study?

In principle, of course, the study of the syntax-semantics and syntax-morpho-syntax interfaces could be carried out on any language or any set of languages in any part of the world. Still, the Balkans do present some features that make it an ideal testing ground for especially the historical side of such study, but with interesting synchronic perspectives as well.

First, the Balkans show an interesting variety and mix of languages – there are representatives of five different branches of Indo-European (Albanian, Greek, Indic (via Romani), Italic (via Romance), and Slavic) and a non-Indo-European family (Turkic). Even if the language mix is skewed towards Indo-European, there is still great diversity of structure and history to reckon with here.

Second, especially with regard to the historical enterprise represented here but with synchronic relevance, the Balkans offer the researcher the ability to distinguish between various causes of similarities among languages, especially inheritance, contact, and universality. Hamp (1977: 279) has emphasized that the first two are complementary, not competing, "twin faces of diachronic linguistics", two key ways of understanding the sources of similarities and differences between languages. It is only possible to understand what has been caused by contact if we have a clear idea of what is inherited, and in converse fashion, it is only possible to determine what is inherited if we can eliminate contact-related similarities. Typological perspectives come into play as well here because of how they inform us as to the possibility of independent origin of a given feature in two or more languages; that is, typologically common features need not be inherited, and might reflect simply the ability of speakers to create structures out of existing material guided by universals.

Third, again primarily on the historical side of the ledger, we are in the fortunate position of having a very deep history involving most of the languages, in terms of both direct attestation and comparative evidence based on related languages. As for direct attestation, we have records of Greek since the 15th century BC (Mycenaean Greek) but also a wealth of material on Greek of the Classical and Hellenistic periods; for Balkan Romance, we have Latin, attested since the 7th century BC and with a vast amount of materials from the Classical era and beyond; in the case of Slavic, there are the Old Church Slavonic texts that date from the 9th century AD, but also some indirect testimony in the form of loanwords into the various languages, including Albanian, from the time the Slavs entered the Balkans in the 6th century; as for Indic and Romani, the evidence of Old Indic as seen in Sanskrit, with texts dating to about 1200 BC, and of Middle Indic (the Prākrits) provides a key historical basis for understanding the development of Romani; finally, as for Albanian, except for some earlier traces, it is attested substantially only via texts from the 16th century.[3] Our knowledge of the prehistory of Albanian especially, though the same can be said for the other languages, comes primarily from the Comparative Method and the way in which it allows for a reasonable "triangulation" of Albanian prehistory through comparisons with corresponding features of other Indo-European languages. As a result, even in the absence of direct attestation, comparative evidence gives a fairly clear

---

[3] The same can essentially be said for Turkish; while Old Turkic inscriptions are attested from the 8th century, the most relevant variety of Turkish for the Balkans — Ottoman Turkish — has texts only as early as roughly the 13th century.

picture of what the language was like before the intense contact leading to the Sprachbund.

Fourth, as noted in various places already, the Balkans show the effects of intense contact among speakers of different languages, and of multilingualism, a result of speaker contact. Friedman and Joseph (to appear, 2019) refer to the important effects in the Balkans of mutual multi-lateral multi-directional multilingualism,[4] and its role in shaping the languages of the Balkan Sprachbund. Contact and multilingualism bring out universals – language is stripped down to its essentials, and universal aspects of communication and structure come to the fore because the words and structures one is used to using with fellow speakers do not work with speakers of another language.

Thus in all these ways, the Balkans provide important insights into all of the leading themes of the studies in this volume: They allow us to tease apart the universal and the particular, the particular being especially where details of history, whether the genealogy sort of history or the contact sort of history, cannot be ignored. They show us, moreover, the value of paying attention to dialects and the relevance of geography, and the facts of concern here lend themselves well to showing the value of formalism in extending our understanding of structure. We thus invite the reader to share in what the Balkan languages have to offer on the intellectual front as far as linguistics is concerned.

Venice, Italy/Columbus, USA
9 June 2018

---

[4] Thus with their own "4-M model" in language contact (rivaling that of Myers-Scotton 1993, referring to four morpheme types and how they behave in contact situations).

References

Asenova, Petya. 2002 [1989]. *Balkansko ezikoznanie. Osnovni problem na balkanskija ezikov săjuz* [Balkan linguistics. Fundamental problems of the Balkan Linguistic Unionn]. Veliko Tărnovo:Faber.

Bisang, Walter. 2004. Dialectology and typology – an integrative perspective. Dialectology meets typology. *Dialect grammar from a crosslinguistic perspective*, ed. by Bernd Kortman, 11–45. Berlin: Mouton de Gruyter.

Bisang, Walter. 2006. Contact-induced convergence: Typology and areality. *Encyclopedia of Language and Linguistics*, ed. by Keith Brown, Vol. 3, 88–101. Oxford: Elsevier.

Friedman, Victor A. and Brian D. Joseph. To appear, 2019. *The Balkan Languages*. Cambridge: Cambridge University Press.

Hamp, Eric P. 1977. On Some Questions of Areal Linguistics. *Proceedings of the 3rd Annual Meeting of the Berkeley Linguistics Society*, ed. by K. Whistler et al., 279–282. Berkeley: Berkeley Linguistic Society.

Heine, Bernd and Tania Kuteva. 2006. *The changing languages of Europe*. Oxford: Oxford University Press.

Hock, Hans Henrich. 1988. Historical Implications of a Dialectological approach to Convergence. *Trends in Linguistics: Historical Dialectology*, ed. by Jacek Fisiak, 283–327. Berlin: Mouton de Gruyter.

Joseph, Brian D. 1983. *The Synchrony and Diachrony of the Balkan Infinitive: A Study in Areal, General, and Historical Linguistics*. Cambridge: Cambridge University Press [Reissued in paperback, 2009].

Kiparsky, Paul. 2008. Universals constrain change, change results in typological generalizations. In J. Good (ed.) *Linguistic universals and language change*, 23–53. Oxford: Oxford University Press.

Meyers-Scotton, Carol. 1993. *Duelling languages: Grammatical structure in codeswitching*. Oxford: Oxford University Press.

Seliščev, Aleksandr. 1925. Des traits linguistiques communs aux langues balkaniques: Un balkanisme ancien en bulgare. *Révue des études slaves* 5.38–57.

Trubetzkoy, Nikolai S. 1923. Vavilonskaja bašnja i smešenie jazykov. *Evrazijskij vremennik* 3.107–124.

Trudgill, Peter. 2011. *Sociolinguistic typology: Social determinants of linguistic complexity*. Oxford: Oxford University Press.

Part I: **Contact Phenomena, Causes and Types of Explanations**

Petya Asenova
Balkan Syntax: Typological and Diachronic Aspects

Abstract: According to the principles of Eurolinguistics, the Balkan linguistic union (BLU) forms part of the European linguistic union (SAE). The tendency to view the field of Balkan linguistics as a sub-field of Eurolinguistics has gained momentum for the past two decades specifically on the basis of the fact that similarities between Balkanisms and Europeanisms are most conspicuous in the realm of syntax and also pertain to grammatical categories. This paper offers some considerations in this respect and argues that while Europeanisms are mostly innovations, Balkanisms are manifested on all language levels with morphology being particularly relevant for establishing the existence (or non-existence) of a language union. As an areal-typological unity of languages, both SAE and BLU represent a linguistic union (Sprachbund) and are suitable objects for the application of areal and typological research methods. However, the areal continuum of the Balkan Sprachbund is characterized by common historical development (as demonstrated by its archaic morphological traits), as well as by cultural and linguistic convergences.

Keywords: Balkanism, Linguistic union, Europeanism, Bilingualism, Convergence

1 Preliminary considerations. Balkan linguistics and Eurolinguistics

Possible objections notwithstanding, the beginning of Balkan linguistics can be traced to the 18th century. Moreover, if it is accepted that its first manifestation is not the widely known conclusion by Johann Thunmann (1746–1778) from 1774 concerning the relationship between Illyrian and Thracian, and the language relations on the Balkan Peninsula (Thunmann 1774), but rather the observations of Dimitrie Cantemir (1673–1723) made about half a century earlier, in 1716 (Cantemiri 1716: Caput IV. De lingua Moldavorum) concerning the mixture of Aromanian with Albanian and Greek, and about the ways the speakers of these languages communicated (Kostov 1999–2000), we have just recently celebrated

---

Petya Asenova, (University of Sofia), petyaass@gmail.com

https://doi.org/10.1515/9783110375930-002

the three-hundredth anniversary of Balkan linguistics. This birth date for Balkan Linguistics is suitably placed between the period marking the emerging interest in language in ancient Greece 2500 years ago (provisionally taking the 5th century BC as its starting point) and the official proclamation of Eurolinguistics some twenty years ago.

The coining of the term "Eurolinguistics" belongs to the remarkable Balkan linguist Norbert Reiter (1928–2009), who used it first in 1991 (Reiter 1991). According to him, Eurolinguistics marks a further stage in the development of Balkan Studies ("Die "Eurolinguistik" ist eine konsequente Weiterentwicklung der Balkanologie"); the latter equipped the former with its basic linguistic tools (Reiter 1997).

Prior to the establishment of Eurolinguistics, much research in the domain of areal typology and the theory of linguistic unions aimed at grouping the European languages in a specifiable number of language types or linguistic unions (e.g. Lewy 1942 [1964]; Décsy 1973; Haarmann 1976, the latter posits seven such types/unions). In such cases, Trubetzkoy's (1928) term *Sprachbund* ("linguistic union") is applied in its broad and relative sense, even metaphorically so, without consistently abiding by historical and sociolinguistic criteria and the hierarchy of commonalities in the structure of the languages.

Eurolinguistics has as its subject matter the study of the European linguistic union or, as it is known, Standard Average European (SAE), i.e. the European (or Indo-European) linguistic invariant as defined by B. L. Whorf, the tertium comparationis he used in the description of the Amerindian languages, Hopi in particular. As Haspelmath (2001: 1504) puts it, "To give Whorf his due, it must be added that he was not interested in demonstrating that SAE languages form a Sprachbund."

Within the framework of Eurolinguistics, the Balkan linguistic union (henceforth BLU) is part and parcel of the European linguistic union, which logically makes the treatment of Balkan linguistics part of Eurolinguistics, a tendency that has been gaining momentum for the past two decades. This justifies a comparison between the objects and methods of analysis of the two cognate linguistic disciplines, particularly in view of the contributions of Balkan linguistics to the domain of Eurolinguistics (cf. Hinrichs 2009).

2 Objects of analysis

The similarities observed in the Balkanisms (the common specificities of the languages of the BLU) and the Europeanisms (the common specificities of the SAE) are manifested in the fact that both are realized on the level of syntax and are related to some grammatical categories. Europeanisms are mostly innovations; the same also goes for the Balkanisms: indeed, the majority of them are innovations, too.

However, the differences between them are substantial. Balkanisms occur on all linguistic levels, starting from the phonological and going to the textual, but the morphological similarities are of particular importance to the BLU because the latter are relevant to the existence (or non-existence) of a linguistic union (if we adhere to Trubetzkoy's definition). Moreover, among Balkanisms, there are existing archaic features (archaisms) of Indo-European origin (e.g., the rich modal-temporal system and the status of the simple past tenses).

3 Research methods

Any linguistic union functioning as an areal-typological unity is the optimal object to which to apply areal and typological methodology in its analysis.

The areal continuum of SAE is certainly more extensive than that of the BLU. Still, the areal continuum of the BLU, geographically bound by three seas, is accompanied by common historical development, and cultural and linguistic symbiosis. The processes of that symbiosis have been manifested by direct, mostly oral, language contacts, mutual influence, and interference (e.g., the occurrence of the future tense forms) which led to the simplification of the language systems (e.g., the replacement of the infinitive in an identical manner). Together with the expected parallels between languages of different origin and development, and subject to typological analysis, the occurrence of the parallels between the Balkan languages has been historically documented to a great extent in their written monuments. This is why the typological method of research of the BLU can be conveniently extended with the application of the historical and comparative-historical method aiming at proving the convergent origin of specific Balkanisms. The application of the diachronic approach to typology results in a kind of diachronic typology (Asenova 1990). Eurolinguistics also poses a like question of "How did the SAE come into being?" and takes into account the significance of a diachronic approach oriented towards "Proto-Indo-European structures", "common substratum of a pre-Indo-European population", "contacts" (Haspelmath 2001:1506): these are all issues of different relevance at different times in the history of Balkan linguistics. The objective historical possibilities do not allow for more precise answers to be given to questions related to the convergence processes operative in the Balkans; such questions should not be reduced merely to "Who borrowed from whom?", and should not be limited to providing general chronological observations such as "from late antiquity to the early Middle Ages" and "from the Renaissance to the Enlightenment".

The Eurotype model, as put forward by Martin Haspelmath (Haspelmath 2001:1493), consists of twelve "major Standard Average European features": syntactic and morpho-syntactic parallels between Romance, Germanic and Balto-Slavic languages, the Balkan languages and the easternmost Finno-Ugric languages, as opposed to other languages in the world. On the basis of nine of these features the author defines "degrees of membership in the SAE", represented on a "cluster map". The selected morpho-syntactic features are as follows (Haspelmath 2001: 1504ff.):

1. Definite and indefinite articles

2. Relative clauses with (underlined in (1)) relative pronouns:

    (1) a. *Gruaja   e dyshimtë   të cilën e përshkrova*   (Alb)
           woman.DEF   LNKR suspicious   LNKR which.ACC her described.1SG
        b. *Podozritelnata žena,   kojato   opisax*   (Bulg)
           suspicious.DEF woman   whom.DEF   described.1SG
        c. Η ύποπτη   γυναίκα την οποία   περιέγραψα   (Grk)
           the suspicious woman   the-whom.ACC described.1SG
        d. *Femeia suspectă   pe   care   am   descris-o*   (Rom)
           woman.DEF suspicious OBJ.MRKR whom have.1SG described-her.ACC
           'The suspicious woman whom I described'

3. 'Have'- perfect

4. Participial passive

5. Dative external possessors:

    (2) *Majkata   mu mie kosata*   (Bulg)
        mother.DEF him.DAT washes hair.DEF
        'His mother washes him the hair' (literally: 'The mother washes to-him the-hair'

6. Negative pronouns and lack of verbal negation (see below for examples);

7. Relative-based equative constructions, cf. the examples in (3), for 'as big as strong', alongside those in (4) for 'beautiful as you (are)'; cf. also (Hinrichs 2009: 20):

(3) a. *sa i   madh   aq edhe i fort* (Alb)
 so LNKR big   as and LNKR strong
 b. *tolkova goljam, kolkoto i silen* (Bulg)
 so   big   as.DEF and strong
 c. τόσο μεγάλος όσο ισχυρός (Grk)
 so   big   as strong
 d. *pe cât de mare pe atât și de puternic* (Rom)
 on how from big on much and from strong

(4) a. *xubava kato tebe* (Bulg)
 beautiful like you.ACC
 b. *e   bukur si ty* (Alb)
 LNKR beautiful like you.ACC
 c. (τόσο) όμορφη σαν εσένα (Grk)
 (so) beautiful like you.ACC
 d. *frumoasă ca tine* (Rom)
 beautiful like you.ACC

8. Subject person affixes as strict agreement markers: 'you/PL work': *rabotite* (Bulg, with no overt subject with which the verb agrees) vs. ***ihr** arbeitet* (German)

9. Intensifier-reflexive differentiation (cf. also Hinrichs 2009:20), e.g. *se* : *sam* (Bulg), ο ίδιος : τον εαυτό (Grk), as in (5):

(5) a. *Vetë Papa na priti në audiencë* (Alb)
 self Pope us hosted in audience
 b. *Samijat papa ni dade audientsija* (Bulg)
 self.DEF Pope to.us gave audience
 c. Ο ίδιος ο Πάπας μας έδωσε ακρόαση (Grk)
 the self the Pope to.us gave audience
 d. *Însuși Papa ne-a acordat o audiență* (Rom)
 himself Pope to.us-has granted an audience
 'The Pope himself gave us an audience'

(6) a. *Presidenti mbron veten   /   Presidenti*
 President.DEF protects self.ACC President.DEF
 mbrohet (nga sulmet) (Alb)
 protects.NONACT.3SG from attacks
 b. *Predsedateljat se zaštitava* (Bulg)
 President.DEF self protects
 c. *Prețedintele se apără* (Rom)
 President.DEF self protects

d. Ο πρόεδρος υπερασπίζεται   τον εαυτό του   (Grk)
The President protects.NONACT.3SG the self.ACC his
'The President protects himself (from the attacks)'

Although the "major Standard Average European features" are not of the same rank – 1, 3, 4, 8 above are categorial and the others are syntactic structures – they represent explicitly the common characteristics of the European languages. According to their areal distribution, however, the nucleus of the SAE is formed by French and German, which possess nine of the features, whereas the languages of the BLU fall into three different groups with a decreasing proximity to the nucleus: Albanian in the layer closest to the nucleus – with eight features – followed by Greek and Romanian – with seven features – and last Bulgarian, essentially the periphery of SAE with five features. Despite the recognition that "the existence of Balkan Sprachbund has been universally accepted" and "nobody questions the validity of the Balkan Sprachbund" (Haspelmath 2001:1492), the Balkan Sprachbund is "scattered" in the southeastern edge of the SAE and is not represented in its entirety as an areal-typological group of languages; therefore, the BLU cannot be considered an independent part of the SAE. To a great extent, this is also due to the interpretation of linguistic facts. Anyone familiar with the Balkan languages can easily determine that seven (with the exception of numbers 6 and 8 here) of the selected "major Standard Average European features" are well represented in all BLU languages; for instance, in Bulgarian, apart from the Slavic type 'be'-perfect, the 'have'- perfect is also used on a dialectal basis, as is an indefinite article, and Albanian does not have SAE feature 6 (negative pronouns and lack of verbal negation); compare *niemand [Ø] kommt* (German) 'nobody comes' and Albanian *askush nuk vjen* 'nobody comes' (literally, 'nobody not comes').

Double negation is a distinguishing feature of the BLU, as in (7):

(7) a. *Nikoj ništo   ne vidja*   (Bulg)
nobody nothing not saw.3SG
b. *Askush nuk pa   gjë*   (Alb)
nobody not saw.3SG thing
c. *Nimeni nu a   văzut nimic*   (Rom)
nobody not has.3SG seen nothing
d. Κανείς δεν είδε   τίποτα   (Grk)
nobody not saw.3SG nothing
'Nobody saw anything' (literally, 'Nobody did not see nothing')

Its absence in the Romance languages seems rather random; cf. Italian *Nessuno viene* 'No one came' (with the prounoun in preverbal position) but *Non ho visto nessuno* 'I did not see anyone (literally, 'no one', with the pronoun *nessuno* in postverbal position), as opposed to French where negative pronouns such as *personne* 'no one' construe with verbal negation, at least in the literary language: *Personne ne vient* 'No one came', *Personne n'a rien vu* 'No one saw anything' (literally, 'nothing').

Moreover, most of the "further likely SAE features" of Haspelmath (2001: 1501ff.) are attested in the BLU, certainly his 3.2., to start with (analytical forms of adjectives in comparative constructions are a major Balkanism), but also his 3.3. ("A and B" conjunction), 3.4 (comitative-instrumental syncretism), and 3.5 (suppletive second ordinal).

In a similar way to the situation with Europeanisms, the major Balkanisms are not evenly distributed over the Balkan area. "Degrees of Balkanization" have been posited within the boundaries of the BLU: a distinction can be drawn between first- and second-degree Balkan languages (Schaller 1975), a nucleus of the BLU is recognized by some (Georgiev 1968), and a central Balkan area is observed by others in which attenuation of Balkanisms occurs the more distant a language is from the nucleus (Gołąb, 1964; Asenova 2002 [1989]). On the basis of the representation of 12 grammatical (classical) Balkanisms in the separate groups of Balkan languages (Greek, Albanian, Balkan Slavic, Balkan Romance, Balkan Romani), an index of Balkanization can be computed (Lindstedt 2000).

Haspelmath's Eurotype model subsumes substantial material from many languages, yet does not allow an in-depth treatment of facts that are pivotal for the conclusions. However, the approach to the SAE employing the above-mentioned and well-known methods of Balkan linguistics is truly impressive and, in the long run, leads to the conclusion that Balkanisms and Europeanisms cannot be identified with each other. Every language type delineates a separate linguistic area or "union", so that the BLU is not a part of the SAE. It can certainly be claimed that in the individual Balkan languages, sporadic Europeanisms occur. The latter, being of predominantly syntactic character, are not relevant to the existence of a linguistic union; therefore, the notion of a linguistic union cannot be equally applied both to the BLU and the SAE.

Although, as Haspelmath asserts, "areal typology is only in its infancy" (Haspelmath 2001:1505), areal-typological methods of research lead to a convergence between Eurolinguistics and Balkan linguistics.[1]

---

[1] In this respect new vistas are offered by geolinguistics, as shown in Leschber (2005:116-125).

4 Balkanism or Europeanism?

None of the "major Standard Average European features" (probably with the exception of the *habeo*-perfect) is related to the so-called major Balkanisms. Nonetheless, Balkanisms occur outside the Balkan area, a fact that has been discussed extensively in Balkan linguistics. It has also been pointed out that Balkanisms are not unique linguistic peculiarities. Such claims are sometimes used to lessen the value of the BLU and to "demystify" it (following the expression of Hinrichs).

Balkanisms are to be found everywhere in Europe, particularly in the Romance area: comparative research by Aronson (Aronson 2007) shows that e.g., the use of the future in the past tense (futurum praeteriti) in the function of a conditional is characteristic of the Romance languages, English and Dutch, and outside Europe – of Georgian. Apparently, this relates to a universal linguistic tendency. Analytic degrees of comparison and the elimination of the goal/location opposition are dominant features in the Romance languages much as the *habeo*-perfect is found across the non-Slavic languages. Other features such as evidentiality are limited to the boundaries of the Balkans. According to Aronson, only two of the so-called Balkanisms – merger of the dative and the genitive and the absence of an infinitive (or its weakening) are truly characteristic only of the Balkan area within the general context of the European area. From among the European languages, it is only in English that the infinitive is absent, as it is in Bulgarian and Greek. In a truly compromising manner, Aronson identifies all the Balkanisms in English, and even speaks of "English as a Balkan Language"; however, English is not a Balkan language because it is not a vernacular in the Balkans (Aronson 2007:10–12).

Concerning each of the above-mentioned features, it is logical to pose the question: is it a Balkanism or is it a Europeanism? The possible answers can be arrived at if we compare in a more precise way the Balkan with the European type. So let us focus our comments here on some of the observations offered by Aronson concerning Balkanisms/ Europeanisms.

4.1 Futurum praeteriti = conditionalis irrealis[2]

The development of the futurum praeteriti in the Balkan and the Romance languages, and also in English, is analogous to the development of the future tense forms. In all the languages, both future tenses – futurum exactum and futurum

---

[2] It should be pointed out that such a case of a Balkan-European parallel was analyzed some fifty years ago in Gołąb (1964), whereby the primacy of the modal function is asserted (Gołąb 1964:1 80-193).

praeteriti – start with similar verbal periphrases consisting of an infinitive and an auxiliary (equivalent to *habeo* 'have' or *volo* 'want') in the present or the imperfect. The morphologization of the verbal syntagm of both future tenses ends up, however, with a different result: in the Romance languages the auxiliary is transformed via agglutination into a verbal inflexion, grammatically marking tense, person, and number, e.g. Fr. *chanterai / chanterais*, It. *canterò / canterei* 'I will sing / you will sing'; in the Balkan languages the auxiliary is transformed into an adverbal (contact) morpheme (traditionally identified as a particle) indexing only future tense, i.e. an invariant element, whereas the other grammatical categories (person, number, tense – present or imperfect) are realized by the inflexion on the main verb. This gives the type $volo_{part} + V_{pres/impf}$, e.g. 'I will write' / 'I would write' [lit. will wrote-Impf]': *šte piša / šte pišex* (Bulg), θα γράφω / θα έγραφα (Grk), *do (të) shkruaj /do (të) shkruaja* (Alb). Thus, the similar source material of the Balkan and the Romance languages has been "reprocessed"/"reelaborated" by means of different configurations of the constituents.

Semantically, the futurum praeteriti forms are double-marked both for the future and for the imperfect: the two tenses whose temporal semantics are interwoven with hypothetical modality. The conditional form $volo_{part} + V_{impf}$ is concentrated in the so-called "central Balkan area", according to Gołąb in southwestern Macedonia, according to Asenova in the southwestern part of the Balkan peninsula: northern Greek, southern Albanian, Aromanian, southwestern Bulgarian. However, apart from that, in various Balkan languages there is yet another conditional form with a lower degree of grammaticalization, in which the auxiliary is inflected as a past tense and the main verb is the infinitive (as in Albanian and Romanian) or a substitute for the infinitive (as in Bulgarian and Aromanian), giving the type $volo_{impf} + V_{inf}$, as in:

(8) *kisha për të shkruar* 'I would write/I had to write' (Alb)
 aş cânta 'I would sing' (Rom)
 štjax da piša 'I would write' (Bulg)
 vrea (s-) cîntu 'I would sing' (Arom)

There exists an independent parallel between English and the Balkan languages in the future tense forms and the forms of the conditional / futurum praeteriti of the second type.

4.2 Analytic degrees of comparison

Some necessary specifications should be made at this stage with other characteristics. In relation to the analytic degrees of comparison, Balkanisms are not identical with Europeanisms either. In the Balkan languages, the analytic forms also replace the suppletive comparatives,[3] whereas suppletion is preserved in both the Germanic and the Romance languages; compare:

(9) a. *good – better – best* (English); *bon – meilleur* (French), with suppletion, but *dobăr* 'good' – *po-dobăr* lit. 'more good'– *naj-dobăr* lit. 'most good' (Bulg); *i mirë – më mirë – më i mirë* (Alb); καλός – καλύτερος / πιο καλός –ο πιο καλός / ο καλύτερος (Grk); *bun – mai bun – cel mai bun* (Rom), with no suppletion
b. *bad – worse – worst* (English); *mauvais – pire* (French), with suppletion, but *loš* 'bad'– *po-loš* literally 'more bad'– *naj-loš* literally 'most bad' (Bulg); *i keq– më keq – më i keq* (Alb); κακός – πιο κακός / χειρότερος – ο πιο κακός / ο χειρότερος (Grk); *rău – mai rău – cel mai rău* (Rom).

4.3 Absence or weakening of the infinitive

As far as the absence of the infinitive (or its weakening) is concerned, it is not a Balkanism in itself; rather, the identical means of its substitution is a Balkanism, usually defined as "analytic subjunctive". On this point, see below Section 5.2 (and the papers in Part III, this volume).

4.4 Europeanisms, Balkanisms, and the East

What is interesting from a typological point of view is that Europeanisms, with few exceptions, are not present in "the eastern Indo-European languages (Armenian, Iranian, Indic); as a matter of fact, these are language groups that are not included in the SAE (Haspelmath 2001: 1493). Even more interesting is the fact that it is in those languages that major Balkanisms can be found. If the Balkanisms in western Armenian can be accounted for in terms of the geographical and historical links of the Armenian language with the Balkan Peninsula, then their presence in the Iranian languages obviously reflects typological universals attested outside the Balkans. Historico-typological research on the Iranian languages during the second half of the 20th century has determined that features similar to those in the languages of the Balkans occurred in much more distant times than in the Balkan languages, e.g.:

---

[3] The first author who drew attention to the phenomenon was Vasilev (Vasilev 1968: 92-96).

- convergence of the functions of the dative and the genitive (in Old Persian, 6th – 4th centuries B.C.);
- the postposed unstressed article -*ē* – (in Middle Persian, 3rd century B.C. – 8th century A.D.).

Moreover, a great number of "Balkanisms" are present in contemporary Farsi: merger of the dative and the genitive; the postposed definite article; a *volo* ('want'-based) future tense; and finite modal constructions instead of the infinitive. In Tajik, a branching aspectual-temporal system of "auditive" mood has developed on the basis of the perfect, i.e. a mood of "non-evidentiality", cognate to the renarration in Bulgarian and similar but not identical to the one in Lithuanian (Edel'man 2004).

According to Edel'man, the similarities in the Iranian and Balkan innovations are caused by some common "development vector", cognate with the processes of pidginization and creolization observed in various multilingual regions of the world under conditions of intense contacts among languages of different sociolinguistic status (Edel'man 2004: 382).

Hinrichs (2012) comes close to Edel'man's conclusion concerning the simplification of linguistic structures in the process of oral and multilingual communication. On the basis of the data from *The World Atlas of Language Structures* (WALS 2005), he analyzes Balkanisms such as the definite article, the cases, the future tense, the comparative degree and the evidential in comparison with typologically similar phenomena in the languages of the world. He is convinced that such an approach would bring about new revelations concerning the etiology of the Balkanisms, particularly if treated within the theory of creolization.

5 Syntax and functional convergence

The tendencies in the development of Balkan linguistics have shifted from a quest for explanations of the origin of specific Balkanisms, a tendency characteristic of the beginnings of the field, to investigation of the reasons for the formation of the BLU. From the possible ways in which the BLU could have been formed – Indo-European heritage, independently occurring typological similarities, mutual influences – the last is undoubtedly of utmost importance. Although the analysis of mutual influences presupposes a historical approach to linguistic phenomena, it nevertheless makes it necessary to abandon the search for superficial similarities among the languages, which, as an approach, has already exhausted its potential.

For the past 50 years or so, the BLU has generally been viewed as a supersystem which unites the Balkanisms in their interdependencies and hierarchy. This is an approach whose explicit manifestations should be rightly linked with the

First Congress of Balkan studies, held in Sofia in 1966. In the organization of that system there can be discerned phenomena which exemplify "not so much similarities of form, but rather similarities of function" according to Joseph (1983: 202), related to the "syntactic consequences of the replacement of the infinitive" (such as 'hard to do': Alb. *vështirë për të bërë* = Rom. *greu de făcut*[4] ≠ Rom. 'hard that it-be-done' *greu să se facă*; Grk. 'hard that I-understand' δύσκολο να καταλάβω). The Balkan languages, despite the differences among them, present similarities of the functions defined by Joseph as "functional convergence" ("represent more of a functional convergence among these languages", Joseph 1983: 230:233).

The term "functional convergence" can illuminate many other phenomena in the system of BLU which come as a result of convergence. I try here to single some of them out.

5.1 The definite article

The postposition of the definite article in the Balkan languages is considered a partial Balkanism: in Greek the definite article is preposed. Typologically, agglutination, the result of a morphologized syntagm in Albanian, Bulgarian, and Romanian, stands in opposition to the isolation of the article seen in Greek. Despite this difference in form, in all the Balkan languages the definite article displays common and specific functions with respect to other European languages (for details cf. Asenova 2002:130–140):

a) the expression of genericity:

(10) a. *Detsata   sa radostta na života*   (Bulg)
         children.DEF are joy.DEF of life
     b. Τα παιδιά είναι η χαρά της ζωής   (Grk)
         the children are the joy of.the life.GEN

b) the correlation with the temporal-aspectual content of the utterance: the verbal forms related to definiteness, punctualness, and completeness, characteristic of the semantics of the aorist and the perfective aspect, preferably construe with articulated adverbial forms and vice versa; the semantics of

---

[4] In Albanian and Romanian, these are structures of preposition +participle form (in traditional grammar, infinitive and supine, respectively) which correspond to the Greek-Bulgarian parallel of preposition+verbal nouns: *lud za vrăzvane* 'so crazy as to need being tied' (literally 'crazy for tying') = τρελός για δέσιμο. Gabinskij accounts for them by introducing the term "secondary infinitivity" (cf. Gabinskij 2008).

the imperfect and the imperfective aspect correspond to the use of adverbial forms with a zero article; compare (11a) *esen-ta* with (11b) *esen*:

(11) a. *Esen-ta   tja dobi   momčana rožba* (P. P. Slavejkov)
       autumn-the she acquired-AOR male child
       'In the autumn she gave birth to a male child.'
   b. *Esen idvaše   tuk da gnezdi* (E. Stanev)
       autumn came-IMPERF here that nestles.3SG
       'Each autumn she came here to nestle.'

It can be shown that the aorist blocks adverbs expressing habitualness and repetitivity such as those illustrated in (12)/(13) from Bulgarian and Greek; without the article, the adverb would be construed as habitual, leading to a conflict with the aorist in the same clause.

(12) a. *Sutrin-ta, kogato Tom se săbudi, toj se počudi kăde se namira* (Bulg)
       morning-the when Tom REFL awoke-AOR, he REFL wondered where was
       'When Tom awoke in the morning he wondered where he was'
       (M. Twain, *The adventures of Tom Sawyer*, transl. by Nellie Dospevska)
   b. **Sutrin, kogato Tom se săbudi,   toj se počudi   kăde se namira*
       morning when Tom REFL awoke-AOR, he REFL wondered where was

(13) a. Το χειμώνα   κρύβομαι   (Grk)
       the winter   hide-PRES-1sg
       'In winter, I hide' (for more details cf. Asenova 2010).
   b. *Χειμώνα   κρύφτηκα
       winter   hid-AOR-1sg

c) the distribution of the definite article with syntactically distinct functions, as already established for Bulgarian in Ivanchev 1978 and Norman 1978.

The placement of the article distinguishes on the surface between an adverb and an adjective because in the BLU there is no special adverbial word-formation process, e.g. via suffixation, so that the adverb coincides with a form of the adjective. Compare (14):

(14) a. *Ujku   e   kapi drerin shpejt / Ujku   e   kapi drerin e   shpejt*
       wolf.DEF it.ACC caught deer quickly wolf.DEF it.ACC caught deer LNKR quick
                                                                            (Alb)
       'The wolf quickly caught the deer' / 'The wolf caught the quick deer'

b. *Lupul   a prins   repede cerbul / Lupul   a prins*
wolf.DEF has.3SG caught quickly deer.DEF wolf.DEF has.3SG caught
cerbul rapid   (Rom)
deer.DEF quick
'The wolf quickly caught the deer' / 'The wolf caught the quick deer'

c. *Vălkăt dogoni   bărzo stadoto / Vălkăt*
wolf.DEF caught.up quickly flock.DEF wolf.DEF
dogoni bărzoto stado   (Bulg)
caught.up quick.DEF flock
'The wolf quickly caught up with the flock.' / 'The wolf caught up with the quick flock.'

d. Ο λύκος πρόφθασε γρήγορα τα κοπάδια. / Ο λύκος πρόφθασε τα
the wolf caught.up quickly the flocks   the wolf caught.up the
γρήγορα κοπάδια   (Grk)
quick flocks
'The wolf caught up quickly with the flocks.' / 'The wolf caught up with the quick flocks.'

d) possessee marking in the external possessor construction (for relevant details see Krapova 2012: 118–125):

(15) a. *i   mbushi   gotën*   (Alb)
him.DAT filled.3SG glass.ACC.DEF

b. *napălni mu   čašata*   (Bulg)
filled.3SG him.DAT glass.DEF

c. του   γέμισε   το ποτήρι   (Grk)
him.GEN filled.3SG the glass.ACC

d. *îşi   umplu   paharul* (Rom)
him.DAT filled.3SG glass.DEF
'He filled his glass'.

Its absence indicates a dative (oblique) object (*podade mu čaša Ø voda* (Bulg) 'He. handed to.him a glass of.water'). In Albanian, Greek and Romanian, the function of the definite article to convey inalienable possession has been grammaticalized, but it is not unknown in Bulgarian either:

(16) a. σήκωσε το χέρι, ανασήκωσε το λαιμό   (Grk)
raised.3SG the hand stretched.3SG the neck

b. *ngriti   dorën,   zgjati   qafën*   (Alb)
raised.3SG hand.ACC.DEF stretched.3SG neck.ACC.DEF

c. *ridică   mâna,   întinse   gâtul*   (Rom)
   raised.3SG hand.DEF stretched.3SG neck.DEF
   'He/she raised his/her hand, he/she stretched his/her neck'
d. *Rătsete   gore, robski sin!* Čelata   *gore! – vikna im Johan*
   hands.DEF up   slave's son foreheads.DEF up   cried to.them Johann
                                                                 (H. Smirnenski)
   'Hands up, son of slave! Raise your foreheads!' Johann cried out to them'
   (Asenova 2001: 128–129).

5.2 Infinitive replacement

It has already been mentioned that it is not the absence of an infinitive (or its weakening) that is a Balkanism but rather its replacement by subordinate structures of the same type, modal or declarative. If the phenomena considered so far are Balkan manifestations of the universal that "yesterday's syntax is tomorrow's morphology", then the substitution of the infinitive is a movement from the morphological form to the syntactic structure. Neither in Bulgarian, which historically did not have a subjunctive, nor in Greek, where the subjunctive inflexion has become phonetically identical with the indicative, nor either in Albanian or Romanian, is subjunctive modality conveyed via a reduced paradigmatic oppositions but rather via a subordinate conjunction that has turned into an adverbal (contact) morpheme. This is why the constructions that have replaced the infinitive have been defined as 'analytic subjunctives'. In independent (main) clauses, the modal conjunctions *të* (Alb), *da* (Bulg), να (Grk), *să* (Rom) together with the verbal tenses may convey different modal meanings – imperative, optative, dubitative (see also Bîlbîie & Mardale, this volume). The analytic Balkan subjunctive not only performs modal functions which are otherwise absent in the BLU (e.g., the optative and the dubitative) but it also functions in the domain of the imperative, and in Albanian of the optative, too. Several examples serve to illustrate the point, showing strict, impatient command (with present tense), palpably nuanced when in competition with true imperative forms; see examples (17)-(18) and (19)-(22) featuring optatives and dubitatives:

(17) a. *Trăgvaj i   veče   da   ne se   vrăštaš   tuka!*   (Bulg) (D. Talev)
        go.IMP and anymore CONJ not REFL come.2SG here
        'Go and you should never come back!'
     b. *Da   si   vărviš – zapovjada glasăt – mahaj se!* (E. Stanev)
        CONJ REFL.DAT go.2SG ordered   voice.DEF get.out.IMP REFL.ACC
        'Go you away' ordered the voice. 'Get away!'

(18) a. Να   προσέχεις στα λόγια σου!   (Grk)
        CONJ attend.2SG to the words your
        'Pay attention to your words!' (i.e., 'Mind what you are saying!')
    b. *Tu să   taci...   marşi   de aici!*   (Rom)
        you CONJ be.silent.IMP march.IMP from here
        'You should keep your mouth shut... get out of here!'

Optatives:
        - (with present tense):

(19) *Po s'ka   gajle! Të   na   rrojnë djemtë   dhe me çupa pas!* (Alb)
    but not has fretting CONJ us.DAT live.3PL boys.DEF and with girls after
    'Don't worry! May our boys be healthy, wealthy, and may the girls follow suit, too!'
        - (with imperfect):

(20) a. Ah, *da pristigneše vednăž tazi djavolska telegrama!* (Bulg) (D. Dimov)
        ah CONJ arrived.3SG once this damned   telegram
        'Well, may this wretched telegram come once and for all!'
    b. Αχ! Να μπορούσα   εγώ να   γίνω   η νύφη! (N. Kazantzakis)
        ah   CONJ could.1SG I   CONJ become.1SG the bride
        'Oh, if only I could be the bride!'
        - (with pluperfect):

(21) *Po-harno   da beše   otišăl   v ada!*   (Bulg) (Elin Pelin)
    CMPV-hard   CONJ was.3SG   gone.out to hell
    'You'd better have gone to the infernal parts!'
    - Dubitatives (with perfect):

(22) a. *Të   ketë   qenë Kozmai?*   (Alb)
        CONJ have.3SG.SUBJ been Kozma.DEF
        'Could it have been Kozma?'
    b. *Să-l   fi   pierdut oare venind spre baltă?*   (Rom)
        CONJ-him be.3SG.SUBJ lost   really coming to marsh.DEF
        'Could he have lost his way while he was coming to the marsh?'

The analytical subjunctive of the Balkan languages is realized as a universal mood which can function practically in the domain of all moods, including those which possess their own forms.

5.3 Repetition constructions

Constructions with repetition directly related to lexis show some interesting features of syntax that are characteristic of the interaction between the speakers of the various Balkan languages. The construction in question involves the repetition of lexemes of various lexico-grammatical classes – nouns, pronouns, numerals, verbs (usually in the imperative) – and brings about the formation of adverbs and adverbial expressions (Asenova, Kacori, Dukova 1990). This phenomenon can be viewed as a specific kind of conversion whereby the repetition "transfers" the lexeme from one category to another. Here are some examples with repetitions of different word types:

- pronouns : *koga (i) koga* (Bulg) = *kur kur* (Alb) = πότε πότε (Grk) = *când și când* (Rom) (lit. 'when (and) when)' = 'sometimes';
- numerals: *edin po edin* (Bulg), ένας ένας (Grk), *një nga një* (Alb), *unu câte unu* (Rom) 'one by one, individually';
- verbs (in imperative forms): *kaži-reči* (literally 'say-IMP-speak-IMP'), *idi-dojdi* (literally 'come-IMP-go-IMP') (Bulg) 'so and so', τρίψε τρίψε (Grk) 'with all that rubbing' (literally 'rub-IMP-rub-IMP');
- nouns: *mëngjes mëngjes* (Alb) = πρωί πρωί (Grk) (literally 'morning morning') = *rano rano* (Bulg) (literally 'early early') = 'early morning'.

The function of repetition as a kind of conversion becomes particularly discernible when the semantics of the adverb has become separated from the semantics of its constitutive elements, i.e. phraseologization has taken place, e.g.: *duar duar* (Alb) (literally 'hand hand') = 'differently', *mendje mendje* (Alb) (literally 'mind mind') = 'not constantly', χέρι χέρι (Grk) (literally 'hand hand') = 'immediately'. According to Burkhart (1985), such repetition constructions in the Balkan languages are a fact of language, not just of speech.

6 Syntax in bilingualism

On the territory of the Balkan Peninsula there are still dialects that are isolated from the languages they belong to and function in a foreign language environment[5]. Such data are extremely useful since they allow the researcher to observe

---

[5] The data used in this study comes mainly from field studies in Bulgaria carried out by a French-Bulgarian team within the framework of the "Rila 2/11 Program", 2005–2007, in settlements of speakers of Munten-Oltentia dialects of Romanian spoken in the Vidin-Nikopol region,

bilingualism in action and to reconstruct convergent processes in the past which have brought about the occurrence of the BLU (Joseph 2001; see also Asenova 2008 for details and references).[6]

Some syntactic characteristics of the BLU are manifested to a greater degree in isolated dialects that exist in a state of bilingualism. For example, the tendency towards analyticity in the Greek and the Romanian dialects in Bulgaria is at a more advanced stage than in literary Greek and Romanian, respectively. This state of affairs cannot be explained only in terms of the influence of the analytical Bulgarian language: probably the language contacts have only stimulated the intrinsic potential for analyticity found in the northern dialects of Greek and in the Muntenia-Oltenia dialects of Romanian in the territory of Bulgaria. The Bulgarian dialects in Aegean Thrace and in the region of Gora in Northern Albania, together with the northern Greek and the Albanian dialects in whose milieu they exist, are part of the area with conditioned obligatory doubling of the object. The samples of Bulgarian dialects spoken in Romania published in M. Mladenov (Mladenov 1993) also show such doubling although they are outside the above-discussed area.

6.1 Prepositional merger

In the special case of the isolated Balkan dialects it cannot be proved that the source of interference is the contact language. Still they react as other languages do in regions of language contact by undergoing changes not reproducing models of the local language. As a rule, such changes are directed towards simplification of the system (Zvegintsev 1962: 225). For example, one can observe that the syntax of some isolated Balkan dialects shows a tendency towards an increased use of one preposition transformed into a universal marker of syntactic relations after having subsumed the functions of several other prepositions.

In the Greek dialects in Bulgaria the all-purpose preposition is *pe* (< από 'from'), which replaces σε 'to, in, at, on', για 'for', and particularly με 'with', compare:[7]

---

of northern Greek dialects spoken in Burgas, Sozopol, Pomorie, Nessebur, and Karlovo, and of southern Albanian spoken in the village of Mandrica, the county of Ivaylovgrad (also in 2010), together with data collected in earlier years.

6 More stable effects of bilingualism, especially code-switching and code-mixing, are not a focus of attention here.

7 These examples and others from the dialect are given in transcription because as the dialect is not generally written. The locale for these examples and others below is given in parentheses.

(23) a. *kserume pe peðia* (Pomorie)
   know.1PL PE children
   'We have known (Greek) since childhood'
   b. *eroteftikane   pe ton andra tis* (Pomorie)
   fell.in.love.3PL PE the man her
   'They have fallen in love with her husband'
   c. *eprepe   na   fiji   pe to strato* (Burgas)
   must.3SG.PST CONJ leave.3SG PE the army
   'He had to escape from (service in) the army
   d. *naxume   pare-ðose pe   tis ɣermanus* (Burgas)
   CONJ.have.1PL take-give PE the Germans
   'We had dealings with the Germans'
   e. *pe sindaksi   moni* (Pomorie)
   PE pension.FEM alone.FEM
   '(He lives) only on his pension'
   f. *pe olus tis patriotiðes* (Burgas)
   PE all   the compatriots
   'to all compatriots'.

In the Albanian of the village of Mandrica the preposition in question is *dë* (< *ndë*), marking location, goal, genitive relation, and comitative:

(24) a. *rron   dë Mandrica*
   live.3SG DË Mandrica
   'He lives in Mandrica'
   b. *pjela   dë Mandricë*
   born.1SG DË Mandrica
   'I was born in Mandrica';
   c. *kle   sekretar dë sävet-i*
   was.3SG secretary DË municipality-DEF
   'He was secretary of the municipality';
   d. *martrova   dë një buri*
   married.1SG DË a man
   'I married a man'
   e. *gel   dë Gërxhaluku*
   go.1SG DË Kărdžali
   'I go to Kărdžali'.

In the Muntenia-Oltenia dialects of Romanian in Bulgaria, the preposition *de/dă* 'of' has taken over the functions of the prepositions *din* 'from', *a/la* 'to', *cu* 'with', *în* 'in', and *pentru* 'for'; see (25):

(25) a. *fată de sat* (= *din*)
    girl DE village
    'a girl from the village'
  b. *s-a   dus dă Tărnovo* (=*la*)
    REFL.3SG-has.3SG led DĂ Tărnovo
    'I went to Tărnovo'
  c. *s-a   însurat dă bulgar* (= *cu*)
    REFL.3SG-has.3SG married DĂ Bulgarian
    'She married a Bulgarian'
  d. *pâine dă săptămână* (= *pentru*)
    bread DĂ week
    'bread for the week'.

6.2 Interrogative constructions

In cases of bilingualism, of course, syntactic models are transferred from one language to the other; for example, the interrogative phrase, most probably due to its proximity to the internal world of the speaker, becomes most susceptible to the influence of the socially dominant language: in all the dialects under consideration it is formed by the respective interrogative marker(s): a) the interrogative particles *li* and *dali*, from Bulgarian, in the Greek, Albanian, and Romanian dialects in Bulgaria, as in (26); b) the interrogative particle *a*, from Albanian, in the Bulgarian dialects in Albania, as in (27); c) by means of intonation, in the Bulgarian dialects of Greece and Romania:

(26) a. *ðen ksero   dali tin ɣnorizete*   (Pomorie)
    not know.1SG QN her.ACC know.2PL
    'I don't know whether you know her'
  b. *ku banonish li?*   (Mandrica, 2007)
    where live.2SG QN
    '(Are you asking) where you live?'
  c. *Ka Viskuke, ama ishte li vërtet, nuk e di*   (Mandrica, 2010)
    from Viskuke but was QN truth not it.ACC know.1SG
    '(He is) from Vithkuq, if it is true, I do not know' (literally, 'from ... is it true? I ...')

(27) a. *a go   sakaš, a go   ne sakaš?*   (Golo Bărdo)
    QN him.ACC love.2SG QN him.ACC not love.2SG
    'Do you love him or don't you?'

b. *Kakov je,* a *je xubav?*   A da   ti   *donesem otsa?* (Gora).
   what is QN is handsome QN CONJ you.DAT bring.1SG father
   'What is he like? Is he handsome? Shall I bring your father?'

6.3 Word order

Even with the foregoing, still the most immediate divergence from the syntax of the mother tongue in bilinguals can be observed in word order: the Bulgarian dialects in Romania and Albania adopt the characteristic use of the initial phrase clitic of the local language and the sequence modified / modifier in the nominal group. In the Romanian and Albanian dialects in Bulgaria, the Bulgarian model can be identified, i.e. modifier – modified. While in Romanian these are sporadic divergences, in Albanian this is a point of definite restructuring, e.g.: *maze bilja* 'the elder girl' instead of *bija e madhe*, *zezë rush* 'black grapes' instead of *rrushi i zi*, *vjetrë verë* 'old wine' instead of *verë e vjetër*; *(Ata zalahitna) vetyët gljufa* '(They speak) their own language' instead of *(Ata flasin) gjuhën e tyre*.

At first glance, such a superficial syntactic phenomenon leads to a deeper restructuring process, namely the elimination of the copulative article linking element (*i* in (28a), *e* in (28b)) outside the noun phrase:

(28) a. *Mërtora jam,*   *tashi jam*   *dare*
        married am.1SG now   am.1SG separated   instead of:
        Unë jam   *i*   *martuar, tani jam*   *i*   *ndarë.*
        I   am.1SG LNKR married now am.1SG LNKR separated
        'I am married; now I am separated (from my wife)'
    b. *Nuk pënon,*   *e*   *mëmë ishte sëmurë*
        not work.3SG my mother was sick   instead of:
        Nuk punoj,   *nëna*   *ime*   *është e sëmurë*
        not work.1SG mother.DEF my.FEM is   LNKR sick
        'I am not working; my mother is ill'.

As a result of this, in the Albanian dialect of Mandrica there is no category of gender and the conviction of the higher educated speakers is that in Albanian there is no gender. Thus, Dimitar Babrikov (52 years of age in 2010) gave us the following example:

(29) *Një gruvë   isht   mirë. Një xhako isht mirë. Këzani isht mirë.*
     one woman is good one man is good child was good
     'One woman is good. One man is good. The child is good'

Such morpho-syntactic restructuring of gender is attested also in a folk song (recorded in 2010 from Maria Dieva, born in April, 1929), i.e. incorporated into conventional usage:

(30) a. *më   shpunë (dë) ljartë kodra*
      me.ACC led.3PL DË   high hill
      'That they took me to a high hill'
    b. *dë nji sellë pruva*
       DË one deep gully
       'Of a deep gully'.

Therefore, the oldest possible chronology should be dated to no more than two hundred years ago, approximately the time when the Albanians settled in Mandrica (Shuteriqi 1965:108). Then the natural question that arises is whether it is possible for bilingualism to cause such a major change after a period of no more than a couple of generations.

These observations on the dialects in a state of bilingualism highlight the major role of syntax as an vehicle for systemic change.

7 Conclusion

In the hierarchy of the linguistic system primacy is given to morphology. The major Balkanisms pertain to morphology and morpho-syntax . They are the determinant ("sprachbundbindend" – Birnbaum, 1965: 43) characteristic of a linguistic union, the latter according to Trubetzkoy is characterized by "eine Ähnlichkeit in der Grundsätzen des morphologischen Baus". The characteristics of the SAE are of a syntactic nature. This statement does not devalue the role of syntax: syntax is the point of intersection for convergence, which explains why syntactic Balkanisms predominate. Syntactic similarities in and of themselves are not relevant to the determination of the existence or non-existence of a linguistic union, yet there does not exist a linguistic union without syntactic similarities.

References

Aronson, Howard. 2007. *The Balkan Linguistic League, „Orientalism", and Linguistic Typology.*
    (The Kenneth Naylor Memorial Lecture Series, No. 4.) Ann Arbor: Beech Stave Press.
Asenova, Petya. 1990. Quelques remarques sur les types convergents. *Diachronica* 7 (1). 1–8.

Asenova, Petya 2001 Observations sur la structure du texte balkanique. *Zeitschrift für Balkanologie* 37 (2). 119 -135.
Asenova, Petya. 2002 [1989]. *Balkansko ezikoznanie. Osnovni problemi na balkanskija ezikov săjuz* [Balkan linguistics: Fundamental problems of the Balkan Linguistic Union]. Veliko Tărnovo: Faber.
Asenova, Petya. 2008. Konservatism i neologija v uslovijax jazykovyx kontaktov [Conservatism and neology in language contact]. *Linguistique balkanique* XLVII, 2–3. 125 -132.
Asenova, Petya. 2010. Temporal'nost'/aspektual'nost' i determinirovanost' ['Temporality'/'aspectualty' and determination]. In *Glagolnata sistema na balkanskite ezici. Sbornik dokladi ot Meždunarodna naučna konferencija. Velikotărnovski Universitet "Sv.sv. Kiril i Metodij", 30.IV – 2.V.2009*, 51–62. Veliko Tărnovo: Faber.
Asenova, Petya, Toma Kacori, and Ute Dukova. 1990. Povtorenieto – vid konversija v balkanskite ezici [Repetition: a type of conversion in the Balkan languages]. *Săpostavitelno ezikoznanie/Contrastive Lingustics* XV (4–5). 102–105.
Birnbaum, Henrik. 1965. Balkanslavisch und Südslavisch. – *Zeitschrift für Balkanologie*, III /1. 12–63.
Cantemiri, Dimitrie. 1716. *Descrierea stării de odinioară și de astăzi a Moldovei* (*Descriptio antiqui et hodierni status Moldaviae*). Critical edition by Dan Slușanschi, 2007, Institutul cultural român.
Décsy G.1973. *Die linguistische Struktur Europas. Vergangenheit, Gegenwart, Zukunft*. Wiesbaden: Harrassowitz Verlag.
Edel'man, Joy J. 2004. Ob istoriko-tipologičeskih paralleljax iranskix i balkanskix jazykov [On the historical-typological parallels between Iranian and Balkan languages]. *Papers of Russian scholars. IX Congress of the Association Internationale d'Études du Sud-est européen (AIESEE). Tirana 30.08. – 03.09.2004*, 375–383. Saint Petersburg: Nauka.
Haarmann, Harald. 1976. *Aspekte der Arealtypologie. Die Problematik der europäischen Sprachbünde*. Tübingen: Verlag Günter Naar.
Haspelmath, Martin. 2001 The European linguistic area: Standard Average European. – Martin Haspelmath, Ekkehard Konig, Wulf Oesterreicher & Wolfgang Raible (eds.), *Language Typology and Language Universals. An international handbook*, Vol. 2, 1492–1510. Berlin & New York: Walter de Gruyter.
Hinrichs, Uwe. 2009. Geschichte, Stand und Perspektiven der Eurolinguistik. *Eurolinguistik. Entwiklungen und Perspektiven. Akten der Internationalen Tagung vom 30.09.-2.10.2007 in Leipzig. Eurolinguistische Arbeiten. Band 5*. Herausgegeben von Uwe Hinrichs, 1–29. Wiesbaden. Harrassowitz Verlag.
Hinrichs, Uwe. 2012. Die Balkanismen in geolinguistischer Sicht. Ein erster Schritt. In Thede Kahl, Michel Metzeltin & Helmut Schaller (eds.), *Balkanismen heute – Balkanisms Today – Балканизмы сегодня*, 47–63. Wien: LIT Verlag.
Gabinskij, Mark A. 2008. *Balkanskij infinitiv – očerednoj etap diskussii. Antikritičeskij obzor*. Chișinău: Central'naja tipografija.
Georgiev, Vladimir. 1968. Le problème de l'union linguistique balkanique. In *Actes du Premier congrès international des études balkaniques et sud-est européennes*. Sofia: BAN.
Gołąb, Zbigniew. 1964. *Conditionalis typu bałkańskiego w językach południowosłowiańskich ze szczególnym uwzględnieniem macedońskiego*. Wrocław-Kraków-Warszawa.
Ivanchev, Svetomir. 1978. *Prinosi v bălgarskoto i slavjanskoto ezikoznanie*. Sofia.
Joseph, Brian D. 1983. *The synchrony and diachrony of Balkan infinitive. A study in areal, general, and historical linguistics*. Cambridge: Cambridge University Press.

Joseph, Brian D. 2001. Is Balkan comparative syntax possible? In Maria Luisa Rivero and Angella Ralli (eds.), *Comparative Syntax of Balkan Languages*, 17–43. Oxford: Oxford University Press.

Kostov, Kiril. 1999–2000. Eine Aussage des Fürsten Dimitrie Cantemir über die Sprachkontakte auf der Balkanhalbinsel. *Linguistique balkanique*. XL (2). 127–131.

Krapova, Iliyana. 2012. On the Syntax of Possession in the Balkan languages: the elusive nature of the External Possessive construction. In Thede Kahl, Michael Metzelin, Helmut Schaller (eds.), *Balkanismen heute – Balkanisms Today – Балканизмы сегодня*, 113–136. Wien: LIT Verlag.

Leschber, Corinna. 2005. Novi tendentsii v arealnata lingvistica: metodi i resultati [New tendencies in areal linguistics: methods and results]. In Julia Stojanova, Gergana Dacheva, Neda Pavlova, Vladimir Milanov (eds.), *Littera scripta manet. Sbornik v chest na 65-godishninata na prof. d-r Vassilka Radeva* [Festschrift for prof. Vassilka Radeva], 16–125. Sofia: University publishing house „Sv. Kliment Ohridski".

Lewy, Ernst. 1942 [1964]. *Der Bau der europäischen Sprache*. Tübingen: Niemeyer.

Lindstedt, Jouko. 2000. Linguistic Balkanization: Contact-induced change by mutual reinforcement. In Dicky Gilbers, John Nerbonne, Jos Schaeken (eds.), *Languages in Contact. Studies in Slavic and General Linguistics*, vol. 28, 131–146. Amsterdam-Atlanta: Rodopi.

Mladenov, Maksim Sl. 1993. *Bălgarskite govori v Rumănija*. [Bulgarian regional varieties in Romania]. Sofia: Izdatelstvo na Bălgarskata akademija na naukite.

Norman, Boris. Ju. 1978. O sintaksičeskih funkcijax artiklja v bolgarskom jazyke [On the syntactic functions of the article in the Bulgarian language]. *Vestnik Belorusskogo gosudarstvennogo universiteta. Filologija, žurnalistika, pedagogika, psihologija*, 45–51. Minsk.

Reiter, Norbert. 1991. Ist Eurolinguistik Gotteslästerung. In *Fragen der Linguistik*, ed. by Elisabeth Feldbusch, Reiner Pogarell & Cornelia Weiß, Band I. 109–113. Tübingen: Max Niemeyer Verlag.

Reiter, Norbert. 1997. "Eurolinguistik – ein Schritt in die Zukunft". *Symposion im Jagdschloß Glienicke (Berlin, 23.-26.4.1997). Südosteuropa Mitteilungen* 37. Jahrgang. Heft 3. 227–229.

Schaller, Helmut W. 1975 *Die Balkansprachen. Eine Einführung in die Balkanphilologie*. Heidelberg. Universitätsverlag Winter.

Shuteriqi, Dh. 1965 Fshati shqiptar i Bulgarisë, Mandrica. Studim dhe tekste. *Studime filologjike* 1. 103–112.

Thunmann Johann Erich. 1774. *Über die Geschichte und Sprache der Albaner und der Wlachen*. Hamburg. Helmut Buske Verlag (1976, facsimile edition).

Trubetzkoy Nikolay. S. 1928. Proposition 16. *Actes du Premier Congrès International des Linguistes*, 17–18. La Haye.

Vasilev, Christo. 1968. Addenda und Corrigenda zu Sandfelds Linguistique balkanique. *Zeitschrift für Balkanologie*. VI.1.92–96.

Zvegintsev, Vladimir A. 1962. *Očerki po obščemu jazykoznaniju* [Essays in general linguistics]. Moskva: Izdatel'stvo Moskovskogo universiteta.

Victor A. Friedman
Parallel Universes and Universal Parallels: Balkan Romani Evidential Strategies

Abstract: The article examines the use of particles of interrogative origin to mark evidential strategies in three distinct and separate (albeit ultimately related) Balkan Romani dialects or groups of dialects in Macedonia, Bulgaria, and Serbia.[1] The use of the respective particles to render meanings belonging to the evidential complex (admirativity, dubitativity, and neutral nonconfirmativity) show typological parallels to developments involving interrogative markers in other languages. At the same time, the presence of evidential strategies in contact languages offers the possibility of adducing how accounts of contact

---

[1] The most widely accepted classification of Romani dialects has four major groups called Balkan, Vlax, Central, and Northern (cf. Matras 2002). Since both Vlax and Balkan Romani dialects are spoken in the Balkans, the term *Balkan Romani* is ambiguous. All the Romani dialects discussed in this article are in the Balkan group and are thus Balkan Romani dialects both geographically and taxonomically.

Note: The field work on which this article is based was conducted while I was in the Republic of Macedonia in 2008-2009 with a fellowship from the John Simon Guggenheim Foundation and a Fulbright-Hays Post-Doctoral Fellowship and in 2012 with support of a Title VIII Research Scholar Award from the American Councils for International Education: ACTR/ACCELS and an East European Studies Fellowship from the American Council of Learned Societies, funded in part by the National Endowment for the Humanities. I hereby express my gratitude to all of these organizations. I also wish to thank my Romani consultants, Elez Beslim, Ljatif Demir, Denis Durmiš, Enisa Eminovska, Azbija Memedova, Engo Serbez, Sali Salievski, and their families and friends. I am grateful to Mozes Heinschink and Petra Cech for the Romani examples from Serbia. I also thank Sasha Aikhenvald for bringing the Tatar example to my attention, Teija Greed for additional information on Tatar, and Kagan Arik for the Turkish example and information on other Turkic languages. I thank Besmir Fidahić for the Bosnian/Croatian/Serbian/Montenegrin example. I thank Marjan Markovikj for the discussion of Serbian versus Macedonian usage. Finally, I am grateful to the Center for Research on Language Diversity of La Trobe University, where I was an honorary visitor in 2016 and was able to complete the writing of this article. None of these organizations or individuals are responsible for the opinions expressed herein. I use the following abbreviations: 2pl = 2nd person plural; 2sg = 2nd person singular; 3sg = 3rd person singular; ABL = ablative; ACC = accusative; AOR = aorist; DAT = dative; DEF = definite article; F = feminine; FUT = future; G = genitive; IMP = imperfect; ITR = intransitive marker; L = *l*-participle; LF = long form (present); M = masculine; N = neuter; NEG = negative marker; OPT = optative; PL = plural; PX = proximal; PRS = present; Q = interrogative particle; SP = subordinating (modal) particle; VOC = vocative.

Victor A. Friedman, University of Chicago and La Trobe University, vfriedm@uchicago.edu

https://doi.org/10.1515/9783110375930-003

induced change can be elucidated by typology without conflating the two types of explanation.

Keywords: admirative, contact linguistics, dubitative, interrogative, typology

1 Introduction

As Hamp (1977) argued in the context of typology, and Joseph (2001) argued in the context of formal syntax, areal linguistics (or contact linguistics) is an historical discipline, the mirror image of genealogical linguistics. Anthropological linguists have seriously questioned the distinction between change during transmission and change via diffusion (Enfield 2005), while sociolinguists adduce new evidence for the difference (Labov 2007). Bisang (2004, 2006) argues for an integrative approach to language change utilizing typology, dialectology, sociolinguistics, and contact linguistics. This article contributes to Bisang's argument by examining evidential strategies (cf. Aikhenvald 2003) in a variety of Romani dialects, both in and out of contact with other languages that possess evidential strategies. At issue are borrowed evidential markers, borrowed particles reinterpreted as evidential markers, and native grammatical distinctions reinterpreted in a manner consistent with evidential concerns. The relevant data demonstrate how typological (universal) and areal (contact) explanations can be used together in a nuanced fashion, and without conflation, to account for language change. Additional relevant material from Turkic and Slavic is adduced to support the argument that contact and typological linguistics can be mutually informative without being conflated. In concrete terms, the data demonstrate a typological connection between interrogation and dubitativity and between epistemological uncertainty and evidential strategy. At the same time, areal factors operating independently but with parallel results are at work.

2 The Evidential Complex

At issue here are different meanings that form a constellation that I shall call the *evidential complex*. There are three basic functions of evidential strategies in the Balkans (and elsewhere) that can, in a sense, be compared with Bühler's (1934) classic three functions of language: emotive (or expressive), addressive, and communicative. In its communicative function, the evidential strategy serves to mark the information as more or less vouched-for (confirmed), i.e. the speaker's degree of certainty, commitment, or responsibility concerning the information. It is frequently the case that such a relationship is determined by the source of the evidence (witnessing, hearsay, inference, etc.), but as numerous examples demonstrate, literal "source of evidence" – first adduced by Kashgari (Dankoff 1982) for Turkish, and Lunt (1952) and Jakobson (1957/1971) for Macedonian – is not always the determining factor (Johanson 1971, Friedman 2014 and references therein).[2]

The other two functions derive conceptually from this communicative one, which I describe as the opposition confirmativity/non-confirmativity (Friedman 2014). If the speaker discovers something to be worthy of confirmation that, previously, said speaker did not consider to be the case, the discovery evokes surprise. This contrary-to-expectation function, when applied to a non-confirmative evidential strategy, can be described as emotive (expressive), insofar as the strategy involves an infelicitous (in Austin's 1962 sense) use of a non-confirmative form for the purpose of confirmation, i.e. 'I did not expect this to be the case, but, to my surprise it is'. This type of usage, which is basic in Albanian, is referred to as admirative.[3] This function can, in Bühler's terminology, be described as emotive or expressive. This description is especially appropriate since expressive language often uses infelicity to create its effects, and, moreover, the admirative does not require an addressee, just as an exclamation of surprise does not.

The third function, Bühler's addressive, is usually associated with imperatives and vocatives. In describing the evidential complex, however, this function can be described as corresponding to the dubitative, which, by its very nature, requires a previous statement. The dubitative is an expression of felicitous disbelief (irony, sarcasm, etc.) that refers to a previous statement.[4] Thus, while the neutral (communicative) evidential strategy marks the speakers willingness or desire to confirm or withhold personal confirmation from the narrated event, and the admirative (emotive/expressive) is an expression of confirmation using a non-confirmative form to convey surprise, the dubitative is an active denial of a real or putative previous statement.

---

[2] The recent literature on the concept *evidential* has become too vast to cite, and, moreover, too diffuse.
[3] See Friedman (2012a, 2012b) and the references therein. The term 'admirative' precedes the term 'mirative' by almost a century, and the latter has a more dubious status (Hill 2012).
[4] By its very nature, the dubitative cannot refer to an actual event, since it presumes non-existence of some state of affairs.

3 Case 1: Kriva Palanka and Barutči Subdialects of Macedonian Arli Romani

Our first case study involves the Arli Romani dialect of Kriva Palanka (Turkish Egri Dere Palanka), spoken in northeastern Macedonia, and the Barutči Arli dialect of Skopje (Turkish Üsküb). The name *Arli* derives ultimately from Turkish *yerli* 'local, settled'. As the name implies, these Romani speakers have been in stable contact with the relevant Balkan languages for centuries. Until the middle of the twentieth century, the language with the highest prestige was Turkish, and, moreover, as these Romani speakers, like 90% of the Roms in Macedonia today, are Muslim, their association with Turkish was especially strong.[5] The language of most of the peasantry with which these Romani speakers were in contact was Macedonian.[6] In the case of the Barutči Arli, as their name implies (cf. Turkish *barut* 'gunpowder'), the speakers originally lived and worked around an Ottoman gunpowder factory. The factory was located in the village of Jurumleri (Turkish *Ürünleri* cf. Turkish *ürün* 'product'). Some families relocated to Skopje at some time in the relatively distant past, and theirs is the second oldest Arli dialect in Skopje.[7]

In the course of field work in Macedonia, I was testing for a wide variety of Romani dialectal features, among which was whether there was a Romani equivalent for any of the kinds of evidential strategies used in the main contact languages, Macedonian and Turkish.[8] It was in this context that I discovered a usage corresponding to the Macedonian dubitative use of its unmarked past.[9]

---

[5] Strictly speaking, Serbian became the prestige language with the annexation in 1913 of most of the territory that became the Republic of Macedonia, and it was replaced by Macedonian in this regard in 1944. However, as late as the 1970s, Turkish retained its high prestige as the language of old urban families, especially Muslims.

[6] While all of the Balkan languages were represented with significant populations of speakers in Macedonia until World War Two, there was considerable variation among specific, local contact situations.

[7] The oldest is Topaanli. For details on the seven traditional Arli dialects of Skopje, see Friedman (2017).

[8] Albanian is an important contact language for Romani in western Macedonia, but not for the dialects under consideration here.

[9] In Standard Macedonian and the dialects on which it is based, the inherited synthetic aorist and imperfect are marked for confirmativity, while the old inherited perfect using the auxiliary 'be' with what used to be a resultative participle, in -*l*, has become the unmarked past. This unmarked past, by virtue of its contrast to a marked confirmative, can be deployed in various (non-confirmative) evidential strategies. In the southwestern dialects, a new perfect using the auxiliary 'have' and what used to be the past passive participle (now a verbal adjective) has

The interviews were conducted in Macedonian, in which all the relevant Romani speakers (and, indeed, most adult Romani speakers in Macedonia) are completely bilingual.[10] For the purposes of trying to elicit evidential usage, one of the scenarios I constructed was one in which two people are conversing on the telephone. Speaker A claims that he is in (calling from) America. Speaker B, convinced or knowing full well that Speaker B is lying, retorts with speaker A's original statement, but using a dubitative, which in Macedonian involves repeating the statement and shifting the tense into the equivalent using a verbal *l*-form (unmarked past or 'have' -perfect with an *l*-auxiliary).[11] The original Macedonian is given in (1):

(1) A: *Jas sum vo Amerika.*
       I   am   in America
       'I'm in America.'
   B: *Abe ti si bil vo Amerika! Lažeš!*
       VOC you are L.M in America! lie.2sg.PRS
       'Oh, sure, you're in America! You're lying!'

The Kriva Palanka Arli Romani of (1) is given in (2):

(2) A: *Me sijum ki Amerika.*
       I   am   in America
       'I'm in America.'
   B: *Abe tu hinjan li t-i   Amerika! Hohavea*
       VOC you are   *li* in-F.DEF America lie.2sg.PRS.LF[12]
       'Oh sure, you're in America! You're lying!'

---

restricted the old perfect entirely to non-confirmative uses. This is an on-going process that is spreading north and east (Friedman 2014 and fieldwork).

10 We can note here in passing that some Romani speakers have an identifiable ethnolectal accent when they speak Macedonian, arguably comparable to the relationship of ethnolectal African American Vernacular English to Standard English, albeit the differences between the two varieties are less noticeable in the former case than in the latter. Many educated Roms, however, speak exactly the same Macedonian as educated ethnic Macedonians.

11 The unmarked past is formed by using the present tense of 'be' in the first two persons and zero in the third person plus the verbal *l*-form, which agrees with the subject in gender (singular) or number (plural).

12 Balkan Romani distinguishes long forms of the present tense, which end in *-a* from short forms, which do not. Although this is frequently described as marking an opposition indicative/subjunctive (e.g., Matras 2002), usage is quite variable. The long form is clearly preferred, however, for progressive meaning.

The particle *li* looks like the Slavic interrogative particle, an analysis which will be confirmed below. It is important to note here that the intonation of dubitative usage is declarative and not the interrogative intonation associated with the interrogative use of *li*. Confirmation that this dubitative strategy does indeed come from an interrogative particle is found in the Barutči Arli equivalent of (1) and (2), which is given here as (3).

(3) *Abe tu injan mi ki Amerika. Hohavea!*
    VOC you are *mi* in America. lie.2sg.PRS.LF
    'Oh sure, you are in America! You're lying!'

Although most Romani dialects in Macedonia (and many others in contact with various Slavic languages) borrow the Slavic interrogative particle *li*, the Barutči dialect has borrowed the Turkish interrogative particle *mi* in this dubitative function. This connection between interrogativity and the evidential complex is also seen in Sliven Romani, to which we now turn.

4 Case 2: Sliven Romani

The town of Sliven, which is in the northwestern quadrant of southeastern Bulgaria, is known in Bulgaria for its significant Romani population.[13] Into the twentieth century, both Turkish and Bulgarian were significant contact languages, although the district now has fewer Turks than it does Roms (Bulgarian Census 2011:24). Kostov (1963:123, 132–133) discusses the use of *li* in the Sliven dialect of Romani used as an evidential marker.[14] According to Kostov (1963:132), *li* can be suffixed to any preterite finite Romani verb form (imperfect, aorist [perfect], pluperfect) to render either reported or non-confirmative speech as in examples (4) and (5)

(4) *phirim-li* (Kostov 1963:123)
    go.1sg.AOR *li*
    'They say I have gone'

---

[13] According to the 2011 census, 11.8% versus 4.9% for Bulgaria as a whole (Bulgarian Census 2011:24).
[14] Kostov (1973:107–108) repeated some of this material in a published article on Balkanisms in Romani. Kostov (1963:123) writes 'some Romani dialects', but he only specifies and supplies examples from Sliven.

(5) *oda vakerjas mangi,   či tu phirsas-li.* (Kostov 1963:133)
   he said.3sg.AOR me.DAT   that you go.3sg.IMP-*li*
   'he told me that, apparently, you were/are going.'

Kostov speculates that the origin of this *li* is the Bulgarian *l*-participle, whose functions in finite verb forms are much like those of the Macedonian *l-form* in terms of marking nonconfirmativity (as noted by Kostov, cf. also Friedman 2002). Igla (2004, 2006) expands on Kostov's results in Sliven Romani. She cites a number of examples in which *-li* is attached to each verb form in an extended narrative, but of particular significance is an example of admirative usage given here as (6):

(6) *O Devla, ta oda mandar   da butrašadi   isja-li!*
   O God.VOC and they me.ABL and more.scared was/were.3sg/pl.IMP-*li*
   rivisejlu-li   u šošoj. (Igla 2006:61)
   cry.3sg.AOR-*li* the rabbit
   '"Oh my God, they are more timid than I am!" the rabbit cried out'

In this example, a rabbit is expressing surprise at seeing frogs jump into a river. This is a typical admirative that in Bulgarian, as in Macedonian, would be rendered by the *l*-form of 'be'. Moreover, since this is part of a second-hand story (here, a folk tale), the verb of speaking is also modified by *li*. According to Igla (2006:58), as also Kostov (1973:108), the present/imperfect opposition is neutralized with the addition of *li*.[15] For our purposes here, the significance lies in the use of *li* to render the evidential complex. Igla (2006:56) also speculates that the origin is the Slavic interrogative marker rather than the Bulgarian *l*-participle. Given the evidence we have adduced in Section 3 above, it seems most likely that Igla is correct.

---

[15] The shape of the form varies between the two sources, which Igla, quite plausibly, attributes to innovation. For our purposes here, however, the fact of *li* usage is what is significant. I have argued elsewhere (Friedman 2002, 2012a) that evidential strategies in Balkan Slavic always have some sort of past reference (either to a previous state of affairs or real or putative statement), since they cannot be used felicitously with genuine present or future meaning, e.g. one cannot look at the sky, see it suddenly cloud over, and exclaim 'It's going to rain!' with an admirative *l*-form in Balkan Slavic. Further research is needed, however, to determine whether these same restrictions apply to the Romani phenomena discussed here.

5 Case 3: Arli in Serbia

Numerous examples of *li* have been recorded in Serbia by Mozes Heinschink (Heinschink Collection, personal communication) that are relevant to evidential usage. In these examples, *li* functions as an emphatic rather than an interrogative particle. The effect is frequently admirative as can be seen in examples (7) and (8). In example (7) a king has learned that his unwed daughter is pregnant, and he is furious about his loss of reputation. In (8), a snake wins a king's daughter's hand in marriage by solving three tasks, and the girl is frightened at the prospect of wedding a snake:

(7) *"Ah", vakerol, "kurvo jek, tu kaljardžan mo muj!*
 ah says.3sg.PRS whore.VOC one you blacken.2sg.AOR my face
 Odova li kerdan tu, jek thagareskiri rakli!"
 this *li* did.2sg.AOR you one king.GEN.F girl
 "Ah", he says, "you whore! You have brought shame upon me! YOU did that, a king's daughter!" (Niš Xoraxane; Heinschink Collection Nr.1207, pc Heinschink)[16]

(8) *Oj kada dikhla, i rakli, so-j li ov, oj lija*
 she when saw.3sg.AOR the.F girl what-is *li* he she took.3sg.AOR
 te daral lestar
 SP fear.3sg.PRS him.ABL
 'When the girl saw what he turned out to be, she grew afraid of him.' (Kruševac Arli, Heinschink Collection Nr.2297, pc Mozes Heinschink)

In these examples, the particle *li* attaches to a nominal form, but it clearly has an admirative illocutionary effect and is not interrogative. In example (7), the *tu* referring to the king's daughter is in focus position, but the *li* is marking the topic of the sentence. In example (8), *so* 'what' can be interrogative, but here it is functioning as a complementizer.

---

[16] Heinschink (p.c.) describes this dialect as "quite Arlesk". In so doing, he is flagging the problems with defining the Arli dialect group in strictly linguistically taxonomic terms. For our purposes, however, the dialect can be taken as part of the larger Arli complex.

6 Influences and Parallels

The examples in Section 5 are from Serbia, where Albanian was spoken as far north as Niš until 1878 and Turkish was a prestige language there and further to the north during the nineteenth century. It is also worth noting that *Xoraxane* are Muslim. Still, Serbian has been the major prestige and contact language for much longer than Macedonian in the Republic of Macedonia. That said, however, we can note that *li* can function as an emphatic marker in the former Serbo-Croatian, as can be seen in example (9), which was used by a Bosnian Serb. As can be seen, this usage is highly colloquial, and, moreover, is unlikely to occur except in speech or imitations of speech (e.g., in drama):[17]

(9) Pa pička vam   materina,   jesam li rekao da mi   pošaljete
    and cunt you.PL.DAT mother's.F am   li said-L SP me.DAT send.2pl.PRS
    vod   vojnika   sad, jebem   li vam   hljeb   i boga!
    platoon soldier.GEN.PL now fuck.1sg.PRS li you.PL.DAT bread.ACC and god.ACC
    'And your mother's cunt, I said *li* to send me a platoon of soldiers now, I fuck *li* your bread and god!' (more idiomatically: 'You stupid mother-fuckers, I told you to send me a platoon now, God fucking damn you to hell!')

Example (9) is interesting on two counts. First, for our purposes, the particle *li* clearly has an emphatic, not an interrogative, illocutionary force. Second, although the speaker is addressing a single person in the actual utterance, it is clear that he intends as his addressees all those who in any way were responsible, as the second singular of politeness is excluded in this context. It is also worth noting that in example (9) the *li* modifies a verb rather than a nominal. The use of *li* as an emphatic declarative marker in the Arli of Serbia is much like the usage in the former Serbo-Croatian. In both cases, the *li* functions to express a kind of shocked surprise, on the border with dubitativity, but in fact admirative.

The difference between dubitative and admirative usages in the Macedonian and Serbian Romani dialects adduced here is reflected in, and arguably due to, a difference between Serbian and Macedonian expressive uses of *li*. The Serbian usage is known in Macedonia, but as a Serbian expression.[18] In Macedonian,

---

[17] This example was from a conversation recorded during the Yugoslav Wars of Succession. The speaker is a soldier. I thank Besmir Fidahić for bringing this example to my attention.

[18] A salient example of the Serbism in Macedonian is provided by the wire-tapping scandal called the "Bombs" (Macedonian *Bombi*) released in 2015 (Prizma 2015). In this example, spoken by a Macedonian government minister, the final word, *mater* is a Serbian accusative, which thus marks the interjection as a Serbism:

expressive *li* functions dubitatively much as in Kriva Palanka and Barutči Romani, as seen in example (10):

(10) Kako da ne, toj li kje ti   ja   napravi   kolata...
how SP not he *li* FUT you.DAT it.ACC fix.3sg.PRS car.DEF.F
(Marjan Markovikj, pc)
'Oh sure, he'll fix your car alright...'

An important difference between the Romani usage and Macedonian, however, is that the Macedonian occurs before the verb (or after the noun or pronoun) rather than post-verbally. Post-verbally, Macedonian *li* will be interpreted as interrogative rather than dubitative. The Romani examples from Macedonia are thus much closer to the dubitative usage of the Macedonian *l*-form (unmarked past) that they have been used to translate.

A typological parallel to admirative usage of the type occurring in Sliven Romani can be seen in Turkic languages in the use of negative interrogative optatives to express surprise, as in example (11a) in Tatar and its Turkish translation in (11b):

(11a) Kič   belän Färid kil-ep   ker-mä-sen-me? (Nasilov et al. 2001:218)
Evening with   F.   come-CVB enter-NEG-OPT-Q'

(11b) Akşamleyin   Ferit gel-ip   gir-me-sin mi? (Kaghan Arik, pc)
Evening.with F.   com-CVB enter-NEG-OPT-Q'
'Unexpectedly Farid showed up this evening'.

Here again we see a connection between an interrogative marker and admirative illocutionary force. In these examples, the converb meaning 'come' combines with the negative interrogative optative to express suddenness and unexpectedness. The same usage also occurs in Central Asian Turkic languages such as Kazakh, Kirghiz, and Uzbek (Kaghan Arik, pc). Typologically, this usage can be compared with the two types of expressions in English. The use of *go and* to express suddenness is parallel to the use of *come+converb marker* in Turkic, cf. *He went and did it*. Similarly, the English use of a negative interrogative conditional

---

Se iznervirav   dopolnitelno so   ova kopilevo   od   Bitola Vlado Talevski,
ITR annoy.1sg.AOR additionally with this bastard.PX.DEF from B.   V.   T.
pička li mu   mater (ZS, Bomb 6, segment 7, Prizma 2015)
cunt *li* him.DAT mother.ACC
'I'm completely fed up with that mother-fucking bastard from Bitola, Vlado Talevski.'

in the expression *wouldn't you know it!*, is not a question but an expression of (often exasperated) surprise.

7 Conclusion

The dubitative usage of *li* and *mi* in Arli Romani dialects of Macedonia is arguably typologically connected to the evidential use of *li* in the Sliven Romani dialect of Bulgaria and also to the emphatic use of *li* in the Arli Romani dialects of Serbia. It is the Barutči Arli use of the borrowed Turkish interrogative particle *mi* combined with the equivalent use of *li* in Kriva Palanka Arli that supports the interpretation of Sliven Romani *li* as being of interrogative origin rather than based on the *l* of the Bulgarian *l*-participle. In both Macedonia and Bulgaria, the respective Romani dialects are in intimate contact with languages that have evidential systems. The Sliven Romani evidential strategy appears to express more meanings of the evidential complex than that of Macedonia, but in both cases the respective usages are clearly part of the evidential complexes of the relevant contact languages. Moreover, a related use of *li* in Macedonian arguably served as a model for the development of *li* as a dubitative marker in the relevant Romani dialects of Macedonia, although the Romani usage is distinct in its modification of the finite verb. In the Serbian case, local Arli usage could be directly based on Serbian usage. Here the transition from interrogative marker to expressions of surprised dismay is semantically related to the meanings expressed in the evidential complex and argues for a typological connection between interrogativity and meanings such as admirativity and dubitativity. The examples from Turkic languages – which, like Macedonian and Bulgarian, have evidentiality encoded in the verbal system – give additional evidence of interrogatives involved in admirative expressions. In the case of the various dialects of Romani, it is a combination of the typological connection of interrogativity to the evidential complex plus contact with relevant languages that leads to parallel developments whose explanation involves both areal and typological factors.

References

Aikhenvald, Alexandra Y. 2003. Evidentiality in Typological Perspective. In A.Y. Aikhenvald and R.M.W. Dixon (eds.), *Studies in Evidentiality*, 1–31. Amsterdam: Benjamins.
Austin, John Langshaw. 1962. How to Do Things with Words. Cambridge: Harvard University.
Bisang, Walter. 2004. Dialectology and typology – an integrative perspective. *Dialectology meets typology. Dialect grammar from a crosslinguistic perspective*, ed. by Bernd Kortman, 11–45. Berlin: Mouton de Gruyter.

Bisang, Walter. 2006. Contact-induced convergence: Typology and areality. *Encyclopedia of Language and Linguistics*, ed. by Keith Brown, Vol. 3, 88–101. Oxford: Elsevier.

Bühler, Karl. 1934. *Sprachtheorie*. Jena: Gustav Fischer.

Bulgarian Census. 2011. BulgarianBulgCensus2011final_en.pdf <www.nsi.bg/census2011/> (downloaded 19 January 2016).

Dankoff, R. (ed. and transl. with J. Kelly). 1982. Mahmud al-Kāšğarī, *Compendium of the Turkic Dialects (Dīwān luğāt at-Turk)*, Part I. Cambridge: Tekin.

Enfield, Nick J. 2005. Areal Linguistics and Mainland Southeast Asia. *Annual Review of Anthropology* 34.181–206.

Friedman, Victor A. 2002. Hunting the elusive evidential: The third-person auxiliary as a boojum in Bulgarian. In Victor A. Friedman & Donald L. Dyer (eds.), *Of all the Slavs my favorites: Studies in Honor of Howard I. Aronson on the occasion of his 66th birthday*. (Indiana Slavic Studies 12 [2001].), 203–230. Bloomington: Slavica.

Friedman, Victor A. 2012a. Perhaps Mirativity is Phlogiston, but Admirativity is Perfect. *Linguistic Typology* 16(2).505–527.

Friedman, Victor A. 2012b. Enhancing National Solidarity through the Deployment of Verbal Categories: How the Albanian Admirative Participates in the Construction of a Reliable Self and an Unreliable Other. *Pragmatics and Society*. 3(2).189–225.

Friedman, Victor A. 2014. *The Grammatical Categories of the Macedonian Indicative*. Columbus: Slavica. 2nd revised edition.

Friedman, Victor A. 2017. Seven Varieties of Arli: Skopje as a Center of Convergence and Divergence of Romani Dialects. *Romani Studies, Series 5*, 27(1).29–45.

Hamp, Eric P. 1977. On some Questions of Areal Linguistics. *Proceedings of the 3rd Annual Meeting of the Berkeley Linguistics Society*, ed. by K. Whistlers et al., 279–282. Berkeley.

Hill, Nathan W. 2012. "Mirativity" does not exist: ḥdug in "Lhasa" Tibetan and other suspects. *Linguistic Typology* 16.389–433.

Igla, Birgit. 2004. Spreženie na glagola v Slivenskija romski dialekt. *Andral* 35–36.19–50.

Igla, Birgit. 2006. Zur Renarrative im slivener Romani. *Balkansko ezikoznanie* 40(1).55–63.

Jakobson, Roman. 1957/1971. *Shifters, Verbal Categories, and the Russian Verb*, Cambridge: Harvard Department of Slavic Languages and Literatures (Reprinted in 1971. *Selected Writings 2*, 130–147. The Hague: Mouton.)

Joseph, Brian D. 2001. Is Balkan Comparative Syntax Possible? *Balkan Syntax in a Comparative Light*, ed. by Maris-Luisa Rivero & Angela Ralli, 17–43. Oxford: Oxford University Press.

Johanson, Lars. 1971. *Aspekt im Türkischen*. Uppsala: Uppsala University.

Kostov, Kiril. 1963. Grammatik der Zigeunersprache Bulgariens: Phonetik und Morphologie. Doctoral dissertation, Humboldt University of Berlin.

Kostov, Kiril. 1973. Zur Bedeutung des Zigeunerischen für die Erforschung Grammatischer Interferenzerscheinungen. *Balkansko ezikoznanie* 16(2).99–113.

Labov, William. 2007. Transmission and diffusion. *Language* 83(2).344–387.

Lunt, Horace. 1952. *A Grammar of the Macedonian Literary Language*. Skopje: Državno knigoizdatelstvo na NR Makedonija.

Matras, Yaron. 2002. *Romani: A Linguistic Introduction*. Cambridge: Cambridge University Press.

Nasilov, Dimitrij M., Xoršid. F. Isxakova, Šaxrijor S. Safarov, and Irina A. Nevskaja. 2001. Imperative sentences in Turkic languages. *Typology of imperative constructions*, ed. by Viktor Xrakovskij, 181–220. Munich: Lincom Europa.

Prizma. 2015. Kompleten materijal od site bombi što gi objavi opozicijata. <http://fokus.mk/kompleten-materijal-od-site-bombi-shto-gi-objavi-opozitsijata/> (accessed 5.VI.2016).

Andrey N. Sobolev
Areal Typology and Balkan (Morpho-)Syntax

Abstract: This paper presents the author's individual views on the state of affairs and presents theoretical, methodological and practical results, obtained in the last decade, in the field of comparative-historical and comparative-contrastive Balkan linguistics and especially with regard to (morpho-)syntax. The major theoretical issues of Balkan linguistics, e.g. principles of genetic, areal, social or contact determination or restriction in language evolution, are addressed. The historical, structuralist and functionalist methods of research in Balkan dialectology (collecting the (morpho-)syntactic data, their mapping, systemic and contrastive analysis) are applied. I first promote a new definition of a (Balkan) Sprachbund, as "a language group defined by functional, not substantive properties". Further, a number of general, areal, particular and universal (morpho-)syntactic phenomena are presented, including (1) redundancy in Balkan grammar; (2) contact-related convergent syntactic structures; (3) two-language-contact-induced morpho-syntactic changes; (4) borrowability hierarchies in the (history of the) Balkan languages. It is claimed, for example, that Balkanisms ("the shared common Balkan features") should be opposed to anti-Balkanisms: "features that were never shared (borrowed) despite similar conditions of contact"; that the causes of Balkan convergence are to be seen in multiple language shifts (substratum phenomena) rather than in balanced bi- or trilingualism; that although a cross-linguistic comparison of (morpho-)syntax involving Balkan languages is truly possible, the study of "comparative (morpho-)syntax of the Balkan languages" can, but should not necessarily discover parts of "comparative Balkan (morpho-)syntax". In conclusion, the major tasks and desiderata of contemporary Balkan linguistics are summarized.

Keywords: Balkan linguistics, Sprachbund, areal typology, (morpho-)syntax, redundancy, convergent syntax, taxis, language change in contact, borrowability hierarchies, Albanian, Balkan Romance, Balkan Slavic, Modern Greek

---

Note: The research is supported by the Russian Scientific Foundation (project "Between separation and symbiosis: the languages and cultures of South-Eastern Europe in contact", Nr. 14-18-01405)

Andrey N. Sobolev, St. Petersburg State University, Russian Academy of Sciences, Philipps-Universität Marburg, sobolev@staff.uni-marburg.de

https://doi.org/10.1515/9783110375930-004

1 Introduction

As the pioneering work by Kopitar (1829), Miklosich (1861) and especially Sandfeld (1930) showed already long ago, some of the languages in the Balkan area, especially Albanian, Balkan Romance (Dacoromanian, Aromanian, Meglenoromanian and Istroromanian) and Balkan Slavic (Bulgarian, Macedonian, and Eastern Serbian dialects), share a considerable number of common features, so-called Balkanisms (Seliščev 1925; Hinrichs 1999), resulting from convergent development.

It is clamed in Sobolev and Rusakov (2008: 6) that the *convergent development* of these languages is evident as much in the area of *mundus sensibilis* as in the sphere of *mundus intelligibilis*, changing both language substance and linguistic function.[1] The effects in language substance under contact influence are seen in the borrowing of linguistic elements (units), which integrate form and meaning: lexeme and idiomatic phrases larger than words, inflectional and word-formative morphemes, and morphonological mechanisms. For a sound system, the corresponding contact-induced change is the borrowing of a phoneme as a phonological unit and its acoustic-articulational nature (e.g. emergence of interdental spirants in Aromanian and dialects of Macedonian under Greek influence). In such cases, the phonemes are usually borrowed together with foreign words and morphemes in which they originally occur. We find the formal-syntactic realization of substantial contact-induced change in the sphere of word order and morpheme order (e.g. incorporating a direct object pronoun into the imperative verb form in a Northern Greek dialect due to Albanian influence (Lopashov 2006)).

Contact-induced alteration of linguistic function comprises interlingual identification of the elements (units) of two languages and changing one of the elements under the influence of the matching element in the other language. It should be mentioned here that interlingual identification is an analogical process, not considerably different from the processes active in monolingual language change (Croft 2000: 145–156). Both separate elements and constructions can be subject to identification, e.g. prepositional usage in one language can be identified with a case form in another or a synthetic verb form can be identified with an analytic one or even with a free syntactic construction (Sobolev 1990; Rusakov 2013). It is

---

[1] Substance can be seen as the ways of marking distinctive function and categorial grammatical meanings, i.e. the inventory of sounds and phonemes, word order, suprasegmental phenomena, morphological mechanisms, inflections and affixes, syntactic and content words (the latter only in obvious cases of their being a part of grammar). Function can be thought of as all kinds of functions and meanings, ranging from the distinctive function in phonology through abstract-grammatical to concrete-grammatical and even lexical meanings.

important to recognize that there is no fundamental difference between internally conditioned semantic shift and contact-induced calquing. A change in the function of an element of language A due to influence of the identification with an element of language B is characterized by its beginning to be used in the context analogical to language B constructions. Such processes were present during the diffusion of a large number of classic Balkanisms, for instance variants of future tense formation and other.

A *group of languages* relevant to such linguistic study is in practice any combination which exceeds two in number by any feature, for example state (languages of the Republic of Macedonia), geographical (languages of the geographical area of "Macedonia" not restricted by current political borders), religious (Muslim languages, Judaic languages, etc.), genetic (Indo-European or Turkic languages or other). In this context, a group of languages that share common features that cannot be explained by genetic relationship and are not restricted to lexical borrowings (Thomason 2000) is of particular interest. Since Trubetzkoy's (1928) terminological proposal, many definitions of a *Sprachbund*, or *convergent language group* have been given, one of the most recent by Joseph (2010: 620): "A Sprachbund can be defined as any group of languages that due to intense and sustained bilingual contact share linguistic features, largely structural in nature but possibly lexical as well, that are not a result of shared inheritance from a common ancestor nor a matter of independent innovation in each of the languages involved."

According to Sobolev and Rusakov (2008: 8), for a group of languages to be recognized as convergent, or a Sprachbund, it is necessary and sufficient to contain *correspondences in function of linguistic units* that are *regular*, i.e. *constitute a constant or definite pattern*, at all levels of language structure; convergences in substance are to occur in this case as inevitable accompanying features. If the languages, speakers of which live in close territorial adjacency, do not manifest such systematic correspondences, they are to be acknowledged as a (geographic-) areal group. It is possible to think that a (geographic-)areal group can develop into a convergent one, and conversely a convergent group can disintegrate into a (geographic-)areal one, in the way that supposedly has been happening in the Balkans.

Balkan studies, being *per definitionem* an areal discipline, cannot avoid using methods of *linguistic geography* and *dialectology* (cf., e.g., Duridanov and Mladenov 1989), mapping and comparing the data from different geographical dialects of different languages of the Balkans, thus making a Balkan Language Atlas (BLA) a desideratum. The history of the BLA projects, which have never come to fruition, reveals their principal theoretical defect: the authors intended to cartographically represent the *similarities*, although the theoretical basis of a language geography is built on the concept of a language (primary dialectal) *differentiation* (Sobolev 2004). What Balkanology needed at the end of the 1990s was a *minimal (but sufficiently large) number* of *maximally deep* descriptions of the Balkan dialects, which constituted a representative corpus of the relevant data allowing the comparison not of selected Balkanisms, but of the whole language systems or their parts within the framework of the whole systems. The *Small Dialectological Atlas of the Balkan Languages* (Sobolev (ed.) 2003; 2005a; 2005b; 2006; 2009; 2013) revealed the spatial distribution of the fundamental grammatical and lexical features of the representative[2] Balkan dialects to the south of the Danube and singled out the main linguistic subareas of the Balkan Peninsula.[3]

Generally, the basic interference mechanisms are universal and all contact situations can be reduced to two principal types – *language conservation* and *language shift*. In language conservation, interference processes act firstly on the lexical level and only afterwards does the phonetic and grammatical influence

---

[2] Although we see all the advantages of a dense network of points, we are forced for practical reasons to pick out a minimal number of the *representative dialects* for each Balkan language, i.e. category members, that are better representatives of the whole category than the others. We *understand* the diasystem of a single language *theoretically* as the totality and product of the systems of all its territorial units, but we *describe* it *practically* as the totality and product of a minimal number of its representative dialects. A representative dialect of a particular language is a dialectal unit, purposefully selected by the implementing of a linguistic procedure, a unit which belongs to the core of a large dialectal area of a single language and implements consequently all the characteristic development tendencies of this area; our list of representative dialects includes the Croatian neo-štokavian younger *i*-dialect; Serbian Zeta-Lovćen dialect; Serbian Timok dialect; West-Macedonian Ohrid dialect; South-West Bulgarian Pirin dialect; Bulgarian Rhodopi dialect; Bulgarian Moesia dialect; Albanian Middle-Geg Dibra dialect; Albanian Middle-Tosk dialect; Northern Greek West Macedonian dialect; Southern Greek Peloponnesos dialect; South-Aromanian Pindos Non-Farsherot dialect (Sobolev (ed.) 2003; 2005a; 2005b; 2006; 2009; 2013; Sobolev 2004).

[3] Areal linguistics data provides the possibility to speak about Balkan linguistic space as an uninterrupted continuum of Balkan dialects, which did not historically have barriers for borrowing and distributing of structural innovations, formal and semantic elements from one language into another. It is possible to talk about dialect structure of the Balkan linguistic community (disengaged from its genetic subdivision) manifested lexically and grammatically. The borders go often from north-north-east to south-south-west, while it appears that the West South Slavic area, when seen typologically and as an area in the general Balkan context, is a part of Balkan linguistic West (which includes also Albanian and Aromanian dialects, partly along with Slavic dialects of Western Macedonia). This Western area is most clearly in opposition to Balkan East or South-East (predominantly consisting of Greek – Bulgarian – East-Macedonian), which indicates the depth of this segmentation of the linguistic landscape of the peninsula in the course of history as we know it (from Illyrian – Thracian, Latin – Greek opposition to the well-known similar subdivision of Turkish dialects into the Western and the Eastern group) (Sobolev 2003a).

of the donor *language start*, usually coinciding with a change in language domination (Thomason and Kaufman 1991). As for the past language shift, one can reconstruct it combining linguistic and historical data from areas where it is supposed to have happened. For example, influence of East Romance languages on South Slavic and vice versa was realized in Bulgaria and Macedonia indubitably as a consequence of partial transition of the Vlachs to the usage of Balkan Slavic (Bulgarian or Macedonian)[4] in the period from the 9th to the 13th – 14th centuries (Chernyak 1998: 195–201). Results of this influence include: transition of Balkan Slavic nominal inflection to analyticity (Sobolev 1991; cf. Wahlström 2015: 16, 21), ways of expressing possessive relationships, development of a special way of marking definiteness on the left member of the noun group, and perhaps postposing the article. It is fairly difficult to localize the center of contacts geographically and to precisely define dialectal features of the donor language, and in the long run research is hindered by the unsolved issue of Romanian ethnogenesis; still some successful attempts have been made in this direction (Gołąb 1964; Tsykhun 1981; Mladenov 1987; Lindstedt 2014).

The most *topical research* leading to a deeper insight in the history and future of the Balkan Sprachbund is being done on *Balkan language contact in multilingual communities* (from the microlevel of families, *mahalas* or villages to the macrolevel of geographic areas, regions and states), providing us with reliable data concerning speech behavior of the Balkan bi- and triliinguals during various historical periods. For example, the language contacts on the border between Albania, Montenegro, Serbia and Macedonia are of special interest (Curtis 2012; Dombrowski 2013; Sobolev and Novik 2013; Sobolev 2015), where constant cross-ethnic communication existed, when "ethnic" Slavs were speaking Albanian and "ethnic" Albanians were speaking Slavic, and a change of languages occurred: the Albanians assimilated with Slavs and Slavs albanised.

It is not the aim of Balkan linguistics to collect a certain set of (grammatical) features that are to be claimed to comprise the group, but rather to discover general or specific regularities, *dominants* or even *constants* in the structure and development of the region's languages (Sobolev 2013a: 59–63). There is no doubt that dialects provide us with absolutely reliable data to resolve this issue (Sobolev 2014).

---

4 "…the scheme of Bulgarian ethnogenesis should be presented this way: 1st stage – assimilation of proto-Bulgarians in the territory of Lower Moesia and Scythia Minor and 2nd stage – assimilation of Romaioi, mostly Vlakhs, in the territory of Thrace and Dacia dioceses" (Chernyak 1998: 195).

2 The general: Redundancy in Balkan grammar

Up to the 1980s, our discipline was concerned with a search for a kind of *genetic dominant* of Balkan language development, i.e. a language which was a source of so-called Balkan linguistic features (Balkanisms). From the theories of a paleo-Balkan substratum (Kopitar 1829) through hypotheses of determinative Greek (Sandfeld 1930) or Romance (Solta 1980) influence, by sorting out all possible variants and overcoming the opposition of national "autochtonists" who saw the source of the most evident exoticisms of their languages in their inner potential (cf., e.g., Mladenova 2007 and discussion in Sobolev 2009b), Balkanistics grew to admit the original cause to be "long-term intimate contacts between languages of the Balkans" (Joseph 1992). It did reveal that some of the convergent innovations of Balkan languages are of communicative-pragmatic nature and emerge "when speakers of different languages try to communicate with each other in the most efficient manner" (Friedman 1994: 86). The structuralist generation turned to the search for intrasystem dominant factors in Balkan languages, assigning this role at first to the analytism of the linguistic structure, and then to the ambivalence of the grammatical structure (Tsiv'yan 1979: 230, 284).

It is important to mention that the Generative Syntax approach, looking for generalities with predictive force as well, turns out to be purely descriptive in the case of Balkan Slavic languages, i.e. Serbian, Macedonian and Bulgarian. Concluding the handbook analysis of the interaction of negation and pronominal clitics in Slavic, Kosta (2009: 309) states, for example, that "the Bulgarian system seems to prefer a position [of Neg] higher in the clause than the other Slavic languages... Neg has also some prosodic features in Bulgarian and Macedonian relevant for the description of syntax of clitics." A Balkan dialectologist can offer some facts, see e.g. (1), for future generativist analyses, making even these modest generalizations about the "height" of negation questionable (Sobolev 2001; Sobolev 2003):

(1) a. *Iê   go   səm   ne=r'ukʌ-lʌ.*   (Rhodope Bulgarian)
     1Sg.Nom 3Sg.Acc be.2Sg. Neg.=call-Participle.F
    Iê   nə=sôm   go   r'ukʌ-lʌ.
     1Sg.Nom Neg.=be.2Sg 3Sg.Acc. call-Participle.F
    'I didn't call him.'
   b. *nə=mô   sʌ   mlogu   trôsə-lə.*
     Neg.=1Sg.Acc be.3Pl   a lot   search-Participle.Pl
    'They didn't search for me a lot.'

Along this line of *searching for the general* in Balkan grammar, we are allowed to assign the role of the common constant for Balkan grammar to the *redundancy* in marking grammatical meanings, i.e. multiplication of grammatical category markers combined with a specific role for syntactic words.[5] Economy (down to the usage of a linguistic zero) and redundancy might be seen as two opposing and competing strategies of coding messages in natural languages. The main ways of coding grammatical information in Balkan languages, leaving suppletion aside, are: lexical meaning of content words (cf. kinship terms, personal pronouns), order of constituents, intonation contours, morphonological alternation (including inner flexion), inflexion, prefixation and suffixation, and synsemantic syntactic words. In addition to usual, typical and expected cases of marking grammatical meaning units with one mechanism (cf. Macedonian aorist *dojd-ov* 'I came'), each Balkan language or dialect provides a proliferation of diverse combinations of different mechanisms, as well as various strategies of decomposing those combinations. Remarkably impressive is the Balkan strategy of combining synsemantic lexical units with inflexion (Gjinari et al. 2007; Sobolev 2012); cf. for example:

- Albanian dialectal *i Muhurraku* 'an inhabitant of Muhurr village';
- double marking of gender in Albanian dialectal *i lam#* Masc. ~ *e lame* Adjective/Participle Fem. 'washed' and *kali i tiji* / *i saji* 'his/her horse';
- double marking of referentiality (definiteness) in Greek αυτά τα ψάρια 'those (the) fish' and Aromanian *peșțăl' aeșță* 'that fish, Pl.';
- double marking of a beneficiary in Albanian *i njeriut* 'to/for a person', and even triple and quadruple marking of an indirect object, or the semantic role of a recipient in Aromanian; cf. (2):

(2) L'i   dzāk-u   a   li   mulear-i
    she.Dat say-1Sg Art.Dat/Gen   Def.Dat   woman-Dat
    '(I) am telling (this) woman'

- comparatives such as Serbian *po deblji* 'thicker', *po bolji* 'better';
- possessives such as Macedonian *tatko mi moj* 'my father' and Aromanian *n'uma-lā a lor* 'their name'.
- infinitive in Romanian *a vorbi* 'to speak';
- 3rd person singular aorist mediopassive in Albanian dialects with *u*-particle and a special set of flexions *u vrati* 'was killed'.

---

[5] In postulating redundancy as dominant in Balkan grammar development, it is necessary to keep in mind that many linguistic strategies for expressing grammatical meanings are essentially redundant (agreement, for instance), that redundancy is basically characteristic of inflectional languages, and that quite often redundancy emerges as a result of the most general analogical processes (see, e.g., Russian *ikhniĭ* 'their', etc.)

It is reasonable to suppose that redundancy increases because of intensive interlingual contact between audiences of low competence, by summation of marking mechanisms, augmentation of "alien" mechanisms by "own" mechanisms, and not only by substituting them with "own" ones.

Those mechanisms may undergo economization, for example through eliding inflexion and introducing syntactic and synsemantic lexical means, as in Aromanian (3a), which was the source of the following construction to some West and South Macedonian dialects, (3b) (Sobolev 2008, cf. Asenova and Aleksova 2008):

(3) a. *u*   *m'esku*   *pri*   *nve'astă tu-ać'a o'ară* (Aromanian)
       she.Acc treat to.3Pl on.DirObj.Anim bride   in this time
       'The bride is being treated to food and drink during this time'
    b. *j'aska gu*   *v'idu*   *na*   *st'efo*   (dialectal Macedonian)
       I   he.Acc saw   on.DirObj.Anim Stefo
       'I saw Stefo'.

It can be argued that such strategies of grammatical marking emerge under two conditions: first, when it is necessary to code the message in a way that can be understood by a less competent audience, and second, when there is no dominance of one culture or language over another, i.e. in a situation that can be labeled 'coordinate bilingualism'. If this is indeed the case, it highlights the importance of searching for other still unknown but contact-related convergent (morpho-)syntactic structures.

3 The areal: Contact-related convergent (morpho-)syntactic structures

In a series of monographs and studies (e.g., Sobolev 2001; Ylli and Sobolev 2002; 2003; Bara, Kahl and Sobolev 2005; Voss 2006; Sobolev 2003b; 2005; 2006a; 2009a), the puzzles of grammar fragments of the Balkan languages have been solved within the dialectological and areal-typological framework, describing, analyzing, mapping and bringing to light Balkan areal dependencies against the general typological perspective. *Case*, especially *instrumentalis* in the nominal field and *tense*, especially *taxis*, in the verbal field, both grammatical (morpho-syntactic) categories represented by the Balkan-specific system (inventories) of grammaticalized forms and syntactically free constructions and their unique intrasystemic and areal distribution, proved to be suitable examples of heuristic capacities of linguistic geography applied to Balkan Sprachbund. A short discussion on taxis serves here as example.

Following Khrakovskij (2003: 39–40; 2009: 21–22), taxis, or relative time, is a category marking with special verb forms temporal localization (simultaneity, anteriority, posteriority) "of one situation P1 relative to another situation P2, the temporal localization of which is characterized in its relation to the time of speech". Situation P1 is denoted by a syntactically dependent, and situation P2 by a syntactically independent (so called "main") verb form.

Balkan languages allow both the dependent and the main taxis forms to be finite or non-finite, the latter being of particular typological interest and hard to derive historically from a single language source. Combinations of a *non-finite dependent* with a finite main form are rather diverse, because the dependent situation may be expressed by a converb (adverbial participle, gerund construction), as well as by a whole range of non-finite non-gerund forms, for example by a combination of some preposition with a verbal noun or by a combination of an indefinite article with a verbal noun or participle. The dependent temporal situation may be in this case localized as preceding or simultaneous with the main situation, and taxis forms and constructions may be characterized as single subject and multiple subject. In the first case, the subject is engaged in action both in the dependent and in the main situations, while in the second the subjects of both actions might have different reference. The few previous comparative studies of Balkan taxis (Sandfeld 1930: 122–125; Tsiv'yan 1979: 13, 116, 163; cf. also Topolinjska 1995–1997) failed to distinguish between the temporal, referential and areal (dialectal) variants of the construction's dependent part.

Searching in dialects for both *isomorphic and isofunctional* inter-Balkan taxis units[6] as part of the postulated comparative Balkan syntax, one can focus on non-finite specific taxis forms and constructions, like the gerund (adverbial participle), combinations of a verbal noun with a preposition meaning 'with', and combinations of an indefinite article with a verbal noun or a participle,[7] which all may express taxis meaning of simultaneity or anteriority and combine with either finite or non-finite forms expressing the main action.

---

[6] The first step in the inter-Balkan identification of forms and constructions is to establish their isofunctionality, and the second their isomorphism.

[7] One can leave aside negative forms and constructions (such as Albanian *pa ardhur* 'before coming' and Macedonian *ushte nevlezen* 'before entering'), which are not considered here, as well as semi-predicative participial phrases or the so-called predicative adjunct (such as Macedonian *sednat na klupa* 'sitting on the bank').

The *gerund* (the adverbial participle), suffixal in the majority of Balkan languages and analytic in Albanian (4a,b), is the most widespread specialized taxis form for simultaneous and anterior actions, but still not omnipresent; cf. its surprising absence in West Macedonian as revealed by (4c):

(4) a. *Tu hec   për rrug e   gjet   lopën.* (Gheg Albanian)
       walk.Gerund on road 3Sg.Acc found.Aorist.3Sg the cow
       'Walking on road, he/she found the cow.'
   b. *Vərv'ēštim Vôlku   pu pôk'ê, si   našôl adnô pun'g'ê*
       walk.Gerund Volku on road   himself found one purse
       s   pari.   (Rhodope Bulgarian)
       with money
       'Walking along the road, Volko found a purse with money.'
   c. *So   odejne   Rade po pət si   najde edno k'ese*
       with walking Rade on road himself found one purse
       so pari.   (West Macedonian)
       with money.
       'Walking along the road, Rade found a purse with money.'

Less widespread is the analogous usage of 'with' + verbal substantive (cf. the West Macedonian example above), which appears to be a feature of the southern part of the Balkans, while the combination of an indefinite article with a verbal noun or a participle (used to express anteriority) is limited in terms of territory and does not occur in the East, cf. (5):

(5) *Ună   beare,   il' kădzu   arău şi   muri.* (Aromanian)
    Indef drink.VerbalSubst him fall.Aorist.3Sg bad and die.Aorist.3Sg
    'Having drunk a mouthful, he felt bad and died.'

Different reference for the subject of the non-finite form (gerund and verbal substantive) and that of the finite main form is well recorded for South-Western and Southern areas,[8] as in (6):

(6) a. Ερχόντας   ο άντρας   στο σπίτι, η γυναίκα του άρχισε να
       come.Gerund the husband in the home, the wife his started Sbjv
       τον μαλώνει   (Northern Greek)
       him scold.3Sg

---

[8] In standard forms of some Balkan languages, e.g. in Bulgarian, the "mismatched agents" are not accepted as correct (Dimitrova 2000: 33).

'After the husband came home, his wife started to scold him.'
b. *Nji   të   fakt'ume,   ne h'ikim në shp'ai.*   (Gheg Albanian)
   Indef Art flash.VerbalSubst we went to house
   'After the lightning, we went into house.'

A range of grammatical features of Balkan taxis forms and constructions makes it possible to correct some of typological generalizations, like those concerning neutralization of simultaneity/anteriority opposition in non-finite taxis forms or single-subject versus multiple-subject oppositions (Nedjalkov 1998: 422, 436), the usage of non-finite forms in the main part of a taxis construction (where both the dependent and the independent taxis forms are non-finite verb forms) being the most interesting feature of some Balkan languages and dialects cross-linguistically. Areally restricted, found only in Albanian and Aromanian dialects, the main action in the past which is preceded by another action can be expressed by a verbal substantive (in Albanian built out of the article + participle) accompanied by an indefinite article with no finite form in the clause at all. In spite of this form carrying substantive morphological features (and articles first of all) there is no doubt about its essentially verbal quality (e.g., it can undergo passivization, and it can be accompanied by a subject in the nominative or a direct object in the accusative). The dependency relationship between the forms of a taxis pair in this case is marked formally by the fixed word order (dependent form – main form), and semantically by the first form having the meaning of anteriority relative to the second form. A different word order or other taxis meanings of those forms are apparently impossible:

(7) a. *Një   të   thënë   burr-i,   një   të   vajtur.*   (Albanian)
       Indef Art say.Participle man-Def Indef Art leave.VerbalSubst
   b. *Me   të   thënë   burr-i,   një   të   vajtur.*   (Albanian)
       with Art say.Participle man-Def Indef Art leave.VerbalSubst
       'After having said (this), the poor man immediately left.'
   c. *Ună videari,   ună   irutipsiri.*   (Aromanian)
       Indef see.VerbalSubst   Indef   love.VerbalSubst
       'Fell in love at the first sight.'

The temporal localization of the P2 situation is relative to the moment of speech, being localized in the past, although it is not marked on the non-finite verb form which in fact functions in contexts reserved, as a rule, for finite forms. Still, there is no evidence that it can be used as the only verb form of a simple non-elliptic sentence. In Sobolev (2005: 73–74), it is argued that we are dealing here with a typologically extremely rare case of combining a non-finite dependent and non-finite main form expressing posteriority.

The segment presented here of comparative (morpho-)syntax of Balkan dialects shows the areal and intrasystemic distribution of isosemantic taxis forms, whose isomorphism is not given at all and whose isofunctionality is in no case absolute. One can claim that pan-Balkan (morpho-)syntax is actually not existent, although full isosemanticism, full isofunctionality and even full isomorphism can be found in pairs of languages or dialects, such as Albanian and Aromanian, or Aromanian and West Macedonian, sometimes showing typologically rare or even exceedingly rare properties.

4 The particular: Contact-induced (morpho-)syntactic changes

Investigating pairs of Balkan languages in contact brings insight into mechanisms of "donating" and receiving (morpho-)syntactic properties, one of the most interesting cases being the direct intensive influence of Greek on Aromanian (for introduction see Chernyak 1990). This influence has lasted for at least a millennium since the moment when that dialect took its shape as a separate linguistic unit (language/dialect) and continues today with a certain intensity for the subdialects in the territory of the modern Hellenic Republic. Although this produces an abundance of material for the study of Romance, Romanian, Greek, and Balkan languages, for contact linguistics, and for general and typological linguistics, no major scientific work in the field has been done, not even a survey that goes beyond examining one usually disputable isolated borrowing (group of borrowings), or an isolated calque (ex. Kramer 1981; Kramer 1993). In Sobolev (2006b), based on the data from the South Aromanian subdialect of Turia, or Kranea (Κρανέα) village in Grevena (on which see Bara, Kahl, and Sobolev 2005), the (morpho-)syntactic changes in Aromanian due to long-term intimate contacts with Greek have been subject to a thorough examination.

For example, although the borrowing of content words obviously proceeds lexeme by lexeme, and not at the level of word classes, the massive inclusion of foreign vocabulary into the recipient language system means progressively less regular implementation of mechanisms for morphological and syntactical adaptation of this vocabulary by the latter. Thus, etymologically Greek adjectives may be integrated into the Aromanian gender and number system (e.g., *fuviroasā* Fem.Sg 'terrific', from Greek *φοβερό-*), but may be invariable as well:

(8) Iasti   fuviro   pravdă.   (Aromanian)
    be.3Sg   terrific   animal.Fem
    'It is a terrific animal (about the bear).'

Etymologically Greek adjectives and participles often take the position before the principal word of an adjectival phrase; cf. the "Greek" and the "Romance" word order, respectively, in these examples:

(9) a. Suntu anapuδi   lukri,   ţi bisearka nu li   va aćali. (Aromanian)
       be.3SG wrong.Pl   work.Pl that church not them like those
       'Those are wrong things, that the church doesn't like.'
    b. Băgam^u leamni   groasi.   (Aromanian)
       put.Imperfect.1Pl   wood.Pl   thick.Pl
       'We put thick pieces of wood.'

Some of the lexico-grammatical classes, smaller than parts of speech, appear to be represented in Aromanian solely by means of etymologically Greek lexemes. Such are, for instance, ordinal numerals and the identifying pronoun "same", both naturally preposed to the determinatum:

(10) a. Lo   si   bagă   prota lingră tu gură omlu. (Aromanian)
        take.Aorist.3Sg Conj   put.3Sg first spoon to mouth man
        'The man started to put the first spoon into his mouth.'
     b. Iδy'a   vakă   ş   iδy'ul^u y'in^u.   (Aromanian)
        same   cow   and   same   wine
        'The same cow and the same wine.'

Borrowing of separate syntactic units (most importantly prepositions and conjunctions) with their grammatical functions is without a doubt the most evident type of grammatical influence of one language on another. However, Greek prepositions get into the Turia dialect usually as the first part of a complex prepositional phrase (an'amisa di 'in between/amidst', δ'ipla di 'near', prot'u di 'before') with its second part being an etymologically Romance preposition di 'of', (11):

(11) Δipla di agru iaraună vali.   (Aromanian)
     Near of field was one valley
     'There was a valley near the field.'

From Greek coordinating conjunctions, the Aromanian language borrowed disjunctive i 'or' and i... i 'either ... or', negative uti 'not; not even', uti ... uti 'neither ... nor'.

There are also adversative *omus* 'but' and causal *epiδ'i* 'because', and many particles (negative interrogative *aray'es*, negative *oh'*, assertative *ne*, demonstrative predicative *na*, and a particle expressing doubt *taha*) on the list of borrowings as well.

Calques of the distributional rules for Greek grammatical units are well demonstrated by means of prepositional syntax. The original Aromanian spatial preposition *la* 'to, by, in, on', which is isofunctional to Greek spatial σε, mimics the functional-semantic range of the latter entering the sphere of indirect objects (where it engages in competition with the original Aromanian synthetic dative-genitive). This new indirect object la-construction often has distributive meaning, cf. (12):

(12) *Mār-ľi   da   la   n'is^i-ľi   ş   unā δrahmi.*   (Aromanian)
     old.Pl-Def give.3Pl to   young.Pl-Def and one   coin
     'The elder gave a coin to the youngsters as well.'

The Aromanian language has at least two ways of expressing noun phrase internal possessive relations. These involve a clitic and a full possessive pronoun (of the type *sokār-n'u* 'my father-in-law' vs. *fičorlu a m'eu* 'my son'); the former is characterized by a number of limitations on its grammatical distribution (observed exclusively with kinship terms and only for singular possessor and possessum). In spite of the obvious redundancy, there is a third way of marking a possessive relation: by a short dative form of the personal pronoun, most probably under Greek influence (e.g. *ο πεθερός μου* 'my father-in-law' and the examples immediately above). This strategy competes quite often with the other two, which are native to Aromanian. However, different noun phrases show different productivity for this new model. For example, in the naming of a close relative of singular number, the construction *h'iľlu-n'i* 'my son', *sora-ľ* 'their sister' is observed only in case of a direct inquiry (e.g., as a direct response to the interviewer's question),[9] while with plural number it appears both in direct inquiry (*frasľi-n'* 'our brothers', *surārli-ţ^a* 'your sisters') as well as in texts freely generated by the informants (*pārindzāľ-nā* 'our parents'). The Greek model of expressing possession appears typical with body parts (*f'aţa-lā* 'his face') but is completely regular also in constructions involving alienable possessions (e.g., *ho'ara-nā* 'our village', *k'asa-ľi* 'their house'). Special attention should be paid to 'doubling' constructions involving both a short dative and a full possessive pronoun (*numa-lā a lor* 'their names').

---

9 Nouns *mumā* 'mother', *m'u(m)-mea* '(my) mother', *af'ei-mea* '(my) father', *tatā* 'father' are not used with dative enclitic *n'i*; however, *k'ir'aua-n'* '(my) wife' (literally 'my lady') is observed.

Emergence of new grammatical models in modern Aromanian under Greek influence is, according to our data, the result of the following processes: (a) massive borrowing of lexemes from different lexico-semantic or grammatical word classes of Greek (from open to closed classes of words), together with their collocational features; (b) borrowing of syntactic word classes (grammatical function units) and/or single syntactic words; (c) calques of the functional-semantic range of Greek grammatical units (or categories), which broaden the functional-semantic range of existing original Aromanian units (or categories); (d) calques of Greek structural schemes and relations, including producing new grammatical units. It should be emphasized that content and syntactic lexemes borrowed from Greek as well as new structural schemes are in the majority of cases lexical and grammatical alternatives to or variants of autochthonous Aromanian forms, used intensively in the dialect (to the exclusion of some conjunctions). Redundant double marking (e.g., *numa-lā a lor* 'their names') can be observed as well, sometimes even realized as mechanical concatenations of native Aromanian and "alien" Greek forms (e.g., *kāć'e epiδ'i* 'because'). Grammatically defective zones within the Aromanian system have been filled by Greek material (as in the case of ordinal numerals).

Nevertheless, the results of the millennium-long "intimate contacts" and bilingualism between Aromanian and Greek, Albanian and Greek (Demiraj 1988; 2013; Spiro 2015), and Slavic and Albanian (Sobolev 1990; Stanišić 1995; Rusakov 2013) are far from being even comparable to the deep structural changes that have occurred in the Balkans to Romance- or Slavic-based varieties, thus demanding other explanations for the causes of Balkan convergence. They can be seen rather in *multiple language shifts* more than in bi- or trilingualism.[10]

5 The universal: Borrowability hierarchies

The evidence of the outcomes of contact-induced changes on the Balkans is highly relevant for the more general discussion of what is borrowable and what is "*donatable*" in language. One of the intriguing questions of contemporary Balkan studies concerns the features that never spread from one Balkan language to other(s), the so-called anti-Balkanisms, cf. Sobolev (2011) for Slavic and Rusakov (2013) for Albanian. The contribution of each Balkan language to the convergence processes should be examined together with the restrictions on structures

---

[10] "Repetition of these processes", as suggested in Matras (2009: 272-273), cannot be considered as the cause, since it leads to similar or the same outcomes of contact.

that can be deemed less "donatable" or on languages that can be classified as less "donation-prone". For example, Seliščev (1925: 51) made an important statement about Balkan Slavic: "Les Slaves furent un élément passif dans les procès d'évolution syntaxique et morphologique. Il n'y a qu'une catégorie linguistique ou toutes les langues balkaniques présentent des éléments slaves" ['The Slavs were a passive element in the processes of syntactic and morphological evolution. There is only one linguistic category where all Balkan languages present Slavic elements']. As argued in Sobolev (2011), the particular tendency of the Slavic grammatical type against the donating Balkan languages is to be explained by the fact that specific Slavic categories such as animacy and verb aspect, impersonality and predicative instrumental are marked inflexionally or via morphological means that occupy a low, if not the lowest, rank on the contact-linguistic scale of borrowability.

One of the most important general findings of language contact studies in the last decades has been that some features are more clearly borrowable than others despite similar conditions of contact. Borrowability as 'a product of inherent semantic-pragmatic or structural properties of the affected categories' means 'the likelihood of a structural category to be affected by contact-induced change [...] (whether matter- or pattern-replication)' (Matras 2007: 34, 31) and borrowability hierarchies, built upon large amounts of data, have become a useful contemporary tool of linguistuic analysis and synthesis. In Adamou and Sobolev (2011), it was claimed that the analysis of convergent and non-convergent features of the Balkan Sprachbund meets with the borrowability hierarchies established for language contact in general (cf. Campbell 2006), bringing some precision to the already existing generalizations:
– consonants > oral vowels > nasal vowels, syllabic sonants
– modal future > aspectual future > future tense
– definiteness > deixis
– core cases > peripheral cases
– plural marker > singular marker, collective, dual.

6 Conclusion and Desiderata

With the crisis of tautological and speculative theories overcome, 21st century Balkan linguistics provides a synthetic, systemic, consistent linguistic and socially relevant description of the Balkan linguistic union (Hinrichs 1999; Friedman 2008; Sobolev 2013a), which has emerged from ages of complex contacts between diverse ethnic groups populating the peninsula. Linguistic theory should formulate consistently, and provide a factual basis for, the theory of a Sprachbund, or a convergent language group, and should be able to demonstrate the applicability of general linguistic and field-specific methods of researching such groups. Such line of research should lead to the creation of a historically, typologically and areally oriented comparative grammar of the Balkan languages and of a comparative Balkan dictionary, as well as to an exhaustive intrasystemic, general typological, historical linguistic and areal analysis. In an interdisciplinary framework, the theory of a convergent language group should be related to contemporary concepts of multi-ethnic, multilingual and multi-religious societies and of the *cultural dialogue* ever-present in societies of this kind. The theory might as well be predictive of the ways to solve the problems of modern multi-ethnic, multilingual, multi-religious and multicultural societies, and of integrative and disintegrative processes in them.

In particular, Balkan linguistics should: solve the problem of interlingual identification of linguistic units and their functions in contact; address the problem of systemicity and reciprocal implicational value of linguistic features and establish the hierarchy of those features; resolve the issue of stable areas of linguistic structure and areas permeable to contact innovation by establishing their relative hierarchy and dependencies between inherent features of a language and contact processes and results, developing a typology of contact-induced changes; describe the role of each of the language groups (and/or languages) as a donor or a recipient in the Balkan language community, with special attention given to minor or extinct languages of the peninsula; establish the interdependency of socio-linguistic situations and the evident results of the contact; and answers to the questions concerning the link between the existence of a linguistic community of a convergent type and the existence of the community of corresponding ethnic groups on levels other than the linguistic ones (on the level of material and spiritual culture above all), to the question of whether the absence of dominant/subordinate relationship between speakers of languages in contact as well as between languages themselves (prestigious and non-prestigious languages and linguistic forms) and between cultures constitutes a necessary condition for the emergence of a convergent language group, and to the question of unlimited permeability of languages and cultures and of unlimited possibility of mutual understanding between representatives of those cultures, etc.

All levels of all languages (in all of their historically recorded standard and substandard forms) and cultures of all large and small ethnic groups of the area that is geographically defined as the Balkan peninsula should be objects of research together with geographical, political, economic, religious, and other constants of the area. To establish linguistic constants and determinants of the Balkan peninsula, including those in the field of (morpho-)syntax, is to be recognized as the main theoretical aim of Balkan linguistics.

References

Adamou, Evangelia and Andrey Sobolev. 2011. Balkan Sprachbund: convergent and non-convergent features. Paper presented at the Conference on linguistic areas, CNRS, Paris, 30. September 2011.

Asenova, Petya and Vassilka Aleksova. 2008. L'aspect balkanique de la nota accusativi personalis. *Zeitschrift für Balkanologie* 44. 1–22.

Bara, Maria and Thede Kahl and Andrey N. Sobolev. 2005. *Yužnoarumynskii govor sela Tur'ya (Pind). Sintaksis. Leksika. Etnolingvistika. Teksty.* München: Biblion Verlag.

Campbell, Lyle. 2006. Areal linguistics: a closer scrutiny. In Yaron Matras et al. (eds.), *Linguistic Areas*, 1–31. Basingstoke: Palgrave Macmillan.

Chernyak, Alexander B. 1990. Arumynskii yazyk. In Agniya V. Desnitskaya (ed.), *Osnovy balkanskogo yazykoznaniya. Yazyki balkanskogo regiona. Čast' I (novogrecheskii, albanskii, romanskie yazyki)*, 192–220. Leningrad: Nauka.

Chernyak, Alexander B. 1998. Bolgarskii yazyk (razdely 1–4). In Agniya V. Desnitskaya and Nikita I. Tolstoi (eds.), *Osnovy balkanskogo yazykoznaniya. Yazyki balkanskogo regiona. Čast' II. Slavyanskie yazyki*, 189–206. Sankt-Peterburg: Nauka.

Croft, William. 2000. *Explaining Language Change*. Harlow, Essex: Longman.

Curtis, Matthew Cowan. 2012. *Slavic-Albanian Language Contact, Convergence, and Coexistence*. Ph.D. Dissertation, The Ohio State University.

Demiraj, Shaban. 1988. *Gramatikë historike e gjuhës shqipe*. Prishtinë: Rilindja.

Demiraj, Shaban. 2013. *Gjuha shqipe dhe historia e saj*. Tiranë: Onufri.

Dimitrova, Stefana. 2000. Sud'ba bolgarskogo predloženiya v poslevoennyi period. *Wyraz i zdanie w językach słowiańskich. Acta universitatis wratislaviensis. Slavica Wratislaviensia*. Vol. CVII. 31–36.

Dombrowski, Andrew. 2013. *Phonological aspects of language contact along the slavic periphery: an ecological approach*. Ph.D. Dissertation, University of Chicago.

Duridanov, Ivan and Maksim Mladenov. 1989. Distributsiya na balkanizmite v bălgarskite dialekti. *Studia z filologii polskiej i słowiańskiej* 25. 93–125.

Friedman, Victor. 1994. Variation and grammaticalization in the development of Balkanisms. In Katherine Beals et al. (eds.), *Papers from the 30th Regional Meeting of the CLS*, Vol. 2. 101–115. Chicago: CLS.

Friedman, Victor. 2008. Balkan Slavic Dialectology and Balkan Linguistics: Periphery as Center. In Christina Bethin (ed.), *American contributions to the 14th International Congress of Slavists*, 131–148. Bloomington, IN: Slavica.

Gjinari, Jorgo et al. (eds.) 2007. *Atlasi dialektologjik i gjuhës shqipe*. V. I. Napoli.

Gołąb, Zbigniew. 1964. *Condicionalis typu bałkańskiego w językach południowosłowiańskich ze szczególnym uwzględnieniem macedońskiego*. Wrocław – Krakow – Warszawa.

Hinrichs, Uwe. 1999. Die sogenannten 'Balkanismen' als Problem der Südosteuropa-Linguistik und der allgemeinen Sprachwissenschaft. In: Uwe Hinrichs (ed.), *Handbuch der Südosteuropa-Linguistik*, 429–461.Wiesbaden: Harrassowitz.

Joseph, Brian. 1992. The Balkan Languages. In W. Bright (ed.), *International Encyclopedia of Linguistics*, Vol. 1. 153–155. Oxford: Oxford University Press.

Joseph, Brian. 2010. Language contact in the Balkans. In Raymond Hickey (ed.), *The Handbook of Language Contact*, 618–633. New York: Wiley.

Khrakovskij, Viktor S. 2003. Kategoriya taksisa (obščaya kharakteristika). *Voprosy yazykoznaniya* № 2. 32–54.

Khrakovskij, Viktor S. (ed.). 2009. *Tipologiya taksisnykh konstrukcii*. Moskva: Znak.
Kopitar, Jernej. 1829. Albanische, walachische und bulgarische Sprache. *Jahrbücher der Literatur*. Band 46. 59–106 (Wien).
Kosta, Peter. 2009. Targets, Theory and Methods of Slavic Generative Syntax: Minimalism, Negation and Clitics. In *Die Slavischen Sprachen, ein internationales Handbuch zu ihrer Struktur, ihrer Geschichte und ihrer Erforschung*. Band 1. Hrsg. von Sebastian Kempgen u.a. Handbuch zur Sprach- und Kommunikationswissenschaft, 282–316. Berlin: Mouton de Gruyter.
Kramer, Johannes. 1981. Griechische Strukturen im Aromunischen. *Balkan-Archiv*. N. F. Bd. 6. 97–105. Hamburg: Buske.
Kramer, Johannes. 1993. Griechische Strukturen in der Balkanromania. In *Balkan-Archiv*. N. F. Bd. 17/18. 71–80. Gerbrunn bei Würzburg: Wissenschaftlicher Verlag Lehmann.
Lindstedt, Jouko. 2014. Balkan Slavic and Balkan Romance: From congruence to convergence. In Juliane Besters-Dilger, Cynthia Dermarkar, Stefan Pfänder & Achim Rabus (eds.), *Congruence in Contact-induced Language Change: Language Families, Typological Resemblance, and Perceived Similarity*, 168–183. Berlin – Boston: De Gruyter.
Lopashov, Yurii A. 2006. Ob odnom albanizme v severnogrečeskom govore. In Aleksandr Rusakov (ed.), *Problemy balkanskoi filologii*, 161–163. Sankt-Pererburg: Institut lingvističeskih issledovanii RAN.
Matras, Yaron. 2007. The borrowability of grammatical categories. In Yaron Matras and Jeanette Sakel (eds.), *Grammatical borrowing in cross-linguistic perspective*, 31–74. Berlin: Mouton de Gruyter.
Miklosich, Franz. 1861. Die slavischen Elemente im Rumunischen. Denkschriften der Kaiserlichen Akademie der Wissenschaften, Philosophisch-historische Klasse. Wien.
Mladenov, Maksim. 1987. Arealna kharakteristika na romanski elementi v balgarskite dialekti. In *Die slawischen Sprachen*. Bd. 12. 75–92. Salzburg.
Mladenova, Olga. 2007. *Definiteness in Bulgarian. Modelling the Processes of Language Change*. Berlin/New York: Mouton de Gruyter.
Nedjalkov, Igor'. 1998. Converbs in the languages of Europe. Johan van der Auwera (ed.), *Adverbial Constructions in the Languages of Europe*, 421–455. Berlin/New York: De Gruyter.
Rusakov, Aleksandr Yu. 2013. Nekotorye izoglossy na albanskoi dialektnoi karte (k voprosu o vozniknovenii i rasprostranenii balkanizmov albanskogo yazyka. In V'ačeslav V. Ivanov (ed.), *Issledovaniya po tipologii slav'anskih, baltiiskih i balkanskih yazykov*, 113–174. St. Petersburg: Ateteya.
Sandfeld, Kristian. 1930. *Linguistique balkanique. Problèmes et résultats*. Paris: Édouard Champion.
Seliščev, Afanasij M.1925. Des traits linguistiques communs aux langues balkaniques: Un balkanisme ancien en bulgare. *Revue des Études slaves*. Tome V, fasc. 1–2. 38–56.
Sobolev, Andrey N. 1990. Zametki o padežnom sintaksise serbohorvatskih govorov kontaktnyh zon. In: *Južnoslovenski filolog*. Knj. XLVI. 13–28. Beograd.
Sobolev, Andrey N. 1991. K istorii utraty balkanoslav'anskogo sklonenija. In: Zbornik Matice srpske za filologiju i lingvistiku. Knj. XXXIV/2. 7–41. Novi Sad.
Sobolev, Andrey N. 2001. *Bolgarskii širokolykskii govor*. Marburg: Biblion Verlag.
Sobolev, Andrey N. (ed.). 2003. *Malyi dialektologičeskii atlas balkanskih yazykov / Kleiner Balkansprachatlas. Probnyi vypusk*. München: Verlag Otto Sagner.
Sobolev, Andrey N. 2003a. *Yužnoslavyanskie yazyki v balkanskom areale*. XIII meždunarodnyi s'ezd slavistov (Ljubljana, avgust 2003). Marburg an der Lahn: Philipps-Universität Marburg, Institut für Slavische Philologie.

Sobolev, Andrey N. 2003b. Nefinitnye taksisnye formy i konstruktsii balkanskikh yazykov. In Aleksander Rusakov et al. (eds.), *Aktual'nye voprosy balkanskogo yazykoznaniya. Materialy mezhdunarodnoi nauchnoi konferentsii* (Sankt-Peterburg, mai 2001 g.). 11–26. Sankt-Peterburg: Nauka.

Sobolev, Andrey N. 2004. On the areal distribution of syntactic properties in the languages of the Balkans. In Olga Mišeska-Tomić (ed.), *Balkan Syntax and Semantics*, 59–100. Amsterdam: Benjamins.

Sobolev, Andrey N. 2005. Ob odnoi balkanskoi taksisnoi konstruktsii s nefinitnoi opornoi formoi. In: *Linguistique balkanique*. Vol. XLIII/1. Sofia. S. 69–74.

Sobolev, Andrey N. (ed.). 2005a. *Malyi dialektologičeskii atlas balkanskih yazykov / Kleiner Balkansprachatlas. Seriya leksičeskaya*. Tom I. Leksika duhovnoi kul'tury. München: Verlag Otto Sagner.

Sobolev, Andrey N. (ed.). 2005b. *Malyi dialektologičeskii atlas balkanskih yazykov / Kleiner Balkansprachatlas. Seriya grammatičeskaya*. Tom I. Kategorii imeni suščestvitel'nogo. München: Verlag Otto Sagner.

Sobolev, Andrey N. (ed.). 2006. *Malyi dialektologičeskii atlas balkanskih yazykov / Kleiner Balkansprachatlas. Seriya leksičeskaya*. Tom II. Čelovek. Sem'ya. München: Verlag Otto Sagner.

Sobolev, Andrey N. 2006a. Južnoslav'anskii instrumental i ego balkanskie ekvivalenty (instrumental'nost' v pole prit'aženiya agentivnosti i pacientivnosti. In: *Makedonska akademija na naukite i umetnostite. Priloi*. Kn. XXXI / 2. 59–71.

Sobolev, Andrey N. 2006b. Grečeskoe grammatičeskoe vliyanie na sovremennyi južnoarumynskii govor Pinda. In: Irina Sedakova et al. (eds.), *Vostok i Zapad v balkanskoi kartine mira. Sbornik pamati V. N. Toporova*, 201–209. Moskva: Indrik.

Sobolev, Andrey N. 2008. On some Aromanian Grammatical Patterns in the Balkan Slavonic Dialects. In Biljana Sikimić and Tijana Ašić (eds.), *The Romance Balkans*. 113–121. Belgrade: SANU.

Sobolev, Andrey N. (ed.). 2009. *Malyi dialektologičeskii atlas balkanskih yazykov / Kleiner Balkansprachatlas. Seriya leksicheskaya*. Tom III. Životnovodstvo. Sankt-Peterburg/München: Nauka/Verlag Otto Sagner.

Sobolev, Andrej N. 2009a. From Synthetic to Analytic Case: Variation in South-Slavic Dialects. In: Malchukov, Andrey and Spencer, Andrew (eds.) *Handbook of Case*. 716–729. Oxford University Press.

Sobolev, Andrey N. 2009b. O kategorii opredelennosti v bolgarskom jayzke (po povodu knigi Olgi Mladenovoi *Definiteness in Bulgarian. Modelling the Processes of Language Change*. [Trends in linguistics. Studies and monographs; 182] Berlin; New York: Mouton de Gruyter, 2007). *Zeitschrift für Balkanologie*. 45. 228–252.

Sobolev, Andrey N. 2011. Antibalkanizmy. In *Južnoslovenski filolog*. Knj. LXVII. 185–195. Beograd.

Sobolev, Andrey N. 2012. On redundancy in Albanian. In Al'vina V. Žugra et al. (eds.), *Sovremennaya albanistika: dostiženiya i perspektivy. Sbornik statei*. 407–412. Sankt-Peterburg: Nauka.

Sobolev, Andrey N. (ed.). 2013. *Malyi dialektologičeskii atlas balkanskih yazykov / Kleiner Balkansprachatlas. Seriya leksicheskaya*. Tom VII. Polevodstvo. Ogorodničestvo. Sankt-Petersburg/München: Nauka/Verlag Otto Sagner.

Sobolev, Andrey N. 2013a. *Osnovy lingvokul'turnoi antropogeografii Balkanskogo poluostrova. Tom I. Homo balcanicus i ego prostranstvo*. St. Petersburg/München: Nauka/Otto Sagner Verlag.

Sobolev, Andrey N. 2014. Theoriebildung in der Dialektologie: historisch-vergleichende Beschreibung. In Peter Kosta, Karl Gutschmidt, Sebastian Kempgen (eds.), *Die Slavischen Sprachen, ein internationales Handbuch zu ihrer Struktur, ihrer Geschichte und ihrer Erforschung.* Band 2. Handbuch zur Sprach- und Kommunikationswissenschaft, 2067–2074. Berlin: Mouton de Gruyter.

Sobolev, Andrey N. 2015. Mrkovići (i Gorana): jazyki i dialekty Černogorskogo Primor'ya v kontekste noveišh balkanističeskih issledovanii. In Bardhyl Demiraj (ed.), *Sprache und Kultur der Albaner. Zeitliche und räumliche Dimensionen. Akten der 5. Deutsch-Albanischen kulturwissenschaftlichen Tagung (6.-9. Juni 2014, Buçimas/Albanien) / Albanische Forschungen.* Harrassowitz Verlag, Wiesbaden, 2015.

Sobolev, Andrey N. and Aleksander Rusakov. 2008. *Substantsial'no-funktsional'naya teoriya balkanskogo yazykovogo soyuza i slavanskie yazyki.* XIV Meždunarodnyi s'ezd slavistov v Ohride, Makedoniya. Sankt-Peterburg: Nauka.

Sobolev, Andrey N. and Novik, Aleksandr A. (eds.). 2013. *Golo Bordo / Gollobordë, Albaniya. Materialy balkanskoi ekspedicii RAN i SPbGU 2008–2010 gg.* St. Petersburg/München: Nauka/Verlag Otto Sagner.

Solta, Georg Renatus. 1980. *Einführung in die Balkanlinguistik mit besonderer Berücksichtigung des Substrats und des Balkanlateinischen.* Darmstadt : Wissenschaftliche Buchgesellschaft.

Spiro, Aristotle. 2015. The Modern Greek Dialects of Albania – A general Description and Clasification. In: Andrey Babanov et al. (eds.), *43rd International Philological Confrerence. 11–16 March 2014. Selected articles*, 396–417. Sankt Peterburg: St. Petersburg State University.

Stanišić, Vanja. 1995. *Srpsko-albanski jezički odnosi.* Beograd: Srpska akademija nauka i umetnosti.

Thomason, Sarah. 2000. Linguistic areas and language history. In Dicky Gilbers et al. (eds.), *Languages in contact*, 311–328. Amsterdam/Atlanta, GA.

Thomason, Sarah and Kaufman, Terrence. 1991. *Language contact, creolization, and genetic linguistics.* Edinburgh: Edinburgh University Press.

Topolinjska, Zuzana. 1995–1997. *Makedonskite dijalekti vo Egejska Makedonija. Kniga 1. Sintaksa.* Tom 1–2. Skopje: Makedonska akademiya na naukite i umetnostite.

Trubetzkoy, Nikolai S. 1928. Proposition 16. In *Actes du Premier Congrès International de Linguistes du 10–15 avril, 1928.* 17–18. Leiden: Sijthoff.

Tsiv'yan, Tat'yana V. 1979. *Sintaksičeskaya struktura balkanskogo yazykovogo soyuza.* Moskva: Nauka.

Tsykhun, Gennadii A. 1981. *Tipologičeskie problemy balkanoslavyanskogo yazykovogo areala.* Minsk: Navuka i tehnika.

Voss, Leluda. 2006. *Die südgriechische Mundart von Kastelli (Peloponnes). Morphosyntax und Syntax, Lexik, Ethnolinguistik, Texte.* München: Biblion Verlag.

Wahlström, Max. 2015. *The Loss of Case Inflection in Bulgarian and Macedonian.* Helsinki: Helsinki University (Slavica Helsingensia. Vol. 47).

Ylli, Xhelal and Andrey N. Sobolev. 2002. *Albanskii toskskii govor sela Leshnya (kraina Skrapar). Sintaksis. Leksika. Etnolingvistika. Teksty.* Marburg: Biblion Verlag.

Ylli, Xhelal and Andrey N. Sobolev. 2003. *Albanskii gegskii govor sela Mukhurr (Kraina Dibyr). Sintaksis. Leksika. Etnolingvistika. Teksty.* München: Biblion Verlag.

Jouko Lindstedt
Diachronic Regularities Explaining the Tendency towards Explicit Analytic Marking in Balkan Syntax

Abstract: Differently from a growing number of linguistic investigations which argue that simplification and complexification of grammars are directly dependent on the type of contact situation as well as the degree of relative isolation of a language, I argue that the effects of the Balkan contact situation were not necessarily simplifying or complexifying. More precisely, the changes that led to structural convergence among the languages of the Balkans represent the effects – explicit analytic marking – of a third type of contact situation apart from the two identified by Trudgill (2011). I elaborate on the properties of this type and show that the rise of explicit marking can be explained on the basis of diachronic regularities that are partly structural, partly sociolinguistic in nature: (a) borrowing increases analytism; (b) convergence of typologically different structures increases analytism; (c) both L2 speakers and bilingual L1 speakers count.

Keywords: Balkans, language contact, structural convergence, grammar simplification, analytic marking, historical sociolinguistics

1 Preamble

A considerable number of recent linguistic studies argue that contact among languages is reflected in their structure in particular ways and that certain types of contact situations simplify grammar, whereas other types of contact situations, and especially the relative isolation of a language, may complexify it (Kusters 2003; McWhorter 2001, 2011; Trudgill 2002, 2011; Dahl 2004: 280–285). In this paper I argue that the changes that made the languages of the Balkan linguistic area converge structurally were neither clearly simplifying nor clearly complexifying. These changes represent a tendency towards a certain syntactic type, that is, explicit analytic marking, whose rise can be explained by two types of diachronic regularities: those that are structural in nature and those that are sociolinguistic in nature. I also argue that the Balkans represent a third type of contact situation besides the two types distinguished by Trudgill (2011).

Jouko Lindstedt, (University of Helsinki, jouko.lindstedt@helsinki.fi

https://doi.org/10.1515/9783110375930-005

2 Simplification, complexification and the Balkan languages

The structural convergence in the Balkan linguistic area (Sprachbund) has been used as an example of both contact-induced simplification and contact-induced complexification (for lists of the relevant structural features, the so-called Balkanisms, see Joseph 2013 and Lindstedt 2000a).

Hinrichs (2004) emphasizes similarities between the Balkan languages and creoles, though he admits that there are also differences. Hinrichs sees the changes that brought about the Balkan linguistic area as examples of "unnatural" change owing to an extreme contact situation (Hinrichs 2004: 142–144); this comes close to McWhorter's (2011) idea of creoles as languages whose normal accumulation of complexity has been interrupted or Dahl's (2004: 281) concept of "suboptimal transmission". As characteristics of the Balkan Sprachbund, Hinrichs (2004: 170) mentions "Kontaktzwänge, Reduktionismus, Vereinfachung, Rekonstruktion, Kreolisierung und weiteren Ausbau". As the sociolinguistic context of this Balkanization of languages, he sees the orally orientated ("oral geprägte") culture of the Balkans, which he compares to the "westafrikanischen Kulturen der vermuteten Substratsprachen der KS" [=Kreolsprachen] (Hinrichs 2004: 163–167).

As for this sociolinguistic explanation, I find Hinrichs's proposal unconvincing. On the one hand, most changes in most languages of the world have always originated in their spoken varieties, and it is difficult to see why the Balkans (or West Africa, for that matter) would have been special in this respect. On the other hand, Southeast Europe was the home of two of the three most important written languages of mediaeval Europe – Greek and Old Church Slavonic – and it is therefore difficult to see what would make the Balkans a region with a distinctively "oral" culture by comparison with other regions in Europe.

But it is also difficult to agree with Hinrichs's characterization of Balkanization as simplification. For instance, the verb systems of the Balkan languages resemble each other, but they are much more complex than those of any creole language; a modern grammar of standard Albanian (Demiraj 2002) distinguishes ten tenses and six moods. Case inflection has been reduced in all Balkan languages to some extent, but only Balkan Slavic has lost case marking completely. What should also be borne in mind is that Balkan Romance is the sole branch of Romance that has *preserved* case distinctions in nouns. And the appearance of enclitic definite articles in several Balkan languages did not simplify those languages, at least for the speaker, because it required obligatory coding of a feature that initially did not have explicit marking. Pidgins and creoles often do not make use of definite articles even when their lexifier languages possess them (Bruyn 1995: 259).

A definite article or the clitic doubling of the object, to give another Balkan example, can, of course, be seen as increasing the *redundancy* of the message to the benefit of the hearer, and Hinrichs does mention this characteristic. Redundancy has also been mentioned by other scholars in connection with Balkanisms (e.g. Hauge 1977). However, Hinrichs seems to think that redundancy is naturally linked to simplification and creolization, whereas Dahl (2004: 5–17) and Trudgill (2011: 62) consider redundancy to increase complexity. Dahl (2004: 9) even defines redundancy with the help of complexity: "A message is redundant if there is a less complex message that could – in principle – transfer the same amount of information, that is, if more communicative resources are spent on it than are theoretically necessary for its successful delivery".[1]

As redundancy and complexity are connected in this fashion, it is natural that in his book *Sociolinguistic typology*, Peter Trudgill (2011: 34, 42) uses Sprachbünde or linguistic areas as examples of the type of contact situation that leads to complexification; his conclusion is thus diametrically opposed to Hinrichs's. Trudgill does not deal with the Balkans in greater detail in his book, but in an earlier article (Trudgill 2002: 710–711) he presents the Balkan loss of the infinitive as an instance of complexification and increasing redundancy. He compares the Greek sentence

(1) θél-o   na   γráp-s-o
    want-PRS.SG1 COMP   write-PFV-PRS.SG1
    'I want to write'

with the corresponding English sentence *I want to write* and notes that the information about the first person singular is marked in English only once, but in Greek twice and therefore in a more redundant fashion. But notice that the subject of the embedded verb could also be different from that of the matrix clause. When this is taken into account, the Balkan pattern is actually more symmetrical than the English system (I use Macedonian here to represent the Balkan system):

(2) sakam da dojdam   – I want Ø to come
    sakam da dojdeš   – I want you to come
    sakaš da dojdam   – you want me to come
    sakaš da dojdeš   – you want Ø to come

---

1 I assume that the hedges "in principle" and "theoretically" are necessary for natural language since once a redundant marker has been fully grammaticalized, there may not be a less redundant grammatical way to express the message in the same synchronic state of the language in question. For instance, an agreement marker may be obligatory in a given language, but in comparing it with other languages, we see that it is not necessary for a functioning human language.

In English, there are syntactic rules defining when the embedded verb can or must appear in the infinitive and when its subject can or must be dropped. In Macedonian and other Balkan languages, the underlying finite forms and their person markings are preserved. Balkan grammar is here rather simpler, not more complicated, than that of most European languages. It can in fact be argued that in the Greek *θélo na yrápso* 'I want to write' or the Macedonian *sakam da dojdam* 'I want to come', there is no real redundancy in the person marking at all, since the first person singular is opposed to all other persons, not only in the matrix verb but also in the embedded verb, independent of the matrix. With clearly modal verbs indicating possibility ('can', 'may') or necessity ('must'), such a distinction between the matrix person and the embedded person is, of course, not valid. But exactly these verbs are often used in the Balkan languages in the unmarked third person singular only, so that it is the lexical verb that shows the person without redundancy.

Notice also that the Balkan loss of the infinitive means that the verb has one inflectional category less, which certainly can count as a paradigmatic simplification.

In general, the grammatical Balkanisms cannot all be unequivocally characterized as simplifying or as complexifying. Several of them, such as the reduction of the case system, recipient/possessor merger, goal/location merger, *relativum generale*, or analytic comparison of adjectives, do decrease the obligatory paradigmatic choices to be made and are in that sense simplifying, but part of the same information must then be encoded syntagmatically. The rise of the analytic *volo* ('want'-based) future meant a similar syntagma-for-paradigm swap. Enclitic articles, clitic doubling and other analytic means of marking the arguments increase redundancy and are in that sense complexifying. Grammaticalized evidentials or the *habeo* ('have'-based) perfect are new verb categories and most clearly complexifying.

However, the essential typological characteristics of the Balkan linguistic area cannot be described along the simple/complex axis at all. What is typical of most Balkanisms is the *explicit analytic marking* of syntactic relations and other grammatical categories by prepositions, pronominal clitics, articles, particles and other function words. Explicit analytic marking can be typologically opposed to inflectional (synthetic) marking, as well as to implicit analytic marking with word order alone and to the absence of marking.

What factors have brought about such a structural type? I propose three diachronic regularities to explain the mechanism of change towards explicit analytic marking in the Balkan languages. My proposals should be considered conjectures, that is to say, informed hypotheses that are not incongruent with what we know about the historical changes in the Balkan languages, their past sociolinguistics and language contacts in general. I hope they give ideas for further research.

3 Borrowing increases analytism

The convergence of the Balkan languages presupposes borrowing. For most Balkanisms, a single source language cannot be indicated, to be sure, but even when structural Balkanisms arose through mutual reinforcement of change among languages (Lindstedt 2000a), having thus multiple sources, the patterns and constructions must have been copied back and forth between languages.

Now, it has long been known that analytic constructions are more likely to be borrowed than inflectional categories. Weinreich (1970 [1953]: 41) wrote: "Significantly, in the interference of two grammatical patterns it is ordinarily the one which uses relatively free and invariant morphemes in its paradigm – one might say, the more explicit pattern – which serves as the model of imitation". Thomason (2001: 69) writes that "less tightly structured features are easier to borrow than features that fit into tightly integrated closed structures", inflectional morphology being an example of the latter. According to Dahl (2004: 127–128), "what is borrowed, or calqued (i.e. translated), in grammar will most frequently be periphrastic constructions or free markers, and less often affixes, although the latter is also observed to happen". He proposes that structures more likely to be borrowed are less "mature"; by mature structures he means a structure that exists in a language only when it has passed through a specific earlier stage (along a grammaticalization path, for instance).

All this is quite uncontroversial, but I surmise that there is an important corollary: the more a language borrows from other languages (beyond mere lexical items), the more analytic it is bound to grow in the long run. If analytic constructions always have a higher probability of entering a language than synthetic constructions do, the former will gradually become more frequent, and this will happen more rapidly if there is large-scale borrowing. This means that an important structural feature of the Balkan languages, their analytism, is a result of those social circumstances that enhanced borrowing among those languages. Of course, these social circumstances in their turn have to be explored and explained, but at any rate, such a simple connection between social context and language structure seems to exist.

Notice that this conjecture does not require the source language of the borrowings to be more analytic than the target language; what is needed is only the right kind of social context for intense borrowing in general. It is the borrowing language that selects the analytic constructions in the source language. Of course, if there are none – if the source language is a polysynthetic language, for instance – the situation is different, but I assume that in such circumstances grammatical borrowing would be rare anyway.

Moreover, the borrowing language may restructure the borrowed pattern so that it becomes more analytic than it was in the source language. To take an example outside the Balkans, Finnish Romani has borrowed from Finnish the periphrastic perfect and pluperfect tenses, which are now opposed to the simple past tense of the type *mekjas* '(s)he left / was leaving', *rakkadas* '(s)he spoke / was speaking'. The Finnish perfect and pluperfect are formed with the present or past auxiliary 'to be', respectively, and the past participle of the verb; being periphrastic constructions, they are likely to be borrowed. However, Finnish Romani has only borrowed the use of the auxiliary 'to be'; the main verb has not been changed into a participle. The Finnish Romani perfects are of the type *hin mekjas* '(s)he has left', *hin rakkadas* '(s)he has spoken', while the pluperfects are of the type *sas mekjas* '(s)he had left', *sas rakkadas* '(s)he had spoken', where both the auxiliary and the main verb are finite; thus, *sas rakkadas* is literally "was spoke". The Finnish Romani periphrastic verb constructions are more analytic than their Finnish models because the auxiliary does not govern the inflectional form of the main verb, but is simply concatenated with it. As a further development, the third-person auxiliary is further generalized optionally for all the persons. The first person singular *som mekjom* 'I have left' is then replaced with *hin mekjom*, where only the main verb shows the person; this is a further move towards analyticity because the tense has received an invariant marker (the examples are taken from Granqvist 2011: 117–124).

All of this means that if an areal group of languages begins to borrow structures from each other, as happened in the Balkans, the degree of analytism in each of them may in the long run become higher than any one language among them had in the beginning. In the Balkans we also see geographically that language varieties spoken in areas of intensive and multilateral contact are more analytic. The contact area of Greek, Albanian, Macedonian, Aromanian, Romani and Turkish in the Central Balkans, around the lakes Ohrid and Prespa and south of them, is the home of the most Balkanized varieties of these languages, as pointed out by Asenova (2002: 17); she sees this centre of Balkanization to be approximately delimited by the river valleys of Shkumbin, Vjosë/Aóos and Vardar/Axiós. This is also the sphere of influence of the western part of the ancient Via Egnatia.

The regularity "borrowing increases analytism" proposed here would not be universally true if analytic structures were also generally lost through obsolescence more quickly than synthetic structures. But what we know about language change certainly does not render this plausible. For instance, in several European languages periphrastic perfects are becoming or have become generalized past tenses or perfective pasts (Lindstedt 2000b: 365–374); we would not expect old synthetic past tenses to recapture the semantic field they have already lost to the new perfects.

The only situation in which this regularity would perhaps not be accurate is when wide-spread childhood bilingualism is involved, because the preference for analytic structures may be linked with adult second-language learning (Trudgill 2011: 40–43). But, unlike Trudgill, I do not believe that the Balkans ever belonged to this type, as I discuss in Section 6 below.

As for the simplification / complexification dimension, borrowed analytic structures simplify the language if borrowing is replacive, i.e. if the new structures supersede old, possibly synthetic structures. But if borrowing is additive, it may introduce new distinctions and thus complexify the grammar. The borrowing of grammatical evidential distinctions from Turkish into Balkan Slavic created a new grammatical category and thus made the structure of the borrowing languages more complex, even though evidentiality is expressed in them by periphrastic verb forms. The borrowing of the *habeo* perfect from Greek and Balkan Romance into Macedonian dialects, in its turn, was first simply additive, but when it caused the old *esse* ('be'-based) perfect to specialize for evidential uses in a growing number of dialects (Graves 2000; Lindstedt 2000b; Bužarovska & Mitkovska 2010), the result was simplification in the sense of greater morphological transparency ("one meaning, one form", Anttila 1972: 100–102; cf. Trudgill 2011: 21).

4 Convergence of different structures increases analytism

The tendency towards explicit analytic marking is manifested in the nominal system of the Balkan languages in the decrease of case distinctions and the increased use of prepositions, although only Balkan Slavic and dialects of Aromanian have completely lost the cases with the exception of the personal and some other pronouns. (The vocative is left out of this discussion as it is not a syntactic case that marks the argument structure of the sentence.) In the linguistic geography of Europe, the Balkans are not unique in this respect; rather they form an intermediary zone between the caseless West and the case-preserving East, as is also shown by comparing Romanian with the other Romance languages. The complete loss of case in Balkan Slavic was a complicated process influenced by several factors (Wahlström 2015).

The remaining case systems in Albanian, Greek and Balkan Romance are remarkably similar, with a genitive-dative case that merges the marking of the possessor and the recipient functions. But another side of the same coin, less often mentioned, is the isosemantism of the most common prepositions, i.e. the fact that their meaning and use is so similar that if one knows the preposition used in one Balkan language, one can usually correctly predict the preposition used in another (Asenova 2002: 97–104).[2] As in other typical Balkanisms, it is the meanings, not the forms of the prepositions that have converged. In Balkan Romance and dialects of Macedonian, a preposition is used even to mark direct objects, especially those referring to humans.[3] Clitic doubling of the direct and indirect objects (see also Kallulli, this volume) is also part of the same picture: the marking of the argument structure of the sentence has moved in an analytic direction, and the markers exhibit a high degree of intertranslatability[4] among the languages, especially among their coterritorial dialects.

Compared with the nominal system, the Balkan verbal system is remarkably complex, with a wide variety of grammaticalized aspectual, temporal, modal and evidential distinctions, part of which are still expressed inflectionally. The oppositions among the past tenses in the Balkan languages are similar, as is the expression of counterfactual conditions (Asenova 2011: 220–274; Gołąb 1964; Lindstedt 2002). But there are convergent analytic forms too, notably the structure "complementizer + finite verb" that is used instead of the infinitive (as discussed in Section 2) and the use of a future auxiliary that has lost part of its verbal inflection or has become an uninflected particle. Their role in the Balkan verbal system is similar to that of the prepositions in the nominal system.

I surmise that the reason the Balkan verbal system has remained more complex than the nominal system is that the common Indo-European inheritance of the Balkan languages already contained similar distinctions: there were aspectually opposed past tenses, there were past participles that could be used to form new periphrastic forms in the same fashion, and there were the copula 'to be' and the transitive possessive verb 'to have' that could be used as auxiliaries in new periphrastic perfects in languages that did not already possess such forms. The different case systems, by contrast, could not be harmonized in the same fashion before they were reduced to a tripartite system of nominative : accusative : genitive-dative, and much of their functional load was shifted to prepositions exhibiting isosemantism among the languages.

I propose the following diachronic regularity: if the corresponding subsystems of two or more languages tend to converge, then the resulting subsystems

---

[2] A notable exception is the Greek preposition *se*, which in its locative use corresponds to several distinct prepositions in other Balkan languages.
[3] The preposition used is *na* in Macedonian and *pe, pi* in Balkan Romance; see, for instance, Markovik' (2007: 91–92) for the Macedonian and Aromanian dialects of the Ohrid-Struga region.
[4] This notion seems to have been introduced to contact linguistics by Gumperz and Wilson (1971).

will be more analytic if they were structurally different to begin with, whereas relatively similar subsystems may reach convergence on a lower level of analyticity.

The regularity proposed does not say anything about why the languages must converge in the first place; some of the sociolinguistic mechanisms behind this are discussed in Sections 5 and 6 below. Nor does this regularity directly explain why Balkan Slavic had to go so far as to lose its case distinctions altogether, although it had already developed a system similar to that in Albanian, Greek and Balkan Romance (Wahlström 2015: 81–85; Gołąb 1997). As shown by Wahlström, the reasons for this further development in Balkan Slavic were certainly manifold, but in the context of this article it can be pointed out that with analytic argument marking, in other words, with prepositions and clitic doubling, an even higher grade of intertranslatability among languages could be attained than with case endings. Exactly why speakers of Balkan Slavic would have striven for high intertranslatability is also discussed in Section 5 below.

On the other hand, the Balkan convergence should not be exaggerated. Albanian and Balkan Slavic, for instance, have both borrowed the category of evidentiality from Turkish, but despite many similarities between them in this respect, there are also substantial differences in the form, meaning and use of the indirect evidentials (Friedman 1986; Makarcev 2014). The regularity proposed in this section does not suggest that strong convergence and intertranslatability are inevitable in a particular kind of contact situation; it only says that *if* convergence is to be attained, then the more different the initial subsystems were, the more analytic structures are required to replace them.

5 Both L2 speakers and bilingual L1 speakers count

The greatest challenge in Balkan linguistics is to anchor the explanations for the convergent development of the languages in their past sociolinguistic context, a context that is known to us only indirectly and through sources that were usually not written for the purpose of recording linguistic observations. The danger of circularity lurks: we explain the observed convergence with past bilingualism, but the convergence is also the proof that such bilingualism must have existed.

A fundamental question is *who* Balkanized the languages: was it (i) the L1 speakers who were influenced by their strong L2 languages? Was it perhaps (ii) the L2 speakers influenced by their L1 languages? Or was it, as proposed by Civ'jan (1965: 14ff., 183ff.), among other scholars, (iii) that L1 speakers were attempting to speak in structures that would be maximally comprehensible to the speakers of another Balkan language? All three explanations are to some extent plausible, but there are also problems with each: in scenario (i), what about the great number of speakers who did not need to learn any L2 well, such as the speakers of the prestige language Greek? In scenario (ii), how could L2 speakers have really initiated changes in a language that had a native-speaker majority, apart from some few situations in which a large-scale language shift occurred? In scenario (iii), how might these bilingual encounters have changed the way anyone spoke in other, monolingual situations?

Questions of this kind are difficult to answer by observing the present-day Balkans, where mutual bilingualism has disappeared with the rise of nation states and only the bilingualism of the dwindling minorities is left. But an indirect way of approaching the problem is first to note that among all the Balkan language groups, it was Slavic that was the most affected by the tendency towards explicit analytic marking, Macedonian being the most Balkanized of all, at least on the level of standard languages. (I think this characterization of Balkan Slavic is uncontroversial at a general level, even if not everyone would agree with the way I counted Balkanization indices in Lindstedt 2000a: 232–234.) What does this fact tell us?

Macedonian is located in the geographical centre of Balkanization (see Sect. 2), which partly explains its high number of Balkanisms. But an explanation valid for all of Balkan Slavic would begin by noting that Slavic was certainly not the most prestigious language in the Balkans during the Ottoman period, but neither was it lowest on the prestige scale. Greek was the prestige language among the Christian population – to the extent that all educated users of Greek irrespective of their native language shared the same "Romaic" identity (Detrez 2008, 2015) – while Ottoman Turkish was the language of the state. On the other hand, the prestige of Slavic was certainly higher than that of Romani and, it is safe to assume, also somewhat higher than that of Albanian and "Wallachian" (Balkan Romance), whose speakers used mainly Greek and Church Slavonic as their written languages. In all, Balkanization was strongest in Slavic, near the middle of this prestige scale, and Greek and Romani, at the two opposite ends of the same scale, clearly possess a lesser number of Balkanisms (Lindstedt 2000a: 232–234).[5]

---

[5] Even now Romani is still not often mentioned among the languages of the Balkan linguistic area; Asenova (2002: 16–19), for instance, does not bring it up in discussing the languages of which the Sprachbund consists. It is true that Romani has fewer Balkanisms than Balkan Slavic, Balkan Romance or Albanian, but no such clear line can be drawn between Romani and Greek. The neglect of Romani is thus mainly a result of the history and sociology of scholarship, not of the objective properties of this language.

I surmise that what makes the middle of the prestige scale special is the *combined* role of L2 speakers and L1 speakers regularly using other languages. Balkan Slavic certainly had more L2 speakers than the languages below it on the prestige scale, especially Romani. In the Central Balkans the direction of the language shift has been from Romance to Slavic (Gołąb 1997). And it is reasonable to assume that the Christian and Muslim Slavs communicated with the Muslim Albanians mainly in Turkish or Slavic. On the other hand, Balkan Slavic had more L1 speakers regularly using other languages than Greek did (or Turkish, for that matter), because the speakers of a prestige language have fewer reasons to learn other languages well.

Weigand (1895: 6) reported that the Aromanians of Monastir (present-day Bitola in Macedonia), "at least the men", knew, besides their native language, Bulgarian and Greek; "most of them" also knew Turkish and Albanian, and many understood even (Judeo)Spanish. From this list we may conclude that Albanian was lower on the local scale of prestige (or at least utility value) than Macedonian (what Weigand called Bulgarian), though we must of course keep in mind that in those Ottoman provinces where there were more Albanian and fewer Slavic speakers, the situation was certainly different.

My conjecture is that grammatical borrowing that favours change towards analytism may occur both when L1 speakers regularly use another language and also when L2 speakers transfer features from their native languages. Furthermore, the combined effect of these two bilingual speaker groups when both are large in a given language community is stronger than if only one group were large. This explains nicely why Balkan Slavic (and especially Macedonian) has developed several Balkan features more than have the other Sprachbund languages. The combined effect of L2 speakers and L1 speakers regularly using other languages also explains why Greek is not the main source of Balkanisms (*pace* Sandfeld 1930, see Lindstedt 2000a: 236–237), or why Romani has not adopted the greatest number of Balkanisms, but the sociolinguistic focus of Balkanization seems to have been around the middle of the prestige scale.

This also fits well with Joseph's (2013: 625) explanation emphasizing "intense, intimate and mutual multilingualism" in the Balkans and describing mutual accommodation in bilingual contact situations, in which L2 speakers have interference from their native languages; L1 speakers also try to use the kinds of patterns in their own language that they know have analogues in the other languages. Notice that in this model an L2 may influence a speaker's L1 not only because the L2 may be a much-used prestige language, but also because the speaker regularly uses L1 with the native speakers of L2 and has therefore been accustomed to accommodating their own L1 usage towards this L2.

This **principle of combined effect** could theoretically mean two different things: either the combined effect of the two kinds of bilingual speakers favours all kinds of explicit analytic marking or else the L1>L2 interference favours one type of feature, the L2>L1 interference another type of feature and the "combined effect" appears only insofar as these types are not distinguished from one another, but counted together. Yet in the latter instance, we would expect to find very different sets of Balkanisms at the two ends of the prestige scale, Greek and Romani, and this does not seem to be the case. It can thus be assumed that *both* L1 speakers regularly using other languages *and* L2 speakers created explicit analytic marking in the Balkan languages, albeit in different proportions.

6 The Balkans: A third kind of contact situation

Trudgill (2011: 40–43) distinguishes two sociolinguistic types of contact situations, which have opposite effects on language complexity. Simplification occurs in contact situations that are dominated by "untutored, especially short-term, *adult* second language learning" (original emphasis; this type is also the main focus of McWhorter 2011). On the other hand, complexity increases "in long-term, co-territorial contact situations which involve childhood [...] bilingualism where young speakers know two or more languages natively or at least extremely well". Trudgill repeatedly gives Sprachbünde as examples of the latter kind.

Now, I have argued that the effects of the Balkan contact situation were neither clearly simplifying nor complexifying, but rather that explicit analytic marking is the property common to most grammatical Balkanisms. This result does not fit Trudgill's two types very well, nor does the Balkan sociolinguistic context correspond to either type. In the Balkans we certainly have a "long-term, co-territorial contact situation", but there is no reason to assume that this situation included much childhood bilingualism, except for some ethnically mixed urban centres. On the other hand, adult bilingualism, especially adult male bilingualism, was not based on "short-term" second-language learning; rather it was a stable property of the linguistic situation.

In the Balkans of the Ottoman period, it was men who were responsible for most of the economic and administrative contacts among different ethnic groups, because men represented the family before the state and religious authorities and traded in products of livestock breeding or crafts. Men also participated in *gurbet*, seasonal work migrations; women could do so more rarely and only until they became married (Hristov 2008: 3). This is not to deny the possibility of female bilingualism or childhood bilingualism at various places and times, but at any rate, the Balkan sociolinguistic situation did not correspond to either of Trudgill's two types.

I propose that there were two crucial sociolinguistic factors that created the specificity of the Balkan situation. In the Ottoman period there was no single lingua franca in the region. Turkish was the state language, and Greek was the prestige language of learning among the Orthodox ("Romaic") population, but neither of them alone combined both state and religious authority as far as the Balkan Christians were concerned. Another important factor was that languages were important symbols of group identity, and large-scale language shifts did not occur. Greek was perhaps on its way to becoming the identity language of the Balkan Christians (Detrez 2008, 2015), but this development was cut short by the new nationalist movements, which finally terminated the Sprachbund formation altogether.

The beginning of the Sprachbund formation must be placed in the last centuries of the Byzantine era,[6] and here we have far fewer facts upon which to construct sociolinguistic hypotheses. Greek was certainly the unrivalled prestige language of the mediaeval Balkans, but Church Slavonic was used as the written language of the Slavic kingdoms; at any rate, the time was much more turbulent than in the later Pax Ottomanica. For six decades during the thirteenth century, Constantinople was the capital of the Latin Empire *(Imperium Romaniae)* founded by the crusaders, and in that time the Greek language was strongly influenced by Western Romance, notably French (Horrocks 2010: 345–359), which may in fact account for some of the apparent Balkanisms in Greek.

To sum up, a third type of contact situation can be posited on the basis of Balkan facts: adult-based long-term, stable, mutual and intense multilingualism which does not lead to outright simplification or complexification, but favours such explicit analytic grammatical marking that increases direct intertranslatability among the languages.

Acknowledgements: I wish to thank the participants of the Balkan panel at the Societas Linguistica Europaea meeting in Split in 2013 and especially the anonymous reviewer of this volume for their useful comments and suggestions. Unfortunately I was able to take into consideration only some of them.

---

[6] Joseph (2013: 618–619) puts the beginning of the Sprachbund formation roughly at 1000 CE.

References

Anttila, Raimo. 1972. *An introduction to historical and comparative linguistics*. New York: Macmillan.

Asenova, Petya. 2002. *Balkansko ezikoznanie: Osnovni problemi na balkanskija ezikov săjuz* [Balkan linguistics. Fundamental problems of the Balkan Linguistic Union]. Veliko Tărnovo: Faber.

Bruyn, Adrienne. 1995. Noun phrases. In Jacques Arends, Pieter Muysken & Norval Smith (eds.), *Pidgins and creoles: An introduction* (Creole Language Library), 259–269. Amsterdam: John Benjamins.

Bužarovska, Eleni & Liljana Mitkovska. 2010. The grammaticalization of the *habere*-perfect in Standard Macedonian. *Balkanistica* 23. 43–65.

Civ'jan, T. V. 1965. *Imja suščestvitel'noe v balkanskix jazykax. K strukturo-tipologičeskoj xarakteristike balkanskogo jazykovogo sojuza*. Moskva: Nauka.

Dahl, Östen. 2004. *The growth and maintenance of linguistic complexity* (Studies in Language Companion Series 71). Amsterdam: John Benjamins.

Demiraj, Shaban (ed.). 2002. *Gramatika e gjuhës shqipe*, I: *Morfologjia*. Tiranë: Botim i Akademisë së Shkencave.

Detrez, Raymond. 2008. Ezik i literatura v "romejskata" obšnost. In Gajda, Stanisław (ed.), *Tożsamość a język w perspektywie slawistycznej*, 151–175. Opole: Uniwersytet Opolski, Instytut Filologii Polskiej.

Detrez, Rajmond. 2015. *Ne tărsjat gărci, a romei da bădat. Pravoslavnata kulturna obštnost v Osmanskata imperija. XV–XIX v.* S.l.: Kralica Mab.

Friedman, Victor. 1986. Evidentiality in the Balkans: Bulgarian, Macedonian, and Albanian. In Wallace Chafe & Johanna Nichols (eds.), *Evidentiality: The linguistic coding of epistemology*, 168–187. Norwood, New Jersey: Ablex.

Gołąb, Zbigniew. 1964. *Conditionalis typu bałkańskiego w językach południowosłowiańskich, ze szczególnym uwzględnieniem macedońskiego* (Polska Akademia Nauk, Oddział w Krakowie, Prace Komisji Językoznawstwa 2). Wrocław – Kraków – Warszawa: Polska Akademia Nauk.

Gołąb, Zbigniew. 1997. The ethnic background and internal linguistic mechanism of the so-called Balkanization of Macedonian. *Balkanistica* 10. 13–19.

Granqvist, Kimmo. 2011. *Lyhyt Suomen romanikielen kielioppi*. [A short grammar of Finnish Romani.] (Kotimaisten kielten tutkimuskeskuksen verkkojulkaisuja 24.) Helsinki: Kotimaisten kielten tutkimuskeskus.

Graves, Nina. 2000. Macedonian – a language with three perfects? Dahl, Östen (ed.), *Tense and aspect in the languages of Europe* (Empirical Approaches to Language Typology 20–6 = Eurotyp vol. 6), 479–494. Berlin: Mouton de Gruyter.

Gumperz, John J. & Robert Wilson. 1971. Convergence and creolization: A case from the Indo-Aryan / Dravidian border in India. In Hymes, Dell (ed.), *Pidginization and creolization of languages*, 151–167. Cambridge: Cambridge University Press.

[Hauge, Kjetil Rå] Hauge, Hetil Ro. 1977. Sintaktični balkanizmi v bălgarskija ezik i ezikova redundantnost. *Bălgarski ezik* 27(5). 380–385.

Hinrichs, Uwe. 2004. Orale Kultur, Mehrsprachigkeit, radikaler Analytismus: Zur Erklärung von Sprachstrukturen auf dem Balkan und im kreolischen Raum. Ein Beitrag zur Entmystifizierung der Balkanlinguistik. *Zeitschrift für Balkanologie* 40(2). 141–174.

Horrocks, Geoffrey. 2010. *Greek: A history of the language and its speakers.* Oxford: Wiley-Blackwell.

Hristov, Petko. 2008. Mobilités du travail (gurbet), stratégies sociales et familiale: Une étude de cas dans les Balkans centraux. *Balkanologie* 11(1–2). 2–14.

Joseph, Brian D. 2013. Language contact in the Balkans. In Hickey, Raymond (ed.), *The handbook of language contact*, 618–633. Chichester: Blackwell.

Kusters, Wouter. 2003. *Linguistic complexity: The influence of social change on verbal inflection.* Utrecht: LOT. (Doctoral dissertation, University of Leiden.)

Lindstedt, Jouko. 2000a. Linguistic Balkanization: Contact-induced change by mutual reinforcement. In Dicky Gilbers, John Nerbonne & Jos Schaeken (eds.), *Languages in Contact* (Studies in Slavic and General Linguistics 28), 231–246. Amsterdam: Rodopi.

Lindstedt, Jouko. 2000b. The perfect – aspectual, temporal and evidential. Dahl, Östen (ed.), *Tense and aspect in the languages of Europe* (Empirical Approaches to Language Typology 20–6 = Eurotyp vol. 6), 365–383. Berlin: Mouton de Gruyter.

Lindstedt, Jouko. 2002. Is there a Balkan verb system? *Balkanistica* 15. 323–336.

McWhorter, John H. 2001. The world's simplest grammars are creole grammars. *Linguistic typology* 5(2/3). 125–166.

McWhorter, John H. 2011. *Linguistic simplicity and complexity: Why do languages undress?* (Language Contact and Bilingualism 1.) Boston: De Gruyter Mouton.

Markovik', Marjan. 2007. *Aromanskiot i makedonskiot govor od ohridsko-struškiot region vo balkanski kontekst.* Skopje: Makedonskata akademija na naukite i umetnostite.

Makarcev, Maksim. M. 2014. *Ėvidencial'nost' v prostranstve balkanskogo teksta.* Moskva – Sankt-Peterburg: Nestor-Istorija; Rossijskaja akademija nauk, Institut slavjanovedenija.

Sandfeld, Kristian. 1930. *Linguistique balkanique: Problèmes et résultats* (Collection linguistique publiée par la Société de Linguistique de Paris 31). Paris: Klincksieck. (Noveau tirage 1968.)

Thomason, Sarah G. 2001. *Language contact: An introduction.* Washington, D.C.: Georgetown University Press.

Trudgill, Peter. 2002. Linguistic and social typology. In J. K. Chambers, Peter Trudgill & Natalie Schilling-Estes (eds.), *The handbook of language variation and change*, 707–728. Malden, MA: Blackwell.

Trudgill, Peter. 2011. *Sociolinguistic typology: Social determinants of linguistic complexity.* Oxford: Oxford University Press.

Wahlström, Max. 2015. *The loss of case inflection in Bulgarian and Macedonian* (Slavica Helsingiensia 47). Helsinki: University of Helsinki, Department of Modern Languages.

Weigand, Gustav. 1895. *Die Aromunen. Ethnographisch-philologisch-historische Untersuchungen über das Volk der sogenannten Makedo-Romanen oder Zinzaren. Erster Band: Land und Leute.* Leipzig: Johann Ambrosius Barth (Arthur Meiner).

Weinreich, Uriel. 1970. *Languages in contact: Findings and problems.* Seventh printing. The Hague: Mouton. (First edition in 1953.)

Part II: **Balkan Syntax and Universal Principles of Grammar**

Raúl Aranovich
Impersonal reflexives in Romance and Slavic: Contact effects in the Balkans

Abstract: In the well-known analysis of Cinque (1988), the generalization that a language will form impersonal reflexives of unaccusatives if and only if it can have accusative pivots follows from Parameter Theory. But the Balkans provide a two-way exception to this prediction. First, impersonal reflexives of unaccusatives are found in Standard Bosnian, Croatian and Serbian in spite of the fact that these are nominative-pivot languages. Second, in Slovene, impersonal reflexives of unaccusatives are disallowed, even though Slovene has accusative pivots. I offer an areal solution to this problem, suggesting that anomalous languages are affected by features from the *Čakavian* dialect of Croatian. I furthermore argue that this is possible because of the relative superficial nature of case marking in these languages.

Keywords: impersonal reflexive, case, unaccusative, Croatian dialects, language contact, Parameter Theory

1 Parameter Theory and Language Contact

There is a broadly accepted theory about substantive language universals, stating that the Language Acquisition Device provides learners with predetermined choices. These parameters, as they are called, may be so fundamental as to affects all kinds of linguistic phenomena (Baker 1996 calls them *Macro-parameters*), or they can be more parochial and subordinate.[1] Often parameters express themselves as clusters of grammatical properties. A classic example is the correlation of null subjects and rich agreement in pro-drop languages. However, in well-defined linguistic areas, a certain feature may come to be shared among neighboring languages that are typologically distinct, resulting in unexpected feature combinations. In Early Modern Irish English, for instance, we find null subjects (from the Irish substratum) but without rich agreement morphology (as discussed in Corrigan 2010).

---
[1] Macro-parameters come close to capturing the "genius" of a language, defining a language type (Baker 1996). I return to the matter of parameters in the conclusions.

Raúl Aranovich, University of California Davis, raranovich@ucdavis.edu

https://doi.org/10.1515/9783110375930-006

In this paper I argue that the distribution of impersonal reflexives in the languages of the Balkans (notice the choice of term here) offers another case in which language contact comes into conflict with Parameter Theory. Evidence from Romance and Slavic languages supports the generalization that unaccusative intransitive verbs can form impersonal reflexives[2] if and only if reflexive passives of transitive verbs retain the accusative marking on the object. Cinque (1988) proposed a parameter to account for this clustering of properties. But two-way exceptions to this generalization can be found among the languages of the Balkans: impersonal unaccusatives alongside nominative objects, and accusative objects without impersonal unaccusatives. I argue that these examples do not constitute a real exception to Cinque's parameterization of impersonal reflexives, but rather superficial phenomena due to intense language contact among varieties with different settings for the parameter.

The paper is structured as follows: Section 2 introduces the most common types of impersonal reflexives, showing that when the verb is transitive the object can be realized in the nominative or the accusative. Section 3 shows that there are languages in which unaccusatives can also form impersonal reflexives, but these are the ones that also have accusative marked objects in impersonal reflexives with transitives. Section 4 discusses Cinque's (1988) account of the generalization in terms of two distinct reflexive pronouns, each with its own properties regarding argument structure. Exceptions to the generalization accounted for by Cinque (1988) are presented in Section 5. Section 6 discusses several possible scenarios under which language contact could have produced the mixed type languages found in the Balkans. The conclusion is that these mixed type languages do not reflect deep exceptions to the parameterization, but the distribution of superficial morpho-syntactic properties, due to contact.

2 Impersonal Reflexives

Impersonal reflexives can be found in Romance and Slavic languages (among others), and share some general characteristics. In impersonal reflexives, the topmost argument is interpreted as an arbitrary human actor, and is not overtly expressed as a subject (hence the term "impersonal"). The construction is formally marked by the presence of a reflexive pronoun (glossed as SE). The examples

---

[2] In this paper, the term "impersonal reflexive" is used with reference to the reflexive marker which occurs in the morphological make-up of the impersonal constructions at issue here.

in (1a-b) show some typical impersonal reflexive clauses, from Bulgarian and Romanian

(1) a. *Tuk se raboti cjal den.* (Bulg)
  here SE work.3SG all day
  'One works all day here.'
  b. *Se muncește.* (Rom)
  SE work.3SG
  'It is worked.'
  (Dobrovie-Sorin 1994)

The predicates in (1a-b) are intransitive (unergatives, to be more specific). But impersonal reflexives can also be formed with transitive predicates. The examples in (2) show that in Bulgarian and Romanian the patient, or logical object, is realized as a nominative argument. As such, it triggers verb agreement, and it cannot be supplemented by any sort of object markers. I refer to this argument as the "pivot", for reasons that become evident soon. There is a long debate in the literature as to whether these nominative pivots in impersonal reflexives are subjects or not, and, if they are, whether it is still acceptable to call these constructions "impersonal" (see Aranovich 2011 for a summary of the arguments, circumscribed to Romance). Here I assume they are subjects, but I still use the term impersonal, because the agent is still an arbitrary human subject.

(2) a. *S'au prins* **hoții** (Rom)
  SE has.3PL caught thieves.def
  'The thieves have been caught.'
  (Dobrovie-Sorin 1994)
  b. **In școala asta se pedepsește prea des* **pe elevi.** (Rom)
  in this school SE punish.3SG too frequently ACC students
  'Students are punished too frequently in this school.'
  (Dobrovie-Sorin 1994)
  c. **Starcite** *se pogrebvat/*pogrebva vâv grobištata.* (Bulg)
  old.men.def SE bury.PL/bury.SG in cemeteries.def
  'One buries the old men in the cemetery.'

In other languages, however, the pivot can be realized as an accusative complement. In that case, it does not trigger verb agreement with the verb, and it is unquestionably not the subject of the clause. The examples in (3) show some sentences with accusative pivots from the Čakavian dialect of Croatian, and also from Venetian (which is included here for reasons that become clear later). The impersonal nature of these sentences is beyond dispute.

(3) a. *Se stavi nuter **juhu*** (Čak)
SE put.3SG in rennet.ACC
'One puts in the rennet (ACC).'
(Houtzagers 1985)
b. *kat se   lŭpi   **trukȉnjo*** (Čak)
when SE peel.3SG maize.ACC
'when the maize is peeled'
(Kalsbeek 1998)
c. *dó'po avę'r kolgá, mę'so su la mę'ſa stǫ majále, sę **lǫ ſbúſa*** (Ven)
after having stretched, put on the table this pig, SE it.ACC punctures
'after stretching, setting the pig on the table, one punctures it…'
(Zamboni, 1974, p. 85)

3 Unaccusatives

So far I have said nothing about substantive universals. To see an interesting clustering of features, one needs to consider impersonal reflexives of unaccusative predicates. While all the languages under consideration seem to have impersonal reflexives with unergatives like *work*, as in (1), unaccusatives like *die, arrive*, or statives and adjectival passives are restricted to occur in impersonal reflexives of languages that have accusative pivots. This generalization is summarized in the Impersonal Unaccusative Condition.

(4) **Impersonal Unaccusative Condition (IUC):** *A language has Impersonal reflexive passives of unaccusatives if and only if it also has accusative pivots in impersonal reflexives of transitives.*

Thus, in Romanian and Bulgarian, impersonal reflexives of unaccusatives/adjectival passives are disallowed, as in (5), but in Venetian and the Čakavian dialect of Croatian they are allowed.[3] This is shown in (6) and (7).

---

[3] Not all "unaccusatives" are excluded from this construction. Verbs like *xodja* 'go, walk' can form an impersonal reflexive, as the following example shows. This example is in contrast with (5a), with the verb *pristigam* 'arrive' (a reviewer suggests this may be an effect of the generic aspect in these sentences, a matter that I must leave for further research).
(A) *na učilište se xodi peša.* (Bulg)
to school SE go.3SG on.foot
'One goes to school on foot.'

(5) a. *Na učilište se **pristiga** peša. (Bulg)
    to school SE arrive.3SG on.foot
    'One arrives to school on **foot**.'
  b. *Ot seljanite se **e uvažavan**
    by peasant.PL.DET SE is respected
    'One is respected by the peasants.'
  c. *Nu se **este** niciodată **mulţumit**. (Rom)
    not SE is ever satisfied
    'One is never satisfied.'
    (Dobrovie-Sorin 1994)

(6) a. i se je **stalo** odzât va cr^{i}ekve (Čak)
    and SE is stand.PAST back of church
    'and one would stand at the back of the church.'
    (Kalsbeek 1998)
  b. se **mučĩ**
    SE be.silent.3SG
    'people ar not speaking.'
  c. i anke kad bi se nëkamor **šlö**
    and also when would SE somewhere go.PAST
    'and also when one would go somewhere.'

(7) ...ki a g ę' đa maīár béṅ,   ę śę sta béṅ! (Ven)
    here it there is of eating well, and SE is well
    'Here there are good things to eat, and one is well!'
    (Zamboni 1974)

4 Impersonal reflexives and syntactic theory

The IUC is the kind of clustering of grammatical properties that Parameter theory is meant to explain. One approach to the phenomenon within formal theories of grammar is developed in Cinque (1988). Cinque suggests that universal grammar makes available two types of impersonal SE, based on the different modules of the theory: argument SE, and non-argument SE.

Argument SE absorbs an external semantic role. This allows the patient to move to the position of the external argument to receive nominative case, if the predicate is transitive. The leftmost sentence diagram illustrates the properties of Argument SE. Since argument SE cannot absorb an internal role, the reflexive clitic cannot occur with unaccusatives, copulatives, or periphrastic passives. Non-argument SE, on the other hand, licenses a null pronoun with arbitrary reference (pro_{arb}) in subject position, without absorbing a semantic role. If the predicate is transitive, the pivot remains in object position, receiving accusative case. This is shown in the rightmost sentence diagram. Since pro_{arb} can also be an internal argument, unaccusative verbs (and similar predicates) can combine with non-argument SE.

In this way, the clustering of properties summarized in the IUC is accounted for. Nominative-pivot languages have argument SE, while accusative-pivot languages have non-argument SE.

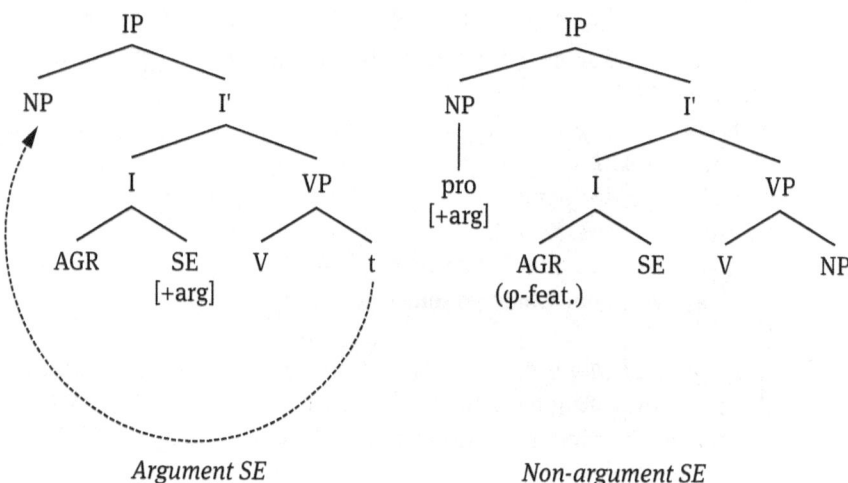

Argument SE   Non-argument SE

5 Exceptions

The UIC work reasonably well for the Romance and Slavic languages at large, but things take an interesting turn when the languages from the Balkans are considered. Here we observe a two-way exception to the UIC. On the one hand, we have the Štokavian dialect of Bosnian, Croatian, and Serbian. Descriptions of the standard (prescriptive or normalized) varieties of these languages classify them as nominative-pivot languages (but according to Belaj 2003 non-standard forms of these languages may have accusative pivots). This is shown in (9a-c). Descriptions of the same register, however, show that impersonal reflexives of unaccusatives like *die* are found, as in (10).

(8)   Qvde se dobro spava.   (BCS)
      here SE well sleep.3SG
      'One sleeps well here.'
      (Bidwell 1965–6)

(9) a. **Himna**   se svira   svaki dan.   (BCS)
       anthem.NOM SE play.3SG every day.ACC
       'The anthem is played every day.'
       (Leko 1988)
    b. *Svira se **himnu** svaki dan.   (BCS)
       play.3SG SE anthem.ACC every day.ACC
       'The anthem is played every day.'
       (Leko 1988)
    c. Jede se samo **bela riba**.   (BCS)
       eat.3SG SE only white.NOM fish.NOM
       'One only eats white fish (NOM)'
       (Djordjević 1988)

(10) Umiralo se za otadžbinu.   (BCS)
      die.PAST SE for country
      'One died for their country.'
      (Djordjević 1988)

Parenthetically, the Kajkavian dialect of Croatian also has nominative pivots.

(11) zë,mja kat sę zörję onda sę puvläči   (Kaj)
      'when you plough the soil, you pull.'
      (Houtzagers 1999)

Slovene, even though not quite within the Balkan language area, provides another intriguing combination of features. Slovene has accusative pivots alongside nominative pivots, as shown in (12). But impersonal reflexives of adjectival passives (or statives/unaccusatives) are disallowed, as seen in (13).

(12) a. Starše se uboga.   (Slo)
        parents.ACC SE obey.3SG
        'One obeys parents.'
        (Rivero & Sheppard 2003, p. 102)

b. *Starši se ubogajo.* (Slo)
parents.NOM SE obey.3PL
'Parents are obeyed.'
(Rivero & Sheppard 2003, p. 96)

(13) *Od časa do časa se je kaznovano od prijateljev (Slo)
from time to time SE is punished by friends
'From time to time one is punished by friends.'
(L. Marušič, p.c.)

As usual, however, there is some disagreement in the literature about these facts. In their impressive survey of impersonal reflexive constructions across the Slavic languages, for instance, Fehrmann et al. (2010) state that Slovene does have unaccusative impersonal reflexives. We now know that some unaccusatives are more unaccusative than others, a fact that needs to be controlled for in studies of this kind. Here I have taken some of those predicates as proxies for the whole class, but I am aware that this is not the best practice. Hopefully more research will clarify disagreements one way or another.

6 Areal explanations

The nice clustering of features that Cinque's (1988) theory of the two SE predicts, then, falls apart in the Balkans. And here is where the issue of the universal and the particular in Balkan syntax comes to the fore. If we are talking about the Balkan languages, properly speaking, it is apparent that the feature that characterizes the Balkan Sprachbund is the presence of argument SE (I have no data on Greek, Macedonian, or Albanian, however). The Čakavian dialect of Croatian is outside the Sprachbund, in this respect, but there are other instances in which the Balkan isoglosses do not seem to extend to the Dalmatian coast. One could speculate that the non-argument SE of Čakavian is due to a Venetian substrate effect (that is the reason why I have Venetian in my sample), but this is difficult to prove without hard diachronic evidence.

Figure 1 shows the geographical location of the three main dialects of Croatian, while figure 2 is a schematic distribution of the two isoglosses that are coming apart in this region. We find impersonal reflexives with accusative pivots in Slovene and Čakavian, and impersonal reflexives of unaccusatives in Čakavian and Štokavian. Only in Čakavian does the clustering of features correspond to a stable universal type, according to the parameters set up in Cinque (1988). The features of the cluster "leak" (so to speak) into neighboring dialects, but in a selective way.

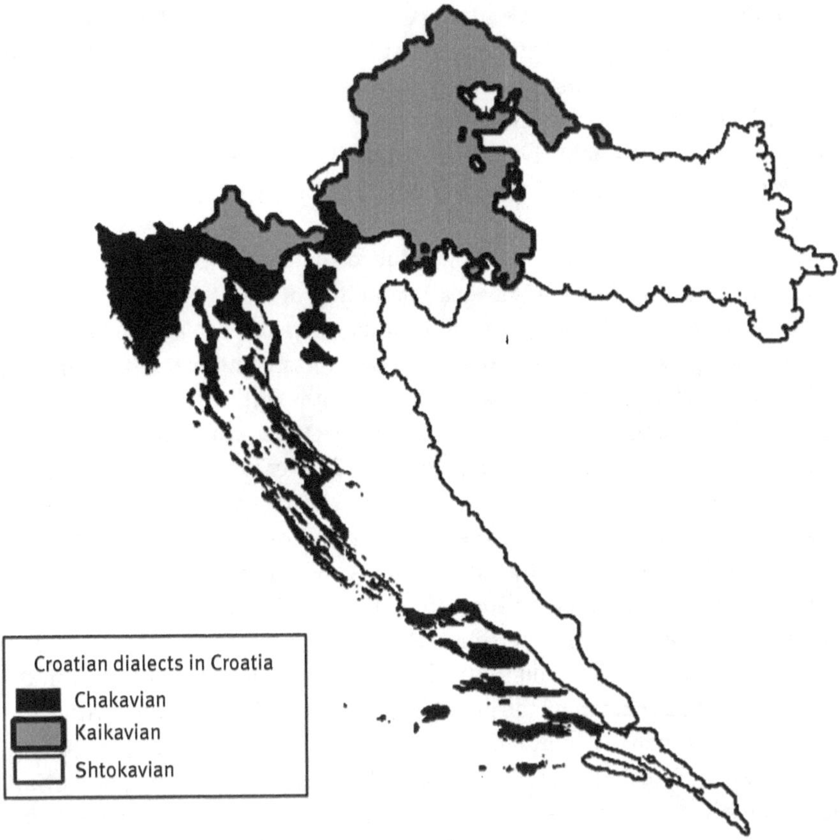

Impersonal reflexives in Romance and Slavic — 95

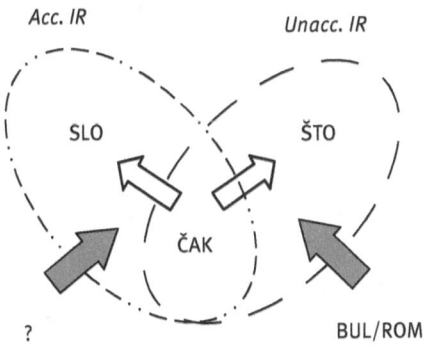

Figure 1: Croatian dialects.
Source: http://commons.wikimedia.org/wiki/File:Croatian_dialects.PNG

Figure 2: Isoglosses and shifts.

How could such a situation have arisen, and what does this say about the validity of the universal principles of grammar (Theta-theory, Case theory, movement – or their translations into more current terminology) that are behind Cinque's tale of two SE? First of all, this is where Balkan syntax becomes really interesting. I have not found these "unstable" types outside the Balkans. So this is a case where an investigation into contact syntax goes beyond mere comparative syntax, as Joseph (2001) urged us to do.

Joseph (2001) suggests that changes due to contact will be of a "superficial" nature, not affecting deep (or universal) properties of the grammars in question. So I am going to describe one possible scenario where this could have happened. This is indicated by the white arrows in Figure 2. Assuming that Čakavian is the outlier, some of its features migrate into languages with Argument SE without affecting the deep properties of the construction. On the one hand, Slovene gets "accusative-marked" subjects in impersonal reflexives. That is, only the superficial coding property of the objects in the Čakavian impersonal reflexive are transferred. On the other hand, the situation in Štokavian may arise through transfer or calqueing of individual lexical items and the constructions they occur in. Štokavian, then, would have adopted particular unaccusative predicates, in a piecemeal fashion, in their impersonal reflexive form.

There is, of course, an alternative. It is possible that the shift went in the other direction, as shown by the gray arrows in Figure 2. In this alternative scenario, non-argument SE would have had a wider distribution than its present one. Through a process of attrition, the peripheral areas (Slovene, Štokavian) would have lost some of the superficial features that make up the cluster (but without changing the deep properties of the construction). In Štokavian, accusative marking on pivots is lost due to contact with Romanian and Bulgarian, resulting in "nominative objects". In Slovene, on the other hand, one has to postulate loss of unaccusatives and passives in impersonal reflexives due to contact with some other language (perhaps Czech or Alpine varieties of Romance). This is a less likely scenario, however, since it would be attrition by negative evidence: a feature is lost because a neighboring language does not have it.

A third alternative mixes and matches from the previous two, getting accusative subjects in Slovene (with non-argument SE), but nominative objects in Štokavian (with argument SE). But of all the alternatives, the first scenario is the most likely, given what we know about language contact in general (Matras 2010). Future work in this area could concentrate on finding hard diachronic evidence, going one way or another. Additionally, research into the specific grammatical properties of impersonal reflexives in the languages of the Balkans should go beyond the coding properties of subjects and objects, and explore their behavioral properties in these languages (raising and control of infinitives, for instance). This is also a matter for further research.

7 Conclusions

To conclude, I have shown that in the Balkans (and its surroundings) the clustering of properties that characterize two deeply distinct impersonal reflexive constructions falls apart. But I also have argued that deep principles of UG can be preserved if, as suggested in Joseph (2001), we take some of these properties to constitute superficial transfers from one language into others, due to the intense contact situation that characterizes a Sprachbund. The exceptions to the IUC that I have discussed here, then, support the view of the Balkans as a linguistic area, and let us speculate on the kind of grammatical features that are likely to be transferred.

In Baker's (1996) approach to parameter setting, linguistic structures are never impacted directly, since parameters capture those properties of a grammar that are most general and abstract. The effects of a parameter may be obscured by other lexical properties or syntactic principles of the language. This also applies to the effects of language contact, as I have argued in this paper. When evaluating the empirical validity of a parameter, then, linguists need to carefully evaluate superficial properties of a language, often having to look past them.

Recently, however, some authors have dealt with exceptions to parameters by postulating "micro-parameters" (Adger et al. 2009). The micro-parametric approach questions the assumption that a language must satisfy a predetermined checklist of grammatical properties to belong to a given type, and that a macro-parametric setting is responsible for such properties. But as I have argued in Aranovich (2013), this is an approach that ends up proposing as many types as there are languages, therefore explaining nothing. By looking at broad classifications, and then trying to pinpoint the sources of apparent departures from those general types, we can gain some insight into the relationship between the general and the particular in syntax. The languages of the Balkans give us a natural setting to develop this line of inquiry.

References

Adger, David, Daniel Harbour, and Laurel J. Watkins. 2009. *Mirrors and microparameters*. Cambridge: Cambridge University Press.
Aranovich, Raúl. 2011. Shifty objects in Romance. In Rodrigo Gutiérrez-Bravo, Line Mikkelsen and Eric Potsdam (eds.), *Representing Language: Essays in honor of Judith Aissen*. Santa Cruz: UCSC Linguistic Research Center. 1–14.

Aranovich, Raúl. 2013. Transitivity and polysynthesis in Fijian. *Language* 89(3): 465–500.
Baker, Mark C. 1996. *The Polysynthesis Parameter*. New York/Oxford: Oxford University Press.
Belaj, Branimir. 2003. On some peripheral types of accusative direct object in Croatian: A cognitive analysis. *Jezikoslovlje* 4 (2): 263–78.
Bidwell, Charles. E. 1964. The reflexive construction in Serbo-Croatian. *Studies in Linguistics* 18: 37–47.
Bidwell, Charles. E. 1965. Serbo-Croatian syntax. *Language* 41(2): 238–59.
Cinque, Guglielmo. 1988. On *si* constructions and the theory of arb. *Linguistic Inquiry* 19: 521–581.
Corrigan, Karen P. 2010. Language Contact and Grammatical Theory. In Raymond Hickey (ed.) *The Handbook of Language Contact*, 106–127. Oxford: Blackwell Publishers
Djordjević, Radmila. 1988. The Reflexive Pronoun/The Verbal Particle 'se' in Serbo-Croatian and its Correspondents in English. *New Zealand Slavonic Journal* 21–38.
Dobrovie-Sorin, Carmen. 1994. *The Syntax of Romanian*. Berlin: Mouton de Gruyter.
Fehrmann, Dorothee, Uwe Junghanns, and Denisa Lenertová. 2010. Two reflexive markers in Slavic. *Russian Linguistics* 34: 203–238
Houtzagers, H. Peter. 1985. *The Čakavian Dialect of Orlec on the Island of Cres*. Amsterdam: Rodopi.
Houtzagers, H. Peter. 1999. *The Kajkavian dialect of Hidegség and Fertöhomok*. Amsterdam: Rodopi.
Joseph, Brian D. 2001. Is Balkan Comparative Syntax Possible? In: María Luisa Rivero and Angela Ralli (eds.), *Comparative Syntax of Balkan Languages*, 17–43. Oxford: Oxford University Press.
Kalsbeek, Janneke. 1998. *The Čakavian Dialect of Orbanići near Žminj in Istria*. Amsterdam: Rodopi.
Leko, Nedžad. 1988. Case of Noun Phrases in Serbo-Croatian and Case Theory. *Folia Linguistica* XXIII. 27–54.
Matras, Yaron. 2010. Contact, Convergence, and Typology. In Raymond Hickey (ed.) *The Handbook of Language Contact*, 66–85. Oxford: Blackwell Publishers
Rivero, María Luisa and Milena M. Sheppard. 2003. Indefinite reflexive clitics in Slavic: Polish and Slovenian. *Natural Language and Linguistic Theory* 21(1): 89–155.
Zamboni, Alberto (1974). *Veneto*. Pisa: Pacini Editore.

Andrea D. Sims and Brian D. Joseph
Morphology versus Syntax in the Balkan Verbal Complex

Abstract: Various Balkan languages have a string of material called here the "verbal complex", in which a verb occurs with various markers for tense, modality, negation, and argument structure. We examine here this verbal complex with regard to its status as a syntactic element or a morphological element. First, we carefully outline the theoretical basis for determining the status of a given entity and we then argue that the verbal complexes display different degrees of morphologization in the different languages. Albanian and Greek show the highest degree of morphologization of the verbal complex, with Macedonian close to them in this regard. Bulgarian shows a lesser degree of morphologization than Macedonian, making for an interesting split within East South Slavic, and Serbian shows an even lesser degree. We argue further that certain aspects of the verbal complex, especially in the languages with the greatest morphologization, represent contact-related convergence, and draw from this a general claim about the role of surface structure in language contact.

Keywords: Albanian, Greek, Macedonian, Bulgarian, Serbian, verbal complex, particle, morphologization, language contact, surface structure

1 Introduction

Most of the languages in the Balkans have a string of material that can be called the "verbal complex" consisting of a verb and various associated elements – what might be termed "particles" for want of a better characterization at this point – marking tense, modality, negation, and argument structure. Examples from a few such languages are given in (1), with dialectal material given for Greek and Macedonian to maximize comparability with the other languages.[1]

---

[1] In this paper, Modern Greek is transcribed with broad IPA. Cyrillic for all relevant Slavic languages is transliterated according to the scientific system.

Note: We thank Iliyana Krapova for her comments on this paper, and Victor Friedman for consultation about Macedonian.

Andrea D. Sims and Brian D. Joseph, The Ohio State University

https://doi.org/10.1515/9783110375930-007

(1) a. *S'   do   të   ja   jep.*   (Albanian)
       NEG   FUT   SBJV 3SG.DAT/3SG.ACC give.1SG
       'I will not give it to him.'

   b. *Nu   o   să   il   dau.*   (Daco-Romanian)
       NEG FUT SBJV 3SG.DAT/3SG.ACC give.1SG
       'I will not give it to him.'

   c. *Đe   θe   na   tu   to   ðóso.*   (dialectal Greek)
       NEG FUT SBJV 3SG.GEN 3SG.ACC give.1SG
       'I will not give it to him.'

   d. *Ne   ḱe   da   mu   go   davam.*   (dialectal Macedonian)
       NEG FUT SBJV 3SG.DAT 3SG.ACC give.1SG
       'I will not give it to him.'

   e. *Neću   da   mu   ga   dam.*   (Serbian)
       NEG.FUT.1SG   SBJV 3SG.DAT 3SG.ACC give.1SG
       'I will not give it to him.'

Elements in these languages seem to line up in the same order, generalizable as in (2)[2]:

(2) NEG – TNS – MOOD – IO – DO – V

This pattern gives the appearance of a template-like order for the relevant elements and suggests convergence as part of the broader Balkan Sprachbund, the well-known result of a long period of sustained and intense contact among the speakers of various languages leading to striking similarities in structure and form in these languages. The similarities in the verbal complex are schematized in (2), although not all elements necessarily occur in any given sentence.

While there are various descriptive issues to be resolved with the verbal complex in each language, for instance regarding the elements that can and cannot occur in it, we approach this construct from a theoretically oriented analytic perspective. In particular, we ask whether the elements that make up the verbal complex are morphological objects or syntactic objects, and accordingly whether the verbal complex itself is a word-level unit or instead is a phrase-level unit. It is important to question the status of the verbal complex in part because surface word order can obscure structural differences. To take a single example

---

[2] Abbreviations in this paper follow the Leipzig Glossing Rules: https://www.eva.mpg.de/lingua/resources/glossing-rules.php; accessed August 9, 2016.

from a different phenomenon, but one that is well understood, Rudin (1988) shows that while multiple WH-fronted structures in Bulgarian (e.g. *Koj kakvo vižda?* lit. 'Who what sees?') and what was then called Serbo-Croatian (e.g. *Ko šta vidi?* lit. 'Who what sees?') seem superficially to be parallel, they nonetheless reflect a structural difference that is revealed by their syntactic behavior when they occur in embedded clauses. In Bulgarian, all of the WH-words in a multiple question must be moved out of an embedded clause. By contrast, for many Serbo-Croatian speakers, only one WH-word can be extracted from an embedded clause, and the other must remain in the lower clause.[3] In terms of Rudin's theoretical framework, this means that all WH-words are in SpecCP in Bulgarian, but only one WH-word can inhabit SpecCP in Serbo-Croatian. A surface similarity between Bulgarian and Serbo-Croatian thus hides a deep structural difference. To the extent that situations of this sort are not uncommon, it is manifestly obvious that surface strings cannot be taken as having any deep reality.

Additionally, once we scratch the surface, it quickly becomes clear that the internal structuring of the Balkan verbal complex differs from one language to another, despite the surface-similar pattern identified in (1) and (2). As we show below, the verbal complex is parallel to multiple WH-fronting in the sense that surface-parallel ordering that is shared among languages nonetheless corresponds to different structures. At the same time, the verbal complex differs in that it reveals not so much different underlying syntactic structures as differences in the morphological versus syntactic status of the elements. As happens with other features of the Balkan Sprachbund, there are piecemeal commonalities and differences from one language to another, but the most interesting dimension of difference from a theoretical standpoint has to do with the extent of morphologization of elements. The question of whether the verbal complex is a morphological or syntactic object thus turns out to have significance, since there are differences among the verbal complexes in the various languages, and some of the differences point to a fundamental divide between those languages in which the verbal complex is substantially morphologized, and those in which it is morphologized less or not at all.

In examining the status of the verbal complex, one of our goals is to justify and explore this construct as a topic of relevance to the Balkan Sprachbund. The verbal complex highlights an important generalization about processes of grammatical convergence in language contact situations, namely that it is surface-oriented. We are not the first to draw attention to surface similarities as being significant to

---

[3] Rudin (1988: 453f.) notes that there is some speaker-by-speaker variation in this regard. Some Serbo-Croatian speakers do accept multiple WH-fronted structures, parallel to the Bulgarian pattern.

the Balkan Sprachbund. Most famously, Kopitar's (1829) description of Albanian, Balkan Romance ('Wallachian') and Bulgarian as being three lexicons with one grammar was based not on deep structural aspects of the grammatical structure, but on surface parallelisms. Our paper is thus in the vein of previous work arguing that the very fact of surface similarities across languages in contact, but with deep structural differences, is evidence of the surface-oriented nature of language contact. However, evidence of morphologization in the languages of the central Balkans additionally raises interesting questions about how language contact and syntactic borrowing intersect with diachronic processes of morphologization. Thus we explore here the theoretical issues raised by the fact that the verbal complex exists at the intersection of morphology and syntax.

2 The relationship between morphology and syntax

The question of whether the verbal complex in each of the various Balkan languages constitutes a word-level unit or a phrase-level unit can only be answered in the context of a model of the morphology-syntax interface. Of course, how morphology and syntax intersect is a major source of debate, with proposals ranging all the way from the claim that they are non-distinct (with morphology usually subsumed to syntax) to the claim that there are fully distinct morphological and syntactic components, each operating according to its own principles. We cannot here rehash the history of thinking on the issue and we simply adopt a position of the latter type. In particular, we assume the framework of inferential-realization morphology and a lexicalist approach to the morphology-syntax interface.[4]

In inferential-realizational models (e.g. Paradigm Function Morphology (Stump 2001) or Network Morphology (Brown and Hippisley 2012)), the combination of a lexeme and morpho-syntactic values licenses rules that perform morphophonological operations on bases, such as affixation. This means that the classical notion of a morpheme as a lexically listed bundle of form and meaning has no status. Such models have the advantage that the meaning of a word need not be exactly the sum of the meanings of its parts. The parts may underspecify, overspecify, or even mismatch the meaning of the whole, and even radical violations of form-meaning isomorphism can be handled easily. Moreover, inferential-realizational models are paradigmatic in the sense that word-forms convey

---

[4] See Stump (2001) for a detailed justification of inferential-realizational morphology, also called Word-and-Paradigm morphology.

meaning by virtue of paradigmatic contrast with other forms of the same lexeme. Thus for example, the English noun form *cat* is interpreted as singular not because it has some zero morpheme that adds the morpho-syntactic value SINGULAR, but because it contrasts with the plural form *cats*. This means that inferential-realizational models are not committed to a concatenative approach, and in fact can accommodate a wide range of morphophonological operations on bases.

Inferential-realizationalism is consistent with a modular grammar architecture that includes an autonomous component for (inflectional) morphology operating according to principles that are at least partly distinct from the principles governing syntax. Inferential-realizational models also tend to accept some version of the Lexical Integrity Principle (Bresnan and Mchombo 1995), also sometimes termed the Principle of Morphology-free Syntax (Zwicky 1990, 1992). In principle, such a model offers a clear definition of what it means for a construction to be 'morphologized'. At the same time, various phenomena pose a challenge to a strict separation of morphology and syntax (and thus to the lexicalist position), requiring more careful thought about the nature of the morphology-syntax interface.

Our goal in this section is to consider how such models answer questions about what constitutes word-like or phrase-like behavior, and how they interpret the empirical properties of constructions. While it is beyond the scope of this article to give a fully formalized model, we summarize arguments that (mostly) operate from the perspective of inferential-realizational morphology. We focus on clitics and periphrasis as phenomena that have received significant theoretical attention exactly because they exist at the morphology-syntax interface and are thus informative about it. Both kinds of pattern are also central to the Balkan verbal complex.

2.1 Some problems with the morphology = synthesis equation

It is fairly uncontroversial that synthetic expression is a matter of morphology. In fact, when linguists talk about 'morphologization' as a diachronic process of language change, they tend to mean the development of a unit that was a free syntactic atom into one that is affixally bound to a stem. Morphology and morphologization are thus equated with synthesis and the development of synthetic expression, respectively. However, once we scratch the surface it becomes obvious that this equation is too simple. Despite a widespread assumption that morphological structure is coextensive with synthetic expression, such a characterization is problematic. Consider, for instance, Zwicky and Pullum (1983)'s well-known criteria for distinguishing between clitics and affixes[5]:

A. affixes show high selectivity with regard to their stem; clitics may show low selectivity with regard to their host;
B. affixed words are relatively more likely to exhibit arbitrary gaps in their inflectional paradigms (i.e. arbitrary restrictions on the combination of a stem and set of morpho-syntactic values); clitics are relatively less likely to exhibit arbitrary gaps in host-clitic combinations;
C. affixed words are more likely to show morphophonological idiosyncrasies (e.g. affixes can trigger or undergo allomorphy that is not purely phonological in nature); clitics are less likely to exhibit such idiosyncrasies;
D. affixed words are more likely to show semantic idiosyncrasies (non-compositionality); clitic-host combinations are more likely to be compositional;
E. syntactic rules may take affixed words as their domain; they cannot take clitic groups as their domain;
F. affixes cannot attach 'outside' of (further from the root than) clitics; clitics must attach outside of affixes.

Zwicky and Pullum (hereafter, Z&P), along with many researchers before and after them, equate clitics with independent morpho-syntactic words and affixes with subparts of words: "... [W]ord-clitic combinability is largely governed by SYNTACTIC considerations. The conditions governing the combinability of stems with affixes are of quite a different sort: they are MORPHOLOGICAL and/or LEXICAL in character..." (Zwicky and Pullum 1983: 503, emphasis original). A logical and common interpretation is thus that Z&P's criteria are diagnostics of syntactic vs. morphological objects.

At the same time, grammatical particles can exhibit mixed properties. In Serbian the feminine accusative singular weak pronoun, normally *je*, and the 3rd person singular auxiliary, also unstressed *je*, are both clearly second position clitics. Their placement (as part of a clitic cluster) is syntactically and prosodically determined and exhibits promiscuous host selection (criterion A). Nonetheless, when these two clitics occur adjacently (accusative preceding the 3sg auxiliary in the clitic cluster), the accusative clitic surfaces as *ju*. The clitic combination thus displays morphophonological idiosyncrasy (criterion C) – allomorphy in the

---

[5] Some of the criteria are diagnostic only in one direction. For instance, the existence of paradigmatic gaps is indicative of affix status, but the lack of such gaps is not necessarily indicative of clitic status, since gaps are relatively rare also in inflectional affixation. Nonetheless, these are the most widely cited criteria when it comes to diagnosing whether a given grammatical element is an affix or a clitic.

accusative clitic occurs in the context of the 3sg auxiliary clitic. This example, along with numerous others, shows that we cannot escape the conclusion that there are formatives that are placed with respect to syntactic phrases that nonetheless exhibit some of the properties of affixes according to the criteria above.

This lack of consistent results when applying the diagnostic criteria has led to further descriptive subdivisions. For instance, Sadler (1997) distinguishes syntactic clitics from phrasal affixation and edge inflection. In her terminology, syntactic clitics are syntactic terminals and form semantically transparent and syntactically accessible constructions with their host.[6] By contrast, phrasal affixes and edge inflection exhibit the syntactic properties of promiscuous host selection and syntactic placement, but the morphophonological properties of an affix. Spencer and Luís (2012) divide clitics further, arguing for a distinction between phrasal affixation and edge inflection. In phrasal affixation, a morphologically generated clitic or clitic cluster is placed syntactically with respect to a phrasal host. (The Serbian allomorphy *je je* → *ju je* qualifies these formatives as phrasal affixes.) In edge inflection, an inflected word-form consisting of both a host and clitic is selected in a given syntactic context (i.e., when the host sits at the edge of a phrase). They summarize a convincing example from Samvelian (2007) of the morphological behavior of edge inflection in Persian *ezafe* constructions. The point here is that a binary distinction into clitics and affixes is insufficient because grammatical formatives may exhibit some traits of each and different combinations of empirical properties occur. (See Aikhenvald (2002) and Spencer and Luís (2012) for a survey.) This highlights that the question of whether something is an affix or a clitic may be descriptively useful, but is ultimately incoherent in theoretical terms. The important issue has to do not with classification, but with determining what the properties of a formative are, and how the elements of grammar architecture interact to produce those properties.

So returning to Z&P's criteria, and the division between syntactic and morphological objects that they are often taken to imply, one thing we can observe is that the criteria themselves are not uniform in what they diagnose. Property A tends to reflect whether a grammatical particle attaches at the lexical or phrasal level. Properties B through D essentially boil down to the claim that affixes show a higher degree of idiosyncratic behavior along a number of dimensions whereas clitics show a greater degree of freedom and regularity. This kind of idiosyncrasy has long been interpreted as indicating composition in the lexicon, rather than the syntax (Chomsky 1970). Properties E and F diagnose objects that are subject

---

[6] However, syntactic clitics do not necessarily motivate an analysis as syntactic functional heads. Sadler argues at length that Welsh pronominal object clitics are syntactic clitics, but nonetheless are best analyzed as morphologically generated objects.

to lexical integrity. Within the criteria there is thus a difference between those that diagnose synthetic objects (criteria A, E-F), and those that diagnose composition in the lexicon or morphological component (B-D). If synthetic objects were always morphological, *and vice versa*, then the formula that equates clitics with syntactic objects and affixes with morphological objects would be justified. However, phrasal affixation and edge inflection throw this equation into doubt, because they tend to exhibit the idiosyncratic properties of morphological objects but do not necessarily form synthetic objects with their hosts.

To the extent that we define affixes as combining with stems to form synthetic objects, Z&P's criteria B through D are consistent with both affixation and morphologically generated clitic + host combinations. As Sadler (1997: 4) notes, these criteria are unable to distinguish between the two, and are thus insufficient by themselves to diagnose affixation in the traditional sense. However, we argue that these criteria are sufficient to diagnose morphological objects. Constructions may exhibit some morphological properties without being fully canonical affixes, highlighting that these notions cannot be conflated. In the following sections we consider a broader notion of what it means for an object of the grammar to be morphological, an understanding that extends beyond synthesis.

2.2 Lexicalism and the notion 'morphological object'

Ackerman et al. (2011) consider in detail the nature of the correspondence between synthetic objects and morphological objects in the context of a lexicalist model. The heart of lexicalism is what they call the Principle of Morphological Integrity: "Syntactic mechanisms neither make reference to a word form's proper subparts nor are able to create new word forms in constituent structure" (326). In other words, syntax has no access to the internal structure of synthetic objects.[7] However, other common tenets of lexicalism are to some degree independent issues, including the Principle of Unary Expression: "In syntax, a lexeme is uniformly expressed as a single morphophonologically integrated and syntactically atomic word form" (326). They argue that the Principle of Unary Expression is not inherent to lexicalism. In other words, there is no conceptual requirement that morphological realizations of lexemes be synthetic objects and syntactically atomic in the sense that is relevant for the Principle of Morphological Integrity. Modular architecture and a distinct morphological component are possible without assuming that synthetic objects are the only output. (See also Ackerman

---

[7] This is essentially a (re)formulation of the Lexical Integrity Principle (see above, Section2).

and LeSourd (1997) for a similar argument.) This raises the possibility of (partly) morphological analyses of phenomena like clitics and periphrasis.

2.3 Clitics as morphology

A number of arguments have been put forward against purely syntactic accounts of clitic cluster exponence and placement.[8] Here we highlight only a few but see Anderson (1992, 2005) and Spencer and Luís (2012) for details and additional arguments.

In an early account, Simpson and Withgott (1986) consider the problem of determining which word-formation happens in the syntax, and which in the lexicon, following the direction set by Chomsky (1970). Their paper is best known for criteria they propose as distinguishing templatic from layered (i.e. hierarchical) morphology, but their exemplification of templatic morphology centers on pronominal clitic clusters in Warumungu (a Pama-Nyungan language of Australia) and other languages. They argue that pronominal clitic clusters in Warumungu exhibit the properties of template morphology and that templates are fundamentally inconsistent with word-formation within the syntactic component because their internal structure is non-hierarchical and limited to the linearized ordering of elements.[9] They therefore take templatic structure as indicating that the cluster is generated in the lexicon (which is to say, in the morphological component), and conclude that the Warumungu clitic cluster is inserted into syntax as a single lexical entry.

An additional argument for this position comes from the fact that clitics do not always exhibit the expected properties of independent syntactic elements. Legendre (2001a) observes that clitic clusters in South Slavic (and other languages) are 'syntactically inert', which is to say, they are not available to be manipulated by syntax and in general do not behave as expected if clitics are

---

[8] At issue here are primarily special clitics. Following the terminology of Zwicky (1977), special clitics are clitics that do not have the same syntactic distribution as corresponding full lexical items or items belonging to the same syntactic category. Some aspects of their syntactic behavior thus require 'special' principles. These are contrasted with 'simple' clitics, which pose no special problems for the morphology-syntax interface. Phrasal affixes and edge inflection are both kinds of special clitics, although the notion of special clitic is broader than these.
[9] Even earlier, Perlmutter (1971) observes that in Spanish, the elements in a clitic cluster are ordered according to a template, leading him to propose a surface filter to account for clitic ordering.

syntactic heads. For example, Macedonian permits subject-verb inversion in questions, as shown in (3).[10]

(3) a. *Katica ja čita knigata.*
    Katica 3SG.F.ACC read.3SG.PRS book.DEF
    'Katica is reading the book.'

   b. *Ja čita li Katica knigata?*
      3SG.F.ACC read.3SG.PRS Q Katica book.DEF
      'Is Katica reading the book?'

As in (3b), the subject normally inverts with the first verbal head (ignoring *li*, which is a clitic; its properties are discussed in Section 4.1 below.) However, when there is an auxiliary clitic, the subject follows the entire auxiliary + lexical verb complex (and any intervening pronominal clitics), not only the auxiliary (e.g. future *ḱe*), as shown in (4) (example from Legendre 2001a: 247).

(4) *Ḱe ti ja dade li Penka knigata?*
    FUT 2SG.DAT 3SG.ACC give.3SG Q Penka book.DEF
    'Will Penka give you the book?'
    (*Ḱe Penka ti ja dade li knigata?)

Legendre argues that "... head movement (to a projection higher than VP) operates as if the auxiliary were not present in the structure. The absence of subject-aux inversion does not make sense if... Macedonian *ḱe* head[s] [a] functional projection of [its] own..." (247). Analyzing *ḱe* as a syntactic functional head thus makes incorrect predictions about syntactic behavior. The data instead suggest that it is part of a larger lexical structure and thereby not visible to the syntax.

In a somewhat similar vein, Anderson (2005: 113) identifies an issue related to the type of Wackernagel clitic sometimes termed 'second word' (2W) clitics, in which the clitics occur after the first word of the domain (as opposed to 'second phrase' clitics, which occur after the first phrasal constituent). In Bulgarian, for instance, definite determiners are prosodically enclitic to the first word in the NP, whether it is a noun or modifier (5).

---

10 Sentence-initial *dali* without inversion is the more usual way of forming yes-no questions in Macedonian, though the use of *li* is possible; *li* is more characteristic of Bulgarian (for relevant discussion, see Englund 1977).

(5) *mnogo=to interesni knigi*
    many=DEF interesting books
    'the many interesting books'
    (cf. *knigi=te* 'the books')

Most syntactic accounts of 2W placement rely on displacement of a word from a phrase to a syntactic position above the clitic; see, for instance, Bošković (2001)'s analysis of 2W clitics in Serbo-Croatian. As Anderson (2005: 113) points out with reference to Bulgarian determiners, this kind of analysis creates two theory-internal problems:

> On the syntactic view, the syntax generates the clitic in the head D position within a DP. A subsequent operation of displacement must then raise precisely the first word of the embedded NP to SpecDP... The syntactic account is motivated by a theory-internal assumption that the syntax must be the locus of description for such facts, so it is perhaps appropriate that it raises some general theory-internal problems... One such problem is the fact that the displacement... crucially involves a single word rather than a complete phrase. As such, it must be the kind of displacement known as 'Head Movement', rather than normal phrasal movement. But the target of the displacement in this case is not a head position, but phrasal: SpecDP. To the extent Head Movement is assumed to have properties distinct from those of ordinary phrasal movement, this presents a conceptual anomaly. Secondly, we can ask what the motivation is for the displacement... Apparently, this is driven only by the needs of the clitic determiner (its presumed prosodic requirements), and not by those of the word that moves. But within at least one version of the sort of theory that is at issue here, movement is only supposed to be driven by the needs of the item that moves, rather than by the resulting configuration.

Thus, Macedonian subject-auxiliary inversion and Bulgarian determiner clitics show that the syntactic properties of clitics can run afoul of theory-internal syntactic principles. Ultimately, we argue that these problems are largely a byproduct of the assumption that clitics are syntactic elements in their own right, rather than parts of larger lexical structures. While much of the focus of the (generative syntactic) literature has been on whether clitic clusters are syntactically or phonologically placed, this framing of the debate partly misses the point. Much of previous work has failed to notice that while clitic clusters are placed relative to syntactic phrases (possibly within prosodic constraints), they may also exhibit the properties of morphological objects (internally, or in combination with a host).

A morphological approach to clitic cluster exponence offers other benefits as well. Sadler (1997) discusses an interesting case of blocking between clitics and full noun phrases. In Welsh, a pronominal object clitic can optionally be doubled by a referentially identical pronoun. However, the clitic cannot double a full noun phrase in the same way. Working in Lexical Functional Grammar, Sadler argues that the clitic + host combination forms a small construction, which is to say, an X^0 (lexical) category that contains adjoined X^0 daughters. She argues that this lexical/morphological status explains the blocking effects: the clitic + host, as a morphological construction, serves to block a full syntactic phrase for the object argument (along the lines of the proposal by Andrews (1990) that morphology blocks syntax). Since the blocking effect is independent of the basic motivation for proposing a small construction analysis, it comes 'for free' in her analysis. Sadler thus offers one way to formalize the idea that clitic + host constructions can form lexical/morphological units that consist of multiple syntactic atoms.

Bonami and Boyé (2007) approach French pronominal clitics from a different theoretical perspective (the inferential-realizational theory Paradigm Function Morphology), but likewise utilize morphological architecture to capture distributional facts surrounding clitics. They argue that French pronominal clitics should be handled as morphological objects, based in part on morphophonological fusion among clitics and conditioning on form (e.g. the object clitic is dropped in the context of dative). The clitics thus exhibit morphophonological idiosyncrasy (Z&P's criterion C). Most interestingly, however, there are also restrictions on clitic combinability (e.g. reflexive and non-reflexive clitics cannot combine). Bonami and Boyé note that pre-existing mechanisms within inferential-realizational morphology for morpho-syntactic feature licensing allow these feature co-occurrence restrictions to be defined in a natural way. To the extent that handling the co-occurrence restrictions in the syntax requires ad hoc principles, this argues for integrating the French pronominal clitics into the system of inflectional exponence.

In summary, clitic-host combinations often exhibit properties that make them anomalous if clitics are syntactic functional heads, but the same properties make clitics fundamentally similar to affixes. Moreover, a morphological analysis of at least some clitics can offer benefits in both general ways (blocking effects) and ways that are specific to the inferential-realizational framework (using independently needed feature-licensing mechanisms to capture clitic co-occurrence restrictions). These arguments and others lead us to the conclusion that at least some clitics are best analyzed as morphological objects.

2.4 Periphrasis as morphology

Finally, before moving on to the main data, we briefly turn to periphrasis. Periphrasis is the phenomenon in which multiple syntactic atoms collectively constitute a grammatical form of a lexeme. To take a widely discussed example, in Latin verbs the passive is sometimes expressed synthetically, as is the perfect tense. However, the intersection of perfect and passive is realized by a periphrastic construction: a past participle form of the lexical verb that inflects for gender and number (e.g. *laudatus* 'praise.MSG') plus a form of ESSE 'be' that inflects for tense, person and number (e.g. *est* 'be.3SG.PRES'). Each component part is an independent syntactic atom, as evidenced for example by the fact that they can be separated. However, only collectively do they express the perfect passive (*laudatus est*). Like clitics, periphrastic constructions have wide-ranging empirical properties (Bonami and Samvelian 2009).

There has been much debate about whether periphrastic constructions belong to the morphology or the syntax. Some approaches have sought to locate periphrastic constructions solely within the syntactic domain, with complementarity between synthetic and periphrastic forms treated as the result of blocking between the morphological and syntactic components (Ackema and Neeleman 2001; Andrews 1990; Bresnan 2001; Kiparsky 2005; Poser 1992). Inferential-realizational models, however, treat periphrastic constructions directly as exponents of inflectional paradigm cells, based primarily on the fact that periphrases are in complementary distribution with synthetic forms and convey morphosyntactic values that otherwise receive synthetic realization (Ackerman and Stump 2004; Sadler and Spencer 2000; Spencer 2001, 2003). Work within this framework has thus generally focused on the morphological aspects of periphrasis.

As with clitics, several arguments against purely syntactic accounts of periphrasis have been raised. Some relate to the internal logic of syntactic analyses (Ackerman and Stump 2004; Ackerman et al. 2011; Börjars et al. 1997). Others are rooted in the logic of inferential-realizational theories: a morphological account of periphrasis "... allows one to maintain a basic assumption of realizational morphology – that every well-formed morpho-syntactic property set is available for morphological realization" (Ackerman et al. 2011: 335). Here we present just a sample.

One major issue has to do with the fact that periphrastic constructions are often not semantically compositional. Popova (2010: 174) gives the following example of non-compositionality in the so-called 'inferential' construction in Bulgarian. The construction can occur in different tenses, including with present time reference (6a) or with past time reference (6b).

(6) a. *V kăštata šte (da) e, kăde drugade.*
   in house.DEF ŠTE (that) be.PRS.3SG where else
   'He must be in the house, where else could he be?'

   b. *Šte (da) go e napisala pismoto.*
   ŠTE (that) 3SG.M.ACC BE.PRS.3SG write.PTCP.SG.F letter.DEF
   'She must have written the letter.'

The inferential construction is probably a reinterpretation of the future tense construction; the latter is formed with the future tense marker *šte*. "The inferential construction has a modal meaning, expressing a supposition on behalf of the speaker... The future tense construction has inherent in it the meaning of predication or supposition and it is easy to see how this might be emphasized" (Popova 2010: 174–175). However, and importantly here, *šte* in the inferential construction is not inherently associated with futurity, as evidenced by its use with both present and past time reference in (6). Given that *šte* is undoubtedly a future marker in future tense constructions, we must either assume that there are two independent *šte* formatives, or we must assume that constructions need not be semantically compositional. Since, to the best of our knowledge, the two *šte* exhibit identical syntactic clitic properties – including different host selection/placement than other clitics (see Section 4.2) – the latter analysis is preferable. Examples of this sort are far from rare.

Non-compositionality motivates an inferential-realizational morphological approach to periphrasis. Spencer (2001) notes that in Slavic languages, several kinds of form-meaning mismatch occur in periphrastic verb constructions, including cumulation, multiple exponence, empty morphemes, deponency and zero exponence. For example in Serbian (and some other Slavic languages), the periphrastic past tense construction (e.g. *napisala sam* 'I wrote') is built with a form of 'be' (e.g. *sam*) that is itself a *present* tense form. The observation that periphrases exhibit semantic non-compositionality and the same kinds of form-meaning mismatches as synthetic forms shows that it can be just as hard to assign grammatical functions to the individual components of a periphrastic construction as it is to assign grammatical functions to the individual morphemes of a word. In this respect, the arguments for treating periphrasis as morphological are the same as those that motivate an inferential-realizational model over an incremental and/or lexical one in general (see Stump 2001).

A different kind of argument comes from what Spencer (2001, 2003) calls the 'underexhaustivity' of the paradigm. Underexhaustivity describes the situation when a component element of a periphrastic construction lacks the full set of forms implied by the set of morpho-syntactic values and their combinations. For example, the Serbian auxiliary derived from HTETI 'want' has only those forms that are used to compose the future tense *((ho)ću, (ho)ćeš*, etc.), and lacks, for example, past tense forms, even though as a lexical verb HTETI 'want' has a full range of tense forms. The forms of the auxiliary are thus limited by virtue of it being a component part of a larger, periphrastic construction. The default assumption is that syntactically separate elements should not condition each other in this way, and all syntactically viable combinations should be generated. Underexhaustivity is a counterexample to this. However, if periphrasis is viewed as the realization of inflectional values, the underexhaustivity of the auxiliary comes 'for free'. The auxiliary is treated as part of the realizational of the lexical verb, so the only auxiliary forms that are licensed are the ones needed for future tense expression. Note that this argument is thus somewhat similar to the one made by Bonami and Boyé (2007) for French clitics, in that independently-needed mechanisms for morpho-syntactic feature licensing within an inferential-realizational model are employed to account for distributional restrictions of grammatical particles.

Finally, patterns of blocking can also argue for a morphological approach to periphrasis, in a way that parallels and extends arguments in the clitic literature. In particular, Bonami (2015) argues that Pāṇinian splits – competition between periphrastic and synthetic realizations that is governed by Pāṇinian ordering, also called Elsewhere ordering or specificity-based ordering – offer strong evidence for the necessity of treating some examples of periphrasis as morphological in nature. Bonami observes that synthesis can function as the specific case that pre-empts the general periphrastic pattern (his example comes from Persian verbs), and crucially, the reverse relationship is also found, in which periphrasis functions as the specific case that pre-empts the general synthetic pattern. In Tundra Nenets, noun inflection for case and number is generally synthetic, including all singular and plural forms, and also the nominative, accusative and genitive dual forms. These three dual cells are realized by the same, syncretic form, indicating a case-underspecified default form. The interesting thing is that this synthetic form is preempted by morpho-syntactically more specific – and periphrastic – forms in the remaining dual cases. In short, the periphrastic forms bleed the 'elsewhere' synthetic form. This interaction suggests direct competition between constructions in a way that is inherent and central to inflectional structure in inferential-realizational models.

These and other arguments have driven an approach that analyzes periphrasis as the realization of inflectional values, generated by principles of morphological structure (Ackerman and Stump 2004; Bonami 2015; Bonami and Samvelian 2009; Popova and Spencer 2013; Sadler and Spencer 2000). The logic lies in large part in the mapping between morpho-syntactic values and morphophonological form: to the extent that periphrases are semantically non-compositional in the same manner as synthetic forms, have only those forms as are dictated by the set of licensed paradigm cells, and enter into Pāṇinian blocking with synthetic forms, the same logic that motivates inferential-realizational models in the first place serves to motivate a (partly) morphological approach to periphrasis. We must therefore consider periphrases that exhibit behavior of morphological objects to have been morphologized, at least in part, even if they consist of separate syntactic atoms. Some possible formal approaches to this issue are outlined as part of the discussion of Macedonian and Bulgarian in Section 4 below.

2.5 Summary

In this section we have developed an understanding of what it means for a construction to be 'morphologized' that is rooted in an inferential-realizational approach to morphological structure and a lexicalist interface to the syntax. The most important idea to emerge is that 'morphological' cannot be equated with 'synthetic'. While periphrastic constructions by definition consist of at least two syntactic atoms, a degree of morphologicity is nonetheless possible, in terms of integration into paradigmatic structure and the system of realizational rules. The same applies to clitics. We reiterate that clitics and periphrasis are both wide-ranging phenomena, so a declaration that they are universally morphological in nature, or universally syntactic in nature, is not justified. How to handle constructions with mixed properties is an important question for formal theories, and while not all issues are yet solved, recent inferential-realizational analyses have offered possible ways to formalize the morphological properties of both clitics and periphrasis. So without further delay, we turn now to the more empirical side of our discussion, where the theorizing of this section is put to work on data from the verbal complex in three language groups represented in the Balkans: Greek, Albanian, and Slavic. We leave the analysis of Balkan Romance facts to another study (though see Bîlbîie and Mardale (This volume: Section 2.2.2) for some argumentation concerning the status of the Romanian subjunctive marker *să*).

3 The verbal complex in Greek and Albanian

We are not the first to be concerned about the nature of the verbal complex as a construct in a Balkan language. Newmark et al. (1982: 23), for instance, without any argumentation and without couching their remarks in any particular theoretical framework, have this to say about Albanian:

> Verbs are typically thought of as single words, but in Albanian one or more proclitics and auxiliaries may precede the main verb and the whole sequence is then still referred to as 'the verb'.

Similarly, Matzinger and Schumacher (2017: §2.3.2), basing their claim on the fact that weak pronouns can co-occur with full nominal objects, explicitly state, regarding the weak object pronouns, that "it is preferable to describe these pronominal elements as verbal affixes, i.e. as agreement markers belonging to the verb. In other words, Albanian has a polypersonal verb with direct and indirect objects being optionally indicated on the verb."[11]

Such concerns are not limited just to Albanian, as similar issues arise, and have been argued about, for the other languages. Philippaki-Warburton and Spyropoulos (1999), for instance, claim that each piece of the Greek verbal complex is a word, each with its own node and projection in a syntactic tree, whereas Joseph (2002) counters that view with arguments that the whole complex is the word. And, one can ask if the Matzinger and Schumacher argument can be amplified upon and extended into the other languages.

3.1 The Greek verbal complex as a morphological object

We start with the Greek verbal complex, exemplified here in (7a), repeating (1c), and then given in its standard Modern Greek form (7b):

(7) a. Ðe θe na tu   to   ðóso   (dialectal Greek)
       NEG FUT SBJV 3SG.GEN 3SG.ACC give.1SG
       'I will not give it to him.'

   b. Ðe θa tu   to   ðóso   (Standard Modern Greek)
      NEG FUT 3SG.GEN 3SG.ACC give.1SG
      'I will not give it to him.'

We structure the presentation in this section in terms of the criteria of Z&P.

We begin the presentation with the combination of the verb with the weak object pronouns, the innermost elements that always occur immediately adjacent to the verb itself. Based on a verb-doubling construction found in Greek with the negator ðe 'not', giving the meaning 'whether one VERBs or not', there is an indication, consistent with Z&P's criterion E ("syntactic rules may take affixed words as their domain; they cannot take clitic groups as their domain"), that the verb-plus-weak-object-pronoun as a unit is manipulated by a syntactic rule. The relevant construction is illustrated in (8):

(8) θeli   ðe θeli
    want.3SG not want.3SG
    'whether he/she/one wants (to) or not'

---

[11] See the postscript to this paper for more on the co-occurrence of weak pronouns with full nominal objects.

As (9) indicates, this construction appears to be restricted to doubling just one word.

(9) a. *θeli   bira   ðe θeli   bira,   θa pji
       want.3SG beer.ACC not want.3SG beer.ACC FUT drink.3SG
       jati   jortazo.
       because celebrate.1SG
       'Whether he wants a beer or not, he'll drink because I am celebrating.'

   b. *θeli   o   Janis   ðe θeli   o   Janis.
      want.3SG the John.NOM not want.3SG the John.NOM
      'whether John wants (to) or not'

Importantly for understanding the morphological status of the verbal complex, weak pronouns can and in fact must be doubled along with the verb (10).[12]

(10) to   θeli   ðe to   θeli
     it.ACC want.3SG not it.ACC want.3SG
     'whether one wants it or not'
     (NB: *to θeli ðe θeli / *θeli ðe to θeli)

Thus with respect to the doubling that constitutes this construction, the weak pronoun itself does not behave like a discrete unit, and the composite consisting of the verb plus weak pronominal elements, the only parts of the verbal complex suitable for use here,[13] itself behaves like a single word. The rule responsible for the doubling, therefore, treats this composite as a unit.

The remaining evidence for morphological status for the pieces of the verbal complex mostly concerns Z&P's other criteria and in particular various behavioral idiosyncrasies which point towards the complex being morphological in nature.

---

[12] Iliyana Krapova pointed out to us that if weak pronouns also cannot be stranded under deletion of the verb (in a gapping structure), even when the weak pronouns have an appropriate prosodic host, this is further evidence that the pronoun and verb form an inseparable unit for purposes of syntactic operations. This is indeed true for Greek. We thank her for this comment.

[13] The markers θa and na are excluded on semantic grounds because the construction is future-like and modal-like as it is, and negation is already there as part of the construction itself. The insertion of other phonologically "minimal" material, like the 2SG nominative pronoun si 'you', that could in principle occur after the first verb, yields ungrammatical results: *θelis si ðe θelis 'whether you want or not' (note too that *θelis si ðe si θelis, is also hopeless, but there, si intervening between ðe and the verb dooms it from the start).

In particular, with regard to the Greek weak object pronouns, as argued in Joseph (2002), they:

i. are selective: with some rare exceptions,[14] they occur only with verbs, not with other hosts (Z&P criterion A);
ii. show idiosyncratic morphophonology: in the combination of 2SG.GEN /su/ + a 3rd person accusative pronoun, e.g /to/ 'it.N' or /tus/ 'them.M', the /u/ of the 2SG form can be elided to give, e.g. [sto], [stus], etc.,[15] and in the combination of the future marker /θa/ with a 3rd person accusative pronoun, e.g. /θa + to/ 'FUT + it.ACC', etc., there can be otherwise unexpected voicing of /t/ to [d], giving [θa do] (Z&P criterion C);[16]
iii. show idiosyncratic involvement in argument structure and consequently in semantics: in particular, in the expression in (11),

(11) pame na tin pesume s to krevati
go.1PL SBJV her.ACC fall.1PL in the bed
'Let's go for some sleep in the bed'

which is literally "let's-go that we-fall her in the bed", there is a weak "object" pronoun *tin* occurring with a verb that outside of this expression is intransitive (meaning 'fall', as in 'X falls from a tree' or 'someone falls down'); here, however, anomalously the verb appears to be transitive, with an apparent direct object in the form of the accusative weak pronoun *tin*. In this case, then, idiosyncratically the weak pronoun is not contributing anything to the argument structure nor to the meaning, and yet it is there, a seeming object but actually not indicating an object at all.

Turning now to the other elements in the Greek verbal complex and applying the criteria to them, we find the following:

---

14 For instance, there are a few particles and adverbs that have imperative-like semantics and take (postposed) weak object pronouns; an example is *kalos ton* 'welcome (to) him', with the accusative *ton* occurring after *kalos* 'welcome' (otherwise an adverb meaning 'well').
15 As discussed in Joseph (2002), the issue here is the elision of /u/ without lip-rounding; in cases where an unstressed /u/ is elided in fast speech between /s/ and /t/, as in the verb *sutaro* 'shoot (a ball)', the /s/ is rounded: /sutáro/ 'shoot.1sg' → [s^{w}táro].
16 The voicing would be motivated if a nasal was involved synchronically, as nasals in Greek trigger voicing on voiceless stops. As it happens, diachronically, there was an historical stage in which θa ended in a nasal, having the form θan. This is the historical source of the synchronically unexpected voicing. However, there is no trace of the nasal anymore, e.g. it is not found before vowel-initial verbs where it might be expected to have remained, so there is no basis for setting up an underlying nasal for θa in present-day Greek.

a. Future *θa*: it is selective in host attachment, allowing attachment only to verbs or weak pronouns that follow it in the verbal complex; it occurs in idiosyncratic combinatory morphophonology (cf. *θa do* above in (ii)); and it is involved in idiosyncratic semantics in the expression *ti θa pi* 'what does it mean?' (literally: "what FUT (it-)says")
b. Negative *ðen*: it is selective in host attachment, like *θa*, allowing attachment only to verbs or elements that can follow it in the verbal complex string (i.e., *θa* and weak pronouns); and it is involved in idiosyncratic semantics and morpho-syntax in the expression *ðen mu les* 'Tell me!' (literally: "NEG me.GEN say.2SG.IND", i.e. 'you do not tell me', thus seemingly an imperative though not imperatival from a formal standpoint and with no semantic negation despite a formal marker of negation).
c. Subjunctive *na*: it provokes the occurrence of a special negation marker, *mi*, as opposed to the indicative *ðen*; and it shows idiosyncratic combinatory morphophononology – like /θa to/ giving [θa do] above in (a) (and (ii)), the combination of *na* with a 3rd person object pronoun allows for otherwise unmotivated voicing of the initial /t-/ of the pronoun, e.g. /na + to/ → [na do] (and see Bîlbîie and Mardale (This volume: Section 2.2.3) for additional argumentation concerning the status of *na*).

As argued in Section 2 above, these kinds of idiosyncrasies indicate that the elements of the verbal complex are generated as a unit within the morphological component (or lexicon, depending on perspective), with a high degree of host selectivity and invisibility to syntactic rules further suggesting synthesis. The conclusion to be drawn for Greek from this assemblage of facts is that the verbal complex represents a fully morphologized, even synthesized, construct.[17]

3.2 The Albanian verbal complex as a morphological object

Except for the Verb-NEG-Verb copying construction, which is particular to Greek and does not have a direct analogue in Albanian, the same sort of reasoning that

---

[17] And it is entirely appropriate to call it "morphologized" and not just "morphological", because in earlier stages of Greek, some of the relevant pieces – or their historical sources – had greater integrity and independence; for instance, weak object pronouns could be positioned relative to a clause, or at least various sentence connectives – see Pappas 2004 – and the source of future marker *θa* was originally a fully inflected verb, with the same form as the verb 'want' (see Section 5 below on the relevant developments).

indicates that the Greek verbal complex is a morphological object can be given for the Albanian verbal complex, repeated here in (12) from (1a):

(12) S'   do   të   ja   jep.
     NEG FUT SBJV 3SG.DAT/ACC give.1SG
     'I will not give it to him.'

We give the argumentation here in a more schematic form.

First, the elements in the Albanian verbal complex show a high degree of selectivity as to co-occurrence; for the most part, the verbal complex modifiers do not occur outside of the context of the complex. The future marker *do* has the same shape as its etymological source, the 3sg present tense form of the verb *dua* 'want', and there is an element *do* that occurs in indefinite pronouns, e.g. *kushdo* 'whoever' (cf. *kush* 'who?'), which is also best identified etymologically with the 2/3SG of the verb *dua* 'want',[18] but it is not clear that there is any reason to connect these forms synchronically. In fact, *do* 'future' behaves differently from *do* 'you/he want/s' in that it allows the elision of the subjunctive subordinator *të* whereas the verb 'want' does not; thus, *do të shkoj* can mean both 'I will go' (literally "will that I-go") and 'you want me to go' (literally, "you-want that I-go"), whereas *do shkoj*, with the *të* elided, can mean only 'I will go' and not 'you want me to go'.[19]

The strongest evidence for morphologized status comes with the weak pronouns and the fact that they show special portmanteau realizations – tantamount to special morphophonology – in certain combinations with one another, e.g. DAT.3SG *i* + ACC.3SG *e* → *ia*, DAT.3SG *i* + ACC.3PL *i* → *ia*, DAT.1SG *më* + DAT.3SG *e* → *ma*, inter alia, and with the subjunctive marker, e.g. *të* + *e* → *ta*; the realizations here are unexpected, in that based on other aspects of Albanian phonology, one might expect [ie] to remain, *i* + *i* to end up as [i], and *të* + *e* to yield simply *t'e* with the *ë* elided.

Moreover, as noted above, the future marker *do* allows complete elision (deletion) of the subjunctive marker *të* with no change of meaning or grammaticality, only the stylistic difference of *do shkoj* being more colloquial than (future) *do të shkoj*. This elision is thus a special feature of the combination of future *do*

---

[18] For a typological parallel, cf. Spanish *cualquier* 'any', where the second element is based (historically at least) on the verb *quiero* 'want'.
[19] What makes this situation somewhat complicated is that the future marker itself derives historically from the 3sg present form of the verb 'want', but via a different route. And there are formal differences synchronically in that in some dialects, the 3sg present form (2SG too) has been inflectionally regularized to *don* 'wants' (with 2/3SG – *n*) but the future *do* remains as *do*.

with the subjunctive marker, and is as much an idiosyncrasy of future *do* as it is of subjunctive *të*.

The conclusion to be drawn from this idiosyncratic behavior together with the selectivity shown by the various elements of the Albanian verbal complex is that the complex is a synthetic object. This is much as Newmark et al. (1982) say (see in Section 3 above), though not in so many words, and it accords with the conclusion about the parallel entity in Greek.

3.3 Summary

It must be admitted that the evidence cited in Sections 3.1–3.2 from Greek and Albanian is compelling to different degrees. While all the evidence points in the same direction, towards recognizing the morphologization of the respective verbal complexes, it is not clear, for instance, that one lone morphophonological idiosyncrasy with the second person singular genitive pronoun *su* is enough in itself to require a categorization of all the weak pronouns as affixes. Still, all in all, it seems fair to say that the accumulation of the evidence from Greek and Albanian points to a high degree of morphologization, even synthesis. We believe that the data can be accounted for fairly straightforwardly in theoretical terms as affixation, for which a garden-variety inferential-realizational theory will do. This result becomes especially interesting in the light of the evidence from South Slavic.

4 The verbal complex in Macedonian, Bulgarian, and Serbian

We now turn to the verbal complexes in the South Slavic languages of the Balkans – Macedonian, Bulgarian and Serbian. The languages differ substantially in the extent to which elements in the verbal complex exhibit synthesis and attachment to the verb so the picture that emerges is a continuum of morphologization. While Greek and Albanian, as just discussed, exhibit a high degree of synthesis within the verbal complex, Serbian falls on the other end of the continuum, with no attachment of elements to the verb. Macedonian and Bulgarian represent intermediate points, with the verbal complex more morphologized in the former than in the latter. As in Greek and Albanian, the elements of the verbal complex in all three languages are prosodically dependent, with the exception of the lexical verb. The facts surrounding the pronominal and auxiliary clitics in the complex are already well established, and we focus here only on those issues that are most directly relevant to the question of morphologization. However, readers are referred to Franks and King (2000) and Friedman and Joseph (in prep) for a fuller description of the facts.

4.1 The Macedonian verbal complex as a (mostly) morphological object

As already observed, dialectal Macedonian has a surface word order that parallels the order of elements seen above in Greek and Albanian. Example (13a) repeats (1d); compare this to the verbal complex template, repeated as (13b).

(13) a. *Ne ḱe da mu go davam.*
NEG FUT SBJV 3SG.M.DAT 3SG.M.ACC give.1SG
'I will not give it to him.'

b. NEG – TNS – MOOD – IO – DO – V

By contrast, in Standard Macedonian, *ḱe* combines with the verb (plus any object clitics) without modal *da* (14).[20] *Da* can follow *ḱe* in suppositional clauses, as in (15) (example from Kramer 1986: 76), although Friedman (1993: 285) marks this construction as 'colloquial'.

(14) *Ḱe mu ja dadam knigata.*
FUT 3SG.M.DAT 3SG.F.ACC give.1SG book(F).DEF
'I will give him the book.'

(15) *Ḱe da imaše edno osumnaest godini.*
ḰE DA have.IMPF.3SG about eighteen years
'He must have been some eighteen years old.'

In the standard language, *da* occurs at the beginning of the clitic group.[21] The order of elements for the standard language can thus be distilled to the template

---

20 The negated future is also typically formed with *nema da* (with the negated form of 'have') rather than *ne ḱe*.
21 A reviewer commented that modal *da* and complementizer *da* may need to be distinguished, along the lines of Franks and King (2000: 81, table 2.16). They say that "... *da* as complementizer

in (16), (adapted from Franks and King 2000: 81), and exemplified in (17) (from Friedman 1993: 285).

(16) da – ne²² – ḱe/bi²³ – AUX – DAT OBJ – ACC OBJ – e/se²⁴ – V

(17) ... da   ne   ḱe   sum   si   mu   go   dal?
      ... that NEG FUT AUX.1SG REFL.DAT   3SG.M.DAT 3SG.M.ACC gave
      '(They didn't say) ...that I won't have given it to him (did they)?'

The order of elements in the verbal complex thus differs somewhat within Macedonian, with the pattern in (13a) more closely matching the surface order of elements found in Greek and Albanian. From a contact perspective, it is unsurprising that a regional variety, rather than the standard one, should be more closely similar to languages with which Macedonian has been in historical contact, since Balkan contact has been characterized by intense multilingualism at the local – thus, dialectal – level. However, other than this difference, the relevant facts are largely the same, and in the following discussion we give examples from the standard language.

---

is initial; modal *da* follows hypothetical *ḱe*" (81). We admit that this is an area in which the facts are not entirely clear to us. Mišeska Tomić (2006: 243) lists a 'subjunctive' marker in two different places within the clitic cluster. These two placements are the same as those identified by Franks and King, but Mišeska Tomić identifies *da* before *ḱe* as modal rather than as a complementizer. Friedman (1993: 285) likewise labels *da* in examples like (17) as subjunctive, but he lists only one position in the cluster (initial). He does not mention the possibility of *da* after *ḱe* except in examples like (15), and thus appears to treat the difference as a function of construction type and register or dialect. Kramer (1986) argues that there is no evidence for two *da* in Macedonian, in contrast to Serbian, although her discussion in general focuses more on semantic properties than formal syntactic ones. Here we base our discussion on Friedman, but these sources do not lead to a clear answer on whether two *da* need to be distinguished with regard to the verbal complex.
22 The position of the negative marker *ne* depends on the scope of negation. In particular, *ne* precedes *da* if it takes scope over the entire clause, and occurs after *da* if it has narrower scope, over the VP. This affects the meaning of the sentence (Friedman 1993: 290). Here we include the latter position, since *ne* in this position is clearly part of the verbal complex.
23 *Bi* is a conditional marker. Like *ḱe*, its form is invariant.
24 These are the third person forms of 'be' – singular and plural, respectively. Since the third person auxiliary has a null form, these forms occur only in the copula function, but in that function they are positioned within the clitic cluster.

In Macedonian the clitic cluster is strictly adjacent to the verb, appearing to the left of the finite verb (see (14) above) and to the right of a non-finite verb, including the imperative, (18).²⁵

(18) *Donesete mu   ja   knigata.*
     bring.IMP 3SG.M.DAT 3SG.F.ACC book(F).DEF
     'Bring him the book.'
     (**Mu ja donesete knigata.*)

Paralleling Greek and Albanian, nothing can intervene between the elements of the verbal complex.²⁶ In fact, the only things that can intervene between *da* and the verb are members of the cluster (Kramer 1986: 8), making *da* functionally part of the verbal complex. We note that analyses of *da* as a preverbal morpheme go back at least to Gołąb (1954) and Maslov (1956) (as cited in Kramer 1986: 54–55). The clitic cluster (including *da* and with limited exceptions *ne*) is thus inseparable from the verb, even though it sometimes appears obligatorily to the left of the verb and sometimes equally obligatorily to the right of it. Additionally, as shown in (14) above, the cluster can also appear in absolute sentence-initial position when proclitic to the verb. This again makes Macedonian similar to Greek and Albanian (but different than Bulgarian, as we will see), suggesting that the clitic-first pattern is a Balkanism (Alexander 1994: 4).

The extent of cohesion of the verbal complex can be observed in the behavior of the question particle *li*, which is phonologically enclitic but not a part of the verbal complex in Macedonian (Englund 1977: 116). *Li* strictly follows the first prosodic word in the clause and is strongly associated with focus. When anything other than the verb is focused, it is fronted and serves as the prosodic host for *li* ((19), from Friedman 1993: 287). Otherwise, *li* appears immediately after the verb (20).

(19) *Vo Bitola li ḱe   odiš?*
     to Bitola Q FUT go.2SG
     'Is it BITOLA you will be going to?'

---

25 The placement of clitics in non-verbal predicates (e.g. *Tatko mi e.* / 'He is my father.') is less rigid. See Mišeska Tomić (1996) and Franks and King (2000: 85–88) for some discussion. Also, Friedman observes that in the *beše* pluperfect, clitic pronouns may either precede or follow the auxiliary, and that "[t]he sense of past resultativity is stronger when the auxiliary is closer to the verb" (Friedman (1993: 286), citing Koneski (1967)).

26 Friedman (1993) notes that some 'old-fashioned' phrases (curses and blessings) are exceptions to this generalization. This is what we might expect from the fact that there used to be greater syntactic freedom of movement; word orders that are no longer licensed in the language became frozen in set phrases.

(20) a. Ќe   odiš   li vo Bitola?
       FUT go.2SG Q   to Bitola
       'Will you go to Bitola?'
       (*Ќe li odiš vo Bitola?)

   b. Ti   go   dade   li?
      2SG.DAT 3SG.M.ACC gave.3SG Q
      'Did s/he give it to you?'
      (*Ti li go dade? *Ti go li dade?)

With two possible exceptions, *li* cannot be placed internally to the cluster or between the cluster and the verb. The first exception has to do with emphatic negation. Rudin et al. (1999) observe that *li* can immediately follow the negator *ne*, but only when *ne* receives independent lexical stress as a result of emphatic negation (21a). In neutral negation, *ne* does not receive independent stress and is phonologically proclitic to the verb, like the rest of the verbal complex. *Li* then follows the verb (21b).[27] (Stress is indicated with capital letters and the prosodic word with square brackets.)

(21) a. [NE] li [ti   GO   dade]?
        NEG Q 2SG.DAT   3SG.M.ACC gave.3SG
        'Did s/he really <u>not</u> give it to you?'

   b. [ne ti   GO   dade] li?
      NEG 2SG.DAT 3SG.M.ACC gave.3SG Q
      'Didn't s/he give it to you?'
      (*ne li ti GO dade? / *ne ti GO li dade?)

This variable placement of *li* relative to *ne* suggests that the negator is sometimes a part of the verbal complex, and sometimes not.[28] Crucially, *li* can directly follow *ne* only when the latter has its own lexical stress, which offers independent evidence of it not being part of the verbal complex when emphatically stressed. We therefore consider it to be a pseudo-exception.

---

27 We can see that it is lexical stress on *ne* that matters for placement of *li*, not just any stress, by the fact that when *ne* is stressed by virtue of being the antepenultimate syllable within the verbal complex, it does not host *li*: [NE sakaš] li da odiš? 'Don't you want to go?' (Rudin et al. 1999: 556). Stress is always antepenultimate within the prosodic word in Macedonian.

28 This behavior is paralleled in Greek, where the negator *ðen* may, but need not, receive its own stress; stressed *ðen* carries emphasis; however, in Greek there is no other indicator like Macedonian *li* that could provide independent confirmation of the stressed negator being outside of the verbal complex.

The other exception has to do with non-finite verbs – the condition in which the clitic cluster follows the verb. In all of the examples above, the clitic cluster precedes the verb. The question is: When the cluster follows the verb, where is *li* placed? The relevant type of sentence seems to be quite rare for several reasons: there are restrictions on fronting of verbal participles in Macedonian (Rudin et al. (1999: 576), citing Embick and Izvorski (1997)); when there is a finite auxiliary in the clause the clitic cluster attaches to it, reducing the occurrence of clitic clusters following non-finite lexical verbs; and it is hard to form a question phrase with *li* that also contains an imperative (which, recall, behaves as a non-finite verb). However, Victor Friedman (personal communication) suggests the example in (22). The relevant part is B's response, which includes the question particle *li*.

(22) A: *Davajkji mu   go   stapot,   sliznal   i   padnal.*
       giving   3SG.M.DAT 3SG.M.ACC baton.DEF, slipped.M.SG and fell.M.SG
       'While giving him the baton, he slipped and fell.'

   B: *Davajkji li mu   go?   A   jas mislev deka*
      giving Q 3SG.M.DAT 3SG.M.ACC But I   thought that
      sliznal   porano!
      slipped.M.SG earlier
      'While giving it to him? I thought he slipped earlier!'

Notice that *li* is enclitic to the non-finite verb and precedes the dative and accusative object clitics. It is unclear whether this ordering is consistent throughout Macedonian, but for at least some speakers it appears to be an exception to the generalization that the clitic cluster is strictly adjacent to the verb.[29]

What does the placement of *li* tell us about the cohesiveness of the Macedonian verbal complex? As part of an argument that the syntactic placement of *li* is the same in Macedonian and Bulgarian, Rudin et al. (1999) analyze *li* as attaching to a prosodic word domain in Macedonian that consists (potentially) of several syntactically separate elements, i.e. the grammatical elements of the verbal complex. This is shown by the bracketing in (21). This analysis allows them to posit that the only difference between *li* in Macedonian and Bulgarian has to do with the size of the domain to which *li* is prosodically enclitic. (The Bulgarian facts are discussed

---

[29] Rudin et al. (1999: 576) cite a similar example: *Predupreden li si bil za toa?* 'Were you WARNED (really) about that?' Here, *li* separates the adjectival participle *predupreden* 'warned' from the auxiliary verb clitic *si*. However, as noted in footnote 25 above, the placement of clitics in non-verbal predicates is not as rigid as with verbs. The importance of this example for the placement of *li* is thus not fully clear.

below.) However, as far as we can see, there is an equally viable analysis positing that *li* attaches to a lexical level (X^0) unit in both languages. In this approach, differences in *li* placement in the two languages relate to what constitutes a lexical unit. Analyses along these lines have been sketched by Spencer (2000) for Macedonian (separately from the question of *li* placement) and Sadler (1997) for Welsh pronominal clitics (see Section 2.3 above), which bear partial resemblance to Macedonian clitics. Here we try to at least give the flavor of the accounts.

Spencer (2000: 379–381) argues that since only verbs can host the clitic cluster in Macedonian, this motivates an analysis of the clitics as exponents of morpho-syntactic properties of the verb. In other words, in Macedonian the paradigm of the verb includes auxiliary and object clitics. Working within Paradigm Function Morphology, Spencer shows that this can be formalized in terms of a(n Extended) Paradigm Function that defines realizational rules realizing the combination of an inflected verb and clitic-realized morpho-syntactic properties. In essence, the clitics are generated as affixes, albeit ones that attach to already-inflected words. Whether the cluster is positioned before or after the cluster is treated as morphological conditioning based on the properties of the verb (whether it is finite or not). Since the combination of verb and pronominal and auxiliary clitics is output by the morphology as a single lexical unit, this naturally captures the fact that they are syntactically inseparable.

Sadler (1997)'s analysis of Welsh pronominal clitics captures some of the same insights about clitics and verbs forming lexical units. However, she takes a somewhat different approach that has some advantages when applied to Macedonian. Remember that the essence of her analysis is that the clitic cluster and verb are each generated as separate morphological objects, and each forms a lexical level (X^0) construction in syntax. However, the clitics are functional categories that do not project to a maximal projection, and instead attach as a lexical sister to the verb, forming a(nother) lexical level (small/X^0) construction with it. This is congruent with the essence of Spencer's proposal that the clitic cluster is morphologically generated as a unit and then affixed to the already inflected verb. And like in Spencer's analysis, the fixed, templatic order of elements in the clitic cluster are a direct result of the fact that it is morphologically generated as a unit. While we haven't worked out the details, we expect an analysis of Macedonian along the lines of either Spencer's or Sadler's would be able to handle the syntactic 'inertness' noted by Legendre (2001a). Also, note that the Macedonian clitics do not exhibit allomorphy depending on the verb that it combines with and there are no lexical exceptions to cluster-verb combinability (Z&P's criteria C and B). Sadler's account as extended to Macedonian precludes morphophonological interactions of this sort on principle, since the clitic cluster and the verb are generated as independent morphological objects. Spencer's account does not preclude allomorphy, but does not require it either.

Admittedly, neither Spencer's nor Sadler's analysis has an obvious way to account for the placement of *li* between a non-finite verb and following clitic cluster (22), given that it is clear that *li* is not generated as part of the verbal complex/clitic cluster. Both analyses would somehow need to assume that *li* can be inserted into the middle of a lexical unit. At the same time, we note that Rudin et al. (1999)'s analysis faces equal problems, since when the verb is non-finite, it must posit either that *li* gets inserted into the middle of a prosodic word, or that *li* is enclitic to a stressed syntactically-minimal word. Both options contradict the analysis made of finite verbs. Of these three, Sadler's approach, as extrapolated to Macedonian, seems to offer the greatest possibility for a viable solution, since the boundary between the verb and clitic cluster is visible to the syntax (unlike Spencer's account, in our understanding), and the account is not oriented to the boundaries of the prosodic word (unlike Rudin et al.'s). Moreover, an analysis that locates the difference between Bulgarian and Macedonian in the extent of morphologization has the advantage of also being able to explain why no other elements can intervene between the clitics and the verb. This is something that Rudin et al.'s analysis offers no direct account of.

Finally, it is worth briefly considering two other arguments, from Kramer (1986: 7), for considering the verbal complex in Macedonian to be syntactic. First, she posits that since the cluster appears both before and after the verb, placement of the cluster must be according to syntactic rules. Second, she observes that the future marker *ḱe* has been 'deparadigmaticized' in the sense that it has a frozen form and no longer inflects for person and number. Although she does not elaborate on the argument, the idea seems to be that its invariant form allows it to be treated as a purely syntactic particle. And indeed, the loss of person-number marking on *ḱe* resulted in loss of multiple exponence of person-number; multiple exponence is a diagnostic of morphological objects (Spencer 2012). In the construction *ḱe* (*da*) V, it localizes person-number marking to the finite verb (either lexical verb or auxiliary).[30] It is thus not necessary to assume that the future has constructional status.

However, Kramer's observations are not actually in conflict with a morphological account of the kind sketched above. First, Anderson (2005: 85) observes that in Macedonian and similar languages, "...the order which is strictly required under one set of circumstances [finite lexical verb] is replaced by another under a complementary set of conditions [non-finite verb]... Parallel to these cases are

---

[30] Also, since the meaning of the construction can be parceled out to the individual components, the construction does not exhibit distributed exponence either. Distributed exponence was proposed by Ackerman and Stump (2004) as a criterion for identifying that a periphrastic construction is morphological, although this criterion has been criticized (Brown et al. 2012; Spencer 2012).

examples in word-level morphology where the same affix may show up either as a prefix or as a suffix, depending on specific factors... What is notable is that in each case, the position of the affix is not at all free," making the placement of the clitic cluster rather unlike syntactic phenomena like scrambling. So while variability in placement of an affix relative to the root is unusual in morphology, it is not unheard of (see Nevis and Joseph 1993, for instance, on word-internal Wackernagel-like second positioning of the reflexive marker in Lithuanian), and in fact its lack of freedom of movement is unusual from a syntactic perspective. As we have already seen, there are at least a couple of different models for how to account for this fact in a fundamentally morphological way. Second, while the frozen form of *ḱe* does not force us to recognize a constructional status for the future in our analysis, neither does it preclude it. And when we take into account the cohesion of the clitic cluster with the verb (high selectivity, non-separability), the evidence tips in the direction of recognizing at least some degree of morphologization.

To review, it is clear that the grammatical elements in the verbal complex are not canonical affixes. They occur on either side of the verb,[31] depending on its finiteness, do not induce allomorphy within the cluster or in the verb, and there are no lexical exceptions that we are aware of. At the same time, the grammatical particles always take verbal hosts (i.e. have high host selectivity) and with the possible exceptions of the negative *ne* when independently lexically stressed, and the placement of *li* when the clitic group follows the verb, they are strictly adjacent to the verb. They also exhibit a fixed, templatic order within the clitic cluster. The clitic cluster is thus partly synthesized. These properties are surprising if the clitics each form their own maximal projection in the syntax, and instead indicate some amount of morphologization. An analysis of the clitic cluster as a morphologically generated object that combines into a lexical unit with the verb (whether along the lines of Spencer's analysis or Sadler's) seems likely to offer a good account of the intermediate status of the Macedonian verbal complex between syntax and morphology.

4.2 The Bulgarian verbal complex as a morphological object?

Like the other languages, Bulgarian has a series of grammatical elements that can occur before the verb and form a (surface-descriptive) verbal complex with it; see

---

[31] Interestingly, variable ordering of objects in Greek in postposed contexts (after nonfinite forms) can be observed, i.e. *ðos mu to ~ ðos to mu* 'give.IPV.SG me.GEN it.ACC' ~ 'give it me', suggesting that the postposed pronouns are less synthetic with the verb (though still adjacent).

(23a) (examples from Franks and King 2000: 59). However, no subjunctive marker occurs between the future marker and object clitics. The future formed with *ne šte* is actually formal and archaic and *njama da* is the more prevalent way to form the negative future (23b). Here a subjunctive marker does occur, but negative and future are synthetically expressed, *njama* being historically *ne + ima* 'have'.

(23) a. *Ne šte ni ja četeš.*
    NEG FUT 1PL.DAT 3SG.F.ACC read.2SG
    'You won't read it to us.'

  b. *Njama da ni ja četeš.*
    NEG.FUT SBJV 1PL.DAT 3SG.F.ACC read.2SG
    'You won't read it to us.'

As for the other elements in the verbal complex, the dative and accusative objects and verbal auxiliaries are clitics. The order of clitics can be extrapolated as in (24), illustrated in (25) (Franks and King 2000: 61–62). These elements appear in the same surface order as in the other languages.

(24) *šte* – AUX – DAT OBJ – ACC OBJ – e^{32}

(25) *Šte ste mu go kazali li?*
    FUT AUX.2PL 3SG.M.DAT 3SG.M.ACC told.PL Q
    'Will you have told him it?'

While the negator *ne* and the subjunctive marker *da* do not bear lexical stress, neither is generally considered to be part of the clitic cluster in Bulgarian. However, even the elements that are superficially similar to the verbal complexes of Macedonian, Albanian, and Greek turn out in Bulgarian to be less cohesive than these examples suggest.

The first issue has to do with the placement of the clitic cluster, which is prosodically conditioned in Bulgarian. Bulgarian object and most auxiliary clitics (but not *šte*, as we see below) are always verb-adjacent. The clitic cluster is syntactically proclitic to the verb by default, but prosodically enclitic. When there is a suitable leftward prosodic host the clitic cluster appears to the left of the verb (26a), but when there is not, the cluster appears after it, with the verb becoming the prosodic host (26b) (Franks and King 2000: 63).

---

[32] This is the third person singular auxiliary verb. As in other Slavic languages, it occurs at the end of the cluster, rather than in the position of other auxiliaries.

(26) a. *Vera mi go dade včera.*
Vera 1SG.DAT 3SG.M.ACC gave.3SG yesterday
'Vera gave it to me yesterday.'

b. *Dade mi go Vera včera.*
gave.3SG 1SG.DAT 3SG.M.ACC Vera yesterday
'Vera gave it to me yesterday.'

This means that Macedonian and Bulgarian are similar in both having verb-adjacent clitic clusters. However, placement of the cluster before or after the verb is prosodically conditioned in Bulgarian, rather than morpho-syntactically conditioned as in Macedonian. Prosodic conditioning is suggestive that placement in Bulgarian is as a second position (Wackernagel) phrasal phenomenon. We assume that clitic positioning in Bulgarian is thus best treated via a combination of attachment to the head of the VP (i.e. above the lexical level) and a prosodic constraint.

Second, some elements of the verbal complex are discrete units structurally. In addition to *da* and *ne*, *šte* behaves differently than other auxiliary clitics. For instance, the full-form auxiliary BĂDA can intervene between *šte* and other clitics in interrogatives (27) (example adapted from Spencer 2000: 362). (*Li* also here intervenes; we return to its placement below.)

(27) *Šte bădeš li se vărnal do 5 časă?*
FUT AUX.2SG Q REFL returned.M.SG by 5 hour.DEF
'Will you have returned by 5 o'clock?'
(**Šte se bădeš li vărnal do 5 časăt?*)

Like *da* and *ne*, *šte* can also serve as a leftward prosodic host for the cluster (see (25) above), an unexpected property if it is itself a member of the cluster. Instead, its appearance in the verbal complex reflects the interaction of a phrasal domain of attachment and prosodic requirements that happen to sometimes place *šte* at the head of the cluster, rather than true unity with the other elements in the verbal complex (Hauge 1999[1976]).

Third and finally in this vein, the placement of the question particle *li* in Bulgarian demonstrates that elements can intervene into the cluster itself, or between the cluster and the verb, in contrast with Macedonian. This is particularly clear in negative contexts. The negator *ne* always throws stress onto the following morpho-syntactic word, even if it is a clitic. *Li* follows the leftmost stressed element,[33]

---

[33] Actually, it is ambiguous between taking the leftmost stressed element as host, or the leftmost prosodic word. Rudin et al. (1999) make the latter analysis. This issue has no bearing

meaning that it can intervene between a stressed clitic and the host verb (28a), or between two clitics when the leftward clitic is stressed (28b,c) (adapted from Franks and King 2000: 60).

(28) a. *Ne mu li izpratix kniga?*
     NEG 3SG.M.DAT Q sent.1SG book
     'Didn't I send a book to him?'

   b. *Ne mu li ja izpratix?*
     NEG 3SG.M.DAT Q 3SG.F.ACC sent.1SG
     'Didn't I send it to him?'

   c. *Ne si li mu go kazal?*
     NEG AUX.2SG Q 3SG.M.DAT 3SG.M.ACC said
     'Had you not said it to him?'

In principle, *li* can separate any two members of the verbal complex, assuming the necessary stress conditions. This is thus another way in which the verbal complex is not as cohesive a unit in Bulgarian as in Macedonian, and much less so than in Albanian and Greek.

The 'core' cluster has at least two properties in common with affixation: parallel to inflectional morphology, the cluster selects a verbal lexical head (Z&P criterion A), and clitic ordering within the cluster is invariant. Despite this, the Bulgarian verbal complex is not a coherent unit of analysis structurally. The clitic facts show that it is not synthetically bound and does not exhibit lexical integrity. In comparison to Macedonian – and, e.g., a Sadler-esque analysis in which clitics are adjoined as sisters to the lexical verb – a crucial difference in Bulgarian is that the clitic cluster must be assumed to attach at a higher (above lexical) level, in order to account for the separability of the cluster.

Spencer (2000) formally captures the ordering of both *šte* and the cluster elements (other auxiliary and object clitics) in Optimality Theory. He proposes an a series of constraints, including INITIAL(ŠTE), stating that *šte* must be initial in its syntactic/prosodic domain, that is ranked above both ALIGN(CL) (have a leftward prosodic host) and INITIAL(CL) (align the left edge of the cluster with the left edge of the domain). This captures the generalization that while *šte* often appears on the surface as a member of the verbal complex, it is subject to different rules of placement and ordering than other members of the verbal complex. Legendre

---

here, however, with the only relevant thing being that *li* can (and often must) be inserted after a stressed pre-verbal clitic.

(1996, 1999, 2001b) also offers a formal analysis along similar lines, in the spirit of Anderson (1992, 1995, 2005)'s analysis of clitics as phrasal affixes.

This is not the end of the story, however. The complex structure of Bulgarian verbs offers additional evidence of morphologization in a different sense. The issues can be illustrated with the negated future perfect, for which Popova and Spencer (2013) argue that morphological constituency and syntactic constituency mismatch.[34] They analyze the future perfect form, e.g. *šte săm mislila* (29a), as being composed of a perfect form *săm mislila* (29b) nested formally and semantically inside the future construction *šte* + V (29c), as shown schematically in (29d).

(29) a. *Do utre   šte   săm   mislila   veče   za   statijata.*
by morning FUT AUX.1SG.PRS think.F.PTCP already about article.DEF
'By tomorrow I will have thought about the article already.'

b. *Mnogo păti   săm   mislila   za   statijata.*
many times AUX.1SG.PRS think.F.PTCP about article.DEF
'I have thought about the article many times.'

c. *Mnogo păti   šte mislja   za   statijata.*
many times FUT think.1SG.PRS about article.DEF
'I will think about the article many times.'

d. [*šte* [*săm mislila*]ᵥ]

While (29a) is semantically compositional in a way that reflects the formal constituency, crucially, the nesting need not reflect syntactic constituency. Popova

---

34 Semantic non-compositionality is also relevant here. For example, the emphatic renarrated mood is constructionally related to the renarrated mood (i).

(i)
	Renarrated	Emphatic Renarrated
Present/Imperfect	*săm pišel*	*bil săm pišel*
Aorist	*săm pisal*	*bil săm pisal*
Present Perfect	*bil pisal*	--

Spencer (2003: 264) argues that the emphatic renarrated is "... a non-compositional extension of a construction [i.e. renarrated] which is already pretty non-compositional...", and that this reflects the paradigmatic morphological structure of the constructions. His reasoning seems to be that while the form is identical to the pluperfect in some other Slavic languages, in Bulgarian the pluperfect has a different form. The forms in the right column are thus available to be assigned a different grammatical function. Emphatic renarrated happens to be the paradigmatic contrast that gets expressed by the available form. Notice that this description rests fundamentally on treating the construction *as a whole* as a realization of a combination of lexeme and morphosemantic values and in paradigmatic contrast to other forms of the verb.

and Spencer argue that the perfect (e.g. *săm mislila*) is similarly morphologically nested inside the negated future (e.g. *njama da mislja*) to form the negated future perfect (e.g. *njama da săm mislila*), based in part on the fact that an alternate form for the perfect (*băda mislila*) is also inherited by the negated future perfect (alternate form: *njama da băda mislila*). The posited morphological structure is thus a composition of the two constructions, with *njama da* as a unit. (Notice that the nesting relationship is the same as in the future and future perfect constructions – the negated future perfect form replaces *mislja* in the negated future construction with *săm mislila*.) Syntactically, however, *da* introduces a subordinate clause and serves as prosodic host for *săm* and any other verbal clitics in the clause. The syntactic constituency must therefore be [*njama* [*da săm mislila*]], and *njama* can be separated from *da* (30).

(30) Utre   po tova vreme njama   v nikakăv slučaj da
      morning at this time   NEG.FUT.3SG   in no case   DA
      săm   dal   statijata   na redaktora.
      AUX.1SG   give.M.PTCP   article.F.DEF to editor.M.DEF
      'There is no way I will have given the article to the editor by this time tomorrow.'
      (*Utre po tova vreme njama da v nikakăv slučaj săm dal statijata na redaktora.)

The emphatic renarrated construction is thus interesting because morphophonologically, its parts (auxiliary and lexical verbs) are discrete syntactic atoms and do not cohere with other elements of the Bulgarian verbal complex, as we saw above. At the same time, the construction behaves like a morphological object – it is an exponent of morpho-syntactic properties and the realization of a paradigm cell of the verb. This sort of data shows that elements of the (surface-oriented) verbal complex, like *da* and *săm*, form part of paradigmatically structured, morphological constructions, even though they do not form synthetic units.

Although they do not look at Bulgarian, Bonami and Webelhuth (2013) propose an analysis of verb constructions that is designed to handle this kind of data, and specifically, to make periphrases maximally parasitic on existing syntactic and morphological mechanisms, while also optimizing the ability of morphological and syntactic structures to function independently. They build an interface between the lexicalist syntactic framework Head-driven Phrase Structure Grammar (HPSG) and the inferential-realizational morphological framework Paradigm Function Morphology. In periphrases consisting, e.g., of an auxiliary and participle, the auxiliary subcategorizes for the participle, as part of the lexical representation for the periphrastic construction as a whole. On the morphological side, the component elements of periphrastic constructions are generated by realizational rules – the same mechanism used to generate synthetic forms – including referrals to independently existing forms where relevant. For instance, an auxiliary might be referred to the copula for its form, to the extent that the auxiliary and the copula exhibit the same morphological behavior. On the syntactic side, relating the component parts of the periphrasis via valence allows the model to piggyback on independently existing mechanisms for syntactic functional relations, to the extent that the syntax of the periphrastic construction is the same as 'normal' syntax in the language. Crucially, however, and differently from purely syntactic accounts, the periphrases are treated as lexical representations and constructional units, with morpho-syntactic values associated to the construction as a whole and inflectionally realized as such.[35] The analysis is thus fundamentally morphological in nature. Popova and Spencer (2013) offer an analysis of Bulgarian verb constructions that applies Bonami and Webelhuth's approach.

To sum up, the verbal complex exhibits less synthesis in Bulgarian than in Macedonian. Elements like *da* and *ne* are generally not considered part of the clitic cluster because they exhibit signs of forming distinct syntactic and prosodic units, and while *šte* often appears at the head of the cluster, it is likewise positioned there by distinct principles. *Da*, *ne*, and *šte* can also serve as prosodic hosts for the cluster, which is surprising if they are part of the cluster themselves, and *li* can in principle intervene between any elements in the verbal complex (subject to restrictions created by stress requirements). All of these facts suggest that the verbal complex is not a coherent unit structurally. At the same time, the auxiliaries and lexical verb (sometimes also including *da*) form constructional units that cannot be reduced to the individual syntactic elements. This is a different notion of morphologization – one that extends beyond synthesis – but as argued in Section 2, it is one deeply embedded in a lexicalist, inferential-realizational model of inflection. We suspect that morphologization of the Bulgarian type is prerequisite to synthesis – constructional status precedes the development of a fixed order of elements. If the Balkan verbal complex is at least in part a Sprachbund phenomenon, it is unsurprising that Bulgarian should show some morphologization, but not synthesis, since it lies on the periphery of the core contact zone.

---

[35] Bonami (2015) builds on this work, adding the observation that periphrasis has a lot in common with idioms. Following work within HPSG on idioms, he proposes to capture periphrasis through 'reverse selection' – i.e., the elements of the periphrasis mutually select each other through bidirectional valence. He also solves a problem of competition between synthesis and periphrasis that the earlier paper faced by having periphrastic realizational rules stated at the level of the paradigm function, rather than at the level of rule blocks. This is able to capture the fact that periphrasis competes with synthesis as a whole, not with individual affixes.

4.3 The Serbian verbal complex as a (mostly non-) morphological object

Finally, we look very briefly at some relevant facts of Serbian, as a point of contrast to both Macedonian and Bulgarian. Serbian is well known for having second position clitics, with the order of elements within the clitic cluster as in (31), illustrated in (32).

(31) li – AUX – DAT – ACC/GEN – se – je

(32) Da li si   mu   ga   dala?
      DA Q AUX.2SG 3SG.M.DAT 3SG.M.ACC gave.F.SG
      'Did you give it to him?'

As in the other Slavic languages, *li* is the yes/no question particle, *se* is a particle used for various agent-backgrounding functions (e.g. reflexive, passive, impersonal), and *je* is the third person singular 'present' auxiliary clitic. Only the third person singular auxiliary occurs at the end of the cluster; all other present auxiliaries, as well as future and conditional/irrealis auxiliaries, occur in the AUX slot. The negator must occur immediately before the finite verb, whether this is the lexical verb (present tense) or auxiliary (past, future, conditional). Negation thus shows high selectivity with regard to its stem, behaving as a prefix for much the same reasons that Zwicky and Pullum (1983) argue that *n't* is affixal in English.[36] This means that while its position sometimes lines up with the surface order of the Balkan verbal complex ((33), repeated from (1e)), *ne* is not part of the Serbian clitic cluster, and its positioning is governed by different principles from the other grammatical elements of the verbal complex. This is evident in sentences like (34), where the accusative object clitic *ga* must follow the negated verb.

(33) Neću   da   mu   ga   dam.
      NEG.FUT.1SG SBJV 3SG.DAT 3SG.ACC give.1SG
      'I will not give it to him.'

(34) Ne vidim   ga   ovde.
      NEG see.1SG 3SG.ACC here
      'I don't see him/it here.'

---

[36] This means that unlike in Bulgarian, *ne* cannot itself host the clitic cluster, although *ne* + a finite verb can host the cluster.

Notice that in (33), *da* is also not a part of the cluster. It introduces a subordinate clause and can serve as host for the cluster (here *mu ga*).

In contrast with Macedonian and Bulgarian, the clitic cluster in Serbian is not required to be verb-adjacent. It instead occurs in second position within the clause, with a leftward prosodic host. While the definition of what constitutes 'second position' has been the subject of much investigation and exhibits dialectal (perhaps idiolectal) variation, what matters here is that the clitic cluster exhibits promiscuous host selection. This can be seen in (35), where the verbal auxiliary clitic *sam* can attach to whatever stressed constituent happens to be at the beginning of the sentence (marked with brackets), and cannot occur in any other position in the sentence.

(35) a. *[Kupio]   sam   Vesni   zanimljivu   knjigu.*
       bought.M.SG AUX.1SG Vesna.DAT interesting.ACC book.ACC
       'I bought Vesna an interesting book.'

   b. *[Vesni] sam kupio zanimljivu knjigu.*
   c. *[Zanimljivu knjigu] sam Vesni kupio.*
   d. **Sam kupio Vesni zanimljivu knjigu.*
   e. **[Vesni] [kupio] sam zanimljivu knjigu.*

Moreover, although Serbian has a general preference for *da*-clauses over functionally equivalent infinitival constructions (36a), in infinitival structures clitic climbing is possible (36b).[37] Here *joj ga* climbs out of the lower clause. This underlines the fact that the positioning of elements of the verbal complex does not depend on the verb.

(36) a. *Marija će   da   joj   ga   predstavi.*
       Marija FUT SBJV 3SG.F.DAT 3SG.M.ACC introduce.3SG
       'Marija will introduce him to her.'

   b. *Marija joj   ga   neće   predstaviti.*
       Marija 3SG.F.DAT 3SG.M.ACC NEG.FUT.3SG introduce.INF
       'Marija will not introduce him to her.'

In short, *ne* and *da* do not cohere with the other elements of the (surface-descriptive) verbal complex and while the auxiliary and object clitics (+ *li*) do

---

[37] For discussion of clitic climbing in the Balkan languages, see Krapova and Cinque (this volume).

form a templatically ordered clitic cluster, they do not form a unit with the verb. In Serbian the verbal complex is thus not a coherent unit of analysis.

It is worth pointing out that there is some allomorphy within the clitic cluster. As noted in Section 2.1, the accusative clitic, which is normally *je*, is realized as *ju* when preceding the third person singular auxiliary clitic *je*. The third person singular auxiliary clitic *je* also drops when preceded by *se*.[38] This is the kind of morphophonological idiosyncrasy that Z&P's criteria diagnose as indicative of morphological objects (their criterion C). However, there is no reason to think that the cluster forms any kind of morphological construction with the verb, certainly not that it realizes a verbal paradigm cell. In the system of Anderson (1992, 2005), the entire cluster (but not together with the verb or any prosodic host) is thus treated as a single morphologically generated object that is positioned with respect to a phrasal domain ('phrasal affixes'). Importantly, positioning of the cluster in Serbian is purely prosodic and syntactic, unlike in the verb-adjacent languages Bulgarian and Macedonian.

5 The verbal complex and the Sprachbund – and contact – (re)considered

The evidence presented in Section 3 from Greek, Albanian, and Section 4 from Balkan Slavic shows that as far as the verbal complex is concerned, for all the interesting similarities, there are real and quite significant differences evident across these languages. Particularly noteworthy is the fact that Bulgarian and Macedonian differ with respect to the conditions for preverbal vs. postverbal positioning of weak pronouns, and with regard to interruptability of the pronouns by the question marker *li*. Moreover, they both differ from Serbian in requiring verb-adjacency for the weak pronouns. Greek and Albanian show no possibility for interrupting the weak pronouns.

Thus the geographically adjacent Albanian, Greek, and Macedonian all converge on a set of characteristics for the verbal complex that point towards a high degree of synthesis. Since these are strings that are safely assumed to have once been syntactic in nature (see footnotes 17 and 26, and discussion below regarding Greek), this is evidence of morphologization. Moreover, Albanian and Greek are especially convergent here, showing the highest degree of morphologization in the verbal complex, with Macedonian diverging from them, analytically

---

38 In usage there is some variation in this regard, but here we describe normative standard practice.

speaking, due to the fact that *li* can intervene between post-verbal weak pronouns and the verb and due to an absence of any telling morphophonological idiosyncrasies involving elements in the Macedonian verbal complex. Furthermore, and quite importantly, the geographically more remote Bulgarian and Serbian diverge from this core clustering within the Balkans that the other languages constitute here. This geographic dimension is suggestive, and would seem to indicate that contact among the speakers of the converging languages is what is responsible for the convergence.

If contact is indeed involved in this convergence – and it is hard to argue otherwise, though we offer some evidence below suggesting what the limits are of the contact-related influence – then it would *appear* that one has to reckon here with contact effects of a nonsuperficial nature and especially with the borrowing of processes, as opposed to specific forms. We examine this claim in some detail in what follows, but first, it is important to see why it is an interesting claim in the first place.

Heine and Kuteva (2005), in arguing for "contact grammaticalization", say that in a situation in which there is "grammaticalization" in a contact zone – as with the parallel morphologization seen with the verbal complexes in the central Balkans – what is borrowed, what is replicated across languages, is the set of processes of grammaticalization evident in the donor language, so that the chain of events that led from, say, a periphrastic construction in one stage of a language to a "grammaticalized" structure in a later stage is replicated in a contact-affected language. Since processes are by nature abstractions, such a view is at odds with the characterization given in Section 1 of borrowing and of contact effects more generally as an inherently surface-oriented phenomenon. In what follows, we attempt to reconcile this surface-oriented view of language contact with the facts of the verbal complex in the Balkans.

First, it is fair to ask whether the processes were indeed borrowed. Among the facts that make the Greek verbal complex appear to be a word-level unit is morphophonology, in particular the behavior of the combination of the second person singular genitive pronoun *su* together with third person pronouns (*su t-* > *st*) and the synchronically unexpected voicing of the initial *t-* of third person object pronouns after *θa* and *na*. And for Albanian, the portmanteau realizations of the pronouns are particularly telling. These effects, however, are language-specific developments and could not in themselves have been borrowed.

Further, there are empirical chronological considerations arguing against a borrowing (replication) of the processes. One of the pieces of the verbal complex is the invariant marker for futurity, Greek *θa*, Bulgarian *šte*, etc., and this marker in each case derives from a present tense verb that at an earlier stage was fully inflected for person and number of the subject, e.g. 2/3SG Greek *θeleis/θelei* (phonetically, [θelis/θeli]). In Greek, for instance, skipping a few of the intermediate steps, the progression was from 3SG *θelei na grapsei* for '(s)he will write' (literally "(s)he will that (s)he writes") to *θel na grapsei* to *θe na grapsei* to *θa na grapsei* and ultimately to *θa grapsei* ([θa ɣrapsi]), by a series of regular sound changes and well-motivated analogies, and similar sorts of changes define the emergence of the invariant marker in the other languages as well.³⁹ Asenova (2002[1989]) gives dates for the appearance of distinct phases in the reduction of this future auxiliary that shows significant differences in the period at which each step in the reduction is to be found in each language. Specifically, she states that the *θe na grapsei* reduction is found from the 14th century in Greek, whereas the corresponding Balkan Slavic *šte/ḱe da piša(m)* is found from the 16th century, Albanian *do të shkrojë* from the early 18th century, and Balkan Romance *o să scriu* from the mid-18th century.⁴⁰ And the fully reduced form without the subordinating element *na/da/të/să* is attested from the early 16th century for Greek, the early 15th century for Slavic, the mid-18th century for Albanian, and the early 19th century for Romanian. These dates do not line up as we might expect if the reductive processes were borrowed (replicated) across the languages. To take the earliest fully reduced form – Slavic – as the starting point, just for the sake of argument,⁴¹ one has to admit that once a process of reduction has done its work, so to speak, what remains is not the process itself but rather the result of the process. Thus after the 15th century in Slavic territory, what would have been available to be passed to another language was not the process of reduction but the outcome of the reductive process. Thus it is hard to see how the process of reduction could be borrowed as only the results are evident, not the process itself. We thus conclude that we must reckon with a certain degree of historical independence to the specific developments leading to morphologized verbal complexes in the different languages here.

In defense of a contact-based approach, one might argue that it was not the process of reduction that was borrowed but the idea of reduction. While it is hard to see how an abstraction like such an "idea" could be borrowed (as if it

---

39 See Joseph and Pappas (2002) for detailed discussion of this progression.
40 These last two dates may be affected, of course, by the rather late attestation of these languages and the scarcity of older materials in general; substantial documents from Albanian and Romanian are known from roughly only the mid-16th century (1555 and 1521, respectively) and then of a somewhat limited nature.
41 There is admittedly an anomaly in Asenova's chronology for Slavic in that the reduced form occurs earlier in her reckoning than the fuller form; this is most likely a matter of attestation as far as the fuller form is concerned. For what it is worth, the fuller form in Greek, while occurring early enough, is not all that robustly attested, in part, perhaps, because it was ambiguous between a future reading and a volitional reading ('he will write' versus 'he wants to write'), as also in Slavic.

were "in the air" in a speech community, so to speak), we do give a reasonable scenario below as to how that might happen, working from the evident results of the reductive process(es).

Still, one might ask whether it is perhaps the case that contact is simply irrelevant here and whether it might not be more reasonable to say that the parallel synthesis in the verbal complexes of the different languages is just a coincidence. To this, we say no. As we see it, such a claim amounts to a denial of the geography and moreover it strains credulity when one considers the significant number of convergent features in the Balkan languages in general and especially among Greek, Albanian, and Macedonian, features which taken together are what motivate the notion of a Sprachbund involving these languages in the first place.[42]

So it must be asked how the convergence in the verbal complex came to be. Vital to our account is a recognition that what can be borrowed is, to reiterate, present in surface structure, in the output of the grammar that speakers produce. By this we mean not the actual surface forms, but rather patterns that are derivable from surface forms, patterns that can be "read" off of the surface. That is, in a social context of fairly intense contact, where there is mutual multilingualism so that speakers of one language have a reasonable command of the language(s) of their neighbors, and have a sense of what the pieces of the other language do, cross-language matching up of elements at the templatic level can easily occur. In this way, patterns can be transferred between languages, being read off of output essentially by speakers imposing an analysis on the elements in the other language that correspond to known entities in their own language. This matching and pattern imposition process does involve some level of abstraction, to be sure, but crucially what is borrowed is not a process per se but rather an analysis. As we envision this process, it is abstract, but it is not deeply syntactic; speakers are not borrowing strictly surface form but rather patterns – surface *structure*, that is – evident from the surface forms. The surface here gives a target structure for speakers of a language to aim at, in the case of the verbal complex yielding a particular surface ordering of elements.

At this point, it is useful to recall Kopitar's (1829) dictum from Section 1, regarding there being one grammar but three lexicons for the Balkan languages

---

[42] See Sandfeld (1930) for what is still the best collection of these convergent features; Friedman (2006) is perhaps the best concise statement of the evidence for the Balkan Sprachbund, though see also Joseph (2010), and Friedman and Joseph (in prep). These features are not just structural in nature but also lexical, and among the lexical items are numerous discourse markers, indicating that the speakers of the different languages were indeed speaking to one another; see Friedman and Joseph (2014) for a discussion of these conversationally based loanwords ("ERIC loans", in their formulation, for those "Essentially Rooted In Conversation").

he was examining. The "one grammar" here can be a template, an ideal surface string,[43] for the order of elements, and that gets realized with different lexical material. An informal characterization of what was going on, as we see it, is that essentially speakers were saying "OK, I recognize that you treat, for instance, your weak object pronouns as verb-adjacent; well, I can do that too in my language". And by doing so, such a speaker was either accommodating to (= adopting) the particular feature of the other, or was selecting from among variants in his/her own language that match the other's pattern; in either case, for either motivation, there is a facilitating of communication between the speakers through the use of a shared structure.

Then, once the ordering of elements is fixed in this way, ordinary processes of language change can operate, much as Joseph (2001) argues with respect to the Greek future and as suggested earlier in this section. The workings of such processes can lead independently to synthetic structure to greater or lesser degrees, for reasons that are particular to specific speech communities and their social (etc.) circumstances. Nonetheless, the original impetus will have been language contact and the borrowing of structure will have been achieved through the cross-language matching of elements of structure in comparable entities in the respective languages.

There is also the possibility for cross-language analogies to play a role. Such a mechanism may be behind the possible absence of the subjunctive marker *të* in the future tense in Albanian, where the pattern of two independent but related variants for the future in Greek could have been the model for its allowable absence in Albanian, if Albanian speakers recognized a relation between the two variants and were in a position to equate them with their own future tense[44]:

Greek: θe na grapso   :   θe grapso
                           : :
Albanian: do të shkruaj :   X,   X → do shkruaj

A similar mechanism, perhaps with Albanian as the model, though Greek would have been possible too, may have been at work in Macedonian, where the standard language now has simply the invariant future marker *ќe* with a finite verb to

---

[43] Note that for Kopitar, working at the time he did, there was not a coherent notion of deep structure and surface structure.

[44] These future variants are of independent origin within Greek; the type with subjunctive marker *na* shows the regular replacement of the earlier infinitive by a finite clause introduced by *na*, while the type without *na* resulted from a reanalysis of an infinitival form as finite, due to the merger of the infinitive ending with 3SG ending. This is a Greek-particular development, not found in other languages.

form the future, e.g. *ke dojdam* 'I will go' whereas dialectally the modal marker *da* can occur as well, e.g. *ke da dojdam*. Similarly, the emergence of evidentiality dialectally in Aromanian under heavy Macedonian influence, as described by Friedman (1994), is based on a recognition by Aromanian speakers of parallel structures in Macedonian that could be used in a novel way in Aromanian.

In the general view of Balkan language contact being advocated here, the convergence becomes a mix of contact-induced impetus and some borrowing with language-particular developments. For a complex contact situation like the Balkans, such a scenario is probably closer to the truth than any single-cause account would be, and it mirrors the multiple-causation account given in Joseph (1983: Ch. 7) for the parallel infinitive-loss and replacement developments in the various Balkan languages.

In this regard too, one can also think of contact scenarios, such as that proposed by Friedman (1999) for the development of evidentiality in the Balkans, in which what occurs might be termed "contact-induced 'enhancement' of native possibilities". Friedman argues that Turkish influence did play a role but not through the importation of completely new material and new categories from Turkish into Balkan Slavic languages, but rather by native tendencies already present in Slavic being enhanced and given a chance to develop through contact with Turkish, a language with grammatical expression of evidentiality. By contact, outright borrowing (actually, calquing) seems to have been involved in the further spread of evidentiality to Aromanian from a Macedonian model.

All of this suggests that the areal pattern of morphologization and synthesis within the verbal complex follows in parallel to other contact patterns that we find in the same region. So in some sense, there is nothing particularly special about the areal distribution of the verbal complex. It does, however, highlight the way in which speakers in contact situations can be sensitive to the ordering and other surface-structural properties of grammatical elements. When speakers recognize and import structural properties that are related to morphologization (e.g. verb-adjacency of weak object pronouns), the result may be convergent grammaticalization. We hypothesize that it is exactly this kind of observational power that has led to the areal distribution of morphologization in the verbal complex.

6 Conclusions

In this paper we have explored theoretical issues raised by the Balkan verbal complex by virtue of its positioning at the intersection of morphology and syntax. Parallelisms in the content and order of functional elements formed the basis for the cross-linguistic comparison and motivated the idea of the verbal complex as a Balkan contact phenomenon in the first place. However, the differences across languages are ultimately at least as interesting as the similarities. We have argued for a broad notion of morphologization, as well as the idea that morphologization processes proceed in piecemeal fashion, resulting in the frequent occurrence of both morphological and syntactic properties in constructions synchronically. This conceptualization has allowed us to explore the question of morphologization in the Balkan verbal complex in a relatively fine-grained (if necessarily non-comprehensive) way. While there are idiosyncratic differences in the verbal complexes of the individual languages, the overarching pattern that emerged was one of decreasing morphologization as we move outwards from the core Sprachbund contact zone. We find a high degree of synthesis in Albanian to Greek, with progressively less morphologization in Macedonian, Bulgarian and Serbian. This offers an interesting window into the questions of contact that have to do with morphologization processes. We argued here that while contact is very likely involved in the pattern of convergent morphologization, it is not the *process* of morphologization that is borrowed from one language to another (contra Heine and Kuteva 2005). Rather, we need assume nothing more than that the *outcomes* of morphologization in the source language serve as the basis for structural calquing in the borrowing language. So while 'extent of morphologization' is a rather abstract kind of contact effect, we ultimately find that this parallels and is no more exotic than other contact outcomes that are firmly established as part of the Balkan Sprachbund. We offer the verbal complex as a member of that canon.

Postscript: Object doubling and the verbal complex

By way of a postscript, we look briefly at object doubling, a phenomenon that touches on the verbal complex, and the issue of morphologization, but in a different light from the discussion above. Our observations here are by necessity speculative and in need of further investigation. But we offer them as consideration of what implications morphologization of the verbal complex may have for broader issues and debates.

As noted above in Section 3, Matzinger and Schumacher (2017) observe that in Albanian, the weak object pronouns can co-occur with full nominals as objects, either nouns or strong forms of pronouns, as in (37):

(37) a. *E   pashë   Gjonin.*
       him.ACC.WK saw.1SG John.ACC
       'I saw John.'

b. *Më pa mua Gjoni.*
   me saw.3SG me.ACC.STR John.NOM
   'John saw me.'

This construction is actually found in other Balkan languages; examples are given in (38) from Greek, in (39) from Macedonian, and in (40) from Bulgarian (though see below for clarification of the status of such examples from Bulgarian):

(38) a. *To pino efxaristos ena uzaki.*
   3SG.WK.ACC drink.1SG gladly an.N.ACC ouzo.DIM
   'I would gladly have an ouzo.' (literally: "it I-drink gladly an ouzo")

   b. *To pino afto efxaristos.*
   3SG.ACC drink.1SG it.STR.ACC gladly
   'I would drink it gladly.' (literally: "it I-drink this gladly")

(39) *Mu go davam molivot na momčeto.*
   3SG.M.DAT 3SG.M.ACC give.1SG pencil.DEF to boy.DEF
   'I give the pencil to the boy.' (literally: "to-him it I-give pencil-the to boy-the")

(40) *Kučeto ja goni edna kotka.*
   dog.DEF her.ACC.F chases one cat.F
   'It's the dog that is chasing a cat.' (Guentchéva 1994:111)

This phenomenon, known in the literature as "Clitic Doubling" or "Object Reduplication" or "Object Doubling", has attracted much attention over the years; the vast literature is summarized admirably and insightfully in Anagnostopoulou (2006); see also Kallulli (this volume). One reason for the considerable interest is that object doubling presents analytic challenges to assumptions and claims made within generative syntax; in particular, sentences like those in (37) – (40) appear to show two potential accusative case-marked entities – the weak object pronoun (e.g. *e* in (37)) and the full nominal object (e.g. *Gjonin* in (37)) – but only one accusative case-licensing entity, namely the verb. The Balkan data thus offer a typological point of contrast to Spanish and other Romance languages where object doubling is possible only when there are two distinct case-licensers (e.g. a verb that licenses the clitic object and a preposition that licenses the full nominal). The Balkan facts also contrast with the pattern in Welsh, discussed by Sadler (1997), where pronominal clitics block full noun phrases, and object doubling does not occur in this context.

There turn out to be a number of ways in which the relevant object doubling facts can be handled, in part depending on other sorts of assumptions that are made within a given theoretical framework for syntax. However, assessing these requires a full evaluation of these other assumptions and the constructs they require and depend on. Such an evaluation is beyond the scope of this paper, and in any case, it is covered well in Anagnostopoulou (2006). However, among the possibilities is one that bears on the morphological versus syntactic status of the weak object pronouns. In particular, if case licensing is a syntactic requirement and the weak object pronouns are morphological in nature, occurring say as agreement markers,[45] then one could in principle exclude the weak object pronouns from a case-licensing requirement. So we cannot help but wonder whether the theoretical issues raised by Balkan object doubling are in fact obviated by the independent evidence in this paper for the reanalysis of object pronouns as affixes to the verb. In other words, is there object doubling at all, or instead an emergent agreement system? We note that object doubling is most grammaticalized exactly in those languages were there is also the most synthesis among elements of the verbal complex, including object pronouns.

Any full exploration of this idea would need to account for object doubling in Bulgarian. As noted in Section 4 above, we find little evidence in support of an affixal analysis of weak object pronominals in Bulgarian, in part because they can be separated from the verb by *li*, which is not structurally part of the clitic cluster. However, we also note that object doubling is not required in Bulgarian except in the impersonal existential use of *ima/njama* 'there is / there is not', literally "has/not.has". Thus in the Bulgarian sentence in (41), no weak pronouns doubling the objects are required.

(41) *Davam moliva na momčeto.*
 give.1SG pencil.DEF to boy.DEF
 'I give the pencil to the boy.'

However, object doubling can, but need not, be used to disambiguate case relations (Stojanov 1983: 192–193). More important here is the claim in Leafgren (2002: 197) that object doubling in Bulgarian serves a pragmatic function, marking *aboutness*, most typically in a contrastive setting (i.e., 'about X as opposed to Y').

---

[45] They could be marking agreement in that their properties (gender, number, case) match those of the full nominal, but they would be atypical agreement markers – different for instance from the agreement that verb endings show with the person and number of the subject or the agreement in gender, number, and case between articles or adjectives and nouns – in being sometimes optional.

(42) Banan ne običam da go   jam.
banana NEG like.1SG that 3SG.M.ACC eat.1SG
'I don't like to eat bananas.' (Leafgren (2002: 176); context = discussion of markets)

In this way, the presence of a doubled pronoun serves as an overt marker of topicality.[46] Object doubling in Bulgarian is thus fundamentally discourse-oriented, rather than grammatical. This is exactly the pattern that we would expect if 'object doubling' and morphologization were related.

Ultimately, we cannot explore this idea in any detail here and leave it for future work. However, we raise the question of the proper analysis of the object pronominals as a way to demonstrate that the question of whether the verbal complex is morphologized bears on larger theoretical issues. We think that the relevance of verbal complex morphologization for licensing of object doubling is an issue that merits further work. Moreover, it underlines the importance of considering the structural properties of the relevant elements, since these may not be obvious from the surface string of elements.

References

Ackema, Peter, and Ad Neeleman. 2001. "Competition between syntax and morphology." In *Optimality-theoretic syntax*, edited by Géraldine Legendre, Jane Grimshaw and Sten Vikner, 29–60. Cambridge, MA: The MIT Press.
Ackerman, Farrell, and Philip LeSourd. 1997. "Toward a lexical representation of phrasal predicates." In *Complex predicates*, edited by Alex Alsina, Joan Bresnan and Peter Sells, 67–106. Stanford, CA: CSLI.
Ackerman, Farrell, and Gregory T. Stump. 2004. "Paradigms and periphrastic expression: A study in realization-based lexicalism." In *Projecting morphology*, edited by Louisa Sadler and Andrew Spencer, 111–158. Stanford, CA: CSLI.
Ackerman, Farrell, Gregory T. Stump, and Gert Webelhuth. 2011. "Lexicalism, periphrasis and implicative morphology." In *Non-transformational syntax: Formal and explicit models of grammar*, edited by Robert D. Borsley and Kersti Börjars, 325–358. Malden, MA: Wiley-Blackwell.
Aikhenvald, Alexandra Y. 2002. "Typological parameters for the study of clitics, with special reference to Tariana." In *Word: A cross-linguistic typology*, edited by R.M.W. Dixon and Alexandra Y. Aikhenvald, 42–78. Cambridge: Cambridge University Press.
Alexander, Ronelle. 1994. "The Balkanization of Wackernagel's law." *Indiana Slavic Studies* 7: 1–8.

---

[46] The geographic distribution is interesting too, in that there is a west-to-east trend, with a decrease in frequency as one moves east within Bulgarian-speaking territory. The end result is that object doubling is relatively infrequent in eastern Bulgarian (Keremedčieva 1993: 297–299).

Anagnostopoulou, Elena. 2006. "Clitic doubling." In *Blackwell companion to syntax, vol. 1*, edited by Martin Everaert, Henk van Riemsdijk, Rob Goedemans and Bart Hollebrandse, 519–581. Oxford: Blackwell.

Anderson, Stephen R. 1992. *A-morphous morphology*. Cambridge: Cambridge University Press.

——. 1995. "Rules and constraints in describing the morphology of phrases." In *CLS 31: Papers from the 31st Regional Meeting of the Chicago Linguistic Society, vol. 2*, edited by Audra Dainora, Rachel Hemphill, Barbara Luka, Barbara Need and Sheri Pargman, 15–31. Chicago: Chicago Linguistic Society.

——. 2005. *Aspects of the theory of clitics*. Oxford: Oxford University Press.

Andrews, Avery D. 1990. "Unification and morphological blocking." *Natural Language and Linguistic Theory* 8: 507–557.

Asenova, Petya. 2002[1989]. *Balkansko ezikoznanie: Osnovni problemi na balkanskija ezikov sâjuz* [Balkan linguistics: Fundamental problems of the Balkan Linguistic Union]. Veliko Tărnovo Faber.

Bîlbîie, Gabriela and Alexandru Mardale. This volume. The Romanian subjunctive from a Balkan perspective.

Bonami, Olivier. 2015. "Periphrasis as collocation." *Morphology* 25(1): 63–110.

Bonami, Olivier, and Gilles Boyé. 2007. "French pronominal clitics and the design of Paradigm Function Morphology." In *On-line proceedings of the Fifth Mediterranean Morphology Meeting (MMM5), Fréjus, 15–18 September 2005*, edited by Geert Booij, Luca Ducceschi, Bernard Fradin, Emiliano Guevara, Angela Ralli and Sergio Scalise, 291–322. Bologna: Università degli Studi di Bologna.

Bonami, Olivier, and Pollet Samvelian. 2009. "Inflectional periphrasis in Persian." In *Proceedings of the 16th International Conference on Head-Driven Phrase Structure Grammar*, edited by Stefan Müller, 26–46. Stanford, CA: CSLI.

Bonami, Olivier, and Gert Webelhuth. 2013. "The phrase-structural diversity of periphrasis: A lexicalist account." In *Periphrasis: The role of syntax and morphology in paradigms*, edited by Marina Chumakina and Greville G. Corbett. Oxford: Oxford University Press and British Academy.

Börjars, Kersti, Nigel Vincent, and Carol Chapman. 1997. "Paradigms, periphrases and pronominal inflection: A feature-based account." In *Yearbook of morphology 1996*, edited by Geert Booij and Jaap van Marle, 155–180. Dordrecht: Kluwer.

Bošković, Željko. 2001. *On the nature of the syntax-phonology interface: Cliticization and related phenomena*. Amsterdam: Elsevier.

Bresnan, Joan. 2001. "Explaining morphosyntactic competition." In *The handbook of contemporary syntactic theory*, edited by Mark Baltin and Chris Collins, 11–44. Malden, MA: Blackwell.

Bresnan, Joan, and Sam Mchombo. 1995. "The Lexical Integrity Principle: Evidence from Bantu." *Natural Language and Linguistic Theory* 13(2): 181–254.

Brown, Dunstan, Marina Chumakina, Greville Corbett, Gergana Popova, and Andrew Spencer. 2012. "Defining 'periphrasis': Key notions." *Morphology* 22(2): 233–275.

Brown, Dunstan, and Andrew Hippisley. 2012. *Network morphology: A defaults-based theory of word structure*. Cambridge: Cambridge University Press.

Chomsky, Noam. 1970. "Remarks on nominalization." In *Readings in English transformational grammar*, edited by R. Jacobs and P. Rosenbaum, 184–221. Waltham, MA: Ginn.

Embick, David, and Roumyana Izvorski. 1997. "Participle-auxiliary word orders in Slavic." In *Annual workshop on formal approaches to Slavic linguistics, vol. 4: The Cornell meeting, 1995*, edited by Wayles Browne, Ewa Dornisch, Natasha Kondrashova and Draga Zec, 210–239. Ann Arbor: Michigan Slavic.

Englund, Birgitta. 1977. *Yes/no-questions in Bulgarian and Macedonian*. Stockholm: Almqvist & Wiksell International.
Franks, Steven, and Tracy Holloway King. 2000. *A handbook of Slavic clitics*. Oxford: Oxford University Press.
Friedman, Victor A. 1993. "Macedonian." In *The Slavonic languages*, edited by Bernard Comrie and Greville Corbett, 249–305. London: Routledge.
———. 1994. "Surprise! Surprise! Arumanian has had an admirative!" *Indiana Slavic Studies* 7: 79–89.
———. 1999. "Evidentiality in the Balkans." In *Handbuch der Südosteuropa-Linguistik*, edited by Uwe Hinrichs, 519–544. Wiesbaden: Harrassowitz.
———. 2006. "The Balkans as a linguistic area." In *Encyclopedia of language and linguistics*, edited by Keith Brown, 657–672. Oxford: Elsevier.
Friedman, Victor A., and Brian D. Joseph. 2014. "Lessons from Judezmo about the Balkan Sprachbund and contact linguistics." *International Journal of the Sociology of Language* 226: 3–23.
———. in prep. *The Balkan languages*. Cambridge: Cambridge University Press.
Gołąb, Zbigniew. 1954. "Funkcija syntaktyczna partykuly da w językach południowoslowiańskich (bułgarskim, makedońskim i serbo-chorwackim)." *Biuletyn Polskiego Towarzystwa Językoznawczego* 13: 67–92.
Hauge, Kjetil Rå. 1999[1976]. "The word order of predicate clitics in Bulgarian." *Journal of Slavic Linguistics* 7(1): 89–137.
Heine, Bernd, and Tania Kuteva. 2005. *Language contact and grammatical change*. Cambridge: Cambridge University Press.
Joseph, Brian D. 1983. *The synchrony and diachrony of the Balkan infinitive: A study in areal, general, and historical linguistics*. Cambridge: Cambridge University Press.
———. 2001. "Is there such a thing as 'grammaticalization'?" *Language Sciences* 23(2-3): 163–186.
———. 2002. "Defining "word" in Modern Greek: a response to Philippaki-Warburton & Spyropoulos 1999. " In *Yearbook of morphology 2001*, edited by Geert Booij and Jaap Van Marle, 87–114. Dordrecht: Kluwer.
———. 2010. "Language contact in the Balkans." In *Handbook of language contact*, edited by Ray Hickey, 618–633. Oxford: Blackwell.
Joseph, Brian D., and Panayiotis A. Pappas. 2002. "On some recent views concerning the development of the Greek future system." *Byzantine and Modern Greek Studies* 26: 247–273.
Kallulli, Dalina. This volume. Balkan clitic doubling revisited: Micro-variation, typological generalizations, and a true universal.
Keremedčieva, Slavka. 1993. *Govorăt na Ropkata*. Sofia: MicroPrint.
Kiparsky, Paul. 2005. "Blocking and periphrasis in inflectional paradigms." In *Yearbook of morphology 2004*, edited by Geert Booij and Jaap van Marle, 113–135. Dordrecht: Springer.
Koneski, Blaže. 1967. *Gramatika na makedonskiot literaturen jazik*. Skopje: Kultura.
Kopitar, Jernej. 1829. "Albanische, walachische und bulgarische Sprache." *Jahrbücher der Literatur* 46: 59–106.
Kramer, Christina. 1986. *Analytic modality in Macedonian*. Munich: Otto Sagner.
Krapova, Iliyana, and Guglielmo Cinque. This volume. "Universal constraints on Balkanisms. A case study: The absence of Clitic Climbing." In *Balkan syntax and (universal) principles of grammar*, edited by Iliyana Krapova and Brian D. Joseph. Berlin: Mouton de Gruyter.

Leafgren, John. 2002. *Degrees of explicitness: Information structure and the packaging of Bulgarian subjects and objects*. Amsterdam: John Benjamins.

Legendre, Géraldine. 1996. "Clitics, verb (non-)movement and optimality in Bulgarian." In *Technical Report JHU-CogSci-96-5*: Johns Hopkins University, Department of Cognitive Science.

———. 1999. "Morphological and prosodic alignment at work: The case of South Slavic clitics." In *WCCFL 17: The proceedings of Seventeenth West Coast Conference on Formal Linguistics*, edited by Kimary N. Shahin, Susan Blake and Eun-Sook Kim, 436–450. Stanford, CA: CSLI.

———. 2001a. "Masked second-position effects and the linearization of functional features." In *Optimality-theoretic syntax*, edited by Géraldine Legendre, Jane Grimshaw and Sten Vikner, 241–278. Cambridge, MA: The MIT Press.

———. 2001b. "Morphological and prosodic alignment of Bulgarian clitics." In *Optimality Theory: Syntax, phonology and acquisition*, edited by Joost Dekkers, Frank van der Leeuw and Jeroen van de Weijer, 423–462. Oxford: Oxford University Press.

Maslov, Jurij. 1956. *Očerk bolgarskoj grammatiki*. Moskva: Izdatel'stvo Literatury na Inostrannyx Jazykax.

Matzinger, Joachim, and Stefan Schumacher. 2017. "The morphology of Albanian." In *Handbook of comparative and historical Indo-European linguistics*, edited by Jared Klein, Brian D. Joseph and Matthias Fritz, 1749–1771. Berlin: de Gruyter Mouton.

Mišeska Tomić, Olga. 1996. "The Balkan Slavic clausal clitics." *Natural Language and Linguistic Theory* 14(4): 811–872.

———. 2006. *Balkan sprachbund morpho-syntactic features*. Dordrecht: Springer.

Newmark, Leonard, Philip Hubbard, and Peter R. Prifti. 1982. *Standard Albanian: A reference grammar for students*. Stanford, CA: Stanford University Press.

Perlmutter, David. 1971. *Deep and surface structure constraints in syntax*. New York: Holt, Reinhart and Winston.

Philippaki-Warburton, Irene, and Vassilios Spyropoulos. 1999. "On the boundaries of inflection and syntax: Greek pronominal clitics and particles." In *Yearbook of morphology 1998*, edited by Geert Booij and Jaap Van Marle, 45–72. Dordrecht: Kluwer.

Popova, Gergana. 2010. "Features in periphrastic constructions." In *Features: Perspectives on a key notion in linguistics*, edited by Anna Kibort and Greville G. Corbett, 166–184. Oxford: Oxford University Press.

Popova, Gergana, and Andrew Spencer. 2013. "Relatedness in periphrasis: A paradigm-based perspective." In *Periphrasis: The role of syntax and morphology in paradigms*, edited by Marina Chumakina and Greville G. Corbett, 191–225. Oxford: Oxford University Press and British Academy.

Poser, William J. 1992. "Blocking of phrasal constructions by lexical items." In *Lexical matters*, edited by Ivan A. Sag and Anna Szabolcsi, 111–130. Stanford, CA: CSLI.

Rudin, Catherine. 1988. "On multiple questions and multiple WH fronting." *Natural Language and Linguistic Theory* 6: 445–501.

Rudin, Catherine, Christina Kramer, Loren Billings, and Matthew Baerman. 1999. "Macedonian and Bulgarian *li* questions: Beyond syntax. " *Natural Language and Linguistic Theory* 17(3): 541–585.

Sadler, Louisa. 1997. Clitics and the structure-function mapping. In *Proceedings of the LFG '97 conference*, edited by Miriam Butt and Tracy Holloway King. Stanford, CA: CSLI Publications Online.

Sadler, Louisa, and Andrew Spencer. 2000. "Syntax as an exponent of morphological features." In *Yearbook of morphology 2000*, edited by Geert Booij and Jaap van Marle, 71–96. Dordrecht: Kluwer.

Samvelian, Pollet. 2007. "A (phrasal) affix analysis of the Persian ezafe." *Journal of Linguistics* 43(3): 605–645.

Sandfeld, Kristian. 1930. *Linguistique balkanique: Problèmes et résultats*. Paris: E. Champion.

Simpson, Jane, and Margaret Withgott. 1986. "Pronominal clitic clusters and templates." In *Syntax and semantics 19: The syntax of pronominal clitics*, edited by Hagit Borer, 149–174. New York: Academic.

Spencer, Andrew. 2000. "Verbal clitics in Bulgarian: A Paradigm Function approach." In *Clitics in phonology, morphology and syntax*, edited by Birgit Gerlach and Janet Grijzenhout, 355–386. Amsterdam: John Benjamins.

——. 2001. "The paradigm-based model of morphosyntax." *Transactions of the Philological Society* 99(2): 279–313.

——. 2003. "Periphrastic paradigms in Bulgarian." In *Syntactic structures and morphological information*, edited by Uwe Junghanns and Luka Szucsich, 249–282. New York: Mouton de Gruyter.

——. 2012. "Sentence negation and periphrasis." In *Periphrasis: The role of syntax and morphology in paradigms*, edited by Marina Chumakina and Greville G. Corbett, 227–266. Oxford: Oxford University Press and British Academy.

Spencer, Andrew, and Ana R. Luís. 2012. *Clitics*. Cambridge: Cambridge University Press.

Stojanov, Stojan. 1983. *Gramatika na săvremenija bălgarski knižoven ezik, tom II: morfologija*. Sofia: BAN.

Stump, Gregory T. 2001. *Inflectional morphology: A theory of paradigm structure*. Cambridge: Cambridge University Press.

Zwicky, Arnold M. 1977. *On clitics*. Bloomington, IN: Indiana University Linguistics Club.

——. 1990. "Inflectional morphology as a (sub)component of grammar." In *Contemporary morphology*, edited by Wolfgang U. Dressler, Hans C. Luschützky, Oskar E. Pfeiffer and John R. Rennison, 217–236. New York: Mouton de Gruyter.

——. 1992. "Some choices in the theory of morphology." In *Formal grammar: Theory and implementation*, edited by Robert Levine, 327–371. Oxford: Oxford University Press.

Zwicky, Arnold M., and Geoffrey K. Pullum. 1983. "Cliticization vs. inflection: English n't." *Language* 59(3): 502–513.

Iliyana Krapova and Guglielmo Cinque
Universal Constraints on Balkanisms. A Case Study: The absence of Clitic Climbing

Abstract: In this paper, we investigate a syntactic gap in the structure of the Balkan languages, the absence of Clitic Climbing, which we argue to be a consequence of a well-known Balkanism, namely the loss of the infinitive. For this purpose, we propose a division of the finite constructions that have replaced the infinitive in three categories: Restructuring (Raising), Control, and Subjunctive-like constructions. We also briefly discuss evidence for the existence of selective Clitic Climbing in older stages and in modern dialects of the Balkan languages.

Keywords: Clitic Climbing, Restructuring, Raising, Control, Infinitive, Balkanisms

1 Introduction

In this article, we consider one syntactic Balkanism and the constraining effects of Universal Grammar on it. Just as Joseph (1980) argued that universal constraints can guide syntactic change, and "lead to a more restrictive, and hence stronger theory of syntactic change" (p. 343), we argue that certain universal constraints can also shed light on certain otherwise puzzling phenomena in areal linguistics, specifically in the Balkan *Sprachbund*.

The phenomenon we consider concerns the apparently unexpected absence, in Albanian, Bulgarian, Greek, Macedonian, and Romanian (the bona fide Balkan languages), of so-called "Clitic Climbing" (henceforth CC), which is otherwise possible in non-Balkan Romance (Italian, Spanish, Catalan, Portuguese, etc.[1])

---

[1] "Clitic Climbing" refers to constructions in which a clitic associated with an embedded verb is actually pronounced on the higher verb. On the very limited scope of CC in French, see Cinque (2002). We find unconvincing the conclusion in Authier and Reed (2008, 2009) that French lacks 'restructuring' altogether (at least formal French), given the existence of CC with *en* and *y* (Kayne 1975, chap.2, fn. 7; Pollock 1978, fn. 18) and of 'long passivization' (Cinque 2002, fn8). Also see

---

Note: For all academic purposes, Iliyana Krapova takes responsibility for sections 2,3,4,5 and Guglielmo Cinque for sections 1,6 and 7.

Iliyana Krapova, (Ca' Foscari University,Venice), krapova@unive.it
Guglielmo Cinque, (Ca' Foscari University,Venice), cinque@unive.it

https://doi.org/10.1515/9783110375930-008

and in the non-Balkan Slavic languages with clitics (Bosnian/Croatian/Serbian (BCS)), Czech, Polish, Slovenian). It is argued that the general absence of CC in the Balkan languages correlates with one well-known Balkanism which they all share, namely the replacement of the verbal infinitive by a combination of a modal particle and an apparently finite verb.[2] In particular, we argue that when a modal particle is present a specific universal constraint (Criterial Freezing – Rizzi 2006) bars CC in these languages.

2 Clitic Climbing and "restructuring"

The existence of CC was first discovered in Romance (Rizzi 1976, 1978, 1982 on Italian, and Aissen and Perlmutter 1976, 1983 on Spanish) and later observed, among other languages, also in those Slavic languages with clitics that fall outside of the Balkan *Sprachbund* area, namely BCS (Progovac 1993, Stjepanović 2004, Aljović 2005), Czech (George and Toman 1976; Veselovská 1995: 372–380; Rezac 2005), Polish (Kupść 1999), and Slovenian (Golden 2003) (also see Franks and King 2000,§6.3). The crucial property of this phenomenon consists in the possibility of locating an argumental clitic of a verb in front of certain classes of functional verbs that take a projection of that verb as their complement. Such classes of functional verbs typically comprise modals, aspectuals, and motion verbs.[3] Examples of CC in non-Balkan Romance and Slavic are given in (1) and (2), respectively:

(1) a. *Gianni lo   {deve/può/comincia a/viene a}*
   Gianni it-CL.ACC {must/can/begins to/comes to}
   leggere (, quell'articolo)   (Italian)
   read-INF (, that article)
   'Gianni must/can/begins to/comes to read that article'
   (Rizzi 1976: 4)

Kayne (1989, Section 12) on French 'easy-to please' constructions, possible with two infinitives if "the higher infinitive [is] of the class that allows clitic climbing [in Italian]" (Kayne 1989: 250), and Kayne (2016), where it is observed that in French "HCI (Hyper-Complex Inversion) is possible to one degree or another with an infinitival embedding only with matrix verbs/predicates of the 'restructuring' type" (p.5).

[2] On the lack of infinitives as a general property of Balkan languages see Sandfeld (1930), Joseph (1983), Asenova (2002), and references cited there.

[3] Although causative and perception verbs also display CC we will not consider them here as they are to be kept apart from modals, aspectual and motion verbs. They add an external argument while functional verbs, like auxiliaries, have no arguments of their own (cf. Cinque 2004, §4.1 for discussion). On motion verbs also see Cardinaletti and Giusti (2001).

b. *El vull   veure* (Catalan)
   him want-1SG see-INF
   'I want to see him'
   (Solà 2010,§1)
c. *Se por ventura as quiserem vender...* (European Portuguese)
   if by chance them want-2SG sell
   'If it happens that you want to sell them (the lands)..'
   (Martins 2000: 185)
d. *Luis las quiere/trató/suele comer* (Spanish)
   Luis them wants/tried/tends eat-INF
   'Luis wants/tried/tends to eat them'
   (Aissen & Perlmutter 1976: 4)

(2) a. *Mila ga   želi   vidjeti* (BCS)
   Mila him-CL.ACC want-3SG see-INF
   'Mila wants to see him'
   (Aljović 2005: 62)
b. *Asi   ho   chtěla   ususit pomalu* (Czech)
   probably him-CL.ACC she.wanted dry-INF slowly
   'She probably wanted to dry him slowly'
   (George and Toman 1976: 241)
c. *Piotr go   chce   kupić w Austrii* (Polish)
   Peter it-CL.ACC want-3SG buy-INF in Austria
   'Peter wants to buy it in Austria'
   (Kupść 1999: 1)
d. *Janez mu   ga   je želel*
   Janez him-CL.DAT him-CL.ACC is wanted
   predstaviti na sprejemu (Slovenian)
   introduce-INF at meeting
   'Janez wanted to introduce him to him at the reception'
   (Golden 2003: 225)

A defining property of CC, at least across Romance and Slavic, is the restriction that the lexical verb out of whose domain the clitic raises must be infinitival or more generally, non-finite.[4] Finite complements do not allow this option, as seen in (3) from Italian:

---

4 As in the case of the Italian gerundive verbal form in the progressive aspect periphrastic construction. See (8) in the text below.

(3) a. *Voglio che **lo** incontri*
    want-1SG that him-CL.ACC meet-SUBJ-2SG
    'I want that you meet him'
  b. ***Lo** voglio che incontri*
    him-CL.ACC want-1SG that meet.SUBJ-2SG

Various proposals have been advanced to account for the possibility of raising a clitic from the embedded verbal domain into a higher one. The phenomenon has been analyzed in terms of fusion between two contiguous clauses. Aissen and Perlmutter (1976) called it "clause union", while Rizzi (1976, 1982) referred to it as "restructuring", a syntactic operation of verbal complex formation which turns a biclausal structure into a monoclausal one. Other accounts, like that of Strozer (1976) or Wurmbrand (1999, 2015) are based on the idea that restructuring verbs take smaller or reduced clausal complements; still others take such constructions to be biclausal, yet allowing inter-clausal transparency as a function of Tense raising (Kayne 1989).[5] See Cinque (2004, fn.1 and 2) for an ample list of references. However, as noted in that work, none of these analyses is able to explain the following three fundamental properties of "restructuring/clause union": (i) why such a phenomenon should exist in the first place, (ii) why it should exist with precisely the classes of modal, aspectual and motion verbs, and more crucially, (iii) why is it that only non-finite but not fully finite complements to lexical verbs allow for CC.

In what follows, we specifically address question (iii), based on data from the Balkan languages, while questions (i) and (ii) constitute part of the background assumptions on which this work is based. Cinque (2004) argued against postulating a transformational operation of "clause union" or "restructuring". Instead, on the basis of the distribution of CC in numerous languages (see the extensive list given in fn. 2 of that article, among which Romance, Slavic, Dravidian, Turkish, Eskimo, etc.), he proposed that the three puzzles can receive a unitary answer if the structure where CC is available is taken to be monoclausal from the start, involving a kind of 'complex predicate' as also assumed in other frameworks (cf. Rosen 1990; Pană Dindelegan 2013). Since so-called "restructuring verbs" realize functional notions pertaining to Tense, Aspect, Modality (root, epistemic, alethic/possibility), Mood (irrealis, evidential, mirative), and Motion (andative, venitive), they can be taken to instantiate specific positions in the universal hierarchy of functional projections proposed in Cinque (1999), a relevant fragment of which is given below (see in particular Cinque 1999: 88ff., 2001: 153):

---

[5] For a different biclausal analysis of "restructuring", see Manzini and Savoia (2005) and Manzini, Lorusso, and Savoia (2017).

(4) [Mod$_{epistemic}$ .... [Tense$_{anterior}$ [Mod $_{possibility}$ [Mod$_{volition}$ [Mod$_{obligation}$ [Asp$_{terminative}$ [Asp$_{inceptive}$ [Mod$_{ability}$ [Asp$_{frustrative/success}$ [Mod$_{permission}$ [Asp$_{conative}$ [Asp$_{completive}$ [V$_{infin}$]]]]]]]]]]]]]

The hierarchy in (4) should read as follows: positions to the left get realized higher on the functional spine of the clause than those to the right. The hierarchy is established on an empirical basis but it has some explanatory power. Among other things, it leads one to expect only certain combinations of functional elements, with interpretations directly deducible from the dedicated functional position the respective element occupies within the hierarchy. In (5a, b) for example, the different interpretations of the reverse ordering of the Italian modals 'can' and 'must', i.e., possibility > root (obligation) for (5a) and epistemic > root (ability) for (5b), derive from the fact that Mod$_{epistemic}$ and Mod$_{possibility}$ are higher than both Mod$_{obligation}$ and Mod$_{ability}$; so whichever modal occupies any of these projections will receive the interpretation corresponding to that projection:

(5) a. *Lo   potrebbe   dover   incontrare*
       him-CL.ACC would.can-3SG must-INF meet-INF
       'He may have to meet him'
    b. *Lo   dovrebbe   poter   incontrare*
       him-CL.ACC would.must   can-INF meet-INF
       'He should be able to meet him'

More generally speaking, the hierarchically higher elements come to linearly precede hierarchically lower elements also in combinations involving Modality and Tense. A case in point is given in (6) regarding the well-known cross-linguistic restriction on the tense properties of epistemic modals, namely that they cannot appear in the anterior tense. This is expected from the hierarchy in (4): since the projection of Mod$_{obligation}$ is lower than that of Tense$_{anterior}$ modals like *dovere* 'must' in (6a), which show up in the anterior tense (*ha dovuto*), must receive a root interpretation and cannot receive an epistemic one. Conversely, if the modal does not bear anterior tense itself but instead precedes (i.e., embeds) a verb in that tense, as does *dovere* in (6b), the only interpretation available to the modal is the epistemic one since Mod$_{epistemic}$ is higher than Tense$_{anterior}$:

(6) a. *Gianni lo   ha dovuto   vedere.*
       Gianni him-CL.ACC has must-PART see-INF
       'Gianni had to see him'   (root)/(*epistemic)
    b. *Gianni lo   deve aver   visto (prima di partire).*
       Gianni him-CL.ACC must have-INF seen (before of leave-INF)
       'Gianni must have seen him (before leaving)' (*root)/(epistemic)

Under such an approach to the structure of the clause, there is no restructuring *per se*. The functional categories that are being accessed in the formation of the clause are already present in the structure and only need to be activated (by the merge of corresponding functional verbs). This derives the inflectional properties of the higher predicate (the modal in (5)), as well as its selectional restrictions (as e.g., in (6)), both determined with reference to the position the predicate occupies on the functional spine of the clause.

According to Cinque (2004), and as the above examples have also illustrated, every clause is uniquely specified for a single **deictic** Tense, thus implying that only the highest functional or auxiliary verb may be finite[6], while all lower verbs belonging to the same clause, whether functional or lexical, should surface in their nonfinite (infinitival, gerundive or participial) form. This can be formulated as an empirical generalization:

(7) In a monoclausal structure, only non-finite verbal forms may qualify as verbal complements of another verb.[7]

Not only is the distribution of deictic (present, past, future) and anaphoric (e.g., anterior) tense captured by this principle but also 'restructuring' effects like CC follow naturally from it and can be viewed in a manner analogous to the distribution of clitics in certain periphrastic constructions, where, too, there is more than one position for the clitic: adjacent to the main verb or to the auxiliary, as in the Italian progressive periphrasis (8):

(8) a. *Io sto   prendendolo*.
       I   stay-1SG catching.it-CL.ACC
    b. *Io **lo**   sto   prendendo*.
       I   it-CL.ACC stay-1SG catching
       'I am catching it'

---

[6] If the clause is subordinate, all verbs can be nonfinite, as in e.g., the Italian subject clause (i):

(i) [Poterlo   leggere] sarebbe   un privilegio.
    Can-INF-CL.ACC read-INF would.be a privilege
    'To be able to read it would be a privilege'

[7] This is a necessary but not a sufficient condition for monoclausality since there are cases where a deictic tense co-occurring with one or more non-finite verbs corresponds to a multi-clausal configuration (e.g., control structures, to which we return).

The principle in (7) may appear problematic in a discussion of the Balkan 'complex predicate' formation strategies. As is well-known, one of the defining properties of the Balkan *Sprachbund* (Sandfeld 1930; Joseph 1983; Asenova 2002) is the complete loss (in Bulgarian, Macedonian, Modern Greek) or considerable reduction (in Romanian and Albanian) of a productive infinitive form in favor of a very productive 'construction' consisting of a modal particle (*da* in Bulgarian and Macedonian, *na* in Modern Greek, *să* in Romanian, and *të* in Albanian) plus an apparently finite verb. This could lead to the conclusion that the functional verbs of non-Balkan Romance and Slavic languages are in the Balkan languages *lexical* verbs, entering a biclausal structure. At first sight, this may appear confirmed by the fact that the *da, na, să* and *të* constructions do not show any CC. The lack of CC however is no sure sign of biclausality. Even in classical CC languages like the Romance languages CC is not ubiquitous: it is highly restricted (if not totally absent) in some northern Italian dialects and in modern French (cf. fn.2), which nonetheless show independent evidence of the presence of "restructuring", i.e. monoclausality with the same class of functional verbs. Analogously, CC is attested in some of the Balkan languages where the infinitive has been retained in specific contexts (see the next section, where we present these contexts), and even in some Balkan varieties that have lost the infinitive entirely (see Section 4). Restructuring/monoclausality should therefore rely on diagnostics other than CC. And as we argue below, some Balkan *da, na, să* and *të* constructions too should be considered monoclausal in spite of the absence of CC and of morphologically marked infinitives.

3 Structural ambiguity of the Balkan "subjunctive"

In this section, we set ourselves the task of identifying the common structures underlying Balkan "subjunctives" which we believe can be successfully analyzed with reference to the universal structure above, and can help us explain the absence of CC in clauses involving a modal particle.

It is well-known that the so-called Balkan "subjunctive" covers a wide range of uses corresponding to either an infinitive (in languages with infinitives) or to a subjunctive in languages with morphologically marked subjunctives like the Romance languages. This ambiguous behavior has been the object of considerable attention in the literature since it involves issues which go beyond the need for a precise description of the grammar of the Balkan languages *per se*. Of theoretical relevance are the questions posed by the mixed behavior of the Balkan subjunctives such as the relation between finiteness and control, types of control (obligatory versus non-obligatory) involved in a two-verb configuration, as well as the precise nature of the understood subject of the second verb (*pro* versus PRO versus trace) (see the papers collected in Rivero & Ralli 2001 and Davies & Dubinsky 2007; see also Roussou 2009, a.o.).

An exhaustive treatment of the Balkan "subjunctive" is of course beyond the scope of this article, but we would like to outline here the essentials of what we believe can be a successful approach to resolving some of the problems posed by the tension between syntax, semantics and morphology of the Balkan "subjunctive".

In this section, we pursue the idea that when compared with Romance, the Balkan "subjunctives" correspond to three distinct constructions: a) a restructuring infinitive-like construction; b) a non-restructuring infinitive-like control construction; and c) a Romance type subjunctive construction. Structurally, these three types can be distinguished in that the latter two are biclausal while the first one is monoclausal. There are both semantic and structural differences between them. First of all, they differ in the type of the first, i.e., higher, verb: only in the restructuring configuration is this verb functional, while in the control and the "true subjunctive" configuration the higher verb can have arguments of its own, independent from those of the second, i.e., lower, verb.

For present purposes, the three structural types can be successfully identified on the basis of the following semantic and syntactic properties: a) interpretation of the understood subject of the lower verb in terms of strict (exhaustive) identity or not; b) possibility or impossibility of Nominative case assignment in the embedded domain; c) presence or absence of deictic Tense on the lower verb. Different correlations of these properties conspire in giving us the three types outlined in the preceding paragraph.

3.1 Pure restructuring, monoclausality and raising

Consider structural type a) first. The class of predicates participating in this configuration includes aspectuals, as well as (non-impersonal) root modals: 'begin', 'start', 'finish', 'manage', 'succeed', 'forget', 'know how', 'can', 'learn' (='come to know how'), 'manage', 'it is possible', all of which arguably lack an argument structure of their own[8] and correspond to restructuring verbs in Romance languages with CC. Cinque (2004) and Grano (2015) argue that such verbs inherit the subject of the lower, lexical, verb as a result of raising, analogous to the raising of the lexical verb's subject to Spec,AuxP in a strictly monoclausal configuration[9]

---

[8] For evidence that those verbs are functional, and are often rendered cross-linguistically with affixes, the reader is referred to Cinque (1999, 2006).
[9] A monoclausal configuration for such clauses has also been proposed by Wurmbrand (1999, 2001, 2015) although she assumes semantic control rather than syntactic raising.

as the one illustrated in the representation below, which is a simplified fragment of the expanded structure in (4) above. FP is the projection of the functional verb.

(9) [$_{CP}$ ... [$_{TP}$... [$_{FP}$ ...DP$_{subject}$ V$_{functional}$ [$_{VP}$ t V$_{lexical}$]

In this configuration, the strict referential identity between the overt subject and the understood subject of the lexical verb (also labeled "exhaustive control" in studies which assume a biclausal configuration of obligatory control – cf. Landau 2000, 2004) is enforced by raising of the lexical subject to the subject position of the respective functional verb. The very nature of this operation excludes the possibility of so-called "partial control", illustrated in (10) from Modern Greek, whereby the understood subject, indicated as ec by Spyropoulos (2007), has a feature specification (manifested on the morphological agreement of the lower verb) which is richer than that of its potential controller (see below).

(10) *I   Zoi   emathe   na   kolimbane [ec$_{i+}$]   (Grk)
     the Zoe-NOM learned PRT swim-3PL
     '*Zoe learned herself and others to swim'
     (Spyropoulos 2007: 167, ex. (22b))

Additionally, the understood subject of the lower verb cannot have 'split antecedents', i.e., more than one antecedent which do not form a constituent. Like partial control, split antecedents are unavailable in restructuring contexts cross-linguistically. The Balkan languages are no different in this respect, as we illustrate with the ungrammatical (11), a fact which suggests that the understood subject is part of an A-chain formed by raising:

(11) *O Janis$_j$ ipe   oti   i Zoi$_i$ emathe   na   kolimbane [ec$_{*j+i}$]
     the John-NOM said-3SG that the Zoe-NOM learned-3SG PRT swim-PL
     *'John said that Zoe has learned them [John and Zoe] to swim'
     (Spyropoulos 2007: 167, ex. (22c))

The 'exhaustive control', alias raising, type[10] can be seen as a direct consequence of the lack of independent temporal deixis on the lexical verb, as already

---

10 While most studies on the Balkan "subjunctive" follow the classical Government and Binding (GB) analysis (Chomsky 1981) from the early 1990's in establishing a general divide between obligatory and non-obligatory control, Spyropoulos (2007) proposes a tripartite distinction,

established by the classical Government and Binding (GB) analysis that goes back originally to Varlokosta (1994). In (12), for example, the "subjunctive" verb selected by the modal/aspectual verb forms a single event with the latter so that the interpretation of the entire sentence is that of knowing how/beginning to perform the driving acitivity. See also the discussion in Landau 2004; Kapetangianni and Seely 2007; Krapova 2001; Spyropoulos 2007. If so, then the data in (12)-(14) come as no surprise: the temporal adverbials cannot have a time reference distinct from the time reference of the modal or aspectual verb, as already pointed out in Varlokosta and Hornstein (1993):

(12) *O Kostas kseri/ arxise simera na odhiji (*avrio)* (Grk)
the Kosta knows-/started-3SG today PRT drive-3SG (*tomorrow)
'Today Kosta knows how/started-3SG to drive (*tomorrow)
(Roussou 2009: 1826, ex. (32a))

(13) *Kosta znae/započva sega da šofira (*utre)* (Bulg)
Kosta knows-/started-3SG now PRT drive-3SG (*tomorrow)
'Now Kosta knows how/begins to drive (*tomorrow)'

(14) a. *Am reușit să plec (*mîine)* (Rom)
AUX-1SG managed PRT leave-1SG tomorrow
'I managed to leave (*tomorrow)'
b. *Încep să citesc /*fi citit*
begin-1SG PRT read-1SG past read
'I'm beginning to (*have) read'
(Alboiu 2007: 198, ex. (23 a,b))

Exhaustive control (i.e., raising) "subjunctives" are consequently untensed in the Balkan languages (Landau 2000, Wurmbrand 2001, a.o.). While most authors take [–T] to be a feature on C, we would like to extend the analogy with Romance restructuring discussed in Section 2. and suggest that such configurations lack a temporal layer on top of the lexical verb (a temporally unsaturated domain, Alboiu 2007: 198). If we keep with Stowell's (1982) original proposal that temporal deixis is strictly dependent on the presence of a CP domain, this amounts to saying that restructuring verbs cannot select an embedded clause (i.e., a CP). This is the first important piece of our monoclausal analysis of Balkan "restructuring". The second piece regards the

---

based on Modern Greek, which is similar in spirit to our proposal: exhaustive control (our 'raising'), partial control, and no control.

unavailability of a distinct subject position for the "emdedded" verb. Indeed, it is often pointed out that modal and aspectual predicates in the Balkan languages do not allow a second Nominative subject, see (15a-c):[11,12]

(15) a. *O Janis   kseri   na kolumbai (*i Maria)*   (Grk)
        the John-NOM know-3SG PRT swim-3SG (the Mary-NOM)
        'John knows how (*Mary) to swim'
        (Kapetangianni and Seely 2007: 144, ex. (23))
    b. *Victor încearca (*Mihai) să cînte*   (Rom)
        Victor try-3SG (*Mihai) PRT sing-3SG
        'Victor is trying (*Mihai) to sing'
        (Alboiu 2007: 190 ex. 9a)
    c. *Ivan znae   (*Marija) da pluva*   (Bulg)
        Ivan know-3SG (*Marija) PRT swim-3SG
        'Ivan can swim (*Maria)'

---

11 Sometimes it is said that obligatory control verbs select a phi-defective I, which does not check Nominative case. Such an approach would be problematic in the face of the Modern Greek example in (i) since the modifying adjective bears Nominative case even though an independent lexical subject is excluded:

(i) *O Janis   kseri na ine   haroumenos   (*o Vassilis)*
    The John-NOM knows PRT be-3SG happy-NOM.SG.M (the Bill-NOM)
    'John know how (*Bill) to be happy'
    (Kapetangianni and Seely 2007: 150, ex. (47/48))

For our analysis (i) does not represent a counterexample since the agreement on the nominal predicate is predicated not of the subject but of the entire A-chain bearing Nominative, which connects the matrix with the lower subject trace:

(ii) [$_{CP}$ ... [$_{TP}$ DPsubject$_j$...[$_{FP}$ ...DPsubject$_j$ V$_{functional}$ [$_{VP}$ t$_i$ V $_{lexical}$]

12 In certain cases, reported from Modern Greek, a second, distinct, subject is apparently possible under specific semantico-pragmatic circumstances, and with verbs like *prospatho* 'try' and *katafero* 'manage/succeed':

(i) *O Kostas katafere   na fiji   o jios tu.*
    the Kostas managed-3SG PRT leave-3SG the son his
    'Kosta managed for his son to leave'

We agree with Terzi (1992: 37–45) that *try* is ambiguous between two lexical items, *try*1 and *try*2, and accordingly, may or may not be restructuring. See also Joseph (1992: 206–212) on this usage, where it is suggested that *try* with a different embedded subject means something like "facilitate things such that...".

Given the absence of alternative morphology on the dependent verb in the above contexts, the obligatory present tense can be taken to be, along the lines of Progovac (1993), the default form of the verb. In other words, we take this default realization (i.e., verbal root + agreement features) to be equivalent to a syntactic infinitive.[13] Each functional verb is inserted in a dedicated functional position within the structural hierarchy of the clause and selects a different segment of the extended projection of VP given in (4) above and repeated here in an abridged form (Cinque 2006: 91, 93):

(4) [$Mod_{epistemic}$ .... [$Mod_{possibility}$ [$Mod_{volition}$ [$Mod_{obligation}$ [$Asp_{terminative}$ [$Asp_{inceptive}$
    'must'   'it's possible'   'want'   'have to'   'stop'   'begin'

[$Mod_{ability}$ [$Asp_{frustrative/success}$ [$Mod_{permission}$ .... [$Asp_{completive}$ [V_{infin}]]]]]]]]]]]
 'can1'   'manage'   'can2'   'finish'

The hierarchy in (4) implies that the "subjunctive" particle does not occupy a single structural position. Rather, it introduces different types of verbal complements to restructuring verbs which belong to the functional field of the same clause. We are aware that such an approach goes against most previous treatments of the "subjunctive" particle, which is usually taken to be the head of a single Mood projection (MP) (Philippaki-Warburton 1994, 1998, Rivero 1994, Giannakidou 1998, 2009 a.o.), or a complementizer, the head of CP (Varlokosta 1993, Roussou 2000, 2010 a.o.). From the point of view of the hierarchy in (4), neither of these approaches can be accepted. We leave the formal elaboration of the proposal for future work, but here we just mention the fact that both of these approaches would have problems accounting for the possibility of multiple particles as in (16). The fact that the only interpretation available in (16) is the one in which the possibility modal takes the deontic ones (ability or permission) in its scope cannot be made to follow from any independent syntactic requirement on the order of clauses. On the contrary, in an approach that postulates a sequence

---

[13] For a similar proposal about Modern Greek, see Iatridou (1993), and Varlokosta (1994), who argue that the lack of temporal properties renders the na+V complex in Greek non-finite.

We are well aware that the issue of finiteness has been a notorious problem in dealing with Balkan "subjunctives" given that they appear to be morphologically finite. As discussed by Spyropoulos (2007: 159), there are three possible approaches to this issue: a) to maintain the strict association between control and nonfiniteness and assume that "subjunctives" in control environments are syntactically nonfinite; b) to maintain the finiteness of the "subjunctive" clause and assume that control can be established with null or overt elements other than PRO; c) to maintain both the finiteness of the "subjunctive" and the strict association between control and PRO and to assume that PRO can be case-marked with its distribution following from the referential properties of both PRO and the "subjunctive" C and T heads. Here we adhere to the first option for reasons that become clear later.

of dedicated functional verbs associated with a specific interpretation, the correct interpretations simply follow from the order of the projections themselves without any further stipulation, thus predicting the two available interpretations in (i) (whereby the first 'can' is interpreted as 'possibility' and the second 'can' as 'ability' or 'permission'), while excluding the opposite combinations in (ii):

(16) [CP [TP pro *možem* [*da* [FP *možem* [*da* [VP *vlezem*]]]]] (Bulg)
     can-1PL PRT can-1PL PRT enter-1PL

   (i) 'It is possible for us to be able to enter'; It is possible for us to be permitted to enter'
   (ii) '*We are able for it to be possible for us to enter'; *We are permitted for it to be possible for us to enter'.

Additional evidence that no CP structure is present in the verbal complement of what we take to be restructuring verbs comes from the fact that "true" complementizers in those Balkan languages which allow them in "subjunctive" contexts are excluded in this configuration (see (17) – Alboiu 2007; Grosu and Horvath 1987; Dobrovie-Sorin 2001 for Romanian, and Turano 1994 for Albanian).[14]

(17) a. *Victor încearcă [ca pe Mihai [să-l ajute]] (Rom)
        Victor try-3SG that PE Mihai PRT-him-CL.ACC help-3SG
        'Victor is trying to help Mihai'
        (Alboiu 2007, p. 197, ex. (20a))

---

[14] Spyropoulos (2007) claims that even in such constructions an overt DP subject or a strong subject pronoun can be licensed in the subjunctive complement (see (i)), which is also true of Bulgarian (see (ii)):

(i) *O Janis   kseri   na xorevi   ki aftos kalo tsamiko.* (Grk)
    the Janis-NOM know-3SG PRT dance-3SG and he good tsamiko-ACC
    'John knows how to dance tsamiko well too'
    (Spyropoulou 2007, 167, ex. (23b))

(ii) *Ivan znae   da tantsuva i toj   vals dobre.* (Bulg)
     John know-3SG PRT dance-3SG and he waltz well
     'John knows how to dance the waltz well too'

However, coreferential subject pronouns are possible in simple clauses as well, cf. (iii), and are in fact emphatic pronouns possibly starting out together with the subject (cf. Burzio 1986: 109–115).

(iii) *Ivan idva   i   toj.* (Bulg)
      Ivan come-3SG and he-NOM
      'Ivan is coming too'

b. *Harrova [që librin ta lexoja] (Alb)
   forgot-1SG that books PRT read-SUBJ-1SG
   'I forgot to read books'
   (Giuseppina Turano, p.c.)

3.2 Biclausal control infinitives

The restructuring modal and aspectual predicates seen in Section 3.1. stand in sharp contrast to the other two structural types identified above: b) control infinitive-like constructions, and c) Romance-type true subjunctive constructions. First, in each of these latter environments, the matrix verb and the embedded one may have independent Tense. This property argues in favor of a biclausal configuration, all the more so considering that in e.g., (18) the higher verbs *očakvam* 'expect' and *otkazvam* 'refuse' can have arguments of their own independent of those of the embedded verbs:

(18) a. *Očakvam <ot vsički>   da dojdat/   da sa pristignali   do 6 časa.*
       expect-1SG from everybody PRT come-3PL/PRT are-3PL arrived by 6 o'clock
       'I expect that everybody comes'/I expect that everybody has arrived by 6 o'clock'
   b. *Otkazax <na Ivan> da   zamina   s nego.*
       refused-1SG to Ivan PRT leave-1SG with him
       'I told John that I am not leaving with him'

(18a) and (18b) differ however in the semantics of the embedded tense and in the overt expression of the embedded subject. Consider first (18b). A major characteristic of verbs like 'refuse' is that they require their complement clause to have a fixed time reference: either simultaneous with respect to matrix tense or future oriented (irrealis). Accordingly, such verbs admit temporal adverbs like *now* and *tomorrow* though not past time adverbials. As a reflex, the embedded verb cannot have a past time reference, cf. (19b):

(19) a. *Otkazvam da zamina   (sega/utre)*
       refuse-1SG PRT leave-1SG (now/tomorrow)
       'I refuse to leave now/tomorrow'
   b. **Otkazvam da săm   zaminal včera*
       refuse-1SG PRT am-1SG left   yesterday
       *'I refuse to have left yesterday'

Other characteristics of this class[15] include the possibility of both partial control and split antecedents, illustrated in (20). Given these restrictions, the structure underlying (20) cannot be a restructuring configuration since as we saw above in relation to Modern Greek (10)-(11), true restructuring predicates require exhaustive control and cannot take split antecedents. (20) thus contrasts with (21) featuring the restructuring predicate 'manage':

(20) **Ivan**$_i$ misli,   če **az**$_j$ otkazvam   ec$_{i+j}$ da otidem   zaedno   na kino.
     John think-3SG that I refuse-1SG   PRT go-1PL together to cinema
     'John thinks that I refuse to go to the cinema together'

(21) ***Ivan**$_i$ misli, če **az**$_j$ uspjax   ec$_{i+j}$ da otidem   zaedno na kino.
     John thinks that I managed-1SG   PRT go-1PL together to cinema
     '*John thinks that I managed for us to go to the cinema together'

In view of this contrast, and considering the properties of the embedded subject, which with predicates like 'refuse' must be null (cf. the ungrammaticality of (22a)), we would like to generalize that a bi-clausal analysis is most suitable to render complements of *refuse*-type verbs. Moreover, such complements are obligatory control structures whose embedded subject is PRO (cf. (22b)):

(22) a. *Az otkazvam ti   da otideš.
        refuse-1SG you-NOM PRT go-2SG
        *'I refuse for you to go'
     b. Az$_i$ otkazvam   [$_{CP}$ [$_{TP}$ PRO$_i$ da   otida]]
        refuse-1SG   PRT go-1SG
        'I refuse PRO to go'

3.3 Biclausal Romance-type subjunctives

Consider now a verb like *očakvam* 'expect' from Bulgarian. Unlike both restructuring and obligatory control verbs, such verbs pose no tense restrictions on the embedded verb (and would thus be [+T] in Landau's 2000 terms). Secondly, they may also take an overt embedded subject which is disjoint in reference from the matrix one. See (23a), which exemplifies both of these properties and recall that

---

[15] This class comprises mostly object control predicates (see Sočanac, this volume), as well as a few subject control predicates like *accept*.

neither property is available for the restructuring type (Section 3.1.) nor for the control type seen above with verbs like *otkazvam* 'refuse' (Section 3.2.). We thus propose that *očakvam* 'expect' *da* + V structures are to be assimilated to a subjunctive structure of the Romance-type (compare (23a) with (23b) from Italian).

(23) a. *Včera očakvax   [ti   da   si   rešil*
        yesterday expected-1SG you-NOM PRT are-2SG do
        zadačite   do utre],
        math-homeworks.DET by tomorrow
        no sega viždam, če šte ti   trjabva   cjala sedmitsa
        but now see-1SG that will you-DAT need-3SG whole week
        'Yesterday I expected that you would do your math homework by tomorrow but now I see that you will need an entire week'
    b. *Mi   aspettavo che tu   facessi   i   compiti oggi*
        me-CL.DAT expect that you-NOM did-2SG ART homework today
        'I expected that you did your homework today'

Confirming evidence that verbs like 'expect' enter a Romance-type subjunctive is the fact that they show the hallmark of the construction, namely the so-called obviation effect, according to which the overt embedded subject cannot be identical to the matrix subject. Compare (24a,b) with (24c) from Italian:[16]

(24) a. **Očakvam az da zamina   utre*   (Bulg)
        expect-1SG I PRT leave-1SG tomorrow
    b. **Mă aștept ca eu să   plec   mâine*   (Rom)
        expect-1SG that I PRT leave-1SG tomorrow
        (Gabriela Soare, p.c.)
    c. **Mi   aspetto   che io   parta   domani*   (It)
        me-CL.DAT expect-1SG that I-NOM leave-SUBJ tomorrow
        'I expect that I leave-SUBJ-1SG tomorrow

---

16 These verbs can also take a regular indicative complement introduced by a regular indicative complementizer in all of the Balkan languages:

(i) a. *Očakvam,   če   šte dojdeš   utre.*   (Bulg)
       expect-1SG that will come-2SG tomorrow
       'I expect that you will come tomorrow'
    b. *Elpizo   oti θa erθi*   (Grk)
       hope-1SG that will come-3SG
       'I hope that he will come'
       (Spyropoulos 2007: 162, (ex. 6))

Cf. *Mi aspetto che tu parta domani* (It)
me-CL.DAT expect-1SG that you-NOM leave-SUBJ.2SF tomorrow
'I expect that you leave tomorrow'

Without the overt embedded subject (*az/eu* 'I') the examples in (24a,b) become grammatical, which we take to mean that the Balkan verbs of the *expect*-type are ambiguous between a Romance subjunctive, exhibiting an obligatory obviation effect (cf. (24c)), and a Romance infinitive (cf. 25b) circumventing the obviation effect by admitting a PRO subject in a control configuration:

(25) a. *Očakvam* PRO *da zamina utre* (Bulg)
 expect-1SG PRT leave-1SG tomorrow
 b. *Mi aspetto* PRO *di partire domani* (It)
 me-CL:DAT expect-1SG to leave-INF tomorrow
 'I expect to leave tomorrow'

Like the other control verbs discussed above, 'expect' can also take split antecedents, as well as exhibit partial control. Observe the parallelism between (26a) and (26b), which repeats (20) featuring the control verb *otkazvam*:

(26) a. *Ivan$_i$ misli* [$_{CP}$ *če az$_j$ očakvam* [$_{CP}$ [$_{TP}$ PRO$_{i+j}$ *da zaminem zaedno utre*]]]
 John thinks that I expect-1SG PRT leave-1PL together tomorrow
 'John thinks that I expect us to leave tomorrow'
 b. *Ivan$_i$ misli* [$_{CP}$ *če az$_j$ otkazvam* [$_{CP}$ [$_{TP}$ PRO$_{i+j}$ *da otidem zaedno na kino*]]].
 John think-3SG that I refuse-1SG PRT go-1PL together to cinema
 'John thinks that I refuse to go to the cinema together'

3.4 Ambiguities with desiderative predicates

What about the class of desideratives? According to a long tradition desideratives/intentional verbs, among which 'want', are classified as non-obligatory control (NOC) predicates. From our point of view these predicates are special since they turn out to be three-way ambiguous. First, they are like 'expect' in entering the control construction See (27a) and (27b), which illustrate the availability of partial control:

(27) a. *Ivan$_i$ iska* PRO$_j$ *da zamine utre*
 Ivan want-3SG PRT leave-3SG tomorrow
 'John wants to leave tomorrow'

b. *Az$_i$ mislja če Ivan$_j$ iska PRO$_{j+i}$ da zaminem zaedno utre.*
 I think that John want-3SG PRT leave-1PL together tomorrow
 'I think that John wants for us [John and me] to leave together tomorrow'

Second, they enter the Romance-like subjunctive one. See (28) illustrating the possibility for a disjoint embedded subject as with *očakvam*-type verbs (cf. (23a) above):

(28) *Ivan$_j$ iska Petăr$_k$ da e veče pristignal*
 John want-3SG Peter PRT is already arrived
 'John wants for Peter to have arrived already'

Third, desiderative verbs plausibly enter a restructuring configuration as well, like 'want' verbs in Romance, where they are three way ambiguous. Romance 'want' verbs can be restructuring, as indicated by the CC test ((29a)) but they also lend themselves to a control structure (cf. (29b) illustrating the possibility for partial control and split antecedents), as well as to a subjunctive structure with obligatory obviation ((29c)):

(29) a. *Lo$_i$ voglio vedere t$_i$*
 him-CL.ACC want-1SG see-INF
 'I want to see him'
 b. *Gianni$_i$ dice che Maria$_j$ vorrebbe PRO$_{i+j}$ andare tutti assieme al cinema.*
 John says that Maria would.like go-INF all together to.ART cinema
 'John says that Mary would like to go all together to the movies'
 c. *Voglio che tu/*io venga*
 want-1SG that you/I come-SUBJ
 'I want you to come'

However, in the Balkan languages CC is not available with restructuring verbs, 'want' included, apart from the few cases found in dialectal varieties, to be discussed in sections 5 and 6. Indirect evidence about the restructuring properties of 'want' also comes from the few instances of CC in Old Church Slavonic (OCS) and Medieval Greek, to be reviewed in the next section. Contemporary Serbian, generally considered as a peripheral member of the Balkan Sprachbund, appears to be the only language which instantiates CC with 'want' verbs allowing this to happen not just with an infinitive but also with a finite *da* + V complex, as in e.g., (30). (See Sims and Joseph, this volume, on other ways in which BCS differs from the "core" languages in the Balkans regarding the verbal complex):

(30) *?Tanja ga   želi   da   vidi*
    Tanja him-CL.ACC want-3SG PRT see-3SG
    'Tanja wants to see him'
    (Progovac 1993: 119)

To summarize, in this section we have shown that when compared with Romance, the Balkan embedded structures containing a "subjunctive" particle correspond to three distinct constructions: a) a restructuring infinitive; b) a non-restructuring control infinitive; c) a Romance type subjunctive. Structurally, these three cases differ in that while the first is monoclausal, the other two are biclausal.

4 Infinitive retention and CC in the Balkan languages and in the "Balkan" dialects of Southern Italy

In this section, we show that the infinitive and CC, to the extent the latter is instantiated in the Balkan languages, are two interrelated phenomena available only with restructuring verbs or a subset thereof. To this end, we briefly review the contexts where the infinitive has been retained in those Balkan languages that still show traces of it in their contemporary form. However, although CC is contingent on the presence of an infinitive, the reverse is not true since the class of verbs with which CC is permitted is smaller than the class of verbs that can combine with an infinitive. This seems universally true,[17] and it is certainly true of the older stages of those Balkan languages which used to have infinitives but have by now entirely eliminated them or have considerably reduced them.

---

[17] For example, Italian CC is available only with restructuring predicates, as mentioned (see section 2) but is unavailable with control infinitives (i):

(i) *La   rifiuto   di vedere.*
    her-CL.ACC refuse-1SG PRT see-INF

See Cinque (2004, n.2) for an overview of languages that overtly show syntactic effects of restructuring.

4.1 Infinitive retention and clitic climbing from a historical perspective: Bulgarian and Greek

In Modern Bulgarian, Macedonian, and Greek, languages with no infinitives, no instances of CC can be detected (31a-c). However, we come back to some instances of CC in dialectal data (see section 5).

(31) a. *Az **go**   moga   da vidja   (Bulg)
    I him-CL-ACC can-1SG PRT see-1SG
    'I can see him'
  b. *Jas **go**   sakam   da vidam   (Mac)
    I him-CL-ACC want -1SG PRT see-1SG
    'I want to see him'
    (Marina Patche, p.c.)
  c. *I Maria **to**   prospathise na grapsi.   (Grk)
    the Maria it-CL.ACC tried-3SG   PRT write-3SG
    'Maria tried to write it'
    (Terzi 1994: 104)

4.1.1 Clitic climbing in the history of Bulgarian

As is well-known, although in the history of Bulgarian the first instances of infinitive replacement by a *da*-construction[18] are found relatively early (Mirčev 1978, 233), the infinitive was a living category until the end of the Middle Bulgarian period (14th c.) and even after (15th c.- 16th c.), as witnessed by the competing occurrences in texts like the Troya legend (Trojanska pritča, a 13th c. manuscript)) and the Wallachian documents (16th c.). Judging by the examples given in the literature, the infinitive would persist most often after modal and auxiliary verbs (Joseph 1983: 120). Mirčev (1978: 234) and Haralampiev (2001: 172) mention instances, from the Troya legend, of *hotjati* 'want', *mošti* 'can', *načęti* 'begin',

---

18 The first uses of the *da*-construction are seemingly related to the use of the particle as a marker of disjoint reference in contexts (e.g., in final clauses) where an infinitive would imply subject identity (strict coreference). Sometimes, however, the two constructions appear to be (near) parallels. For example, in Codex Zografiensis we find *isplъnišę sa dъnьe roditi ei* 'the days arrived [for her] to give-INF birth', while in the same place Codex Assemanius uses a *da*-construction *isplъnišę sa dъnije da roditъ* 'the days arrived PRT give-3SG birth' (Mirčev 1978: 233).

smjati 'dare', *oumjati* 'can =be able to', which would preserve the infinitive even though in a reduced form.[19]

What is interesting for our purposes here is that all of these verbs are restructuring and moreover, a selection of these allowed CC already in Old Bulgarian (OB)/Old Church Slavonic (OCS). From a preliminary empirical study based on electronic corpora it emerges that some pronominal clitics[20] (mostly in *Codex Suprasliensis*) could climb (apparently optionally) in front of modal functional verbs like 'want' (32a-b), 'can' (32c), and 'have to' (32d). The first example is ambiguous between a modal (*volitive*) reading and a future periphrasis, but the others have an unambiguous modal interpretation, including the one in (32d) which contains a non-auxiliary use of *imjati* 'have to'.[21]

(32) a. *čъto **mi** xoštete dati* (Cod.Supr., 3, 36, 205b, 27)
what me-CL.DAT want-2PL give-INF
Τί **μοι** θέλετε δοῦναι
'What do you want to give me/What will you give me'

b. *ašte **mi** se xošti izvjastiti* (Cod. Supr. 4, 33a, 20–21)
if me-CL.DAT REFL want-2SG tell-INF
Εἰ θέλεις **μοι** πληροφορῆσαι
'If you want to tell me'

c. *čto **ti** mogǫt dati ...* (Cod.Supr., 3, 37, 213r, 12–13)
what you-DAT can-3PL give-INF
τί **σοι** δύνανται δοῦναι
'What can they give you?'

d. [Focus *div'no čoudo*] *ti imam sъpovjadati·*
wonderful miracle you-CL.DAT have-1SG tell-INF
(Cod. Supr. 19, 112v, 20–21)
Παράδοξον θέαμά **σοι** ἔχω ὑφηγήσασθαι.
'I have to tell you a wonderful miracle'

---

19 Only in Early Modern Bulgarian did the *da*-constructions replace the infinitive in all contexts but the periphrastic future which was already in stable use since the 14th c. By that time *da* probably had ceased to mark disjoint reference and was reinterpreted as an irrealis marker.

20 According to Večerka (1989: 42), of all pronominal forms only the dative ones of the 1st and 2nd person pronouns were "true" clitics in OCS; the reflexive pronoun, the personal pronouns in the accusative (*mę, tę, sę*), as well as the anaphoric pronoun that would render 3rd person, were at this stage "semi-clitics" and only later evolved into true clitics.

21 Perhaps a similar conclusion can also be made for New Testament Greek, based solely on the original examples for the OB/OCS translations, but we don't discuss this possibility for lack of data.

In their derived position before the modal clitics show second position effects. The fact that in all of these examples the pronoun is an argument of the lower verb but targets a position after the first CP element of the entire clause is a clear indication that we are dealing with a restructuring configuration. Alongside (32a-d), one also finds the more frequent pattern in which the clitic shows up in between the modal and the lexical verb, cf. (33):

(33) *Simone, imatъ* **ti** *něčьto* *rešti.* (Luke 7:40, Mar, Zogr, Assem)
Simon, have-1SG you-CL.DAT somethimg tell-INF
Σίμων, ἔχω **σοί** τι εἰπεῖν
'Simon, I have something to tell you'

Note that in (33), the clitic is again second within its intonational phrase. We will not discuss here the factors underlying the change to second position cliticization in OB/OCS (for a detailed analysis see Pancheva 2005), so we just note that apparently it has been affected by factors such as V-initial, as in (33), presence of a complementizer like *jako* 'that', *jakože* 'as', *ižde* 'where', *e(g)da* 'that ... not'*, ašte* 'if'; an initial wh-word or a relative pronoun like *iže* 'who, which', etc.; fronted discourse material like focalized or topicalized noun phrases, as well as scene setting adverbs/adverbial PPs (for details and examples see Krapova and Dimitrova 2016). Nevertheless, this pattern was obviously unstable since alongside (32a), for example, one also finds (34), in which the clitic does not climb to second clausal positon after the *wh*-word:

(34) *čto hoštete* **mi** *dati*
what want-2PL me-CL.DAT give-INF
(Cod.Supr., 3, 36, 206a, 10);(Mt. 26:15, Mar, Zogr)
Τί θέλετέ μοι δοῦναι
'What do you want to give me/What will you give me'

It is well known that Bulgarian clitics did not remain 2P clitics (i.e., enclitic to the first prosodic word in the clause) but shifted towards preverbal ones (i.e., verbal proclitics) in the later history of the language (for the history of this shift in Bulgarian, see Pancheva 2005). While we can preliminarily take the dubious patterns to be an instantiation of competing strategies for pronoun placement, more evident in contexts where the restructuring verb is ambiguous between a true modal and a future auxiliary, it is significant that in the later history of the language – and this is true already of Middle Bulgarian – the position of the clitic pronoun gets fixed between the modal and the lexical verb. Given that the same ambiguity in clitic placement is found in the original Greek text, these word order changes might well be due to translation effects. Importantly, with the advent of the *da*-constructions no instances of CC are attested in the later history of the language, so substitution of the infinitive by the *da*-construction[22] follows an already well-established pattern of clitic placement.

(35) a. *hoštǫ   da mi   dasi   ousěčenǫ   glavǫ*
   want-1SG PRT me-CL.DAT give-2SG cut-off-ACC head-ACC
   'I want that you give me the head that has been cut off'

---

[22] Restructuring verbs seem to have played a role also in infinitive retention. It is interesting to note that remnants of the infinitive (the so-called short or abbreviated infinitive) are found in standard Bulgarian after the root modal *can* and the aspectual *stop* (in its imperative form), as well as after the negative imperative auxiliary *nedej* 'don't'. Note that most of the short infinitival forms reported here appear under negation although it is not clear what role negation has played in the preservation of the infinitive.

(i) a. *Ne možeš   go   nameri.*
   not can-2SG him/it-CL.Acc find-INF(short)
   'You cannot find him/it'
 b. *Stiga   plaka*
   stop-IMP cry-INF(short)
   'Stop crying'.
 c. *Nedej   mi   govori.*
   don't-IMP me-CL.DAT talk-INF(short)
   'Don't say it to me/Don't even mention it'

The literature reports on dialects (Balkan and Moesian) in which a short form of the infinitive is used with verbs such as *moga* 'can', *smeja* 'dare', *rača* 'want' (Stojkov 1993/2002: 266). See also the data in Sobolev 2003: 68):

(ii) a. *Sigà ni mògă   izdărže   nă tăkvăs svàdbă*
   now not can-1SG bear-INF to such   wedding
   'Now I cannot support (financially) such a wedding'.
 b. *Ni smějă   prudùmă*   (Gabrovo region)
   not dare-1SG utter-INF (a word)
   'I do not dare utter a word'
 c. *Ni mòjăt   gu   izède*   (Sliven region)
   not can-3PL it-CL.ACC eat-INF
   'They can't eat it'
 d. *S ništo   ne mòem ti   pomògna*   (Pirdop region)
   with nothing not can-1PL you-CL.DAT help-INF
   'We can't help in any way'

Haralampiev (2001: 172) also points out that the process of infinitive abbreviation is positionally restricted and must be put in relation to the class of what we here call 'restructuring' predicates. This is evident not just from the first instances of this process in Codex Zografensis and Codex Suprasliensis, but also from the later Troya legend in which the full infinitive occurs with the functional verbs 'want', 'begin', 'can', 'dare', 'know', while the short infinitive (in *-t*) takes place only with a subset of these, i.e., 'can' and 'want' (negative form). Cf. also the examples above.

b. *čto hošteši   da ti   sъtvorjǫ*
   what want-2SG PRT you-CL.DAT make-3PL
   'What do you want to do for you'

4.1.2 Clitic climbing in Medieval Greek and in some modern Greek varieties

As far as the history of Greek is concerned, cases of CC with *thelo* 'want' have been reported from the period of Medieval Greek. As discussed in Pappas (2004), Medieval Greek pronouns could attach to *thelo* rather than to the surviving infinitive in the future periphrasis. There is no evidence that this pattern occurred in volitive constructions, i.e., in those in which the modal verb preserves its modal meaning but such an occurrence would be highly improbable given that the future auxiliary is grammaticalized since the 10th c., i.e. much earlier than its Bulgarian counterpart (14th c.) (Mertyris 2008). The following examples are from Joseph (1983: 64) [23] and Pappas (2004: 92):

(36) a. *kathõ:s to théleis   máthei*   (The Chronicle of Morea 1197, 14th c.)
        as   it want-2SG learn-INF
        'as you will learn it'
        (Joseph 1983: 64)
    b. *opu mɛ θeli   pari*   (Digenēs 1016, 12th c.)
       which me want-3SG take-INF
       'which will take me'
       (Pappas 2004: 92)

As noted in Pappas (2004: 94), other verb types in (Later) Medieval Greek like aspectuals *arxizo/arxo* 'begin', implicational verbs like *tolmo, tharro* 'dare', modals like *mporo* 'can', *elpizo* 'hope' appearing in combination with an infinitive did not allow CC. Just as in OCS, as well as in Middle Bulgarian, the clitic would more often attach in between *thelo* and the main verb, which according to Mackridge (1993: 338) cited in Pappas (2004: 92) can still be interpreted as

---

[23] According to Joseph's analysis, the periphrastic future construction, which made productive use of the infinitive in the medieval period, was reanalyzed, due to a sound change (the loss of the final –*n* of the infinitive), as a V1 V2 finite sequence (*thelo grapho* 'want write') so that the infinitive came to be homophonous with 3sg present indicative (in 15–16th c. colloquial language) which would subsequently give rise to the MG analytic future (*the(lo:) grapho* > *tha grapho* 'I will write'). On the development of the future in Medieval and Modern Greek also see Joseph and Pappas (2002).

attachment to *thelo,* i.e., as a sort of CC or 'argument incorporation' (Joseph 1990) in the future periphrasis, presumably in the absence of conditions relevant for second position cliticization such as the presence of a complementizer or a CP element, fronted constituents etc.

Cases of obligatory CC are reported for the contemporary Greek variety spoken in the Salento Peninsula of Italy (Griko) (see Chatzikyriakidis 2009, 2010a,b, and Baldissera 2012, 2013). However, the phenomenon is observed with only two verbs, namely the equivalents of 'can' and 'finish':

(37) a. *Sa   sòzzane   insultètsi (*sa)*
       you-CL.ACC can-3PL.Past insult-INF (you-CL.ACC)
       'They could insult you'
       (Baldissera 2012: 61)
   b. *To   sotzi   vorasi? Ne, sotzi*
       it-CL.ACC can-3SG buy-INF yes can-3SG
       'Can he buy it? Yes, he can'
       (Chatzikyriakidis 2010a, ex. (43))
   c. *To   spitseo   tse (*to)   torisi   (*to)   avri*
       it-CL.ACC finish-1SG COMP (*it-CL.ACC) see-INF (*it-CL.ACC) tomorrow
       'I will finish seeing it tomorrow'
       (Chatzikyriakidis 2010a, ex. (10))

The noteworthy fact about CC in Grecia Salentina is that these are also the only two verbs that still take an infinitival complement. According to Manolessou (2005), the interesting thing about infinitive retention in Italiot is that the structures show a close correspondence to those of infinitive retention in Medieval Greek (Mackridge 1996) and Early Modern Greek, which is usually taken as an argument in favor of the Koine origin of the Greek dialects spoken in Italy. In Grecanico, the Greek variety spoken in Calabria, the infinitive is retained to a greater extent but CC is unattested even though the contexts where the infinitive is used until present day coincide precisely with the ones described by Rohlfs (1958) for Grecia Salentina.[24]

The above pattern shows that CC is contingent upon infinitive retention but is a phenomenon independent from it in that it is not found with all 'restructuring' predicates taking infinitives.

---

[24] These contexts are: the modal verb *sozo* 'can'; the aspectual *spitseo* 'finish'; the causatives *kanno, afinno,* and the perception verbs *torò* 'see', *akuo* 'hear'. The last two contexts are unavailable in Griko as of today (Baldissera 2012: 59, cit. Remberger 2011).

4.2 Infinitive retention and clitic climbing in Balkan Romance

Moving on to Balkan Romance, Romanian, where the infinitive is still in use, allows CC with the few verbs that have retained the possibility of selecting a bare infinitive complement: the modal verb *putea* 'can/be able' (38a) and, at least until the first half of the 20th c., the verb of 'internal capacity' *şti* 'know' (38b) (Pană Dindelegan 2013: 220);[25] the deontic modal 'have to', as well as the aspectual verbs *termina*, and *ispravi* 'finish' taking a supine *de*-complement (38c). With these structures CC is obligatory and Romanian grammars interpret it as evidence in favor of a complex predicate formation which we take to be a restructuring configuration:

(38) a. *O   pot   vedea*
       her-CL.ACC can-1SG see-INF
       'I can see her'
   b. *O   ştiu   cînta*
       her-CL.ACC know-1SG sing-INF
       'I know how to sing it'
   c. *O   are de terminat*
       her-CL.ACC   has DE finish-SUP
       'He has to finish it'
   d. *Cartea   o   termin   de citit*
       book-DET   her-CL.ACC finished-1SG DE read-SUP
       'The book, I finished reading'
       (Pană Dindelegan 2013, ex. 387)

As discussed in Amman and van der Auwera (2004: 303, fn.19), there is an areal and diachronic North-South cline in Romanian and its varieties. Megleno-Romanian and Aromanian seem to have restricted the infinitive after modal verbs (cf. also Hill and Tomić 2008). Tomić (2006: 540) reports that the Megleno-Romanian infinitive is used only as a complement of the modal verbs *puteari* 'can' and *trăbuiri* 'need to/should'. It is said that there are no infinitives in Aromanian, although Manzini and Savoia (2016) report Aromanian data from locations in South Albania which have infinitival complements with–*re* inflected infinitives

---

25 In Old Romanian bare infinitival constructions also occurred with other verbs such as *căuta* 'try', *cuteza* 'dare'. Some of them are attested in the north-western dialects (Pană Dindelegan, 2013: 220).

(so-called long infinitives) after restructuring modal, aspectual and motion verbs. However, neither of these languages has CC, according to the existing literature.

The only other Balkan Romance language with clitic climbing is Istro-Romanian (Zegrean 2012). Judging from Zegrean's work, this language appears quite parallel to Romanian in terms of both CC and the distribution of the infinitive after the following two classes of verbs:
a) modal verbs: *moręi* 'must', *putę* 'can/may', *vrę* 'want/will', where CC is optional
b) aspectual verbs: *pošnę* 'start', *fini* 'finish', *provęi* 'try', where CC is obligatory.

(39) a. *Io voi   (vo)   putę   (vo)   vedę   (*vo)*[26]
     I will-1SG (her) can-1SG (her) see-INF (*her)
     'I'll be able to see her'
     (Zegrean 2012: 119)
   b. *Io voi   (vo)   pošni   (*vo)   prontivęi.*
     I will   her-CL.ACC start   her-CL.ACC   prepare-INF
     'I will start preparing it'
     (Zegrean 2012: 120)

4.3 More on the independence of infinitive retention and clitic climbing: the case of Albanian

As is well-known, Albanian does not feature a true infinitive in its grammatical system. Some of the functions of the Indo-European infinitive are expressed in some Tosk Albanian dialects, as well as in standard Albanian, by a general non-finite form *për të* + participle (used in purpose clauses and relative clauses), while the Gheg area uses a periphrastic infinitive built up by means of the preposition *me* ('with') and a participle. However, in neither of these varieties is CC attested. See (40), from Krapova and Turano (2015):[27]

(40) a. (*I)   *dua*   *t'i*   *takoj*   (Tosk/Albanian)
     them-CL want-1SG TË+them meet.SUBJ-1SG
     'I want to meet them'

---

[26] The (feminine accusative) clitic pronoun cannot stay in the lowest position after the lexical verb – the canonical position of the direct object, in which full NPs appear.
[27] But see the case of CC with a verb like 'finish' in the variety of Gjirokastër reported in Manzini and Savoia (2007: 325).

b. (*E)   du   me **e**   marr   (Gheg)
   (*it-CL.ACC) want-1SG ME it-CL.ACC take
   'I want to take it'

In Krapova and Turano (2015) it was observed that (leaving aside Exceptional Case Marking (ECM) with perception and causative verbs of Arbëresh) the only type of CC in the Albanian-speaking area is the one found in some Southern Albanian dialects with a sub-type of periphrastic future of the type *kam për të dhënë* (= I have to give) 'I will give'. Clitics, which normally appear in between the particle *të* and the participle (41a), in this kind of future can also precede the auxiliary *kam* 'have', see (41b-c):

(41) a. *ai ka   për të **ju**   thënë diçka*
        he has PËR TË you-CL.ACC.PL said   something
        'He will tell you something'
        (Sami Frashëri, in Demiraj 1985: 840)
     b. *Turqya **u**   ka për të dhënë gjë*
        Turkey them-CL.ACC has PËR TË given something
        'Turkey will give them something'
        (Sami Frashëri, in Demiraj 1985: 840)
     c. *Evropa s'**i**   ka për të vënë në vatrë*
        Europe not them-CL.ACC has PËR TË put in homeland
        'Europe will not take them at home'
        (Sami Frashëri, in Demiraj 1985: 840)

The data reviewed so far show clearly that the presence of an infinitive is a necessary though not a sufficient condition for a restructuring configuration. As we will see in the next subsection, Serbian is particularly revealing in this respect.

4.4 A brief survey of CC in Serbian

As is well-known, in the South-Eastern Serbo-Croatian dialectal area there are (almost) no traces of the infinitive, while the Western varieties preserve it to a greater extent. Infinitive regression has spread not only to the Torlak dialects, which are typologically Balkan also in other respects, but has been extended nearly to Belgrade (Alexander 1983: 18, cit. in Ammann and van der Auwera 2004: 302). The only predicate which seems to almost always require the infinitive even in the eastern dialectal area appears to be *moći* 'can' (*ne mogu ciniti*

'I cannot do') although Tomić (2006: 485) gives a longer list comprising *um(j)eti* 'can/be able to', *sm(j)eti* 'dare', *morati* 'must', *trebati* 'should', *ht(j)eti* with modal or auxiliary uses, and *imati* 'have to'. With all of these predicates CC is attested.[28]

Serbian thus patterns with Old Church Slavonic, as well as with the other Slavic (non-Balkan) languages with clitics, in allowing CC with a more limited set of the restructuring predicates (see, e.g. (42)). Note that differently from Modern Bulgarian, but similarly to OCS, as well as to Old Serbian, Modern Serbian is a second-position clitic language.

(42) *Mila ga mora/želi vidjeti*
 Mila him-CL.ACC must/want-3SG see-INF
 'Mila wants to/must see him'
 (Aljović 2005:62)

If CC is an instantiation of monoclausality, as we have argued so far, it follows that it should be impossible to find a configuration in which a clitic "climbs" from a finite complement of a non-restructuring verb since this necessarily implies a bi-clausal structure.

The constructions that have replaced the infinitives in the Balkan languages are generally taken to be finite constructions representing clauses distinct from the one containing the verb that selects them. But, as we have argued above, there are reasons to doubt that they always represent distinct finite clauses, precisely in those cases where they constitute the complement of a modal, an aspectual or a motion verb.[29] In fact, complements to verbs of the 'restructuring' class behave as infinitives rather than as genuine finite clauses.

For one thing, such verbs are arguably always "functional", in the sense that they necessarily occupy the modal, aspectual and motion projections of the universal clausal hierarchy (even in the absence of such monoclausality

---

[28] According to Wurmbrand (2001) and Todorović (2012), although the frequency and preferences of BCS infinitives vary from region to region, they are allowed with predicates belonging to the class of obligatory (exhaustive or partial) control, as well as to the one we identified in section 2. as Romance-style Balkan subjunctives. In some cases, clitic climbing is disallowed.
[29] Namely 'raising' of the subject of the lexical verb to the subject position of the 'restructuring' verb (similarly to what happens with auxiliaries). For an early differentiation between the *da*-clause complements of modal and aspectual verbs (vs. all others) in Bulgarian, see Krapova (2001). Also see Terzi (1994, 1999) and Dobrovie-Sorin (1994).

diagnostics as CC – Cinque 2004). Secondly, it is not at all clear whether the constructions that have replaced the infinitives in the Balkan languages are fully finite. The verb that follows *da, na, să,* and *të* is typically represented by the stem of the verb followed by person and number agreement morphology and (in some cases) by morphology selected by the higher functional verbs (what Progovac 1993 calls the "default" form of the verb). Tense specifications are severely restricted in these constructions, in ways that appear to comply with the make-up of the universal clausal hierarchy.

5 Absence of clitic climbing: towards an analysis

We take the impossibility of CC out of *da, na, să,* and *të* constructions not to depend on their putative (in fact, rather dubious) finite nature, but from a combinations of two factors: the presence of the *da, na, să,* and *të* particles (which are not present with the infinitive, whenever this is possible) and the position of the clitics themselves, which are subjacent to such particles.[30] That a clitic cannot be extracted, and climb up, from the complement of a "restructuring" verb introduced by *da, na, să,* and *të*, which are subordinators of sort, while it can from an infinitival complement of such a verb (whenever possible in the same variety), is reminiscent of the contrast existing in English between *wh*-extraction of the subject of a tensed clause subjacent to a subordinator/complementizer like *that* (impossible, in most varieties of English) (cf. (43a)) and extraction of the subject of an infinitive (cf. (43b)) or of a finite clause (cf. (43c)) in the absence of a subordinator/complementizer.

(43) a. *Who_i do you believe [*that* ___$_i$ *is telling the truth*]?
 b. Who_i do you believe [___$_i$ *to be telling the truth*]?[31]
 c. Who_i do you believe [___$_i$ *to be telling the truth*]?

Certain Balkan dialectal varieties seem to provide an interesting confirmation that it is the presence of such particles that blocks CC.

As reported in Sobolev (2003, 2004), in the Torlak East Serbian dialect of Kamenitsa, as well as in the Bulgarian Rhodope dialect of Gela, it is

---

[30] They immediately follow *da* in Bulgarian and Macedonian, *na* in Greek, *să* in Romanian, and *të* in Albanian.
[31] This is a case of the so-called Exceptional Case Marking infinitive in English and evidence exists that *who* is the subject of the infinitive, not the object of *believe* (see Chomsky 1981: 98ff).

possible to find the clitic argument of the embedded verb to the left of the matrix verb in a configuration corresponding to CC, but crucially only if *da* is absent:

(44) a. *d'a li ga m'ogu n'ajdem?* (Kamenitsa – Sobolev 2003,68)
  Q him-CL.ACC can-1SG find-1SG
  'Can I find him?'
 b. *i gu nă možaxmă fanăm* (Gela – Sobolev 2003,68)
  and him-CL.ACC not could-1PL catch-1PL
  'And we couldn't catch him'.

The phenomenon of particle omission, which Sobolev (2003: 75) describes as a "synthetic innovation" located in the Central Balkan zone, appears to allow for a clear case of CC, available for example with the verb 'can' in its ability reading. Aware that more data are needed for the description of this phenomenon and abstracting away from its possible origin, we take the examples in (44) to show that CC is available in some Balkan Slavic varieties with verbs which select an apparently inflected embedded verb not introduced by a particle. Therefore, it is not the type of embedded morphology *per se* which allows for CC in these dialects, but rather the absence of one such particle.

We come back to the theoretical question of why such particles should block extraction of the clitics (much like *that* in standard English blocks extraction of the subject following it). Before that we want to point out the analogous case in the Italian Northern Salentino dialect spoken in the areas of Brindisi and Taranto (Puglia), a Romance variety which displays many Balkan features including the replacement of most infinitives with particles followed by seemingly finite verbs (possibly stemming from the medieval Greek substrate of Southern Puglia) (cf. Calabrese 1993 and Terzi 1994). Here too CC is possible if the particle is absent but not if it is present (see (45c) vs. (45b), from Calabrese 1993, note 8; and (46c) vs. (46b) from Terzi 1994: 159):

(45) a. *Maryu voli ku ntʃi lu tai*
  Maria want-3SG PRT him-CL.DAT it-CL.ACC give-3SG
 b. **Maryu ntʃi lu voli ku ddai*
  Maria him-CL.Dat it-CL.ACC want-3SG PRT give-3SG
 c. *Maryu ntʃi lu voli ddai*
  Maria him-CL.Dat it-CL.ACC want-3SG give-3SG
  'Maria wants to give it to him'

(46) a. *voggyu   ku   lu   kattu*
       want-1SG PRT it-CL.ACC buy-1SG
    b. **lu*   *voggyu   ku   kattu*
       it-CL.ACC want-1SG PRT buy-1SG
    c. *lu   voggyu   kattu*
       it-CL.ACC want-1SG buy-1SG
       'I want to buy it'

To summarize, the difference between these peripheral Balkan varieties and the standard Balkan languages has to do with the possibility for the former but not the latter to delete the modal particle. When no modal particle is present (with at least some of the "restructuring" verbs) CC becomes possible.

6 Refining the analysis of the apparent blocking effect of modal particles

The *that*-trace effect illustrated in (43) has been the object of a number of studies since the discovery of the phenomenon by Perlmutter (1968, 1971). Among recent accounts, we think that Rizzi and Shlonsky's (2007) represents a particularly interesting one in that it subsumes the *that*-trace effect under a more general principle of Universal Grammar: Criterial Freezing (Rizzi 2006).

According to this principle a phrase meeting a certain Criterion (i.e., reaching a dedicated position, like the final position reached by an interrogative *wh*-phrase, a topic or focus phrase) is frozen in place and resists further movement to a distinct and higher criterial position. For example, a *wh*-phrase satisfying the *Wh*-Criterion in an embedded question context cannot undergo further focus movement to the main clause as in (47b. = ex. (4) of Rizzi and Shlonsky 2007), an operation which is normally available in Italian to a direct object (cf. 48a. and b. = ex. (3a-b) of Rizzi and Shlonsky 2007).

(47) a. *Mi domandavo quale RAGAZZA avessero scelto, non quale ragazzo*
       'I wondered which GIRL they had chosen, not which boy'
    b. **Quale RAGAZZA mi domandavo___ avessero scelto, non quale ragazzo*
       'Which GIRL I wondered they had chosen, not which boy'

(48) a. *Pensavo che avessero scelto la RAGAZZA, non il ragazzo*
       'I thought they had chosen the GIRL, not the boy'
    b. *La RAGAZZA pensavo che avessero scelto___, non il ragazzo*
       'The GIRL I thought they had chosen ___, not the boy'

In other terms, a certain element cannot satisfy more than one Criterion. This eventually leads Rizzi and Shlonsky (2007, §2) to propose the following principle:

(49) Criterial Freezing: A (feature-bearing element of a) phrase meeting a criterion is frozen in place.

If extended to subject phrases, whose final dedicated position bears a particular 'aboutness' relation with respect to the predicate, and is subjacent to a subordinator/complementizer in embedded contexts, the *that*-trace effect can be seen to follow immediately. (43a), as opposed to (43b) and (43c) is bad because in English subjects necessarily reach the criterial position under *that* in embedded contexts (no other position being available for subjects, e.g. postverbal or clause medial positions).

This has as a consequence that they are frozen in place, no further movement being possible. The Freezing Principle is assumed to be universal, i.e. operative in all languages, including those, like standard Italian and other Romance languages, where no comparable *that*-trace (or rather *che/que/* etc.-trace effect is detectable – Perlmutter 1968, 1971). The reason appears to be that extraction of the subject can in these (null subject) languages occur from a lower position, thus skipping the criterial position which would freeze them and which is arguably filled instead by a null expletive, available in these languages. See Rizzi and Shlonsky (2007) and references cited there.[32]

Returning now to the apparent blocking effect of the 'modal' particles *da, na, să,* and *të* we submit that the absence of CC across them is very much like the impossibility or extracting the subject across *that* in English. As just seen, rather than *that* itself it is the criterial nature of the position of the subject under *that* in English that bars any further movement of the subject. We suggest that the position of the clitics under *da, na, să,* and *të* in Bulgarian, Macedonian, Greek, Romanian and Albanian, respectively, is also a criterial position, one for clitics in these languages (i.e., the dedicated position which they have to reach). The consequence is that if the clitics reach such a position they are frozen there and cannot 'climb' to any higher position.

We have also seen that only if the modal particle is absent, in those varieties where it can be absent after some modal verbs, CC becomes possible (cf. (44), (45c) and (46c) above). We take this fact to exactly match again the English case where when *that* is absent extraction of the subject can take place (cf. (43c) above). Rizzi and Shlonsky (2007) consider the possibility that in such cases deletion of the CP containing *that* may be accompanied by the deletion of the subjacent criterial

---

32 We refer to their article for discussion of further complexities (like the possibility of subject extraction in relatives *The boy that __ left*).

subject position, so that the subject may directly move from its position of Merge to the matrix CP, avoiding the freezing effect of the movement to the embedded criterial subject position, which is no longer there. In the same vein we submit that the deletion of the modal particle is accompanied by the deletion of the subjacent criterial clitic field, which then forces the clitic to move from their position of Merge to the higher criterial clitic field (whence the obligatory character of CC in such cases).[33]

We are thus suggesting that while a standard Bulgarian case like (31a), repeated here as (50a), has a structure like (50b), the Bulgarian Rhodope Gela dialect case in (44)b, repeated here as (51a), has a structure like (51b), where the low criterial clitic field subjacent to the modal particle has been deleted together with the modal particle.[34]

(50) a. *Az go   moga   da vidja
       I him-CL.ACC can-1SG PRT see-1SG
       'I can see him'
    b. *[IP Az_i [Clitic Field go_k] moga [da [Clitic Field t_k] t_i vidja]]

(51) a. I gu   nă možaxmă fanăm
       and him-CL.ACC not could-1PL catch-1PL
       'And we couldn't catch him'
    b. I [IP pro_i [Clitic Field gu_k] nă možaxmă [t_i fanăm]][35]

---

[33] The obligatory character of CC with infinitives in BCS (Stjepanović 2004,§3; Aljović 2005,§2.3) may suggest that the infinitival complements of modal and aspectual verbs do not activate a criterial clitic field (cf. Aljović 2005: 68; but see Bošković 2001 and Stjepanović 2004,§3, for arguments that the obligatoriness may only be apparent).

[34] Perhaps, the modal particle itself is part of the clitic field, so that deletion of the particle brings along the deletion of the entire clitic field. For arguments that the modal particle of Salentino varieties, when absent, is *structurally* rather than just phonologically absent, see Ledgeway (2015).

[35] As mentioned briefly above with reference to ex. (30) above, a potential problem for the analysis just sketched is provided by the apparently optional CC across the modal particle *da* in Serbian varieties of BCS, originally pointed out in Progovac (1993). Note that our analysis is only concerned with the modal ("subjunctive") particle *da* and not with the homophonous indicative complementizer *da* 'that' (for which difference see Todorović 2012).

(i) a. *Tanja želi   da ga   vidi.*
       Tanja want-3SG PRT him-CL.Acc see-3SG
       'Tanja wants to see him'
       (Progovac 1993: 119)
   b. (?)?*Tanja ga   želi   da vidi.*
       Tanja him-CL.Acc want-3SG PRT see-3SG
       'Tanja wants to see him'.
       (Progovac 1993: 119; Todorović 2012: 164)

7 Conclusions

In this article we have tried to show how certain properties and principles of Universal Grammar, such as the functional nature of the classes of modal, aspectual and motion verbs, and the principle of Criterial Freezing, can shed light on an otherwise puzzling negative Balkan feature: the absence of CC in the modern bona fide Balkan languages and on certain aspects of the older stages of these languages, which show a peculiar behavior of modal, aspectual and motion verbs in the longer retention of infinitives and in the selective presence of instances of CC.

We believe this analysis may help clarify the shift to a morphologically finite subordination system in contact situations where only one of the languages or dialects which enter in contact has undergone a (full or partial) infinitive loss. There is a higher probability for this language/dialect to influence the language/

Tomislav Sočanac (p.c.) suggests that the degraded status of such examples could be due to a conflict between criterial freezing and the second-position requirement of the clitic. Criterial freezing is stronger than the clitic requirement forcing the clitic to stay in the lower clause. No such conflict would of course arise with infinitives which do not introduce a criterial position for the clitic, so the only relevant constraint is clitic-second (hence climbing is obligatory).

Alternatively, it could be thought that the examples in (i) parallel once again the English *that*-trace phenomenon, which shows variation in acceptability judgments, with some speakers accepting sentences such as (iia) (while still rejecting extractions of the subject from a *wh*-interrogative sentence like (iib)) (cf. Sobin 1987; 2002, and Rizzi and Shlonsky 2007 for a treatment of this exception within their Criterial Freezing approach):

(ii) a. %Who did you say that would hate the soup?
    (Sobin 2002, 528)
  b. *Who did you ask whether would hate the soup?
    (Sobin 2002, fn.2)

We leave this question open, given the (relative) marginality of such CC and the poorly understood restrictions to which it is subject ("if the matrix verb is in the past or future tense [...] no CC is allowed" (Todorović 2012: 164). See the contrast in (iii) and (iv):

(iii) a. *Tanja je   htela   da ga   vidi.*
    Tanja aux-3SG wanted-part. fem PRT him-CL.ACC see-3SG
    'Tanja wanted to see him'
  b. ?**Tanja ga   je   htela   da vidi.*
    Tanja him-CL.ACC. aux-3sg. wanted-part. fem. PRT see-3SG

(iv) a. *Tanja će   hteti   da ga   vidi.*
    Tanja aux-FUT.3SG want-INF PRT him-CL.ACC see-3SG
    'Tanja will want to see him'
  b. ?* *Tanja će   ga   hteti   da vidi.*
    Tanja aux-3sg. him-CL.ACC want-INF PRT see-3SG

dialect which has preserved the infinitive, rather than the other way around, leading to the use of finite morphology in both languages. Such is also the case reported by Tsiplakou and Kappler (2015) for Cypriot Turkish and Squillaci (2015) for the Romance dialect of Bova (Calabria), both of which have been influenced by Greek (the Greko/Grecanico variety of Calabria, Southern Italy). Greek was at the stage of partial infinitive loss, which means that the tendency of replacement with a finite subordination system is stronger than the preservation tendency.

References

Aissen, Judith and David M. Perlmutter. 1976. Clause Reduction in Spanish. In *Proceedings of the Second Annual Meeting of the Berkeley Linguistics Society*. 1–30. Berkeley, CA: Berkeley Linguistics Society.

Aissen, Judith and David M. Perlmutter. 1983. Clause Reduction in Spanish. In David M. Perlmutter (ed.), *Studies in Relational Grammar*, 360–403. Chicago: University of Chicago Press.

Alboiu, Gabriela. 2007. Moving forward with Romanian backward control. In William D. Davies & Stanley Dubinsky (eds.), *New Horizons in the Analysis of Control and Raising*, 187–212. Dordrecht: Springer.

Alexander, Ronelle. 1983. On the definition of Sprachbund boundaries. The place of Balkan Slavic. In N. Reiter (ed.), *Ziele und Wege der Balkanlinguistik: Beiträge zur Tagung von 2–6 März 1981 in Berlin*, 27–39. Wiesbaden: Harrassowitz.

Aljović, Nadira. 2005. On clitic climbing in Bosnian/Croatian/Serbian. *Forum Bosnae* 34. 58–84

Ammann, Andreas and van der Auwera, Johan. 2004. Complementizer-headed main clauses for volitional moods in the languages of South-Eastern Europe: A Balkanism? In Olga Mišeska Tomić (ed.), *Balkan Syntax and Semantics*, 293–314. Amsterdam & Philadelphia: John Benjamins.

Asenova, Petya. 2002. *Balkansko ezikosnanie. Osnovni problemi na balkanskija ezikov săjuz* [Balkan linguistics. Fundamental problems of the Balkan Linguistic Union]. Veliko Tărnovo: Faber.

Authier, J.-Marc, and Lisa Reed. 2008. Against restructuring in modern French. *University of Pennsylvania Working Papers in Linguistics* 14, 13–27.

Authier, J.-Marc, and Lisa Reed. 2009. On the lack of transparency effects in French. In Pascual José Masullo, Erin O'Rourke and Chia-Hui Huang, eds., *Romance Linguistics 2007: Selcted papers from the 37th Linguistic Symposium on Romance Languages*. 37–49. Amsterdam & Philadelphia: John Benjamins.

Baldissera, Valeria. 2012. *Il dialetto grico del Salento: elementi balcanici e contatto linguistico*. Ph.D Dissertation. Università Ca' Foscari, Venezia. http://dspace.unive.it/handle/10579/3020 (accessed 20 February 2015)

Baldissera, Valeria. 2013. Conservative and innovative tendencies in Griko infinitive complements. In Mark Janse, Brian D. Joseph, Angela Ralli and Metin Bağrıaçık (eds.), *Online Proceedings of the Fifth International Conference on Modern Greek Dialects and Linguistic Theory* (MGDLT5). 35–44. University of Patras. https://biblio.ugent.be/publication/4211390

Bošković, Željko. 2001. *On the Nature of the Syntax-Phonology Interface: Cliticization and Related Phenomena.* Amsterdam: Elsevier.
Burzio, Luigi. 1986. *Italian Syntax. A Government-Binding Approach.* Dordrecht: Reidel.
Calabrese, Andrea. 1993. The Sentential Complementation of Salentino: a study of a language without infinitival clauses. In Adriana Belletti (ed.), *Syntactic Theory and Dialects of Italian*, 28–98. Torino: Rosenberg & Sellier.
Cardinaletti, Anna and Giuliana Giusti. 2001. "Semi-lexical" motion verbs in Romance and Germanic. In Norbert Corver and Henk van Riemsdijk (eds.), *Semi-lexical Categories*, 371–414. Berlin: Mouton de Gruyter.
Chatzikyriakidis, Stergios. 2009. Clitics in Grecia Salentina Greek: A dynamic account. *Lingua* 119, 1939–1968.
Chatzikyriakidis, Stergios. 2010a. *Clitics in four dialects of Modern Greek: A dynamic account.* Ph.D. Dissertation, King's College, London. https://www.stergioschatzikyriakidis.com/uploads/1/0/3/6/10363759/chatzikyriakidis-phdthesis.pdf
Chatzikyriakidis, Stergios. 2010b. Clitic climbing in Grecia Salentina Greek: A dynamic account. In Angela Ralli, Brian D. Joseph, Mark Janse, and Athanasios Karasimos (eds.), *Online Proceedings of the Fourth International Conference on Modern Greek Dialects and Linguistic Theory* (MGDLT4). 208-233, Patras: University of Patras. https://biblio.ugent.be/publication/1011543 (accessed 15 June 2016)
Chomsky, Noam. 1981. *Lectures on Government and Binding.* Dordrecht: Foris Publications.
Cinque, Guglielmo. 1999. *Adverbs and Functional Heads.* New York: Oxford University Press.
Cinque, Guglielmo. 2001. 'Restructuring' and the Order of Aspectual and Root Modal Heads. In Guglielmo Cinque and Gianpaolo Salvi (eds.), *Current Studies in Italian Syntax. Essays offered to Lorenzo Renzi*, 137–155. Amsterdam: Elsevier.
Cinque, Guglielmo. 2002. A Note on Restructuring and Quantifier Climbing in French. *Linguistic Inquiry* 33. 617–636 (also in Cinque 2006).
Cinque, Guglielmo. 2004. Restructuring and functional structure. In Luigi Rizzi (ed.), *The Structure of CP and IP.* 132–191. New York: Oxford University Press (also in Cinque 2006).
Cinque, Guglielmo. 2006. *Restructuring and Functional Heads.* New York: Oxford University Press.
Davies, William D. and Stanley Dubinsky. 2007. *New Horizons in the Analysis of Control and Raising.* Dordrecht: Springer.
Dobrovie-Sorin, Carmen. 1994. *The Syntax of Romanian: Comparative Studies in Romance.* Berlin: Mouton de Gruyter.
Dobrovie-Sorin, Carmen. 2001. Head-to-head merge in Balkan subjunctives and locality. In Maria-Luisa Rivero and Angela Ralli (eds.), *Comparative Syntax of Balkan Languages*, 44–74. Oxford: Oxford University Press.
Franks, Steven and Tracy Holloway King. 2000. *A Handbook of Slavic Clitics.* New York: Oxford University Press.
George, Leland and Jindřich Toman. 1976. Czech Clitics in Universal Grammar. *Papers from the 12th Regional Meeting. Chicago Linguistic Society* 12. 235–249
Giannakidou, Anastasia. 1998. *Polarity Sensitivity as (Non)veridical Dependency.* Amsterdam and Philadelphia: John Benjamins
Giannakidou, Anastasia. 2009. The dependency of the subjunctive revisited: temporal semantics and polarity. *Lingua* 119 (12). 1883–1908.
Golden, Marija. 2003. Clitic placement and clitic climbing in Slovenian. *STUF – Language Typology and Universals.* 56. 208–233.
Grano, Thomas. 2015. *Control and Restructuring.* Oxford: Oxford University Press.

Grosu, Alex and Julia Horvath 1987. On nonfiniteness in extraction constructions. *Natural Language and Linguistic Theory.* 5. 181–196.
Haralampiev, Ivan. 2001. *Istoričeska gramatika na bălgarskija ezik.* Veliko Tărnovo: Faber.
Hill, Virginia and Olga Mišeska-Tomić. 2008. Subjunctive Complements to Verbs in Romance and Slavic Balkan. In Marko Tadić, Mila Dimitrova-Vulchanova, Svetla Koeva (eds.), *Proceedings of the Sixth International Conference Formal Approaches to South Slavic and Balkan Languages. 25–28 September 2008, Dubrovnik, Croatia.* 7–14. Zagreb: Croatian Language Technologies Society – Faculty of Humanities and Social Sciences. https://bib.irb.hr/datoteka/436750.FASSBL6_2008_proceedings.pdf (accessed 16 March 2015)
Iatridou, Sabine. 1993. On nominative case assignment and a few related things. *MIT Working papers in Linguistics* 19. 175–196.
Joseph, Brian D. 1980. Linguistic Universals and Syntactic Change. *Language* 56. 345–370
Joseph, Brian D. 1983. *The Synchrony and Diachrony of the Balkan Infinitive: A Study in Areal, General, and Historical Linguistics.* Cambridge: Cambridge University Press.
Joseph, Brian D. 1990. *Morphology and Universals in Syntactic Change: Evidence from Medieval and Modern Greek.* New York: Garland.
Joseph, Brian D. 1992. Diachronic Perspectives on Control. In Richard Larson, Sabine Iatridou, Utpal Lahiri, & James Higginbotham (eds.), *Control and Grammatical Theory*, 195–234. Dordrecht: Kluwer.
Joseph, Brian D. and Panayiotis A. Pappas. 2002. On some recent views concerning the development of the Greek future system. *Byzantine and Modern Greek Studies* 26. 247–273
Kapetangianni, George and Dimitra Papangeli. 2007. Control in Modern Greek: It's another good move. In William D. Davies & Stanley Dubinsky (eds.) *New Horizons in the Analysis of Control and Raising*, 111–132. Dordrecht: Springer.
Kayne, Richard S. 1975. *French syntax.* Cambridge, Mass.: MIT Press.
Kayne, Richard S. 1989. Null Subjects and Clitic Climbing. In Oswaldo Jaeggli & Ken Safir (eds.), *The Null Subject Parameter*, 239–261. Dordrecht: Kluwer.
Kayne, Richard S. 2016. Clitic Doubling and Agreement in French Hyper-Complex Inversion. Ms., NYU.
Krapova, Iliyana. 2001. Subjunctive in Bulgarian and Modern Greek. In Maria-Luisa Rivero and Angela Ralli (eds.), *Comparative Syntax of Balkan Languages*, 105– 126. New York: Oxford University Press.
Krapova, Iliana and Giuseppina Turano. 2015. On Clitic Climbing in the Balkan Languages from a Synchronic Perspective. In Antonio D'Alessandri & Francesco Guida (eds.), *L'Europa e il suo Sud-Est.* 135–153. Ariccia (RM): Aracne Editrice.
Krapova, Iliana and Tsvetana Dimitrova 2016. "The genitive-dative syncretism in the history of Bulgarian: towards and analysis", *Studi Slavistici* XII. 181–208.
Kupść, Anna. 1999. A Lexical Account of Clitic Climbing in Polish. Ms., Polish Academy of Sciences and University of Tübingen. https://pdfs.semanticscholar.org/96b/5565e339d80342db6 deae7c6e65c6a17d089.pdf?_ga=2.130000716.1746865723.1537605109- 703337119.1528715781 (accessed 15 March 2015)
Landau, Idan. 2000. *Elements of control: Structure and meaning in infinitival constructions.* Dordrecht: Kluwer.
Landau, Idan 2004. The scale of finiteness and the calculus of control. *Natural Language and Linguistic Theory* 22. 811–877.
Ledgeway, Adam. 2015. Reconstructing Complementizer-drop in the Dialects of the Salento: A Syntactic or Phonological Phenomenon? In Theresa Biberauer and George Walkden

(eds.), *Syntax over Time: Lexical, Morphological, and Information-Structural Interactions*. Oxford: Oxford University Press.

Mackridge, Peter. 1993. An editorial problem in the medieval Greek texts: the position of the object clitic pronoun in the Escorial Digenes Akrites. In N. M. Panayiotakis (ed.), *Neogreca Medii Aevi*, 325–342. Venice: Greek Institute of Venice.

Mackridge, Peter. 1996. The Medieval Greek Infinitive in the Light of Modern Dialectal Evidence. In C.Constantinidis, N.Panagiotakis, E.Jeffreys and A.Angelou, eds., *Φιλλέλην: Studies in Honour of Robert Browning*. 191–204. Venice: Greek Institute of Venice.

Manolessou, Io. 2005. The Greek dialects of Southern Italy: An Overview. ΚΑΜΠΟΣ, Cambridge Papers in Modern Greek 13. 103–125.

Manzini M. Rita and Leonardo M. Savoia. 2005. *I dialetti italiani e romanci. Morfosintassi generativa*. Alessandria: Edizioni dell'Orso. 3 Volumes.

Manzini M. Rita and Leonardo M. Savoia. 2007. *A Unification of Morphology and Syntax. Investigations into Romance and Albanian dialects*. London: Routledge.

Manzini M. Rita and Leonardo M. Savoia. 2016. Finite and non-finite complementation, particles and control in Aromanian, compared to other Romance varieties and Albanian. Ms., University of Florence. To appear in *Linguistic Variation*. https://ling.auf.net/lingbuzz/004274 (accessed 20 March 2016)

Manzini, M. Rita, Paolo Lorusso and Leonardo M. Savoia. 2017. Bare finite complements in Southern Italian varieties: Mono-clausal or biclausal syntax? Ms. Università di Firenze.

Martins, Ana Maria. 2000. A Minimalist Approach to Clitic Climbing. In Joao Costa (ed.), *Portuguese Syntax. New Comparative Studies*. 169–190. New York: Oxford University Press.

Mertyris, Dionysios. 2009. "The Grammaticalization of Future in Greek and Bulgarian" In Karasimos Athanasios, Vlachos Christos, Dimela Eleonora, Giakoumelou Maria, Pavlakou Maria, Koutsoukos Nikolaos & Bougonikolou Dimitra (eds.) *Theoretical and Applied Linguistics. Proceedings of the First Patras International Conference of Graduate students in Linguistics (PICGL1)*, Patras, 28–30 March 2008, 222–230. University of Patras, Greece

Mirčev, Kiril. 1978. *Istoričeska gramatika na bălgarskija ezik*. (Treto izdanie). Sofia: Nauka i izkustvo.

Pană Dindelegan, Gabriela. 2013. *The Grammar of Romanian*. Oxford: Oxford University Press.

Pancheva, Roumyana 2005. The Rise and fall of second position clitics. *Natural Language and Linguistic Theory*. 23. 103–167.

Pappas, Panayotis. 2001. *Weak object pronoun placement in Later Medieval and Early Modern Greek*. Ph.D. dissertation, The Ohio State University.

Pappas, Panayotis. 2004. Medieval Greek Weak Object Pronouns and Analogical Change: A Response to Condoravdi and Kiparsky (2001). *Journal of Greek Linguistics* 5. 127–158

Perlmutter, David M. 1968. *Deep and surface structure constraints in syntax*. Ph.D. Dissertation, Massachusetts Institute of Technology. http://hdl.handle.net/1721.1/13003 (accessed 18 March 2015)

Perlmutter, David M. 1971. *Deep and Surface Structure Constraints in Syntax*. New York: Holt, Rinehart and Winston.

Philippaki-Warburton, Irene. 1994. The subjunctive mood and the syntactic status of the particle *na* in Modern Greek. *Folia Linguistica* 28. 297–328.

Philippaki-Warburton, Irene. 1998. Functional categories and Modern Greek syntax. *The Linguistic Review* 15. 158–186.

Pollock, Jean-Yves. 1978. Trace theory and French syntax. In Samuel Jay Keyser (ed.), *Recent transformational studies in European languages*, 65–112. Cambridge, Massachusetts: MIT Press.

Progovac, Ljiljana. 1993. Locality and Subjunctive-like Complements in Serbo-Croatian. *Journal of Slavic Linguistics* 1. 116–144.

Remberger, Eva-Maria. 2011. Morfosintassi verbale dei dialetti neogreci in Calabria. In Walter Breu (ed.), *L'influsso dell'italiano sul sistema del verbo delle lingue minoritarie. (Resistenza e mutamento nella morfologia e nella sintassi)*. 123–148. Bochum: Brockmeyer (Diversitas Linguarum).

Rezac, Milan. 2005. The syntax of clitic climbing in Czech. In Lorie Heggie and Francisco Ordoñez (eds.), *Clitic and Affix Combinations*. 103–140. Amsterdam & Philadelphia: John Benjamins.

Rivero, Maria-Luisa, 1994. Clause structure and V-movement in the languages of the Balkans. *Natural Language and Linguistic Theory* 12. 63–120.

Rivero, Maria-Luisa and Angela Ralli. 2001. *Comparative Syntax of Balkan Languages*. New York: Oxford University Press.

Rizzi, Luigi. 1976. Ristrutturazione. *Rivista di Grammatica Generativa* 1. 1–54.

Rizzi, Luigi. 1978. A Restructuring Rule in Italian Syntax. In Samuel Jay Keyser (ed.), *Recent Transformational Studies in European Languages*, 113–158. Cambridge, Massachusetts: MIT Press. (also in Rizzi, Luigi. 1982, *Issues in Italian Syntax*, Dordrecht: Foris Publications).

Rizzi, Luigi. 2006. On the form of chains: Criterial positions and ECP effects. In Lisa Lai-Sheng Cheng & Norbert Corver (eds.), *Wh-movement: Moving on*. 97–134. Cambridge, MA: MIT Press.

Rizzi, Luigi and Ur Shlonsky. 2007. Strategies of Subject Extraction. In Gärtner, Hans-Martin. and Uli Sauerland (eds.), *Interfaces + Recursion = Language?* 115–160. Berlin: Mouton de Gruyter.

Rohlfs, Gerhard. 1958. La perdita dell'infinito nelle lingue balcaniche e nell'Italia Meridionale. In *Omagiu lui Iorgu Iordan cu prilejul împlinirii a 70 de ani*. 733–744. Bucureşti: Academia Republicii Populare Romîne.

Rosen, Sara T. 1990. *Argument Structure and Complex Predicates*. New York: Garland.

Roussou, Anna. 2000. On the left periphery: Modal particles and complementizers. *Journal of Greek Linguistics* 1. 65–94.

Roussou, Anna. 2009. In the mood for control. *Lingua* 119. 1811–1836.

Roussou, Anna. 2010. Selecting complementizers. *Lingua* 120. 582–603.

Sandfeld, Kristian. 1930. *Linguistique balkanique: Problèmes et resultats*. Paris: Champion.

Sims, Andrea D. and Brian D. Joseph. This volume. Morphology versus Syntax in the Balkan Verbal Complex.

Sobin, Nicholas. 1987. The Variable Status of Comp-Trace Phenomena. *Natural Language and Linguistic Theory* 5. 33–60.

Sobin, Nicholas. 2002. The Comp-trace effect, the adverb effect and minimal CP. *Journal of Linguistics* 38. 527–560.

Sobolev, Andrey. 2003. *Malyj dialektologiceskij atlas balkanskix jazykov*. [Small Dialectological Atlas of the Balkan Languages] Probnuj vypusk. Initial volume. München: Biblion.

Sobolev, Andrey. 2004. On the areal distribution of syntactic properties in the languages of the Balkans. In O. Tomić, ed., *Balkan Syntax and Semantics*. 59–100. Amsterdam: Benjamins.

Sočanac, Tomislav. This volume. Subjunctive complements in the Balkan languages: Problems of Distribution.

Solà, Jaume. 2010. Clitic Climbing and Null Subject Languages. Ms., Universitat Autònoma de Barcelona, Departament de Filologia Catalana. http://filcat.uab.cat/clt/publicacions/reports/pdf/GGT-01-10.pdf

Spyropoulos, Vassilios. 2007. Finiteness and Control in Greek. In William D. Davies & Stanley Dubinsky (eds.) *New Horizons in the Analysis of Control and Raising*, 159–184. Springer.

Squillaci, Maria Olimpia. 2015. 'Greko and Bovese, a case of language contact in the Extreme South of Italy', paper presented at the BA Society, Trinity College, University of Cambridge, UK, 6 February 2015.

Stjepanović, Sandra. 2004. Clitic Climbing and Restructuring with "Finite Clause" and Infinitive Complements. *Journal of Slavic Linguistics* 12. 177–212.

Stojkov, S. 1993/2002. *Bǎlgarska dialektologija*. Sofia: Akademično izdatelstvo "Marin Drinov".

Stowell, Tim. 1982. The tense of infinitives. *Linguistic Inquiry* 13. 561–570.

Strozer, Judith. 1976. *Clitics in Spanish*. Ph.D. Dissertation, University of California at Los Angeles.

Terzi, Arhonto. 1994. Clitic Climbing from Finite Clauses and Long Head Movement. *Catalan Working Papers in Linguistics* 3 (2). 97–122

Terzi, Arhonto. 1999. Clitic climbing from finite clauses and tense raising. *Probus* 8. 273–296

Todorović, Nataša. 2012. *The Indicative and Subjunctive* da-*complements in Serbian. A Syntactic-Semantic Approach*. Ph.D. Dissertation, University of Illinois at Chicago.

Tomić Olga Mišeska. 2006. *Balkan Sprachbund Morpho-syntactic Features*. Dordrecht: Springer.

Tsiplakou, Stavroula and Matthias Kappler. 2015. Is There a Common Cypriot Subjunctive? *Mediterranean Language Review* 22. 139–155

Turano, Giuseppina. 1994. *Dipendenze sintattiche in Albanese*. Padua: Unipress.

Varlokosta, Spyridoula. 1993. Control in Modern Greek. *University of Maryland Working Papers in Linguistics* 1. 144–163.

Varlokosta, Spyridoula. 1994. *Issues on modern Greek sentential complementation*. PhD dissertation, University of Maryland.

Varlokosta, Spyridoula and Norbert Hornstein. 1993. Control in Modern Greek. *Proceedings of NELS* 23. 507–521.

Večerka, Radoslav. 1989. *Altkirchenslavische (Altbulgarische) Syntax*. Freiburg i. Br. : U.W. Weiher.

Veselovská, Lida. 1995. *Phrasal Movement and X^0-morphology*. Ph.D. Dissertation, Palacky University, Olomouc.

Wurmbrand, Susi. 1999. Modal verbs must be raising verbs. In *Proceedings of WCCFL* 18. 599–612.

Wurmbrand, Susi. 2001. *Infinitives: Restructuring and clause structure*. Berlin: Mouton de Gruyter.

Wurmbrand, Susi. 2015. Restructuring cross-linguistically. Proceedings of NELS 45. 227–240 http://ling.auf.net/lingbuzz/002514/current.pdf (accessed 02 April 2015)

Zegrean, Iulia-Georgian. 2012. *Balkan Romance: aspects on the syntax of Istro-Romanian*. Ph.D. Dissertation. Università Ca' Foscari, Venezia. http://lear.unive.it/jspui/bitstream/11707/294/1/Zegrean.pdf (accessed 03 April 2015)

Dalina Kallulli
Balkan Clitic Doubling Revisited: Micro-Variation, Typological Generalizations, and a True Universal

Abstract: The main goal of this paper is to present a case study in comparative Balkan syntax, regarding the phenomenon of clitic doubling, which is pervasive in these languages and which illustrates and highlights the usefulness of the micro-comparative enterprise. While I have discussed this phenomenon before, in this paper, inspired by Kiparsky (2008), I focus on the relation between generalizations drawn in previous work and a true universal, namely what Kiparsky refers to as the "D-hierarchy". While clitic doubling is always the spell-out of agreement with a topic (in the sense: 'given') XP, one of the concerns of this paper is to show how this phenomenon can be brought in line with bigger-picture considerations, such as the relation of argument structure, Case and information structure, and with the vast typological literature on (other well-known cases of) differential object marking, including in particular the objective conjugation in Hungarian, which for all intents and purposes has the same function as clitic doubling in Balkan languages. Crucially, this paper sketches the beginnings of a new approach to the so-called "person-case constraint" effects, a constraint which I argue to be causally related to differential object marking.

Keywords: clitic doubling, argument structure, Case, information structure, differential object marking

---

Note: Parts of the material contained in this paper were presented at the 46th Societas Linguistica Europaea Workshop 'Balancing the Universal and the Particular in Balkan Morpho-Syntactic Convergence', and at the 41st Incontro di Grammatica Generativa. I thank the audiences at these events, an anonymous reviewer, and the editors of this volume for their feedback. Parts of the material contained in this article appear in: Kallulli (2016).

Dalina Kallulli, University of Vienna

https://doi.org/10.1515/9783110375930-009

1 Introduction

The last couple of decades have witnessed a surge of scholarly interest in comparative Balkan syntax, among other linguistic studies.[1] This is maybe not surprising given the change of focus from macro-syntactic to micro-syntactic variation in the field of comparative syntax more generally. The main goal of this paper is to make a case for indulging in comparative Balkan syntax as a particularly useful enterprise in the light of this shift in the field, a shift that is motivated by the idea that the languages under comparison are particularly close to one another, the rationale being that it is easier to search for comparative syntax correlations across a set of more closely related languages than across a set of less closely related languages, since in this way there will be fewer variables to control for, which in turn increases the likelihood of hitting upon the valid correlations (see Kayne 2013 and references therein). The situation within the Balkan Sprachbund, whereby the constituting languages, though quite different in their respective vocabularies – as Tomić (2011: 307) puts it they are "often genetically only remotely related (and in some cases totally unrelated)" – are particularly close in the relevant dimension (i.e. morpho-syntax), makes their comparative study a rather suitable object for linguistic theory; after all, the determination of the ways in which all languages are alike and the ways in which they differ is a key goal of this theory.

Empirically, the focus of this paper is on clitic doubling, a well-known pervasive phenomenon in Balkan languages, as recognized already in Miklosich (1862), and defined and studied as a Balkan Sprachbund phenomenon by Lopašov (1978).[2] This construction is illustrated in (1) with an example from Albanian.

---

[1] Joseph (2001) draws a distinction between 'comparative syntax of Balkan languages' on the one hand, which he defines as an exercise in cross-linguistic syntactic comparison that just happens to involve Balkan languages, and 'comparative Balkan syntax' on the other, which he defines as an exercise in the comparison of contact-related convergent syntactic structures found within the Balkan Sprachbund languages. While this distinction is rather useful for the purposes that Joseph discusses, throughout this paper, I deal exclusively with the former, but because of my goals in this paper, I take the liberty to use both expressions interchangeably, however.
[2] The fact that the phenomenon of clitic doubling is also found in other languages that are not part of the Balkan Sprachbund, such as Spanish or North Italian dialects, does not make it less of a Balkan Sprachbund property, especially since its properties in these languages vary substantially from its properties as manifested in Romance (see Kallulli and Tasmowski 2008b). For instance, one such difference is the fact that, except for Romanian, the Balkan Sprachbund languages violate "Kayne's Generalization" (Jaeggli 1982).

(1) *Eva* **e**   *lexoi*   **letrën**   *deri në fund.*
    Eva CL-ACC.3S read-3SG letter-DET till in end
    'Eva read the letter till the very end.'

While I have discussed this phenomenon before (see Kallulli 2000, 2008), in this paper, inspired by Kiparsky (2008), I focus on the relation between generalizations drawn in previous work and a true universal, namely what Kiparsky refers to as the "D-hierarchy". And while in previous work I have argued that clitic doubling is always the spell-out of agreement with a topic (in the sense of 'given') XP, one of the concerns of this paper is to show how this phenomenon can be brought in line with bigger-picture considerations, such as Givón's (1975) idea that (verbal) agreement is always topic agreement (i.e. agreement with a topic argument), and with the vast typological literature on (other well-known cases of) differential object marking (cf. Bossong 1983–1984, Aissen 2003, Nikolaeva 2001 on Ostyak, Leonetti 2008 on Spanish, Escandell-Vidal 2009 on Balearic Catalan, É. Kiss 2005, 2013 on the objective conjugation in Hungarian, López 2012 on scrambling in German, among others).[3]

The rest of this paper is organized as follows. In section 2, I present a short summary of the Balkan clitic doubling patterns and their theoretical significance especially in view of the by now well-known violations to Kayne's Generalization (Jaeggli 1982). Then, in section 3, I revisit the Albanian and Greek clitic doubling patterns, which on top of violating Kayne's Generalization (see Dobrovie-Sorin 1994; Anagnostopoulou 1994; Kallulli 1995, 2000), serve as a rather good illustration of syntactic micro-variation in this domain. In turn, in section 4 these are juxtaposed to the patterns of the definite objective conjugation in Hungarian, which for all intents and purposes has the same function as clitic doubling (see É. Kiss 2013), and which I contend reflects the workings of the same underlying universal, namely the so-called "D-hierarchy" (Kiparsky 2008), which crucially is to be understood in terms of topic-worthiness, or individuation. Section 5 sketches a novel approach to the person-case constraint (henceforth: PCC), which I contend is causally related to differential object marking.

---

[3] Maybe not surprisingly given the understandable dominance of Romance studies in the early generative literature on clitic doubling (see Kallulli and Tasmowski 2008b on this), this phenomenon has strikingly not been recognized as a form of differential object marking in the literature so far. However, there are strong grounds to consider it as such, as the present paper seeks to establish.

2 Clitic doubling in the Balkan languages: A bird's eye view

As discussed at length in Kallulli and Tasmowski (2008b), clitic doubling in the Balkan languages is an innovation that has arisen within these languages themselves. Even if the first vestiges of this phenomenon may be considered to stem from Vulgar Latin (Friedman 2008), and its (rare) appearance in New Testament Greek is probably due to previous contact with Vulgar Latin (de Boel 2008), neither of these languages disposed of a double series of third person pronouns (i.e. strong versus phonetically reduced clitic ones), with clitics similar in nature to the ones found in the daughter languages. Clear-cut cases of (modern-type) clitic doubling are not attested in Old Church Slavonic either (but see Dimitrova-Vulchanova and Vulchanov 2008), and the phenomenon is not found in any of the non-Balkan Slavic languages. Since the development of clitic doubling in the Balkan languages is thus not genetically determined by an established historical source in any obvious way, it has in all likelihood spread from a well-defined center of innovation inside the region. However, the resulting situation is far from homogeneous: clitic doubling seems subject to strict grammatical constraints in the West and the South of its expansion area, but gets increasingly conditioned by discourse-pragmatic factors towards the North and the East. This situation is represented through (2), with grammatically constrained clitic doubling on the left hand-side becoming freer and pragmatically significant as one proceeds to the right:

(2) Macedonian > Albanian > Romanian > Greek > Bulgarian

The representation in (2) conforms to the environments traditionally recognized to trigger clitic doubling in the specific languages, namely:
- For Macedonian, all definite direct objects and all indirect objects;
- For Albanian, all indirect objects, direct objects instantiated by first and second person pronouns, and all non-focal/non-rhematic direct object DPs;
- For Romanian, all full personal and definite pronouns, preverbal indirect objects and not [–specific] DPs, postverbal direct object DPs that are not [–specific] and are introduced by *pe* and postverbal indirect object DPs which are not [–specific] and/or [–human] Goal;[4]
- For Greek, no obligatory context, except with *olos* 'all';

---

[4] *Pe* is a prepositional-like element that is often viewed as a differential object marker (cf. Hill and Tasmowski 2008, López 2016, and references therein) on a par with the prepositional element *a* in Spanish (cf. Aissen 2003 and references therein).

– For Bulgarian, all objects that are interpreted as Experiencers and objects of *ima*, *njama* 'there is (not)'.

One of the most perplexing aspects of clitic doubling is the fact that across languages, doubling clitics affect interpretation in ways subject to various idiosyncratic constraints that make it very hard, if not altogether impossible, to define their function in a unitary manner. To illustrate, early generative (and non-generative) studies described clitic doubling as sensitive to the feature *humanness* in Romanian and *animacy* in Spanish (Jaeggli 1986, Borer 1984, Dobrovie-Sorin 1990), a view that was already untenable for particular varieties of Romance in the presence of examples like those in (3) below (from Suñer 1988), and also for the languages of the Balkan Sprachbund at large.

(3) a. *Yo lo voy a comprar el*
    I it.CL go.1SG COMP buy the
    diario justo antes de subir. (Porteño Spanish)
    newspaper just before come.up.INF
    'I am going to buy it-the newspaper just before coming up.'
b. *Yo la tenía prevista esta muerte.*
    I it.CL had.1SG foreseen this death
    'I had foreseen it-this death'
c. *Ahora tiene que seguir usándolo el apellido.*
    Now has.3SG COMP continue.INF using.it.CL the surname
    'Now she has to go on using it-the surname.'

The examples in (3) are also important because they invalidate Kayne's Generalization, which informally stated, says that clitic doubling is possible whenever the (doubled) noun phrase can get case by means of some non-verbal device that has case assigning properties, namely prepositions. Simplifying somewhat, the idea was that the doubling clitic absorbs Case, so unless a preposition (or some other case-assigning device) could be inserted, the DP-argument would remain caseless, and the Case Filter (Chomsky 1981) would cause the derivation to crash.[5] Suñer (1988) argues instead that the so-called prepositional

---

5 In an effort to account for the violation of Kayne's Generalization with respect to indirect object clitic doubling in (Standard) Romanian, Dobrovie-Sorin (1994) appeals to the fact that indirect objects in this language bear morphological dative case, which in pre-minimalist Case theory was considered to be inherent, or lexical, and as such, different from structural case that had to be assigned by a governing category. However, further research soon revealed that this phenomenon is quite extensive in the Balkan languages: Albanian and Greek exhibit clitic doubling not

element *a* in Spanish is an animacy marker, which is why it is missing in the examples in (3) even though the direct object DPs here are clitic doubled.⁶ Suñer's claim for Spanish gains more general significance given the fact that, unlike Standard Romanian, the South-Danubian Aromanian and Megleno-Romanian dialects double the direct object in the same contexts as in (3) while lacking a preposition-like element even before animates (see Friedman 2008, Tomić 2008, and references therein). This is illustrated in (4).

(4) a. *nu-lu   ávdu   fiĉórlu*
    not-him.CL hear.1SG boy-the
    'I don't hear the boy'
    (Aromanian; Caragiu-Marioțeanu 1975: 237)
  b. *ieł nu lă   vreà   țela fitšór*
    he not him.CL wanted that child
    'He did not like that child'

With the Balkan patterns coming into the focus of research on the topic, other semantic properties such as *prominence, specificity, presuppositionality, familiarity, definiteness* and *topicality* have increasingly been scrutinized as to their relevance for the phenomenon of clitic doubling (see the contributions in Kallulli and Tasmowski 2008a and references therein).⁷ Be it as it may, the mention of (each of) these notions makes it easy to see how a rather direct connection of this phenomenon to what Kiparsky (2008) refers to as the "D-hierarchy", given in (5), can be established.⁸

---

only of inherently case marked indirect objects, but also of structurally governed direct objects bearing morphological accusative case but that nonetheless do not co-occur with a prepositional element. Moreover, Macedonian, Bulgarian, (and among the Romance languages) Aromanian and Megleno-Romanian can double a purely structurally governed direct object that bears no morphological case, as in (4).

6 Indeed in Aissen's (2003) influential approach to differential object marking, highly 'animated' objects constitute a semantically marked class, and are as such also morphologically marked (by iconicity).

7 Lopašov (1978), who defines the phenomenon of clitic doubling as a Balkan Sprachbund property, considered the preverbal position of the object to be a trigger of clitic doubling, a situation that in current syntactic theory largely falls under the phenomenon of clitic left dislocation. Secondly, Lopašov relates clitic doubling to the definiteness of the associate, acknowledging however that clitic doubling of a strong pronoun is more widespread than that of a non-pronominal DP. Finally, he particularly emphasizes the impossibility of doubling focalized objects (i.e. objects bearing logical accent in his terminology).

8 Kiparsky attributes this formulation of the hierarchy in (5) to extensive discussions by Kenneth Hale in lectures at M.I.T. in the late sixties and Hale (1973), pointing out that Silverstein (1976)

(5) The D-hierarchy:

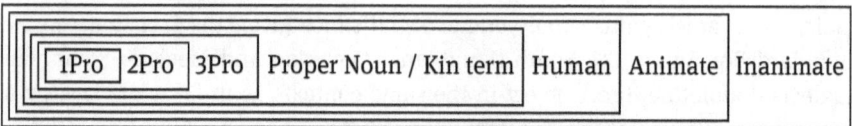

Furthermore, Kiparsky notes, somewhat contra Aissen (2003), that, as Wierzbicka (1981) has shown, the hierarchy involves neither "animacy" nor "agentivity", which makes a direct functional explanation implausible, and that a category related to definiteness, such as individuation or "topic-worthiness" is a more likely candidate.[9]

With these prerequisites in mind, I now turn to a case study of clitic doubling in Albanian and Greek, partially revisiting facts discussed in earlier work by myself and others. To my mind, this subject is a perfect illustration of syntactic micro-variation, and other relevant issues in this context, such as the relation between what Kiparsky (2008) refers to as "typological generalizations" on the one hand, and "true intrinsic universals" (in the sense of Universal Grammar) on the other, one instance of the latter being the D-hierarchy in (5). In a broader (Balkan Sprachbund) context, clitic doubling serves as an illustration of Kiparsky's (2012) idea of grammaticalization as UG-driven analogy.

3 Micro-variation case study: Clitic doubling in Albanian and Greek

Both Albanian and Greek only have object pronominal clitics (i.e. both lack subject clitics). As I have discussed in Kallulli (2000) and as can be seen in all the examples that follow, a striking property of Albanian and Greek clitic doubling, especially when viewed from a Standard Romance perspective, is the already mentioned fact that it violates Kayne's Generalization. In fact, prepositional

---

and Dixon (1979) only documented its application to ergative case systems. He also notes that the hierarchy is actually not always so tidy, and that one somewhat widespread pattern groups kinship terms with the pronouns, and that sometimes "animates" are restricted to higher or intelligent animals, the others patterning with inanimates. Crucially, Kiparsky (2008) argues for this hierarchy being part of Universal Grammar.

9 As an anonymous reviewer points out, the notion of 'individuation' also figures prominently in Hopper and Thompson (1980) research on transitivity, who implicitly build a similar hierarchy based on it.

objects cannot be clitic doubled in these languages. The significance of these two latter facts alone in terms of differential object marking can be made explicit as follows: If prepositional object marking is differential object marking (as in Aissen 2003 and references therein), and clitic doubling presupposed prepositional marking, then there is no need to formulate an explicit condition on clitic doubling as differential object marking. But because Kayne's Generalization is not valid, then clitic doubling itself (i.e. independently of prepositional object marking) is an instance of differential object marking.[10]

Only in Albanian, but not in Greek, dative/genitive DPs, i.e. indirect objects, are invariably clitic doubled.[11] In (6a,b) this applies to (non-quantified) singular definite expressions (note throughout that *v*P-internal scrambling of objects has no bearing on the generalization), in (6c,d,e) to quantificational (and/or non-quantified plural) expressions, and in (6f,h) to questions (note here that the generalization really is about datives, as it holds also for two-place predicates like 'speak' which assign dative but no accusative to their non-subject argument).

(6) a. *Eva *(i) dërgoi Anës / një vajze lule.*
Eva CL.DAT.3SG sent Ana$_{DAT}$ a girl$_{DAT}$ flowers
'Eva sent Anna flowers.'
b. *Eva *(i) dërgoi lule Anës / një vajze*
Eva CL.DAT.3SG sent flowers Ana-DAT a girl-DAT
'Eva sent Anna flowers.'
c. *Eva *(i) dërgoi secilës (vajzë) / çdo vajze lule.*
Eva CL.DAT.3SG sent each-DAT girl every girl-DAT flowers
'Eva sent each/every girl flowers.'
d. *Eva *(i) dërgoi lule secilës (vajzë) / çdo vajze*
Eva CL.DAT.3SG sent flowers each-DAT girl every girl-DAT
'Eva sent each/every girl flowers.'
e. *Eva *(u) dërgoi (gjithë) vajzave lule.*
Eva CL.DAT.3PL sent (all) girls.DAT flowers
'Eva sent (all) girls flowers.'
f. *Eva *(u) dërgoi lule gjithë vajzave.*
Eva CL.DAT.3PL sent flowers all girls.DAT
'Eva sent each/every girl flowers.'

---

[10] I thank an anonymous reviewer for suggesting that the connection between the violation to Kayne's Generalization and differential object marking be thus made explicit.
[11] Albanian and Greek have identical case systems except for the fact that the Greek counterpart of the Albanian dative is the genitive (i.e. the Greek dative has been supplanted by the genitive).

g. *Kujt   *(i)   dërgoi (Eva) lule (Eva)?*
   who.DAT CL.DAT.3S sent Eva flowersEva
   'Who.DAT did Eva sent flowers to?'
h. *Kujt   *(i)   foli Eva?*
   who.DAT CL.DAT.3S spoke Eva
   'Who did Eva speak to?'

Of course datives are also obligatorily clitic doubled when instantiated by full pronouns.[12]

(7) a. *Neve   *(na)   foli.*
       us-FP.DAT us.CL.1PL spoke.3S
       'S/he spoke to us.'
    b. *Juve   *(ju)   foli.*
       you.PL.FP.DAT you.CL.2PL spoke.3S
       'S/he spoke to you (all).'
    c. *Asaj/atij   *(i)   foli.*
       her.FP.DAT/him.FP.DAT CL.DAT.3SG spoke.3S
       'S/he spoke to her/him.'

Likewise, only in Albanian but not in Greek, direct objects instantiated by first and second person (full) pronouns are obligatorily clitic doubled, as shown in (7).[13]

(8) a. *Mua   *(më)   zgjodhi.*
       me.FP me.CL chose.3SG
       'S/he chose me.'
    b. *Ty   *(të)   zgjodhi.*
       you.SG.FP you.SG.CL chose.3SG
       'S/he chose you.'
    c. *Ne *(na) zgjodhi.*
       us-FP us.CL chose.3SG
       'S/he chose us.'

---

12 Note that due to considerable case syncretism, dative and accusative cannot always be told apart for first and second person (full) pronouns in Albanian. In fact, the two forms in which the dative differs are often reduced to the first syllables namely *ne* and *ju*, which are (identical with) the respective accusative forms. Interestingly, the clitic forms are fully identical; compare the examples (7a,b) and (8c,d).
13 Like Greek, Albanian is a null subject, *pro*-drop language.

d. *Ju   *(ju)   zgjodhi.*
   you.PL.FP you.PL.CL chose.3SG
   'S/he chose you (all).'

These facts alone point to clitic doubling as a differential object marking strategy, at least in Albanian, an issue that gains in significance when taking into account the nominative-accusative case syncretism for indefinites, illustrated in (10), versus the lack of such syncretism for definites, see (9).

(9) a. *Libri   u botua.*
       book.**the**-NOM.MASC was published
       'The book was published.'
    b. *Botoi   librin.*
       published.3SG book.**the**-ACC.MASC
       'S/he published the book.'

(10) a. *Një libër   u botua.*
        a book   was published
        'A book was published.'
     b. *Botoi   një libër.*
        published-3SG a book
        'S/he published a book.'

Another aspect of clitic doubling as differential object marking is the fact that, while both definite and indefinite expressions with articles (i.e. overt determiners) can be clitic doubled, bare indefinites cannot; see (11a,b) versus (11c). This fact relates rather directly to the D-hierarchy in (5) above, and it also entails that dative objects cannot be instantiated by bare nouns (recall that dative objects are invariably clitic doubled in Albanian).

(11) a. *(E)   botoi   **librin**.*[14]
        CL.ACC.3S published.3SG book.the-ACC.MASC
        'S/he published the book.'
     b. *(E)   botoi   **një libër** (më në fund).*
        CL.DAT.3SG published.3SG a book   at long last
        'S/he published a book (at long last).'

---

14 Unlike in Greek, the 3rd person accusative clitic in Albanian is underspecified for gender.

c. (*E)   botoi   **libër**   (më në fund).
   CL.DAT.3S published.3SG a book at long last
   'S/he published a book (at long last).'

Note that the fact that both (11b) and (11c) are unspecified for case (recall the nominative/accusative case syncretism for indefinites) further weakens the view that Kayne's Generalization can somehow be tied to (overt) case marking (see footnote 5).

Let me now turn to the function of doubling clitics in cases like (11a,b), cases that, unless more is said, might lead one to believe that clitic doubling is an optional phenomenon. As I have argued in detail in Kallulli (2000, 2008), clitic doubling is an anti-focus operation, in that it serves to encode the topic status of the (direct) object.[15] In other words, a clitic doubled object functions as a familiarity topic, i.e. it is [+given], as illustrated by the complementarity of felicity conditions between the 'minimal pairs' in (12B) and (13B) on the one hand, where a doubling clitic is impossible in the given contexts (i.e. when the VP, or the object DP is focused), versus (14B) and (15B) on the other, where a doubling clitic must be present in Albanian and is strongly preferred in Greek.[16]

(12) A: What did Ana do?   B: Ana   (*e)   lexoi   **librin.**   (Alb)
                                      I Ana (*to)   ðiavase   **to** vivlio. (Grk)
                                      the Anna CL   read   **the** book
(13) A: What did Ana read?   B: Ana   (*e)   lexoi   librin.
                                      I Ana (*to)   ðiavase   to vivlio.
(14) A: Who read the book?   B: Ana   *(e)   lexoi   librin.
                                      I Ana   ?(to) ðiavase   to vivlio.
(15) A: What did Ana do to the book? B: Ana *(e)   lexoi   librin.
                                      I Ana   ?(to) ðiavase   to vivlio.
                                      'Anna read the book'

Thus, it stands to reason that focused objects, such as *wh*-objects, cannot be doubled:[17]

---

15 Note that the clitic doubled object need not be preposed or right-dislocated (see Anagnostopoulou 1994 for Greek, and Kallulli 1999, 2000 for Albanian).
16 As the paradigm in (12) through (15) clarifies, the complementarity of felicity conditions between the doubled and the non-doubled versions is full only in Albanian, but partial in Greek (see in particular (14B) and (15B)).
17 So-called "d-linked" *wh*-phrases (Pesetsky 1987) are an apparent exception to this generalization; see Kallulli (2008) for details.

(16) a. Alb: *Kë/çfarë*   *(*e)*   *pe?*
        [who-ACC/what] CL.3S.ACC saw-you
   b. Grk: *Pjon/ti*   *(*ton/*to)* *iðes?*
        [who/what].ACC him/it-CL saw-you
        'Who/what did you see?'
        (Kallulli 2000:220)

In contrast, the object of a subject question, forming part of the presupposition, must be doubled in Albanian and is strongly preferred doubled in Greek, too:

(17) a. Al: *Kush *(e) pa   fëmijën?*
   b. Gr: *Pios ?(to) íðe to peðí?*
           who   CL   saw the child
           'Who has seen the child?'
           (Kallulli 2000:220)

This link to presupposition is further highlighted when considering the data in (18) and (19) below, which show that even for a so-called "non-factive" verb such as 'to believe' (Kiparsky and Kiparsky 1970), factivity can in fact be triggered by clitic pronouns 'doubling' the clausal complement, though this 'doubled' CP, in turn, can be said to be the complement of an empty D-head corresponding to the pleonastic *it* in English or the so-called 'correlate' *es* in German, which likewise trigger factivity in these languages (for details, see Kallulli 2006).[18] That is, factivity is the correlate of givenness, or topichood, in the propositional domain.

(18) a. *Besova   se   Beni shkoi (por në fakt ai nuk shkoi).*
        Believed- 1SG that Ben left (but in fact he not left)
        'I believed that Ben left (but in fact he didn't).'
        (Kallulli 2006: 212)

---

[18] While the factivity of *believe* is easy to see in sentences like 'I couldn't believe it that John left' and 'I didn't believe it that John left', crucially, factive *believe* doesn't need to be accompanied by either modals, negation, or pleonastic it, as the following example (from Kallulli 2006) shows: *I didn't see John leave my party, but then he called me from his home phone. Now it was obvious. I believed that John left*. Interestingly, however, both in the relevant sentence here (i.e. the underlined one), as well as in the relevant Albanian and Greek sentences, i.e. (18b) and (19b), factive 'believe' needs to be (pitch) accented, as discussed in detail in Kallulli (2006). This is important, because it underlines once again the deaccentedness and thereby givenness of the (factive) CP.

    b. ***E***   besova   se Beni shkoi *(*por në fakt ai nuk shkoi)*.
       CL-3SG.ACC believed-1SG that Ben left   (but in fact he not left)
       'I believed the fact that Ben left (*but in fact he didn't).'

(19) a. *Pistepsa*   *oti o Janis efije (ala stin praymatikotita ðen ejine kati tetio)*.
       Believed-1SG that the Janis left (but in.the reality not happened
                                                                        something such)
       'I believed that John left (but in fact he didn't).'
    b. ***To*** *pistepsa*   *oti o Janis efije*
                                        (*ala stin praymatikotita ðen ejine kati tetio).
       it-CL believed.1SG that the Janis left (but in.the reality   not happened
                                                                                     something such)
       'I believed the fact that John left (*but in fact he didn't).'

In sum, the data discussed so far sufficiently illustrate that (at least direct object) clitic doubling is a topic-licensing operation. Clearly, however, the grammaticalization of this phenomenon is at different points, or stages, across the two languages under investigation (compare for instance Albanian and Greek in (14B), (15B) and (17), among other patterns that have been discussed here). Similarly, it has been claimed that clitic doubling of direct objects in Greek is dependent on definiteness (Anagnostopoulou 1994), though this seems to be a contentious issue among scholars studying this phenomenon in Greek. For instance, Kazazis and Pentheroudakis (1976) provide many examples of such clitic doubled indefinites, one of which is given in (20b).[19]

(20) a. *Do* ***ta***   *pija*   *me kënaqësi* **një** *uiski*.   (Alb)
       FUT SUBJ.CL.3S.ACC drink-1SG with pleasure **a**   whisky
    b. ***To*** *pino*   *eukharistos ena ouiskaki*.   (Grk)
       it drink-1SG with-pleasure one whisky
       'I would gladly drink a whisky.'

Be it as it may, even if in Greek clitic doubling of indefinites is more restricted than in Albanian, it is certainly not the case that definite expressions can always be clitic doubled; recall for instance the (Greek) examples in (12B) and (13B). Crucially, just like clitic doubled definites, clitic doubled indefinites are necessarily interpreted as [+given]/[+topic],[20] i.e. they are 'non-novel' in the sense of

---

[19] To be fair, Anagnostopoulou (1994) does acknowledge this example as a counterexample to her claim that Greek clitic doubling is contingent on definiteness.
[20] This is in fact what the conclusion in Kazazis and Pentheroudakis (1976) boils down to – see also Friedman (2008) for further detail.

Krifka (2001).[21] That the clitic doubled indefinites in the examples in (20) are non-novel indefinites is evidenced by several diagnostics. First, just like the 'doubled' CPs in (18b) and (19b), they are deaccented; that is, the nuclear pitch accent cannot be borne by the clitic doubled expression. Secondly, the indefinite picks up a discourse referent whose existence in the input context is obviously presupposed, as can be seen by the fact that the sentences in (20) can be uttered felicitously in either of the contexts in (21): while the clitic doubled indefinite in (20a,b) function as a kind of quotation in the context of (21a), it stands in a part-whole relationship with the indefinite 'a drink' in (21b), and is presupposed through accommodation in the context of (21c).

(21) a. What about a whisky? / Would you like a whisky?
b. What about a drink? / Would you like a drink?
c. I have just stepped out of work.

Turning to the (other) differences between Albanian and Greek clitic doubling, given that datives in Albanian are invariably clitic doubled, as are direct objects instantiated by 1st and 2nd person (full) pronouns, it seems sensible to describe the function of doubling clitics as mere object agreement markers in such configurations. But if the nature of agreement and topic markers is indeed substantially different, why are doubling clitics employed as means for fulfilling such different functions? I suggest that these two seemingly different functions are not that different after all, and that crucially, clitic doubling is always agreement with a topic (object) DP, which is fully in line with Givón's (1975) original claim that (object) agreement is topic-verb agreement. Furthermore, I hypothesize that PCC effects (Perlmutter 1971) in Albanian as in other languages arise due to the competition for topic-prominence.[22]

---

21 Krifka (2001) argues (contra Heim 1982) for a class of so-called "non-novel" indefinites. These are indefinites that pick up discourse referents that exist in the input context. For a discourse referent to exist in the input context, it must either have been mentioned before in the immediate context, or its existence must in some way be presupposed (e.g. through sensory salience, via world knowledge, or typically through accommodation). Crucially, non-novel indefinites must be deaccented, an idea that is in tune with the well-known observation that across languages, 'given' information systematically correlates with lack of phonetic prominence (Halliday 1967, Ladd 1996, Selkirk 1995, Schwarzschild 1999). For Krifka, evidence for non-novel indefinites stems from adverbial quantification in connection with the so-called "requantification problem" (Rooth 1985, 1995, von Fintel 1994).
22 Also known as the *me-lui constraint (Perlmutter 1971), PCC is a restriction on possible combinations of phonologically weak elements. The PCC was first extensively analysed by Bonet (1991, 1994), who noticed the following properties: (i) it applies in a large range of unrelated languages; (ii) it applies only to phonologically *weak* elements, i.e. clitics, agreement affixes and weak pronouns; (iii) it applies only to combinations of phonologically weak elements; (iv) it

In other words, PCC effects within and across languages are nothing more than effects of the D-hierarchy given in (5) and repeated below for ease of reference; note in particular the proximity of local (i.e. 1st and 2nd) pronouns in this hierarchy, and Kiparsky's point mentioned earlier that "the hierarchy involves neither 'animacy' nor 'agentivity', [...], and that a category related to definiteness, such as 'individuation' or 'topic-worthiness' is a more likely candidate". In sum, PCC effects arise due to competition for the first slot (occupied by 1st and 2nd pronouns) in the D-hierarchy. I return to a more detailed discussion of PCC effects in section 5.

(5) The D-hierarchy:

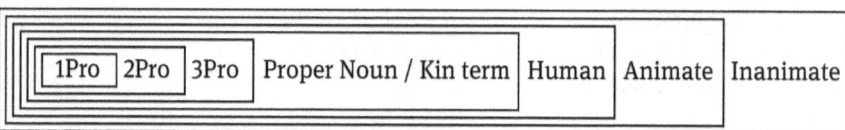

The corollary that I want to specifically add to Givón's (1975) original claim that (object) agreement is topic-verb agreement is the one implicitly contained in the D-hierarchy in (5). I contend that datives and 1st and 2nd person pronouns, just like subjects, are always DPs (i.e., they always contain a D-projection), which is however not invariably the case for (non-pronominal) direct objects. Indeed as I have already pointed out and illustrated in (11c) for Albanian, repeated below for ease of reference, bare singulars can only occur as direct objects, but not as indirect objects.[23] And as also noted earlier, bare singulars cannot be clitic doubled either in Albanian or in Greek. The implication here is that bare singulars are truly bare, in the sense that there is no D-layer projected in their structure.[24] Interestingly, as

---

also applies to combinations where the DO is a reflexive element; (v) it only affects constructions with an external argument. There are at least two versions of the PCC, the *strong* version and the *weak* version. *Strong* PCC refers to the banning of local (i.e., 1st and 2nd) person direct objects in double-object constructions in general, and *weak* PCC to the banning of local person direct objects only when the indirect object is 3rd person. Albanian is a so-called *strong* PCC language, i.e. it disallows local person direct objects in double object constructions.

23 This generalization in fact extends to languages beyond the Balkan Sprachbund which have a three-way formal distinction for the category of definiteness (namely: definites, vs. indefinites with articles, vs. bare indefinites), such as the Mainland Scandinavian languages (see Kallulli 1999, 2005 for detailed discussion).

24 In Kallulli (1999) I relate this difference between dative and direct objects to differences in the respective phrase structure positions they are merged in. Specifically, I argue that DPs are merged in Specifier positions, whereas NPs lacking a D-projection are merged as complements of V⁰. This difference both in terms of size of projection (i.e., presence versus absence of the

I have argued in Kallulli (2005), bare singulars just like their plural counterparts (i.e. existential bare plurals) cannot serve as topics, which in Kallulli (2005) I relate to their property-denoting (i.e. semantic <e,t> type) status.[25] Consequently, datives (and subjects) are presuppositional – or, in Kiparsky's (2008) terminology "topic-worthy"/"individuated" – in a way that direct objects are not,[26] and this is precisely what their marking (via clitic doubling) relates to.[27]

(11) c. (*E)   botoi   **libër**   (më në fund).
      CL.DAT.3SG published-3SG   a book at long last
      'S/he published a book (at long last).'

Since, in spite of its earliest occurrence in Vulgar Latin (Friedman 2008 citing Ilievski 1988) and in the private papyri of the Hellenistic Age (de Boel 2008) clitic doubling in the Balkan languages (including Albanian and Greek) has been largely referenced as a Balkan Sprachbund innovation and as a contact convergence phenomenon – indeed the phenomenon is not attested in the oldest Albanian documents (cf. Friedman 2008 citing Asenova 2002:105)[28] – its degree of grammaticalization especially in Albanian is rather striking, as is the micro-variation observed even when comparing it to just the Greek patterns. Drawing on Kiparsky (2012), I suggest that clitic doubling can be seen as an instance of UG-driven analogy (i.e. a sort of parallel development according to universal principles), which is exactly how Kiparsky defines grammaticalization.[29] In this context, it is not surprising to witness the same effects that the phenomenon of clitic doubling

---

D-layer) and phrase structure position ensures a straightforward mapping to semantics: DPs are individual-denoting entities, NPs are property-denoting entities. (Note here the relation to the notion of "individuation" that Kiparsky (2008) also zooms in on in his accompanying note to (5).)
25 Like in Romance (Longobardi 1994) and unlike in Germanic, bare plurals in Albanian and Greek are incompatible with generic readings; i.e. they necessarily receive an existential interpretation in these languages.
26 From this discussion, it also follows that datives (and subjects), when focused, can only be contrastive topics. The fact that quirky subjects across Balkan languages must be clitic doubled (see Krapova and Cinque 2008) is further evidence of the topic-worthiness of such quirky (i.e. dative and/or accusative) subjects.
27 While subjects are not clitic doubled in any of the Balkan languages, they invariably agree with the finite verb. That is, subject-verb agreement can be viewed as a further stage in this grammaticalization process, or different means of marking "topic-worthiness"/"individuation".
28 The oldest attested extensive written Albanian text is from the 16th century.
29 More specifically, Kiparsky argues that universals constrain change, and change results in typological generalizations (and grammaticalization – and innovation – is optimization). Structural features caused by change (such as e.g. clitic doubling in Balkan languages) are inherently unstable and can be washed out by other changes, or replaced with the opposite feature, hence

produces also in languages beyond the Balkan Sprachbund, such as Hungarian, which uses a particular conjugation, namely the so-called "definite", or "objective", conjugation, which I turn to next.[30]

4 'Balkanosis' beyond the Sprachbund: The Hungarian 'objective' conjugation

Hungarian verbs have two subject agreement inflectional paradigms, the so-called "objective" (or "definite") and "subjective" (or "indefinite") conjugations, reflecting the presence or absence of a definite object, as illustrated in (22) through (24), from Coppock (2013).[31]

(22) *Lát-om   a madar-at.*
    see-1SG.DEF the bird-ACC
    'I see the bird.'

(23) *Lát-ok   **egy** madar-at.*
    see-1SG.INDEF a   bird-ACC
    'I see a bird'

(24) *Vár-ok.*
    wait-1SG.INDEF
    'I'm waiting'

---

recurrent structural features caused by recurrent patterns of change are typological generalizations, not true universals.

30 Indeed object agreement markers in languages like the Bantu ones can also be seen as 'clitic doubling'; see for instance Bax and Diercks (2012) on Manyika Shona.
31 According to É. Kiss (2013), the types of objects eliciting the definite conjugation include nouns with a definite article, possessive constructions, proper names, 3rd person personal pronouns, reflexive pronouns (which have the morphological make-up of possessive constructions of the type 'my body', 'your body'), and demonstratives. Object clauses also trigger the definite conjugation, which É. Kiss ascribes to a presumable overt or covert pronominal head in their structure. On the other hand, the types of objects eliciting the indefinite conjugation include bare nouns, nouns with an indefinite determiner, and indefinite and universal pronouns.

Person also affects the choice of conjugation: the subjective conjugation is used with 1ˢᵗ and 2ⁿᵈ person objects, despite their definiteness:³²

(25) *Lát-nak   engem/téged/minket/...*
 see-3PL.INDEF me-ACC/you-ACC/us-ACC/...
 'They see me/you/us'

While the distribution of the definite conjugation is rather complex (see Bartos 2001, É. Kiss 2002, 2005, 2013, Wechsler and Coppock 2012, Coppock 2013 and references therein), (25) identifies an obvious gap, in that, as Coppock (2013) points out, first and second person non-reflexive, non-reciprocal pronouns are certainly definite, and under the hypothesis that the objective conjugation is governed by definiteness, they should trigger the objective conjugation, contrary to fact. In spite of this, as Coppock (2013) notes, a dominant view on what conditions the use of the objective conjugation is what Coppock and Wechsler (2012) refer to as the *DP-hood hypothesis* (Bartos 2001, building on Szabolcsi 1994, adopted in É. Kiss 2002, pp. 49, 151–157, quoted in Coppock 2013):³³

(26) *DP-hood hypothesis*
 The objective conjugation is used if and only if the object is a DP (or larger).

Coppock and Wechsler (2012) point out several empirical challenges for this view, which I however do not go into. Suffice it to mention that in later work, Coppock (2013) relates the objective conjugation to *familiarity* (i.e. non-novelty), which however is related to a morphological [+definiteness] feature as follows: If the referential argument of a phrase is lexically specified as *familiar*, then the phrase bears the feature [+def], and this feature governs the objective conjugation. (If, on the other hand, the referential argument of a phrase is specified as *new*, then the phrase bears the feature [-def], which governs the subjective conjugation.) She defines the notion 'referential argument' as in (27):

---

32 There are further qualifications, or exceptions, to this generalization, which I will however not go into as they are not important in the present context. For details on these exceptions, see Coppock (2013) and references therein.
33 É. Kiss (2013) attributes to Bartos (2000) the attempt to eliminate the 'exceptions' illustrated in (24) by claiming that the 1ˢᵗ and 2ⁿᵈ person pronouns are indefinite, i.e., they are not DPs but NumPs, but notes that no independent semantic or syntactic evidence has been presented to support their indefiniteness. Indeed É. Kiss provides evidence against the NumP analysis of 1ˢᵗ and 2ⁿᵈ person pronouns, by pointing out that sentences with a 1ˢᵗ person singular subject marginally allow a 1ˢᵗ person plural object (the optimal solution is to use a reflexive pronoun in such cases), in which case the verb must be in the definite conjugation.

(27) *Referential argument*
The referential argument of a phrase is the discourse referent *u* such that: when the phrase combines an expression denoting property P, P is predicated of u.

While this in effect comes quite close (it looks in fact identical) to the trigger of clitic doubling in Albanian and Greek, it does not account for the gap in (25), since the parallelism with Albanian (though not with Greek) breaks down here. Coppock claims that the person effect (i.e. (25)) is explained on the grounds that first and second person non-reflexive pronouns are not anaphoric but rather purely indexical, unlike third person pronouns and first and second person reflexive and reciprocal pronouns. This is also the most problematic part of her account, since, even though she takes familiarity to be broader than anaphoricity (indeed she states that "[f]amiliar discourse referents do not necessarily have a linguistic antecedent, so long as the discourse referent can be found in the associated context", and "[f]amiliarity must be understood here in a broad sense, one that includes givenness purely on the basis of world knowledge"), indexicals are obviously not given in the associated context for her, which is puzzling. Interestingly, É. Kiss (2013) reports that although object noun phrases supplied with indefinite determiners (including the [+specific] *bizonyos* and *egyes* 'certain') require the indefinite conjugation according to all grammars of Modern Hungarian, Peredy (2009) has found certain types of examples in which speakers hesitate whether the indefinite or the definite conjugation is more appropriate, often accepting both, or preferring the definite conjugation. Furthermore, the examples in which the unexpected definite conjugation is accepted, and even preferred, by the majority of speakers (up to 85% of them) all involve a topicalized [+specific] indefinite object, as in (28), taken from É. Kiss (2013):

(28) a. *Bizonyos gyerekeket a társasjátékok lekötik.*
   certain kids-ACC the board-games absorb-DEFO-3PL
   'Certain kids are absorbed by board-games.'
   (Peredy 2009, (13c))
 b. *Egyes nıket a sötét ruhák öregítik.*
   certain women-ACC the dark clothes make.look.old-DEFO-3PL
   'Certain women, dark clothes make look older.'
   (Peredy 2009, (15))

Taken together, these facts suggest that an account of the impossibility of the use of the objective conjugation in (25) along the lines of É. Kiss (2005, 2013), according to which this gap is a manifestation of the Inverse Agreement Constraint (Comrie 1980) which blocks object – verb agreement if the object is higher ranked in the animacy hierarchy than the subject, seems more feasible, as it is more in tune both with phenomena known from other languages, including languages genetically related to Hungarian (e.g. Ostyak), and as it can be easily derived from the universal D-hierarchy in (5). In particular, relying on Nikolaeva's (2001) work on Ostyak, a sister language of Hungarian, which shows that agreeing objects function as secondary topics, É. Kiss (2013) suggests that the objective conjugation in Hungarian is fossilized topic-verb agreement. The object thus competes with the subject for the higher slot in (5), and the objective conjugation is ruled out in this case because of the Inverse Agreement Constraint, in a manner that is quite analogous to the PCC effects observed in Albanian, Greek and other languages, as suggested in Section 3. That is, 1st and 2nd person pronouns objects which trigger the subjective conjugation in Hungarian (i.e. the data in (25)) are no less DPs than e.g. their Albanian (direct object) counterparts, which are invariably clitic doubled, and cannot partake in a clitic cluster given that dative objects, which asymmetrically c-command direct objects (see Massey 1992), are invariably doubled, too.[34]

5 A note on the PCC

In this section I turn to the following interrelated questions. What, if anything, does a language in which all dative objects, local direct object pronouns, and non-local [+given] direct objects are (almost) invariably clitic doubled tell us about the relation between argument structure, Case, agreement, and information structure in natural language? And what, if anything, does the partial suspension, or mitigation, of such a constraint in configurations that would otherwise yield a PCC effect tell us about these relations, and about the PCC itself? Before attempting to answer these questions, and providing the facts presupposed in these questions, let me however turn to a critical evaluation of a prominent line of syntactic approaches to the PCC, namely those accounts that involve feature-checking with the same functional head (Anagnostopoulou 2003, Béjar and Rezac 2003, 2009, Adger and Harbour 2007, Nevins 2007, 2011).

According to Anagnostopoulou (2003) for instance, dative and accusative object clitics (unlike full pronouns) compete for agreement with v^0, which involves the cyclic checking of *person* and *number* features assumed to be distributed as in (29). In *strong* PCC languages first the dative, and then the accusative object clitic checks its features with v^0; the derivation converges if the dative clitic checks the

---

[34] The order within a clitic cluster is invariably dative > accusative in Albanian (and genitive > accusative in Greek).

person feature of v^0, and the accusative clitic its *number* feature. If the accusative object clitic is 1st/2nd person, the person feature of v^0 cannot be checked and the derivation crashes because only φ-complete checking results in structural Case checking. *Weak* PCC languages have Multiple Agree, i.e. *person* is checked simultaneously against both object clitics, which can only occur under non-conflicting feature specifications of the elements partaking in the Agree relation.

(29) 1,2, ACC: +person, number   1,2, DAT: +person
      3 ACC: number   3 DAT: -person

Looking at the Albanian patterns, there emerge two immediate problems for such a Case-based account. First, while languages manifest so-called "anti-agreement" repair strategies to obviate PCC effects – see for instance the radical Albanian case in (31a) where the (otherwise) obligatory direct object doubling clitic has been omitted to avoid a PCC violation – a fact that Anagnostopoulou's (2003) approach is indeed designed to capture since the absence of a clitic is taken to indicate lack of agreement between v^0 and the full pronoun (FP) *in situ*, Albanian also exhibits another strategy, namely reversing the otherwise rigidly fixed dat > acc order within the cluster (see (30)), yielding the (otherwise ungrammatical) order ACC > DAT instead; see (31b). Both (31a) and (31b) while slightly marked stand in stark opposition to the fully ungrammatical (31c), which violates the (strong) PCC.[35]

(30) a. *Kush na   e   bëri   dhuratë këtë njeri?*
        who us-CL 3SG-CL.ACC made present this person
        'Who brought us this guy (as a present)?'
    b. **Kush   e   na   bëri   dhuratë   këtë njeri?*
        who 3SG-CL.ACC us-CL made present   this person

(31) a. *?Kush na   bëri   dhuratë   ty?*
        who us-CL made present   you-SG.FP

    b. *?Kush të   na   bëri   dhuratë (ty)?*
        who you-SG.CL us-CL made present you-SG.FP
        (Intended) 'Who brought you to us as a present?'
    c. **Kush na   të   bëri   dhuratë (ty)?*
        who us-CL you-SG.CL made present you-SG.FP

---

[35] Note that the checking order dat > acc is crucial for Anagnostopoulou (2003), which is why it fails to account for (31b).

A second problem for Anagnostopoulou's Case-based approach involves the fact that in Albanian two dative clitics may co-occur in a clitic cluster, as shown in (32); the first clitic, which is invariably 1st or 2nd person is arguably an ethical dative, and the second clitic, which is invariably 3rd person (hence relevant to the PCC) doubles a (dative) goal DP, namely 'the/my family'.[36]

(32) ... imagjino se çfarë mund të   m'i   bëjnë   familjes   (sime).
     ... imagine that what can   SUBJ me.CL-3SG.CL.DAT do.3P family.the-DAT my
     '... imagine what they can inflict (me) on my family'

Building on the re-interpretation of the "D-hierarchy" by Kiparsky (2008), who to recall posits that it "involves neither 'animacy' nor 'agentivity'", but that "[a] category related to definiteness, such as 'individuation' or 'topic-worthiness' is a more likely candidate", breaking with tradition I take "topic-worthiness"/"individuation" to be an *interpretable* feature on the head of an applicative phrase, in the specifier position of which datives are licensed. Further, I follow Pancheva and Zubizarreta (2017) in assuming that: (i) the applicative phrase is a phase; (ii) there is only one individuation feature per phase; (iii) if there is more than one DP that can agree with the interpretable individuation feature on the head of the phase, and one DP is marked [+author] while the other [-author], the DP [+author] is the one that agrees; (iv) the domain of application of the constraint can be different: Appl^0, v^0, T^0; (v) variation arises from different specifications of the value of the interpretable individuation feature. Finally, the crucial data in (31b) can be accommodated by assuming that whenever this order reversal happens, the accusative clitic has expanded the relevant agreement domain by moving upwards, possibly introducing a new phase with a new interpretable 'topic' feature.

6 Conclusion

I hope to have shown that undoubtedly, clitic doubling is a form of differential object marking. While I agree with López (2016) in that "[i]t seems that our faculty of language – our Universal Grammar, if you will – includes [differential object marking] as a possible ingredient of a natural language", I have described this in terms of what Kiparsky (2008) refers to as a "typological generalization"

---

[36] Indeed Anagnostopoulou (2003: 302) categorically and explicitly rejects the existence of data as in (32) which involve ethical dative clitics partaking in a PCC configuration.

(as opposed to a true universal, in the sense of Universal Grammar), and have related it to the D-hierarchy, which is a "true intrinsic universal" (in the sense of Universal Grammar). Furthermore, I have contended that PCC effects arise as a result of competition for the same slot within the D-hierarchy, a conclusion that is corroborated by the distribution of the Hungarian objective conjugation, which for all intents and purposes is the Hungarian counterpart of clitic doubling in Albanian and Greek. An interesting outcome of this comparison is the idea that both PCC and the Inverse Agreement Constraint are direct consequences of the D-hierarchy. In other words, the D-hierarchy that governs split case assignment, number marking, and agreement (cf. Kiparsky 2008 and references therein) also governs PCC and the Inverse Agreement Constraint. A precise formal implementation of this idea that also covers the observed variation (e.g. the dichotomy *strong* versus *weak* PCC) will have to await future research.

References

Adger, David and Daniel Harbour 2007. Syntax and syncretisms of the Person Case Constraint. *Syntax* 10(1): 2–37.
Aissen, Judith. 2003. Differential object marking: iconicity vs. economy. *Natural Language and Linguistic Theory* 21: 435–448.
Anagnostopoulou, Elena. 1994. On the representation of clitic doubling in Modern Greek. *EUROTYP Working Papers, Theme Group 8*, 5: 1–66.
Anagnostopoulou, Elena. 2003. *The Syntax of Ditransitives. Evidence from Clitics*. Berlin. Mouton de Gruyter.
Asenova, Petya. 2002. *Balkansko ezikoznanie. Osnovni problemi na balkanskija ezikov săjuz* [Balkan linguistics. Fndamental problems of the Balkan Linguistic Union]. Veliko Tărnovo: Faber.
Bartos, Huba. 2000. Az inflexiós jelenségek szintaktikai háttere. In F. Kiefer (ed.), *Strukturális magyar nyelvtan II. Morfológia*. 653–761. Budapest: Akadémiai Kiadó.
Bartos, Huba. 2001. Object agreement in Hungarian: A case for Minimalism. In G.M. Alexandrova and O. Arnaudova (eds.) *The minimalist parameter: Selected papers from the open linguistics forum, Ottawa, 21–23 March 1997*. 311–324. Amsterdam: John Benjamins.
Bax, Anna and Michael Diercks. 2012. Information structure constraints on object marking in Manyika. *Southern African Linguistics and Applied Language Sciences* 30(2): 185–202.
Béjar, Susana and Milan Rezac. 2003. Person licensing and the derivation of PCC effects. In A.T. Perez-Leroux and Y. Roberge (eds.) *Romance linguistics: theory and acquisition*, 49–62. Amsterdam: John Benjamins.
Béjar, Susana and Milan Rezac. 2009. Cyclic Agree. *Linguistic Inquiry* 40: 35–73.
Bonet, Eulália. 1991. *Morphology after Syntax: Pronominal clitics in Romance languages*. PhD thesis. Massachusetts Institute of Technology.
Bonet, Eulália. 1994. The Person-Case Constraint: A Morphological Approach. In H. Harley and C. Philipps (eds.) *MIT Working Papers in Linguistics 22. The Morphology-Syntax Connection*. 33–52. Cambridge, MA: MIT Press.

Borer, Hagit. 1984. *Parametric Syntax: Case Studies in Semitic and Romance Languages.* Dordrecht: Foris.
Bossong, Georg. 1983–1984. Animacy and markedness in Universal Grammar. *Glossologia* 2–3:7–20.
Caragiu Marioțeanu, M. 1975. *Compendiu de dialectologie română.* București: Ed.Științifică și Enciclopedică.
Chomsky, Noam. 1981. *Lectures on Government and Binding.* Dordrecht: Foris.
Comrie, Bernard. 1980. Inverse verb forms in Siberia: Evidence from Chukchee, Koryak and Kamchadal. *Folia Linguistica* 1: 61–74.
Coppock, Elizabeth. 2013. A semantic solution to the problem of Hungarian object agreement. *Natural Language Semantics* 21: 345–371.
Coppock, Elizabeth and Stephen Wechsler. 2012. The objective conjugation in Hungarian: agreement without phi-features. *Natural Language and Linguistic Theory* 30: 699–740.
De Boel, Gunnar. 2008. The genesis of clitic doubling from Ancient to Medieval Greek. In D. Kallulli and L. Tasmowski (eds.), 89–103.
Dimitrova-Vulchanova, Mila and Valentin Vulchanov. 2008. Clitic doubling and Old Bulgarian. In D. Kallulli and L. Tasmowski (eds.), 105–132.
Dixon, Robert M.W. 1979. Ergativity. *Language* 55: 59–138.
Dobrovie-Sorin, C. 1990. Clitic doubling, wh-movement and quantification in Romanian. *Linguistic Inquiry* 21: 351–397.
Dobrovie-Sorin, Carmen. 1994. *The Syntax of Romanian.* Berlin: Mouton de Gruyter.
É. Kiss, Katalin. 2002. *The Syntax of Hungarian.* Cambridge University Press. Cambridge: Cambridge University Press.
É. Kiss, Katalin. 2005. The inverse agreement constraint in Hungarian – a relic of a Uralic–Siberian Sprachbund? In H. Broekhuis et al. (eds.) *Organizing Grammar. Linguistic Studies in Honor of Henk van Riemsdijk.* 108–116. Berlin: De Gruyter.
É. Kiss, Katalin. 2013. *Differential object–verb agreement is (fossilized) topic–verb agreement.* Ms. Hungarian Academy of Sciences.
Escandell-Vidal, Victoria. 2009. Differential object marking and topicality. The case of Balearic Catalan. *Studies in Language* 33(4): 832–885.
Friedman, Victor. 2008. Balkan object reduplication in areal and dialectological perspective. In D. Kallulli and L. Tasmowski (eds.), 35–63.
Givón, Talmy. 1976. Topic, pronoun, and grammatical agreement. In C. Li and S. Thompson (eds.) *Subject and Topic*, 149–188. New York: Academic Press.
Hale, Kenneth. 1973. A note on subject-object inversion in Navajo. In Braj B. Kachru et al. (eds.) *Issues in Linguistics: Papers in honor of Henry and Renee Kahane.* Urbana, IL: University of Illinois Press.
Halliday, Michael. 1967. *Intonation and Grammar in British English.* Berlin: Mouton de Gruyter.
Heim, Irene. 1982. *The Semantics of Definite and Indefinite Noun Phrases.* Ph.D. dissertation, University of Massachusetts, Amherst.
Hill, Virginia and Liliane Tasmowski. 2008. Romanian clitic doubling: A view from pragmatics-semantics and diachrony. In D. Kallulli and L. Tasmowski (eds.), 135–163.
Hopper, Paul and Sandra Thompson. 1980. Transitivity in grammar and discourse. *Language* 56(2): 251–299.
Ilievski, P. 1988. Kon interpretacijata na modelot na udvoeniot objekt vo makedonskiot jazik [On the interpretation of the doubled object in the Macedonian language]. *Balkanološki lingvistički studii.* Skopje, Institut za Makedonski Jazik.
Jaeggli, Osvaldo. 1982. *Topics in Romance Syntax.* Dordrecht: Foris.

Jaeggli, Osvaldo. 1986. Three issues in the theory of clitics: Case, doubled NPs, and extraction. In H. Borer (ed.) *Syntax and Semantics 19: The Syntax of Pronominal Clitics* 15–42. New York: Academic Press.

Joseph, Brian D. 2001. Is Balkan comparative syntax possible? In Maria-Luisa Rivero and Angela Ralli (eds.) *Comparative Syntax of Balkan Languages*, 17–43. Oxford: Oxford University Press.

Kallulli, Dalina. 1995. Clitics in Albanian. University of Trondheim Working Papers in Linguistics 24. Dragvoll: University of Trondheim. [Cand. Philol. thesis]

Kallulli, Dalina. 1999. *The Comparative Syntax of Albanian. On the Contribution of Syntactic Types to Propositional Interpretation.* PhD dissertation, University of Durham.

Kallulli, Dalina. 2000. Direct object clitic doubling in Albanian and Greek. In Frits Beukema and Marcel den Dikken (eds.) *Clitic Phenomena in European Languages.* [Linguistik Aktuell/ Linguistics Today 30] 209–248. Amsterdam: John Benjamins.

Kallulli, Dalina. 2005. On existential bare plural "subjects": they don't exist! *Belgian Journal of Linguistics* 19: 27–57.

Kallulli, Dalina. 2006. Triggering factivity: Prosodic evidence for syntactic structure. In D. Baumer, D. Montero and M. Scanlon (eds.) *Proceedings of 25th West Coast Conference on Formal Linguistics*. 211–219. Sommerville, MA: Cascadilla Proceedings Project.

Kallulli, Dalina. 2008. Clitic doubling, agreement, and information structure. In D. Kallulli and L. Tasmowski (eds.), 227–255.

Kallulli, Dalina. 2016. Clitic doubling as Differential Object Marking. *Rivista di Grammatica Generativa: Research in Generative Grammar* (RGG) 38: 161–171.

Kallulli, Dalina and Liliane Tasmowski (eds.). 2008a. *Clitic Doubling in the Balkan Languages.* Amsterdam: John Benjamins.

Kallulli, Dalina and Liliane Tasmowski. 2008b. Introduction: Clitic doubling, core syntax, and the interfaces. In D. Kallulli and L. Tasmowski (eds.), 1–32.

Kayne, Richard. 2013. Comparative grammar. *Lingua* 130: 132–151.

Kazazis, Kostas and Joseph Pentheroudakis. 1976. Reduplication of indefinite direct objects in Albanian and Modern Greek. *Language* 52: 398–403.

Kiparsky, Paul. 2008. Universals constrain change, change results in typological generalizations. In J. Good (ed.) *Linguistic universals and language change*, 23–53. Oxford: Oxford University Press.

Kiparsky, Paul. 2012. Grammaticalization as optimization. In D. Jonas, J. Whitman and A. Garrett (eds.) *Grammatical Change: Origins, Nature, Outcomes*, 15–51. Oxford: Oxford University Press.

Kiparsky, Paul and Carol Kiparsky. 1970. Fact. In M. Bierwisch and K. Heidolph (eds), *Progress in Linguistics*, 345–369. The Hague: Mouton.

Krapova, Iliyana and Guglielmo Cinque. 2008. Clitic reduplication constructions in Bulgarian. In D. Kallulli and L. Tasmowski (eds.), 257–287.

Krifka, Manfred. 2001. Non-novel indefinites in adverbial quantification. In C. Condoravdi and G. Renardel de Lavalette (eds) *Logical Perspectives on Language and Information*, 1–40. Stanford CA: CSLI.

Ladd, Robert. 1996. *Intonational Phonology.* Cambridge: Cambridge University Press.

Leonetti, Manuel. 2008. Specificity in clitic doubling and in differential object marking. *Probus* 20: 35–69.

Longobardi, Giuseppe. 1994. Reference and proper names: a theory of N-movement in syntax and logical form. *Linguistic Inquiry* 25: 609–665.

Lopašov, J. 1978. *Mestoimennye povtory dopolnenija v balkanskih jazykah* [Pronominal doubling of the object in the Balkan languages]. Leningrad: Nauka.
López, Luis. 2012. *Indefinite Objects. Scrambling, Choice Functions and Differential Marking.* Cambridge MA: MIT Press.
López, Luis. 2016. (In)definiteness, specificity and differential object marking in Romance. In Susann Fischer and Christoph Gabriel (eds.) *Manual of Grammatical Interfaces in Romance*, 241–265. Berlin: De Gruyter.
Massey, Victoria. 1992. *Compositionality and Constituency in Albanian.* PhD thesis, Massachusetts Institute of Technology.
Miklosich, Franz. 1862. Die Slavischen Elemente im Rumänischen. *Denkschriften der Kaiserlichen Akademie der Wissenschaften, Philosophisch-historische Klasse* 12: 1–70.
Nevins, Andrew 2007. The representation of third person and its consequences for Person-Case Effects. *Natural Language and Linguistic Theory* 25: 273–313.
Nevins, Andrew 2011. Multiple agree with clitics: person complementarity vs. omnivorous number. *Natural Language and Linguistic Theory* 29: 939–971.
Nikolaeva, Irina. 2001. Secondary topic as a relation in information structure. *Linguistics* 39: 1–49.
Pancheva, Roumyana and Maria Luisa Zubizarreta. 2017. The Person Case Constraint: the syntactic encoding of perspective. *Natural Language and Linguistic Theory.* Online first.
Peredy, Márta. 2009. A stochastic account for the variation in Hungarian object agreement. Ms. Budapest: Research Institute for Linguistics of the Hungarian Academy of Sciences.
Perlmutter, David. 1971. *Deep and Surface Structure Constraints in Syntax.* New York: Holt, Rinehart and Winston.
Pesetsky, David. 1987. Wh-in-Situ: Movement and Unselective Binding. In E. Reuland and A. ter Meulen (eds) *The Representation of (In)definiteness.* Cambridge, MA: MIT Press.
Rooth, Mats. 1985. *Association with Focus.* Ph.D. dissertation, University of Massachusetts at Amherst.
Rooth, Mats. 1995. Indefinites, adverbs of quantification and focus semantics. In G.N. Carlson and F.J. Pelletier (eds.) *The Generic Book*, 265–291. Chicago IL: Chicago University Press.
Schwarzschild, Roger. 1999. GIVENness, AVOIDF and other constraints on the placement of accent. *Natural Language Semantics* 7: 141–177.
Selkirk, Elizabeth. 1995. Sentence prosody: Intonation, stress, and phrasing. In J.A. Goldsmith (ed.) *The Handbook of Phonological Theory*, 550–69. Oxford: Blackwell.
Silverstein, Michael. 1976. Hierarchy of features and ergativity. In R.M.W. Dixon (ed.) *Grammatical Categories in Australian Languages*, 112–71. Canberra: Australian Institute of Aboriginal Studies.
Suñer, M. 1988. The role of agreement in clitic-doubled constructions. *Natural Language and Linguistic Theory* 6: 391–434.
Szabolcsi, Anna. 1994. The noun phrase. In F. Kiefer and K. É. Kiss (eds.) *The Syntactic Structure of Hungarian.* Syntax and Semantics 27: 179–274. New York: Academic Press, New York.
Tomić, Olga M. 2008. Towards grammaticalization of clitic doubling: Clitic doubling in Macedonian and neighbouring languages. In D. Kallulli and L. Tasmowski (eds.) *Clitic Doubling in the Balkan Languages*, 65–87. Amsterdam/Philadelphia: John Benjamins.
Tomić, Olga M. 2011. Balkan Sprachbund features. In B. Kortmann and J. van der Auwera (eds) *The Languages and Linguistics of Europe: A Comprehensive Guide*, 307–324. Berlin: De Gruyter.
Von Fintel, K. U. 1994. *Restrictions on Quantifier Domains.* Ph.D. dissertation, University of Massachusetts at Amherst.
Wierzbicka, Anna. 1981. Case marking and human nature. *Australian Journal of Linguistics* 1: 43–81.

Lena Baunaz and Eric Lander
Cross-categorial Syncretism and Containment in Balkan and Slavic

Abstract: This paper presents syncretism patterns in the Balkan and Slavic languages between complementizers, (indeclinable) relativizers, and interrogative pronouns. Building on Baunaz and Lander (2017), we claim that complementizers – and the categories they are syncretic with – are internally complex and composed of syntactico-semantic features which are hierarchically ordered according to a functional sequence. The syncretism patterns of Balkan and Slavic are shown to be precisely paralleled by the syncretism data from Romance and Germanic, and are thus compatible with (and additional evidence for) the functional sequence proposed in Baunaz and Lander (2017). Yet, even though the syncretism patterns from Balkan and Slavic support our previous findings, some Slavic languages (Serbo-Croatian, Russian) present a problem in the form of an unexpected morphological containment relation. To account for this *Slavic containment puzzle*, we propose a finer-grained morphological decomposition of some of the items discussed, coupled with a relevant generalization concerning the internal structure of demonstratives.

Keywords: Slavic, syncretism, complementizers, demonstratives, morphological containment

1 Introduction

Syncretism is the phenomenon whereby multiple functions are covered by a single phonological form. For instance, the Latin plural case ending -$\bar{i}s$ has both dative and ablative functions. Rather than positing two separate case endings which happen to be homophonous (dative plural -$\bar{i}s$ vs. ablative plural -$\bar{i}s$), one posits a single ending -$\bar{i}s$ which is syncretic between dative and ablative (see Baerman, Brown and Corbett 2005, Starke 2009, Caha 2009, among others).

In this paper we discuss a phenomenon which might be called *cross-categorial syncretism*. That is to say, we consider cases where there is a syncretism conflating what are normally considered to be distinct categories: demonstrative,

---

Lena Baunaz, (University of Zurich)
Eric Lander, (University of Gothenburg)

https://doi.org/10.1515/9783110375930-010

complementizer, relative pronoun, and interrogative pronoun. Cross-categorial syncretism is present in the (finite) complementizer systems of, for instance, English (*that* is a demonstrative, complementizer, and relative pronoun; see Roberts and Roussou 2003, Kayne 2008, Leu 2015) and French/Italian (*que* and *che* are complementizers, relative pronouns, and interrogative pronouns; see Sportiche 2011 for French, Manzini and Savoia 2003, 2011 for Italian, and Roussou 2010 for similar facts in Modern Greek). The items responsible for non-finite complementation in these languages, moreover, appear to involve a cross-categorial syncretism between complementizers and prepositions (French *à, de, pour*; English *for*). Cross-categorial syncretism also implicates the verbal domain, as in Akan [Niger-Congo] (*sɛ* is the verb 'say', a quotative marker, and a similative marker 'like, as if'; see Lord 1993), Mandarin [Sinitic] (*shuō* is the verb 'say' and a quotative; see Chappell 2008), and Buru [Austronesian] (*fen(e)* is the verb 'say' and a quotative; see Klamer 2000), and even English (*like* is a verb, a quotative marker, and a similative marker).

In previous work we established – primarily on the basis of facts from Germanic and Romance – a particular underlying functional sequence responsible for building the demonstrative, (nominal) complementizer, relative pronoun, and interrogative pronoun. In this paper we extend our approach to the Balkan and Slavic languages, with interesting consequences. On the one hand, the syncretism patterns from Balkan and Slavic support our previous findings, but on the other hand these languages present a problem in the form of an unexpected morphological containment relation.

The theoretical approach taken is nanosyntactic (Starke 2009, 2011; see also Baunaz et al. 2018), meaning that we consider these items to be complex (cf. Sanfelici and Poletto 2014, Leu 2015, among others), with a fine-grained internal structure consisting of multiple syntactic features. Following the cartographic maxim of 'one feature – one head' (Cinque and Rizzi 2008: 50), moreover, these features are merged as heads in a strict, universal hierarchical order (i.e. the functional sequence). One especially important aspect of nanosyntax is that it allows for multiple heads to be spelled out by a single morpheme, that is, phrasal spellout.

The outline of the paper is as follows. In Section 2 we provide some basic background on cross-categorial syncretism in Germanic and Romance and the functional sequence emerging out of the patterns observed. Section 3 is the empirical core of the paper: it presents the relevant syncretism patterns in the Balkan and Slavic languages between complementizer, (the indeclinable) relativizer, and interrogative pronoun. The syncretism patterns are seen to be perfectly compatible with (and thus further evidence for) the functional sequence seen in Section 2. In Section 4, we propose a finer-grained morphological decomposition of some of the items discussed, along with discussion of a relevant generalization concerning the internal structure of demonstratives. In Section 5 we discuss an interesting puzzle of *morphological containment* which arises in Slavic, for which we provide an account. Section 6 concludes the paper.

2 Background: Syncretisms with the nominal complementizer

Baunaz and Lander (2017) discuss patterns of syncretism with the complementizer in Germanic and Romance (as well as some Balkan and Finno-Ugric, which we omit here). We observe that the declarative complementizer (Comp) in these languages often has the same morphophonological form as demonstrative (Dem), relative (Rel), and interrogative (Wh) pronouns (see work cited above), which we take to be cases of cross-categorical syncretism. The data are summarized in (1).

(1) Syncretisms with nominal complementizer (3 SG inanimate/neuter forms)

		DEM	COMP	REL	WH
North Gmc	Swedish	det	att	som	vad
West Gmc	English	that	that	that	what
	(Non-standard) English	that	that	as	what
	Dutch	dat	dat	dat	wat
	German	das	dass	das	was
	Yiddish	jenc	vos	vos	vos
			az	az	
Romance	French	ce(lui)	que	que	que
	Italian	quello	che	che	che
	Spanish	aquél	que	que	qué

Even though we did not perform detailed morphological decompositions of the forms in (1), we still assumed that Dem, Comp, Rel, and Wh elements have a fine-grained internal structure.

As seen in (1), syncretism targets only adjacent cells in the paradigm (as indicated by the shaded areas). The fact that non-adjacent cells are not syncretic is analyzed in terms of the *ABA theorem and can be accounted for by nanosyntactic principles of spellout (Caha 2009: Section 2.3; see also Bobaljik 2007, 2012). For our purposes here the most important concept is that syncretism reflects structural adjacency, revealing which syntactic heads are merged next to each other in the functional sequence. In other words, the patterns in (1) necessitate a linear order of heads such that the functional layer Dem is next to Comp, which is next to Rel, which is next to Wh: Dem | Comp | Rel | Wh.

While syncretism facts can determine what the linear order of functional heads is in a functional sequence, they do not necessarily determine what the hierarchical order is (i.e. Dem > Comp > Rel > Wh vs. Wh > Rel > Comp > Dem). In Baunaz and Lander (2017) we propose a novel way of handling the hierarchy issue, namely identifying something we call the 'nominal core' and studying its behavior with regard to syncretism, a strategy we briefly discuss below. For now, though, observe that the first hierarchy – Dem > Comp > Rel > Wh – lines up with certain findings from (more traditional) cartographic work on the clausal spine (e.g. D > C > Rel in Cinque 2008) and thus this order should be preferred over the other one. In other words, the word-internal or morphological structure we are interested in can be seen to replicate structure at the higher clausal level.

We may assume (following Grimshaw 1991 and later work) that functional structure in the extended projection must be merged on top of a lexical element, in this case a noun (though for our purposes this noun is taken to be 'lighter' than a full lexical noun like *house*).

(2) Dem > Comp > Rel > Wh > ... n

In nanosyntax, structures are taken to be additive or cumulative. This means that the set of syntactic heads making up the Dem structure is a superset of the set of heads making up the Comp structure, that Comp is in turn a superset of Rel, and so on. The relevant structures are given in (3), with the more abstract labels A, B, C, and D for the heads in order to make the concept of cumulative structure clearer.

(3) [D [C   [B   [A   [*n*]]]]]   =   Dem
       [C   [B   [A   [*n*]]]]   =   Comp
             [B   [A   [*n*]]]   =   Rel
                   [A   [*n*]]   =   Wh
                         [*n*]   =   nominal core

The cumulative nature of structure is the key to accounting for the *ABA theorem (see Caha 2009: Section 2.3 in particular).

As for the head n, it is the smallest element of the structure. Features being cumulative, [n] is thus a subset of the structure of the Wh pronoun, which itself is a subset of Rel, and so on. This 'nominal core', contained in all of the structures in (3), essentially classifies the morphological items being built as nominal elements. Being the smallest structure that the fseq can build, this item is expected to be semantically vacuous (or at least, semantically light).

An interesting piece of evidence for the existence of the nominal core can be found in the Germanic and Romance languages. In English, for instance, interrogative/quantificational pronouns and (non-D-linked) demonstratives can be decomposed into at least two components: *whi-ch* (< Old Eng. *hwi-lc*; cf. German *we-lch-*, Dutch *we-lk-*, Swedish *vi-lk-*), *ea-ch* (< Old Eng. *ǣ-lc*), *su-ch* (< Old Eng. *swi-lc*). The second component in each form here (i.e. *-(l)ch/-lk*) expresses something along the lines of 'form', which makes sense from a historical point of view since these morphemes descend from the Proto-Germanic noun **līk-* 'body, form' (see Leu 2015: §6.2.1 and references cited there). This is overt evidence for the light noun being embedded in the structure of the larger pronoun, i.e. *whi-ch*$_{FORM}$. Similarily, Romance quantifiers are often built combining an overt operator with the semantically vacuous bound morpheme *-que/-che* (Fr. *quel-que* 'some', *cha-que* 'each, every'; It. *qual-che* 'some' and *cias-che-duno* 'someone'), which is actually syncretic with (non-bound) Comp, Rel, and Wh, as seen in (4).

(4) Romance nominal cores

		DEM	COMP	REL	WH	n
Romance	French	ce	que	que	que	-que
	Italian	quello	che	che	che	-che

In other words, the bound morpheme *-che* is like Gmc. *-(l)ch/-lk* in being a relatively semantically vacuous element which is found in certain nominal environments (e.g. combined with independently built operators like Fr. *quel-*, *cha-*, It. *cias-*, *qual-*). Crucially the Romance nominal core participates in the syncretism patterns we are interested in and for this reason can be considered part of the functional sequence as in (2) and (3) above. The prosodic dependence and relative semantic vacuousness of Gmc. *-(l)ch/-lk* and Rom. *-que/-che* are two reasons to assign it a very small structure (see Cardinaletti and Starke 1999), and since this small structure is syncretic with the Wh-layer, we have evidence for the hierarchy Dem > Comp > Rel > Wh (i.e. the hierarchy with Wh placed at the structurally smaller end).

3 The core data: Syncretism patterns in Balkan and Slavic

We now extend the approach discussed above to the Balkan and Slavic data. We also make more specific claims about the precise functions implicated in our syncretism patterns. We observe for Balkan and Slavic that declarative complementizers used in (finite) *emotive factive* contexts[1,2] (labeled Comp$_{EF}$ in the table in (5) below) – that is, under predicates like 'regret', 'be surprised', 'be happy', 'be sorry', etc. – are often syncretic with the *indeclinable relativizer* (which we label Rvz instead of Rel; note that relativizers are sometimes called *relative complementizers*). In some languages (Greek, Russian, Serbo-Croatian), moreover, the Comp/Rvz syncretism also includes the neuter singular Wh-pronoun 'what'. The neuter singular Dem pronouns cited in (5) are distal 'that' unless otherwise noted.

(5) Syncretisms with the nominal complementizer in Balkan and Slavic[3]

		DEM$_{PRO}$	COMP$_{EF}$	RVZ	WH$_{PRO}$
Modern Greek		ekíno	pu	pu	tí
Romanian		acel	că	ce	ce
West Slavic	*Polish*	to	że	co	co
				% że	
	Czech	to	že	co	co
East Slavic	*Russian*	to	čto	čto	čto

---

1 With the exception of Yiddish (where *az* is the semi-factive and non-factive complementizer and *vos* the emotive factive complementizer; Taube 1994), in Germanic and Romance factivity with regard to complementizers is not overtly distinct (i.e. there is a syncretism, e.g. Eng. *that*). The languages discussed here often do make this distinction. In some languages there is a complementizer that can be used in both factive and non-factive contexts (MG *oti*, SC *da*, Bg. *če*, and Ma. *deka*). Certain items, however, are always factive when used (MG *pu*, SC *što*, Bg. *deto*, Ma. *što*). As seen in (5), our Balkan and Slavic data suggest that it is the emotive factive complementizer which participates in syncretism with the relativizer and wh-pronoun. For a more fine-grained account of these facts in terms of veridicality, see Baunaz (2016, under review).
2 We also do not consider declarative 'how' complementizers like Ro. *cum*, Ru./Bg. *kak*, SC *kako*, and Cz./Po. *jak*, though it is interesting that these are syncretic with Rel and Wh adverbs meaning 'how'. They also appear to trigger some kind of modality when used.
3 We would like to thank an anonymous reviewer for suggestions on improving our table.

(continued)

		DEM_PRO	COMP_EF	RVZ	WH_PRO
South Slavic	Serbo-Croatian	to	što	što	što
	Bulgarian	tova 'this'	deto	deto	kakvo
	Macedonian	toa 'that (close to hearer)'	što	što	što

3.1 The data in more detail

Modern Greek has two complementizers: *pu* and *oti*.[4] *Pu* introduces epistemic and emotive factive-type of complements (6a, b), while *oti* introduces non-factive complements (6c). *Oti* may also introduce epistemic factive complements (6a), but not emotive factive complements (6b).

(6) a. *Thimame*   **pu/oti** *dhjavaze*   *poli*.   (Grk)
    remember.1SG that   read.3SG   much
    'I remember that he used to read a lot / I remember him reading a lot.'
    (Roussou 2010: 590, (17))
  b. *O   Pavlos lipate   **pu/*oti** i   Roxani   efije*.
    the Paul   is.sad.3SG that   the Roxanne left.3SG
    'Paul regrets that Roxanne left.'
    (adapted from Giannakidou 2009: 1886, (8))
  c. *O   Pavlos ipe   **oti** i   Roxani   efije*.
    the Paul   said.3SG that   the Roxanne left.3SG
    'Paul said that Roxanne left.'
    (Giannakidou 2009: 1886, (7))

---

4 In addition, Modern Greek displays *pos* 'that'. *Oti* and *pos* vary freely: *pos* essentially replaces *oti* in everyday usage (Roussou 2000, 2006, 2012). Complementizer *pos* is syncretic with the relative pronoun *o-pos* 'how', the free relative *o-pos* 'whichever way' and with the *wh*-word *pos* 'how'. Modern Greek also displays *na* under desiderative 'wish'-type of verbs. The status of *na* is still debated, with some viewing it as a complementizer (Roussou 2010) and others as a mood particle (Giannakidou 2009, among others). Because *na* is restricted by tense and agreement – it must always, contrary to *oti/pu*, be adjacent to the verb, it can appear in main clauses, and it can co-occur with other complementizers (*pu*) (whereas *oti* and *pu* cannot co-occur) – we follow Giannakidou (2009) and claim that it is a mood particle.

Pu is syncretic with Rvz, as seen in (7).

(7) O   fititi   **pu**   sinandises   (ine   filos   mu)   (Grk)
    the   student   that   met.2SG   is   friend   mine
    'The student that you met (is my friend).'
    (Roussou 2010: 591, (18a))

Note that *pu* also looks identical to (and is in fact historically derived from) the locative adverb *pu* 'where' and the relative adverb *ó-pu* 'where'. This intersection with locatives (also relevant for Polish and Bulgarian) can be analyzed in terms of syncretism as well, but for reasons of space we cannot discuss this complication here. The important thing to notice is that the kind of *wh*-item we compare across languages in this paper is the interrogative pronoun 'what', and thus in Modern Greek we must consider *tí* rather than *pu* under the Wh-column. In sum, then, Comp$_{EF}$ in Greek is syncretic with Rvz, but not with Dem or Wh.

Romanian has one declarative complementizer, namely *că*. This item appears almost everywhere (but not under predicates selecting the subjunctive mood). In (8) we provide an emotive factive example using *că*.[5, 6]

(8) *Ion   regretă   **că**   Maria   e   bolnavă.*   (Rom)
    Ion   regrets   that   M.   is.IND   sick
    'John regrets that Mary is sick.'

Romanian *că* is not syncretic with anything in the table above. However, there is a syncretism between Rvz and Wh in the form of *ce*, as illustrated in (9) (Grosu 1994, Benţea 2010, among others).[7]

(9) a. *Am   citit cartea   **ce**   a   publicat-o*
       have.1SG   read book.the   that   has   published-CL.FEM.SG
       Paul anul trecut.   (Rom)
       Paul last year.
       'I read the book that Paul published last year.'
       (Benţea 2010: 175, (30b))

---

[5] Romanian subjunctive clauses may be introduced by *ca* when an XP is topicalized. If no topic is present, *ca* is also absent. We do not discuss this here.
[6] *De* may also be classified as a declarative complementizer in Romanian (see Hill 2002). However, not only does it cover the same ground as Fr. *de* and It. *di*, namely *non-finite* complement clauses, it also extends to interrogative and conditional contexts. Because of its broad usage we leave out *de* for the time being.
[7] As a relativizer, *ce* is quite rare and can only be used with subject and direct object relatives (see Grosu 1994, Benţea 2010).

b. ***Ce   ai   auzit?***
   What   have.2SG   heard
   'What did you hear?'
   (Bențea 2010: 173, (25a))

Thus there is a Rvz/Wh syncretism in Romanian, an important fact in its own right as it establishes the adjacency of the Rvz and Wh layers.

The default complementizer in Polish is *że*, with an emotive factive example given in (10a). Hansen et al. (2016: 205–206) write that Comp *że* is historically derived "from the masculine form of the Proto-Slavonic interrogative pronoun *jьže* 'which' which is no longer in use in Polish." This means that the Polish complementizer *że* is historically – but not synchronically – related to an interrogative pronoun, just like Modern Greek *pu*. Note also that Comp *że* can be suffixed with -*by* in irrealis contexts (which agrees in number and person with the subject). For some speakers *że* is syncretic with the relativizer *że* (10b). In this function it is important to note that Po. *że* is possible only in certain contexts, as noted by Murelli (2011: 195), namely when there is some nuance of consecutivity or finality (the relativizer by default being *co* 'that').[8] In addition, Murelli (2011: 195) writes: "In South-Eastern Polish dialects the relative particle *że* is used not only in constructions with a consecutive nuance, but has generalized to an all-purpose (relative) particle." This is illustrated in (10c).

(10) a. *Maria jest   zadowolona   **że**   wyjeżdżasz*   (Pol)
         M.   is   happy   that   leave.2SG
         'Maria is happy that you're leaving.'
    b. % *Takiego człowieka **że**-by spał   z   otwartymi*
         such   man   that-IRR   sleep.PAST.MASC with open
         oczami, jeszcze nie   widziałem.
         eyes I.have   yet.not   seen
         'I still haven't seen a man that slept/would sleep with his eyes open.'
    c. *Ten   chłopak, **że**-smy   go   wczoraj   spotkali.* (SE Pol)
         That lad   that-we.are   CL.M.ACC.3SG   yesterday met
         'The lad we met yesterday.'
         (Laskowski 1991: 275, cited in Murelli 2011: 195, (4.113))

To sum up, Polish Comp$_{EF}$ *że* is not syncretic with anything in the standard language, but is syncretic with the relativizer in southeastern Polish and in some

---

[8] Unfortunately Murelli (2011) does not provide clear examples for (non-standard) Polish. Our informants are very reluctant to accept *że* as a relativizer, but one of our speakers provided us with (10b).

non-standard varieties. Note also that the default relativizer *co* 'that' is syncretic with the *wh*-pronoun *co* 'what'.

There is one complementizer in Czech, namely *že*. It is the complementizer by default, but in (11) we once again provide the relevant context for our proposal, namely *že* under an emotive factive predicate.

(11) *Maruška   je   šťastná,   že   Honza odešel.*   (Cz)
     Mary.NOM is.3SG   happy.FEM   that John   leave.PAST.MASC
     'Mary is happy that John left'

Že is not syncretic with any other items considered here.[9] Just like in Polish, though, there is a syncretism between Rvz *co* 'that' and the Wh-pronoun *co* 'what'.

The default complementizer in Russian is *čto*. In (12a) we provide an emotive factive example. As in Polish, the suffix *-by* (from auxiliary 'be') can appear in irrealis/subjunctive contexts (see Hansen et al. 2016). Contrary to Polish, though, *-by* does not agree in number and person with the subject in Russian. Moreover, *čto* is syncretic with Rvz (12b, c) and Wh (12d).

(12) a. *Mne   zhal',   čto   ty   obidel   Ivana.*   (Ru)
        1DAT.SG   pity   that   you   hurt   Ivan
        'I regret (lit. it's a pity to me) that you hurt John.'
     b. *Eti   bol'shie kartiny, čto   visiat na stene, privezli
         these big   pictures that are   on wall   have.been.brought
         iz   drugogo   goroda.*
         from another   city
         'These big pictures that are on the wall have been brought from another city.'
     c. *On uvidel   staryi dom,   čto   postroil   ego   ded.*
         he has.seen old   house   that had.built   his   grandfather.
         'He has seen the old house that his grandfather had built.'
     d. *Čto   vy   budete   zakazyvat'?*
        what   you.NOM.2PL   will.AUX.2PL   order
        'What would you like to order?'

Čto is partially syncretic (in a sense to be made more precise below) with the distal 3SG demonstrative *to*.

---

9 For some speakers, Czech *že* is syncretic with the relativizer that occurs in the same contexts as Romanian relative *că* and Polish relative *że*, that is, when the relative relation exhibits a nuance of consecutivity or finality (Murelli 2011: 195). Our Czech informants do not accept *že* in this context.

Like Greek, Serbo-Croatian has two complementizers: *da* and *što*. While *da*[10] is the default complementizer, the use of *što* – interestingly for our purposes – is limited to appearing under emotive factive verbs (13a). Crucially, furthermore, Comp *što* is syncretic with both Rvz (13b) and Wh (13c). Note that regional variation as to the use of *što* or *šta* is found among SC speakers (T. Samardzic and T. Sočanac, p.c.).

(13) a. Žalim **što** si povrijedio Ivana. (SC)
regret.1SG that AUX.PAST.2SG hurt.PAST.PART John
'I regret that you hurt John.'
b. *Profesor* **što** *predaje istoriju ima veliki nos.*
professor that teaches history have big nose
'The professor who/that teaches history has a big nose.'
(Mitrović 2012: 1, (1))
c. **Što** *radish*?
what do.2SG
'What do you do?'

Thus SC Comp *što* is syncretic with both Rvz and Wh. In addition, just like Russian *čto*, SC *što* is partially syncretic with the distal 3SG Dem *to*.

Bulgarian exhibits two declarative complementizers: *če* and *deto*. Comp *če* appears everywhere, for instance in semi-factive contexts (14).[11]

(14) *Interesno e* **če** *tuk e zapazen*
interesting be.PRES.3SG that here be.PRES.3SG stored
edinstvenijat original (Bulg)
sole-DEF.M.NOM original
'It's interesting that the only original is stored here.'
(Hansen et al. 2016: 212, (134))

---

10 There is a debate in the literature concerning the status of SC *da*. The general trend nowadays is that there are two homophonous items with the form *da*: declarative *da* vs. modal *da*. The distinction between the two has been established on the basis of (i) their distribution and (ii) their historical development. In particular modal *da* would be historically derived from 2nd and 3rd person singular imperatives of the verb *dati* 'give', namely **dadjъ* (Old Church Slavonic *daždъ*). The origin of 'declarative' *da* is unclear (though it might have been adverbialized from a demonstrative). The reader is referred to Todorović (2012) and Sočanac (2017) and references cited in these works for details.

11 It is interesting for our purposes to note that in earlier stages of the language *če* had a relativization function (see Sonnenhauser 2015 for examples, as well as references cited there).

Under emotive factive verbs, both *če* and *deto* can be used (Krapova 2010), as shown in (15a).[12] The use of one or the other complementizer triggers a subtle change in meaning: the presupposition of the embedded clause gets somewhat stronger when *deto* is selected than when *če* is selected (see Baunaz 2016, under review). Comp$_{EF}$ *deto* is syncretic with Rvz *deto* 'that', as shown in (15b).[13]

(15) a. *Săžaljavam,* **če/deto** *ne možax da dojda.* (Bulg)
   regret.1SG that not could.1SG MOD come.1SG
   'I regret that I couldn't come'.
   (Krapova 2009: 1240, (1a))

   b. *Tova e čovekăt,* **deto** *(go) snimax včera.*
   This is man.the that him.CL.ACC photographed.1SG yesterday
   'This is the man that I photographed yesterday.'
   (Krapova 2009: 1240, (1b))

To sum up, Bg. Comp$_{EF}$ *deto* is syncretic with Rvz (but not Wh or Dem).

Finally, the Macedonian Comp$_{EF}$ is *što* (16a), which is syncretic with Rvz (16b) and Wh (16c).

(16) a. *Mi e milo* **što** *si otide.* (Mac)
   me.DAT is glad that AUX left
   'I'm glad that he (has) left.'

   b. *Profesorot* **što** *predava istorija ima golem nos.*
   professor.DEF that teaches history has big nose
   'The professor that teaches history has a big nose.'

   c. **Što** *e ova?*
   what be.3SG this.NEUT.SG
   'What is this?'
   (Tomić 2006: 419, (fn.2, (ii)))

The default complementizer in Macedonian is *deka*, as it appears with non-factive verbs and semi-factive verbs. As it is not the emotive factive complementizer, we do not include it in our table.

---

12 Some speakers accept *deto* also with semi-factive verbs like 'remember'. When that is the case, the same presupposition shift as the one described here is in order, i.e. the presupposition of the embedded clause is somewhat stronger with *deto* than with *če* (see Baunaz 2016, 2018 for more details).
13 Historically the relative *kădeto* is derived from the interrogative adverb *kăde* 'where' by adding the definite/demonstrative *-to* morpheme. *Deto* is synchronically (partially) syncretic with the relative pronoun *kădeto* 'where, which, whom'.

All of the attested syncretisms in (5) are restricted to adjacent cells: Modern Greek Comp *pu*, Russian Comp *čto*, SC Comp *što*, Bulgarian Comp *deto*, and (non-standard) Polish Comp *że* are all syncretic with at least Rvz and sometimes also with Wh, but never only with Wh to the exclusion of Rvz. If we look a little bit closer at the tables in (1) and (5) we see that the linear ordering of Dem, Comp, Rvz, and Wh can only be the one given in (17), which captures the relevant adjacencies: Bulgarian (and some varieties of Polish) show that Comp and Rvz must be adjacent, and the Czech data demand that Rvz and Wh also be adjacent. Drawing from our previous work, we include (non-standard) English data to show that Dem and Comp need to be adjacent as well (18) (since none of the Balkan/Slavic data happens to show syncretism with Dem).

(17) Dem | Comp | Rvz | Wh

(18) Four crucial syncretism patterns from (1) and (5)

	DEM	**COMP**	**RVZ**	**WH**
Non-standard English	that	that	as	what
Bulgarian	tova	deto	deto	kakvo
% Polish	to	że	że	co
Czech	to	že	co	co

The linear order in (17) is the only one that can capture the data in (1) and (5) accurately. Any other ordering would disrupt this empirical reality: if Comp and Dem were not contiguous, then the English data would not be captured. If the ordering had been Dem | Comp | Wh | Rvz, then the Bulgarian and Polish data would not be captured either, since Comp and Rvz are syncretic in this language, and so on. In Baunaz and Lander (2017: §2.1), we came to the same conclusion, so we can straightforwardly say that the same ordering posited on the basis of data from Germanic and Romance also holds for Balkan and Slavic.

As in Romance, nominal cores can be identified in Slavic and Balkan. In particular, there is a nominal core in Serbo-Croatian, Russian, and Modern Greek that is syncretic across the Comp, Rvz, and Wh layers: SC *ne-što* 'something', *sva-šta* 'everything', *ni-šta* 'nothing', *bilo-šta* 'anything'; Russian *čto-to* 'something' and *ne-čto* 'something (specific)'. Similarly, Czech and Polish have a nominal core syncretic with Rvz and Wh (but not with Comp): Cz. *-co* '-thing', as in *ně-co* 'something', and Po. *co-* as in *co-ś* 'something'. Modern Greek can also form its quantifiers with a bound morpheme which is syncretic with Wh *tí* 'what' (but not with Comp *pu*). Quantifiers like *ká-ti* 'something' and *ti-pota* 'anything' overtly display the nominal core -*ti*- '-thing'. Finally, Romanian also has a nominal core syncretic with Rvz and Wh (but not with Comp): -*ce*- as in **ce**-*va* 'something' or *ori-***ce** 'anything'.

We claim here that these bound morphemes are the Slavic and Balkan counterparts of Romance -*que*/-*che* and Gmc -*(l)ch*/-*lk* discussed earlier: they are semantically quite vacuous and are only found in combination with operators like 'every-', 'some-', etc. As such, these items in Balkan and Slavic present strong supporting evidence for the nominal core hypothesis and the reasoning (based on Cardinaletti and Starke 1999) that they are realizations of the lowest (i.e. smallest) bit of structure than can be built using our functional sequence.

(19) Dem   > Comp   > Rvz   >   Wh   > ...   n
      [DCBA...*n*] [CBA...*n*]   [BA...*n*] [A...*n*]   [*n*]

Thus Balkan and Slavic confirm that the linear ordering Dem | Comp | Rvz | Wh can be assigned the hierarchical order Dem > Comp > Rvz > Wh (rather than Wh > Rvz > Comp > Dem) on the basis of syncretism with the nominal core.

3.2 An emerging puzzle

The tables in (1) and (5) differ in one crucial way. In (5) there are no syncretisms with Dem. Because of this one might wonder if Dem is even relevant to these particular languages and if we should not, perhaps, remove this column from the table completely. On the one hand, this would seriously undermine the universality of our fseq, something to be avoided on general principles. There is also empirical evidence to support keeping the Dem column for Balkan and Slavic: Comp, Rel, and Wh all contain the Dem element *to* (SC *š-to* and Ru. *č-to*). The fact that these items all make use of the same basic morphological ingredients when they are constructed is evidence that they belong to the same 'paradigm'.

(20)   Dem   Comp   Rvz   Wh
      Ru   to   **č-to** **č-to** **č-to**
      SC   to   **š-to** **š-to** **š-to**
      = [_{Comp/Rvz/Wh} *č*- / *š*- [_{Dem} *to*]] (?)

Though the morphological containment shown in (20) is evidence that the functional template Dem > Comp > Rvz > Wh also applies to Slavic, there is something unexpected about the relationship between Dem *to* and Comp/Rvz/Wh *čto/što*. According to our fseq, Dem is the most complex (i.e. the largest) structure, with Comp being the next biggest structure, then Rvz, and finally Wh. However, the containment relation in (20) suggests the exact opposite, namely that Dem is structurally smaller than Comp, Rvz, and Wh, since it is overtly contained *within* these structures. Our fseq predicts instead that if Dem happens to be involved in a morphological containment relation, then the Dem structure should be the one containing Comp, Rvz, or Wh rather than the other way around.

In Section 4, we provide an account of this 'Slavic containment puzzle' (as we call it). We extend our analysis to Bulgarian, Polish, and Czech. Our analysis calls for further decomposition of the morphemes discussed so far, a possibility readily afforded to us by the nanosyntactic approach.

4 Decomposition, demonstratives, and definite markers

We now turn to further decomposition of the Germanic, Romance, Balkan, and Slavic data, showing how some of these data fit the approach developed so far, while others are at first glance problematic.

4.1 Decomposing further in Germanic

In Baunaz and Lander (2017) we mention that many of the forms in the table in (1) are obviously (at least) bimorphemic (e.g. Eng. *th-at*) but that syncretism can be studied without full-fledged decomposition down to the smallest level. While this is true, in this paper we in fact continue to decompose the forms in (1). For instance, if we take English, at least the demonstrative and *wh-* items are straightforwardly decomposable.

(21) Dem   th-at   =   /ð-æt/
     Wh   wh-at   =   /(h)w-ʌt/ (North America), /(h)w-ɒt/ (UK)

The *th*-prefix in the demonstrative form can be put on a par with other such prefixes in Germanic.

(22) Swedish   Dem   det   =   /d-eː(t)/
     Dutch   Dem   d-at   =   /d-ɑt/
     German   Dem   d-as   =   /d-as/

More specifically this prefix has been argued to be an instantiation of the definite article (Def) appearing as a subcomponent of the demonstrative (see Déchaine and Wiltschko 2002, Kayne and Pollock 2010, Leu 2015 (and previous work), Roehrs 2010, among others).

The *wh*-operator is instantiated by *wh*-morphology in many languages. Consider the Germanic forms in (23).

(23) Swedish Wh v-ad = /v-ɑː(d)/
 Dutch Wh w-at = /ʊ-ɑt/
 German Wh w-as = /v-as/
 Yiddish Wh v-os = /v-ɔs/

In some of these languages, moreover, the remaining element when the prefix is removed (Du. *-at*, Ger. *-as*, etc.) is the same as the element which remains when the D-prefix is removed. In German (and Slavic, as we see below) there is also evidence for a third component in the structure, namely agreement (in German the strong adjective ending for neuter nominative/accusative, namely *-(e)s*), which we simply label ΦP here.

(24) Trimorphemic structure for German *was*

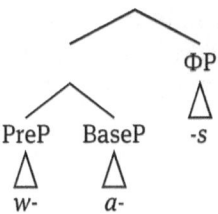

All in all, then, we have a tripartite structure, where the leftmost position (PreP, here corresponding to the morpheme *w-*) is the locus of our fseq (Dem > Comp > Rvz > Wh). The other constituents (BaseP and ΦP) are also assumed to have complex internal structure. Note that we are making crucial use of phrasal spell-out here (a ubiquitous trait of nanosyntactic proposals).

For NP in particular, we note that Caha and Pantcheva (2014) and Taraldsen (2018) have both proposed that prefixes are independent constituents merged as complex specifiers outside of the main extended projection. They also reason that the functional heads making up such prefixes, moreover, must be merged on top of a lexical category, and that this lexical category is a classifier-like noun (distinct from the main lexical N). This is abstractly shown in (25), where the constituent f3P is the prefix structure (PreP in (24)), with the classifier-like noun *n* at the bottom, and the constituent F3P is the base structure (BaseP in (24)), with lexical N at the bottom.

(25)

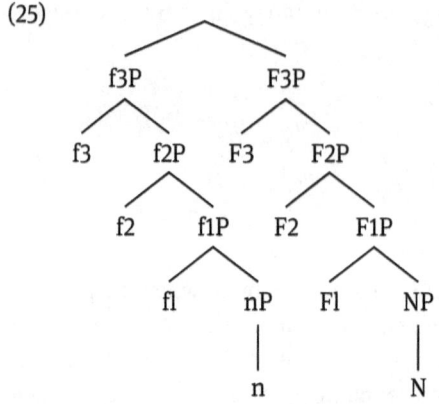

Both Caha and Pantcheva (2014) and Taraldsen (2018) provide interesting evidence from Bantu in favor of such a binominal structure. Without going into detail, we note that our structure closely matches the structure already argued for by these authors on independent grounds (except for ΦP, of course, which is an additional constituent we have proposed for the structures we consider here).

We remind the reader that structures are cumulative, and that this also applies to our double structure made up of PreP and BaseP. This is illustrated in (26).

(26) a. Wh b. Rel

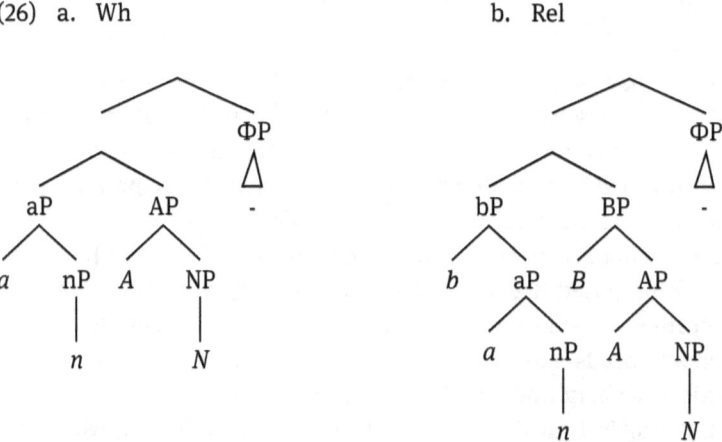

c. Comp

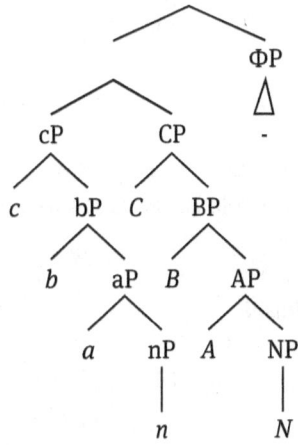

d. Dem

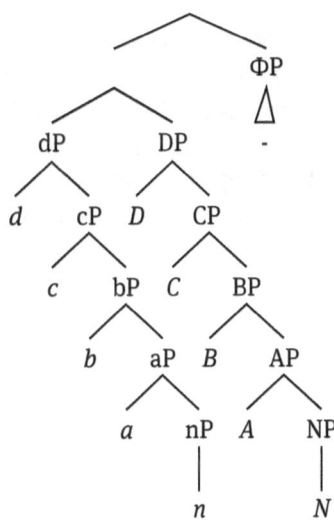

With two fseqs (one for PreP and one for BaseP), we expect that two distinct syncretism patterns should also be possible. Indeed, this is exactly what we observe with, for instance, Dutch Dem/Comp/Rvz /d-/ vs. Wh /ʊ-/ in PreP, as opposed to total syncretism of /-ɑt/ in the BaseP sequence, as shown in (27).

(27) PreP   BaseP
    [d [c [b [a [n]]]]] => **d-**   [D [C [B [A [N]]]]] => **-ɑt**
        [c [b [a [n]]]] => **d-**   [C [B [A [N]]]] => **-ɑt**
            [b [a [n]]] => **d-**   [B [A [N]]] => **-ɑt**
                [a [n]] => **ʊ-**   [A [N]] => **-ɑt**

Another example is English, where PreP has the same basic pattern as in Dutch (Dem/Comp/Rvz *th-* /ð-/ vs. Wh *wh-* /(h)w-/), while BaseP is realized as Dem/Comp/Rvz /-æt/ vs. Wh /-ʌt/.

(28) PreP   BaseP
    [d [c [b [a [n]]]]] => **ð-**   [D [C [B [A [N]]]]] => **-æt**
        [c [b [a [n]]]] => **ð-**   [C [B [A [N]]]] => **-æt**
            [b [a [n]]] => **ð-**   [B [A [N]]] => **-æt**
                [a [n]] => **(h)w-**   [A [N]] => **-ʌt**

4.2 Containment of Def within Dem

Importantly for our purposes here, PreP for demonstratives is in many languages an instantiation of the definite article (Def), e.g. Eng. *th(e)* in *th-at*. That is to say, Def is an integral component in the internal structure of Dem. There is in fact an abundance of crosslinguistic evidence outside of Germanic for the claim that Def is contained within Dem. In Klallam [Salish], for instance, demonstrative forms contain a distinct morpheme encoding definiteness, the suffix *-niɬ*. This is seen in (29) (where PROX and DIST refer to distance from the speaker).

(29) a. tiəw̓ -**niɬ**   (Klallam)
         PROX-Def
         = Dem 'this'
     b. təsə-**niɬ**
         DIST-Def
         = Dem 'that'
     (Montler 2007: 411)

In Tahitian [Austronesian], moreover, the definite article is *te*. Once we decompose the long *ē* of medial and distal *tē-* into *ee*,[14] we see that the definite marker *te* can be isolated in each of Tahitian's three demonstratives.

---

14 "[Long vowels] are the same in quality as [short vowels], but are pronounced as if they were a double vowel. [† ... a long vowel is regarded as a sequence of two identical vowels.]" (Tryon 1970: 2).

(30) a. **te**-ie (Tahitian)
　　　 Def-PROX
　　　 = Dem 'this'
　　b. tēna
　　　 te-ena
　　　 Def-MED
　　　 = Dem 'that (near the person addressed)'
　　c. tēra
　　　 te-era
　　　 Def-DIST
　　　 = Dem 'that (not near the speakers)'
　　　 (Tryon 1970: 9, 24))

In Koromfe [Niger-Congo], an item which "is very simlar to the definite article in English" (Rennison 1997: 81) can be appended with a deictic marker, giving the form "more demonstrative or deictic force" and making it "more akin to the English demonstratives *this* and *that*" (Rennison 1997: 234, 81).[15]

(31) a. HU.SG　　　　　HU.PL　　　　　　　　　　　(Koromfe)
　　　 hoŋ-go　　　 **bɛŋ**-gɛ
　　　 Def-DX　　　　 Def-DX
　　　 = Dem　　　　　= Dem
　　b. Non-HU.SG　　 Non-HU.PL
　　　 koŋ-go　　　 **hẽŋ**-gɛ
　　　 Def-DX　　　　 Def-DX
　　　 = Dem　　　　　= Dem
　　　 (Rennison 1997: 234–235)

In Romanian, the generalization concerning the containment of Def within Dem is straightforwardly instantiated. As seen in (32), the entire Romanian demonstrative paradigm shows morphological containment of the definite article.

(32) Romanian (Savu and Bican-Miclescu 2012)
　　 a. Dem 'that'

	M.SG	F.SG	M.PL	F.PL
NOM/ACC	a.ˈtʃel	a.ˈtʃea	a.ˈtʃej	a.ˈtʃe.le
GEN/DAT	a.ˈtʃe.luj	a.ˈtʃe.lej	a.ˈtʃe.lor	a.ˈtʃe.lor

---

15 Though, as Rennison notes, Koromfe has additional dedicated deictic items with even more "deictic force" (Rennison 1997: 234, 81).

b. Def 'the'

	M.SG	F.SG	M.PL	F.PL
NOM/ACC	-ul	-a	-i	-le
GEN/DAT	-luj	-ej	-lor	-lor

The definite article is not a prefix in Romanian, but this can be accounted for in terms of movement.

Consider now the Italian forms for 'that' in (33).

(33)
	Dem	Def	
M.SG	quel-**lo**	**lo**	(+ word-initial sC- or z-)
	[quel]	**il**	(+ word-initial other C-)
F.SG	quel-**la**	**la**	
M.PL	que-**gli**	**gli**	(PL of *lo*)
	que-**i**	**i**	(PL of *il*)
F.PL	quel-**le**	**le**	

The Italian forms follow our basic generalization, though with some minor complications: (i) there is no M.SG *que-il*, for instance (*quel* being used instead, perhaps simply for phonological reasons) and (ii) the Def element is not actually a prefix but looks more like a suffix (which we assume can be accounted for in terms of movement). Nevertheless, the generalization discussed above regarding Def being morphologically contained within Dem very clearly holds for Italian, with both singular and plural Def being overtly contained within the Dem forms.[16]

As a final set of evidence for our generalization regarding Def-containment within Dem, consider Greek. The N.SG Dem forms *ekíno* 'that', *tuto* 'this', *auto* 'this' are likely candidates for morphological decomposition, especially considering the history of these pronouns (*ekíno* < minimally trimorphemic PIE *h_1e-ki-eno and *tuto* < minimally bimorphemic PIE *h_2u-tod; see Johansson and Carling 2015: §6.1). The crucial question, though, is whether or not Def is an integral morphological ingredient for Dem. We propose that the answer is yes, but that Def is not contained within the morphological structure of Dem, rather it is contained at the phrasal level of DemP. That is, it is a well known fact that Def is required in the presence of Dem in Greek, as seen in (34).

---

[16] Note that BaseP for the Italian demonstratives is spelled out as *que(l)-* /kwe/; the smaller structures (Comp, Rvz, Wh) are all *che* /ke/, on the other hand, which we assume to be a portmanteau morpheme spelling out the constituent containing both PreP and BaseP (see the structure in (36) below).

(34) a. ekíno   to   pédi   (MG)
       Dem.DIST Def child
       'that child'
   b. aftó   to   spíti
       Dem.PROX Def house
       'this house'
       (Holton et al. 2003: 93, 19–20)

The 'stacking' of Dem and Def is also found in languages as diverse as Lakota (Ingham 2003: 90), Hungarian (Kenesei et al. 1997: 95), Koyra Chiini (Heath 1998: 61), Yucatec Mayan (Janssen 2004: 986), Welsh (Dryer 1992: 121), and D(r)ehu (Dryer 1992: 121).

In sum, the claim that Def is a building block in the construction of Dem has support from a diverse set of crosslinguistic morphological evidence.

5 The Slavic containment puzzle

We now turn to Slavic, specifically Serbo-Croatian and Russian. It is clear that SC *što* and Ru. *čto* are easily decomposable into *š-t-o* and *č-t-o*. The first consonant derives historically from palatalization of the *wh-* morpheme *k-* before a front vowel (see the proto-forms below), the second consonant *t-* is the demonstrative root, and *-o* is the neuter singular inflection (i.e. Proto-Balto-Slavic *ki-to > Proto-Slavic *čь-to 'what') (Boban Arsenijević, Tomislav Sočanac, p.c.). Thus we can say that SC *š-* and Ru. *č-* (/ʃ/ and /ş/, respectively) correspond to PreP, *t-* to BaseP, and *-o* to ΦP.

(35) Comp/Rel/Wh in Serbo-Croatian and Russian

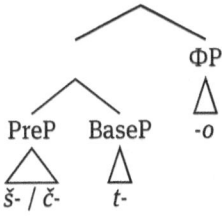

This kind of decomposition can be extended to Polish and Czech as well, if we simply assume that *c-*, spelling the affricate /t͡s/ in both languages, is a portmanteau of PreP and BaseP (again making crucial use of phrasal spellout).

(36) Comp/Rel/Wh-structures in Polish and Czech

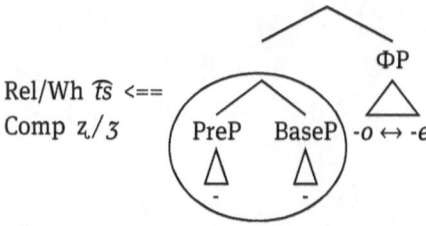

Rel/Wh ts͡ <==
Comp z/ʒ

Interestingly, -o (in t-o and c-o) has the allophone -e after 'soft' consonants like Po. ż- /z/ and Cz. ž- /ʒ/, so also the complementizers Po. ż-e and Cz. ž-e have exactly the same basic structure, with the same neuter singular ending, i.e. ΦP.[17]

The demonstrative form in this languages, on the other hand, is simply t-o, which when compared to (35) above is clearly missing a realization for PreP.

(37) Dem in Serbo-Croatian and Russian

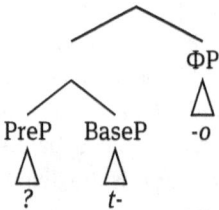

That is to say, Dem in Serbo-Croatian and Russian is only bimorphemic while Comp/Rvz/Wh is trimorphemic; in other words, Dem is smaller than Comp/Rvz/Wh. This is unexpected since our sequence predicts that Dem should be the larger structure. Moreover, Dem to is contained within Comp/Rel/Wh [š-[to]] and [č-[to]], which is the opposite of what we expect. That is, if there is an overt containment to be observed, then Dem is expected to contain Comp, Rvz, and Wh.

On the other hand, this containment puzzle does not make an appearance in Macedonian (Dem toa vs. Comp/Rvz/Wh što[18]) or Bulgarian (Dem tova vs. Comp/Rvz deto vs. Wh kăde). In these languages the Dem form is not contained within the Comp, Rvz, or Wh structures. In fact, as expected, the (so-called 'neutral') definite marker -to in Macedonian is contained within Dem [[to]-a], as well as

---

[17] Thanks to a reviewer for discussion of the data and suggestions.
[18] Deka or oti is the default (broadly, non-factive) complementizer, but here we consider the factive complementizer što (Tomić 2006: 458, fn.86). Deka, interestingly, is also a relativizer in Macedonian.

within Rvz/Wh [š-[to]]. Bulgarian Def -*to* is similarly contained within Comp/Rvz [de-[to]]. Thus these languages do not pose a problem for the containment relation predicted by our fseq.

6 Solving the puzzle

We can account for the containment puzzle with a very simple observation: most Slavic languages do not have definite articles (see, among others, Bošković 2005, 2008, 2009, 2010 on the NP/DP parameter), Serbo-Croatian and Russian being perfect cases in point. In fact, the only Slavic languages with definite articles are Macedonian and Bulgarian (where the neuter singular definite marker is -*to* in both). Because Serbo-Croatian and Russian do not have definite articles, their demonstratives do not have the definite article (PreP) available to them. Thus Dem ends up being smaller than Comp/Rel/Wh, the latter forms having access to a PreP structure (š- and č-) since these PrePs are not dependent on being a DP language.

(38) 'Containment puzzle' in Serbo-Croatian and Russian

	PreP	BaseP	ΦP
Wh	š-/č- (*wh*-marker)	t-	-o
Rvz	š-/č- (rvz-marker)	t-	-o
Comp	š-/č- (EF-marker)	t-	-o
Dem	definite article (not available)	t-	-o

Indeed, the relevant Dem forms in Bulgarian and Macedonian contain Def (i.e. Bg. *to-va* 'this', Ma. *to-j* 'that (close to hearer)', both in the neuter singular), just like the data from Germanic, Romance, Klallam, Tahitian, and Koromfe above.

This accounts for the clear contrast between Serbo-Croatian and Russian on the one hand, where the containment is problematic, and Macedonian and Bulgarian on the other, where the containment is not problematic. As for the other languages at stake, namely Polish and Czech, the containment puzzle is still present, yet in a slightly less obvious guise. Above we mentioned that both Comp (Po. *ż-e*, Cz. *ž-e*) and Rvz/Wh *c-o* can be considered to be underlyingly tripartite structures (they are historically exactly equivalent to SC *što* and Ru. *čto*) as long as the initial consonant is analyzed as a portmanteau morpheme. However, the Dem form is again *to* in Polish and Czech (again historically exactly equivalent to

SC/Ru. *to*). Though we could always assume that *t-* is a portmanteau once again and in this way try to dissolve the containment puzzle, such an analysis might be considered suspect on the grounds that the voiceless stop *t-* is phonologically simpler than the palatalized consonants in the Comp, Rvz, and Wh forms (i.e. Po. /ʑ/ and Cz. /ʒ/, and Po./Cz. /t͡s/), which betray a more complex history; more important, though, is the crosslinguistic evidence from closely related languages like Serbo-Croatian and Russian, where it is clear that *t-o* is not trimorphemic when compared to *š-t-o* and *č-t-o*.

(39) 'Containment puzzle' in Serbo-Croatian and Russian

	PreP		BaseP	ΦP
Wh		c-		-o
Rvz		c-		-o
Comp		ż- / ž-		-e
Dem	definite article (not available)		t-	-o

In other words the containment puzzle is relevant for Polish and Czech as well, but the puzzle can be solved in the same way as it was for Serbo-Croatian and Russian, since Polish and Czech are also languages lacking definite articles.

The basic structure for Slavic NP languages is given in (40), where PreP is not part of the structure.

(40) Dem in SC/Ru (as well as Po/Cz)

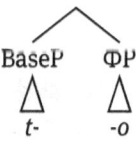

Even though Serbo-Croatian and Russian do not have definite articles, we also do not want to assert that the semantic features responsible for definiteness are completely absent in these languages. Indeed, Slavic demonstratives must still be "disguised definite descriptions" (Bennett 1978: 22), as in other languages. Rather, we believe that these definiteness features are packaged with items elsewhere in the grammatical system (that is, not in the form of distinct, overt Def morphemes found in DP languages), but we leave the specifics of this hypothesis for future research.

7 Concluding remarks

Our paper is based on Baunaz and Lander's (2017) nanosyntactic analysis of complementizers in Romance and Germanic. In nanosyntax, syncretism reflects structural adjacency, that is, forms that are syncretic are taken to reflect a specific ordering of syntactic heads merged in a functional sequence. Here we have shown that (nominal) complementizers in the Balkan and Slavic languages participate in systematic syncretisms with Dem, Rel, and Wh pronouns, verifying previous findings about these patterns in Germanic and Romance and empirically strengthening the proposal that these items are internally complex and built using a single functional sequence. Moreover, there is evidence for a structurally deficient 'light' noun at the bottom of this fseq, which overtly appears as a bound morpheme in the internal morphological structure of quantifiers in these languages.

Following the discussion of the syncretism data, we have proposed to further decompose the forms under observation into at least a tripartite structure made up of a prefix (PreP), a base (BaseP), and an inflectional ending (ΦP). Most interesting is the generalization that demonstratives (in DP languages) have a definite article acting as their PreP, which is backed up by evidence from a typologically diverse range of languages.

We have also looked at a potential problem for our approach, namely the 'containment puzzle' exhibited by languages like Serbo-Croatian and Russian. In these languages it is clear that Comp, Rvz, and Wh *što/čto* show morphological containment of Dem (*to*), even though we expect to find the opposite (Dem containing Comp, Rvz and Wh). We account for this puzzle by referring to the well known fact that, with the exception of Bulgarian and Macedonian, Slavic languages lack definite articles. Thus, the fact that PreP is missing in languages like Serbo-Croatian and Russian can be attributed to independent reasons about the availability of a grammaticalized definite article; indeed, in Bulgarian and Macedonian, which are the only Slavic languages to have definite articles, there is no containment puzzle to speak of.

Acknowledgements: We would like to thank Boban Arsenijevic, Anamaria Bentea, Joanna Blochowiak, Pavel Caha, Goljihan Kachaeva, Iliyana Krapova, Teodora Radeva-Bork, Gabriela Soare, Tanja Samardzic, Tomislav Sočanac, Branimir Stankovic and Bartosz Wiland for their help with the data. We would like to specially thank Iliyana Krapova for showing interest in our work, as well as an anonymous reviewer for interesting suggestions and discussions. Lena Baunaz's research is supported by FWO project 2009–Odysseus-Haegeman-G091409. Eric Lander's research was funded by BOF grant 01D30311 awarded by Ghent University and FWO project 2009–Odysseus-Haegeman-G091409.

References

Baunaz, Lena. 2016. Deconstructing complementizers in Serbo-Croatian, Modern Greek and Bulgarian. *Proceedings of NELS* 46, 1: 69–77.

Baunaz, Lena and Eric Lander. 2017. Syncretisms with the nominal complementizer. *Studia Linguistica* 71: 1–34.

Baunaz, Lena. 2018. Decomposing complementizers: The fseq of Serbo-Croatian, Modern Greek, Bulgarian and French complementizers. In Lena Baunaz, Karen De Clercq, Liliane Haegeman and Eric Lander (eds), *Exploring Nanonosyntax*. Oxford Studies in Comparative syntax, New York: Oxford University Press. 149–179.

Baunaz, Lena, Karen De Clercq, Liliane Haegeman, and Eric Lander (eds). 2018. *Exploring Nanosyntax*. Oxford Studies in Comparative Syntax. New York: Oxford University Press.

Baerman, Matthew, Dunstan Brown, Greville G. Corbett. 2005. *The syntax-morphology interface: A study of syncretism*. Cambridge: Cambridge University Press.

Bennett, Michael. 1978. Demonstratives and indexicals in Montague Grammar. *Synthese* 39: 1–80.

Benţea, Anamaria. 2010. On restrictive relatives in Romanian: Towards a head-raising analysis. *GG@G* 6: 165–190.

Bobaljik, Jonathan. 2007. On comparative suppletion. Ms., University of Connecticut.

Bobaljik, Jonathan. 2012. *Universals in comparative morphology. Suppletion, superlatives, and the structure of words*. Cambridge, MA: MIT Press.

Bošković, Željko. 2005. On the locality of left branch extraction and the structure of NP. *Studia Linguistica* 59: 1–45.

Bošković, Željko. 2008. What will you have, DP or NP? *Proceedings of NELS* 37: 101–114.

Bošković, Željko. 2009. More on the no-DP analysis of article-less languages. *Studia Linguistica* 2: 187–204.

Bošković, Željko. 2010. On NPs and clauses. Ms., University of Connecticut.

Caha, Pavel. 2009. *The nanosyntax of case*. PhD dissertation, University of Tromsø.

Caha, Pavel and Marina Pantcheva. 2014. Locatives in Shona and Luganda. Ms., University of Tromsø.

Cardinaletti, Anna and Michal Starke. 1999. The typology of structural deficiency: A case study of the three classes of pronouns. In Henk van Riemsdijk (ed.), *Clitics in the Languages of Europe*: 145–233. Berlin: Mouton De Gruyter.

Chappell, Hilary. 2008. Variation in the grammaticalization of complementizers from *verba dicendi* in Sinitic languages. *Linguistic Typology* 12, 1: 45–98.

Cinque, Guglielmo. 2008. More on the indefinite character of the head of restrictive relatives. *Rivista di Grammatica Generativa* 33: 3–24.

Cinque, Guglielmo and Luigi Rizzi. 2008. The cartography of syntactic structures. *CISCL Working Papers on Language and Cognition* 2: 43–59.

Déchaine, Rose-Marie and Martina Wiltschko. 2002. Decomposing pronouns. *Linguistic Inquiry* 33: 409–443.

Dryer, Matthew S. 1992. The Greenbergian word order correlations. *Language* 68: 81–138.

Giannakidou, Anastasia. 2009. The dependency of the subjunctive revisited: Temporal semantics and polarity. [Special issue on Mood] *Lingua* 119: 1883–1908.

Grimshaw, Jane. 1991. Extended projection. Ms., Brandeis University.

Grosu, Alexander. 1994. *Three studies in Locality and Case*. London: Routledge.

Hansen, Björn, Alexander Letuchiy, and Izabela Błaszczyk. 2016. Complementizers in Slavonic (Russian, Polish, and Bulgarian). In Kasper Boye and Petar Kehayov (eds.), *Semantic*

functions of complementzers in European languages. Berlin and Boston: De Gruyter Mouton. 175–223.
Heath, Jeffrey. 1998. *A grammar of Koyra Chiini*. Berlin: De Gruyter Mouton.
Hill, Virginia. 2002. Complementizer Phrases (CP) in Romanian. *Rivista di Linguistica* 14,2: 223–248.
Holton, David, Peter Mackridge, Irene Philippaki-Warburton. 2004. *Greek: An essential grammar of the modern language*. London: Routledge.
Ingham, Bruce. 2003. *Lakota*. München: LINCOM.
Janssen, Theo A. J. M. 2004. Deixis and reference. In Geert Booij, Christian Lehmann, Joachim Mudgan, Stavros Skopeteas (eds), *Morphology: An international handbook on inflection and word-formation, Vol. 2*: 983–997. Berlin and New York: De Gruyter.
Johansson, Niklas and Gerd Carling. 2015. The de-iconization and rebuilding of iconicity in spatial deixis. *Acta Linguistica hafniensia: International Journal of Linguistics* 47, 1: 4–32.
Kayne, Richard. 2008. Why isn't this a complementizer? Ms., New York University.
Kayne, Richard and Jean-Yves Pollock. 2010. Notes on French and English demonstratives. In Jan-Wouter Zwart and Mark de Vries (eds), *Structure preserved: Studies in syntax for Jan Koster*: 215–228. Amsterdam: John Benjamins.
Kenesei, István, Robert Michael Vago, Anna Fenyvesi. 1997. *Hungarian*. London: Routledge.
Klamer, Marian. 2000. How report verbs become quote markers and complementisers. *Lingua* 110: 69–98.
Krapova, Iliyana. 2010. Bulgarian relative and factive clauses with an invariant complementizer. *Lingua* 120: 1240–1272.
Leu, Tom. 2015. *The architecture of determiners*. Oxford and New York: Oxford University Press.
Lord, Carol. 1993. *Historical change in serial verb constructions*. Amsterdam and Philadelphia: John Benjamins.
Manzini, Maria Rita and Leonardo Maria Savoia. 2003. The nature of complementizers. *Rivista di Grammatica Generativa* 28: 87–110.
Manzini, Maria Rita. and Leonardo Maria Savoia. 2011. *Grammatical categories*. Cambridge: Cambridge University Press.
Mitrović, Ivana. 2012. Relative clauses in Serbian. Handout for paper presented at Syntax Lab, University of Maryland, 11 September.
Montler, Timothy. 2007. Klallam demonstratives. *University of Columbia Working Papers in Linguistics* 20: 409–425.
Murelli, Adriano. 2011. *Relative constructions in European non-standard varieties*. Berlin and Boston: De Gruyter Mouton.
Rennison, John. R. 1997. *Koromfe*. New York: Routledge.
Roberts, Ian and Anna Roussou. 2003. *Syntactic change: A Minimalist approach to grammaticalization*. Cambridge: Cambridge University Press.
Roehrs, Dorian. 2010. Demonstrative-reinforcer constructions. *The Journal of Comparative Germanic Linguistics* 13, 3: 225–268.
Roussou, Anna. 2000. On the left periphery: Modal particles and complementisers. *Journal of Greek Linguistics* 1: 65–94.
Roussou, Anna. 2006. *Simpliromatiki diktes [Complementizers]*. Athens: Patakis.
Roussou, Anna. 2010. Selecting complementizers. [Special issue *Exploring the left periphery*] *Lingua* 120: 582–603.

Roussou, Anna. 2012. Complements, relatives and nominal properties. Paper presented at *GIST 5: Generalizing relative stategies*. Ghent University, 22–23 March.
Sanfelici, Emanuela and Cecilia Poletto. 2014. On the nature of complementizers : Insights for Italian subject relative clauses. Paper presented at *Going Romance 28*. Lisbon, 4–6 December.
Savu, Carmen and Sebastian Bican-Miclescu. 2012. Romanian demonstratives. Ms., nanosyntax weblab 'The ingredients of demonstratives' convened by Michal Starke.
Sočanac, Tomislav. 2017. *Subjunctive complements in Slavic languages: A syntax-semantics interface approach*. PhD dissertation, University of Geneva.
Sonnenhauser, Barbara. 2015. Functionalising syntactic variance: Declarative complementation with *kako* and *če* in 17th to 19th century Balkan Slavic. *Wiener Slavistisches Jahrbuch* 3: 41–72.
Sportiche, Dominique. 2011. French relative *qui*. *Linguistic Inquiry* 42: 83–124.
Starke, Michal. 2009. Nanosyntax: A short primer to a new approach to language. [Special issue on Nanosyntax] *Nordlyd, Tromsø University working papers on language linguistics* 36: 1–6. http://septentrio.uit.no/index.php/nordlyd/.
Starke, Michal. 2011. Towards an elegant solution to language variation: Variation reduces to the size of lexically stored trees. LingBuzz/001183.
Taraldsen, Tarald. 2018. Spanning vs. constituent lexicalization: The case of portmanteau prefixes. In Lena Baunaz, Karen De Clercq, Liliane Haegeman and Eric Lander (eds), *Exploring Nanonosyntax*. Oxford Studies in Comparative syntax, New York: Oxford University Press. 88–107.
Taube, Moshe. 1994. On factivity, emotivity and choice of conjunction in Yiddish. *Studies in Language* 18, 1: 113–125.
Todorović, Nataša. 2012. *The subjunctive and indicative da-complements in Serbian: A syntactic-semantic approach*. PhD dissertation, University of Illinois at Chicago.
Tomić, Olga Mišeska. 2006. *The Balkan Sprachbund morpho-syntactic features*. Dordrecht: Springer.
Tryon, Darell Trevor. 1970. *Conversational Tahitian*. Canberra: Australian National University Press.

Part III: **Variation in the Sprachbund**

Eleni Bužarovska and Liljana Mitkovska
Modal *habere*-Constructions in the Balkan Slavic Context

Abstract: Balkan languages share a common construction type based on the verb of possession and a subjunctive clause: modal *habere*-constructions. These constructions have not received due attention in the literature because of their restriction to the vernaculars of the Balkans. Balkan Slavic languages differ from other Balkan languages in featuring two variants: inflected and uninflected *habere*-constructions. The paper examines the functional distribution of *habere*-constructions in Balkan Slavic languages through a questionnaire containing situations prompting the use of one of the variants. The investigation confirmed the initial hypothesis that the distinction between the two formal variants is based on semantic and pragmatic considerations. Each variant belongs to a different modality type: inflected constructions express circumstantial obligation, whereas uninflected ones code deontic and epistemic necessity. In addition, uninflected constructions have different discourse functions because they are used in manipulative speech acts. The pragmatization and speech act orientation of the uninflected construction seem to be gradient features of Balkan Slavic languages, but in all languages they are marked with performativity and high speaker involvement. The results show that Macedonian exhibits strict adherence to the functional delimitation between the two variants, which leads to the conclusion that there is a greater degree of correlation between form and meaning.

Keywords: modality, performativity, subjectivity, pragmatization, Balkan Slavic languages

1 Introduction

It is a well-known fact that Balkan dialects were subject to prolonged language contact in the course of history, leading to the convergent development and substantial restructuring of their grammar systems. As a result of the process

---

Eleni Bužarovska, (Ss Cyril and Methodius University, Skopje), elenibuzarovska@t.mk
Liljana Mitkovska, (FON University, Skopje), liljana.mitkovska@fon.edu.mk

https://doi.org/10.1515/9783110375930-011

of Balkan "creolization"[1] these geographically clustered but genetically distant languages obtained a number of common properties, which have been well documented and extensively discussed in the literature.[2] "Classical" syntactic Balkanisms in the verbal system include loss of the infinitive, a *velle* ('want'-based)-future, conditional forms and a *habere*-perfect. However, there is another common construction- type based on the verb of possession. In Balkan and other European languages, the possessive *habere* has acquired modal meanings when immediately followed by the infinitive. Due to the infinitive loss and its replacement by an untensed finite clause in Balkan languages (Joseph 1983), modal *habere*-constructions exhibit an isomorphic structural patterning characteristic of the Balkan Sprachbund.[3]

While *habere*-constructions were previously used to code the future tense under the influence of biblical Greek, today they are restricted to spoken language to express a range of modal meanings. In Balkan Slavic languages (Macedonian, Bulgarian and Serbian), these consist of the verb *ima* 'have' followed by the subjunctive *da*-clause[4] (the mood morpheme *da* + a lexical verb inflected for person and number). Their equivalents in other Balkan languages have functionally similar components: the *kam* + *për të*-construction in Albanian,[5] the *exo* + *na*-construction in Greek, and the *am* + *să*-construction in Romanian. Although distributed across a relatively large territory shared by genetically different languages, the modal *habere*-construction has not been included in the inventory

---

[1] Topolińska (1995b) argues that creolization implies ranking of two language systems in contact whereby the grammar of a higher prestige language undergoes simplification, but the Balkan case seemingly does not involve ranking. She thinks that "the general direction of convergent evolution has followed the once prestigious Romance pattern" (ibid, 240). This may be true for the spoken language, but Greek influence on the Church Slavonic syntax was decisive in the translation of religious texts. As McAnallen (2011: 156) points out: "In many areas of syntax ... OCS Bible translations preserve the source syntax of New Testament Greek quite faithfully."
[2] Here we mention only the scholars investigating Balkan innovations in the verbal system related to our topic, such as Topolińska (1995a, 2000), Friedman (1977, 2000), Joseph (1983), Kramer (1986), Lindstedt (2000), among others.
[3] We are grateful to Andrey Sobolev for pointing out that the subjunctive forms known as 'conjunctive' in Romanian and Albanian can hardly be generalized as "untensed finite clause" like in South Slavic and Greek.
[4] Subjunctive clauses in Balkan Slavic languages are analytic constructions in which the proclitic morpheme *da* governs the verb thus disallowing tensed forms. Semantically, they express non-factual, future-oriented situations (Topolinjska 1995b: 138–142). The particle *da*, similarly to the Greek *na* (Joseph 1990), here is treated as an affixal marker of mood.
[5] In Gheg Albanian (Sobolev, p.c.). the construction is different: *kam* + infinitive (which consists of *me*+ participle).

of "classical" Balkanisms[6] because it occupies a marginal position in the system of modal verbs, especially in Balkan Slavic languages, its functional zone varies from language to language, and it is a feature of spoken language. Therefore, Topolińska's reference to habere modals as "underestimated Balkanisms" (Topolińska 2008: 509) seems well justified.

Balkan Slavic modal *habere*-constructions differ from their non-Slavic functional counterparts by featuring two variants: inflected (1) and uninflected *ima da*-constructions (2). The formal difference between them is signaled by the absence of person and number markers on *ima* 'have' in the uninflected construction as shown in the Macedonian examples (1) and (2).

(1) *Jas imam da odam.*
    I   have.1SG PRT go.1SG
    'I have to go.'

(2) *Jas ima da odam.*
    I   have.3SG PRT go.1SG
    'I shall go.' (I am determined to go)

The uninflected formal variant of the *habere*-type in (2) represents an areal feature found only in these three languages, exemplifying the Balkan tendency for further grammaticalization of modal verbs into modal particles. Thus in Macedonian, the modal inflected *ima* forms a pair with the uninflected *ima*, similarly to the creation of the uninflected *mora* 'must' and *može* 'can' from their inflected counterparts.

The goal of this paper is to examine the distribution of inflected and uninflected *ima da*-constructions in Macedonian with reference to their equivalents in other Balkan Slavic languages and to show that *habere*-modal constructions are used with similar functions in most Balkan languages. The main hypothesis is that a strict formal split between the two variants has taken place in Macedonian, and that this delimitation was caused by discourse factors guided by the principle of formal transparency, "*spiritus movens* in the majority of creolization processes" (Topolińska 1995a: 21). This hypothesis has a potential typological significance: even in the realm of these modal constructions, Macedonian, as geographically central and thus more "balkanized" compared with the other two Balkan Slavic languages, exhibits a greater degree of correlation between form and meaning.

---

[6] For several proposed lists of Balkanisms see Aronson (2007: 4).

To account for the reasons of the split, we place this phenomenon in the realm of pragmatics, attributing a major role to speech acts in discourse. As shown in Mitkovska and Bužarovska (2014), Macedonian uninflected *ima*-constructions are used performatively because they are intended to act on the addressee. In that sense they belong to manipulative speech acts[7] performed by an emotionally involved speaker at the time of utterance. Speaker involvement and speaker commitment constitute the notion of subjectivity (Narrog 2012: 41). Performativity is inherently subjective because a performative utterance is speaker-oriented. These two interrelated pragmatic features–performativity and subjectivity–set uninflected *ima*-constructions apart from inflected constructions employed in stylistically neutral assertions.

Bearing in mind that Balkan languages coexisted in a contact situation for a long time, a number of Balkanisms can be viewed as grammaticalized pragmatic devices (Friedman 2000: 1344).[8] Having retreated from the grammatical systems of the Balkan Slavic under the pressure of a new rival future tense form, *ima*-constructions assumed discourse functions. Today they are used as pragmatic modal devices that mark the illocutionary force of the utterance, expressing speaker involvement and close horizontal distance between speakers in everyday communication.

2 The modal meanings of *ima* in Macedonian

In the course of their development the two rival constructions for coding future events, with *habere* and with *velle*, have specialized for separate non-factual domains: *velle* for future and *habere* for deontic modality. But how these two types of modal meanings map with the two formal variants of the *ima*+subjunctive construction has not received due attention in the grammars of Balkan Slavic languages. The grammars of all three languages mention this pattern pointing

---

[7] Givón's (1990: 806) division of speech acts into manipulative and declarative seems to capture the two essential aspects of the speaker's verbal behaviour with respect to the listener. In declarative speech acts (non-manipulative) the speaker imparts information, in manipulative he/she elicits action. However, 'assertive' speech acts (Searle 1975) is a more common term than 'declarative' speech acts, as declaratives in Searle's classification are performatives.

[8] Friedman (2000: 1347) looks at the three Balkanisms that have not been grammaticalized to the same degree in Bulgarian in contrast to Macedonian: object reduplication, evidential uses of perfect and the resultative *habere*-perfect. He concludes that "whereas the three features ... are treated as discourse functions in Bulgarian, they are either grammaticalized or eliminated in Macedonian."

out its colloquial nature but stop short of explaining the functional differences between the variants. Even Dahl (2000: 323) points out that "its range of uses in the different languages is not quite clear from the sources". The insufficient treatment of this construction in Serbian grammars has been noted by Topolińska (2008). In Bulgarian, Asenova (2002: 206) underlines that the semantic difference between the two variants is not clearly defined in native grammars. In Macedonian, Čašule (1989) and Topolińska (2000) treat these constructions as modal, identifying the modality of two variants (obligation in inflected and certainty in uninflected), while Koneski (2000) considers uninflected constructions to be stylistically marked exponents of future.

In our previous research (Bužarovska and Mitkovska 2011, Mitkovska and Bužarovska 2012, Mitkovska and Bužarovska 2014) we argued that the verb *ima* 'have', when placed in a specific syntactic environment (immediate adjacency of a subjunctive clause), has grammaticalized into a modal verb with two forms in Macedonian: inflected and uninflected. We have also established the meanings of each *ima*-construction type in contemporary Macedonian and the interrelation between the two variants. In determining form-function correspondences of these constructions the exact modal status of both variants was defined in the context of typological categorizations of modality, as well as the place of the uninflected *ima* within the system of deontic verbs: it ranks the highest with respect to the degree of obligation: *ima* 'have-to' > *mora* 'must' > *treba* 'should'.

It was shown that the formal division into two types is pragmatically motivated and that considerable semantic variability exists within each formal type. The inflected form expresses agent-oriented modality (3) for which we use the term 'circumstantial obligation', while the uninflected *ima* has three functions. It is used as a deontic modal of speaker-oriented modality (4) (directive or commissive) or as a marker of epistemic prediction (5), the interpretation depending on the illocutionary force of the utterance, as well as for agent-oriented obligation (6) implying strong speaker certainty. In the rest of this section, the fine distinctions between these functions are further clarified.

(3) *Ne zaboravaj, imaš   da odiš   vo bolnica.*
    not forget.IMP have.2SG PRT go.2SG in hospital
    'Don't forget, you need to go to hospital.'

(4) *Ne smeeš pak da   go propuštiš pregledot.   Ima   da odiš
    not dare again PRT it miss.2SG appointment-the has-impers PRT go.2SG
    na lekar!*
    to doctor
    'You mustn't miss your appointment again. You shall go to the doctor's!'

(5) *Do moreto ima   600 km. Daleku e, ima   da   patuvaš cel den!*
    to sea-the has-impers 600 km far   is has-impers PRT travel.2SG all day
    'It's 600km to the sea. It's far, you are going to travel all day!'

(6) *Nema   beganje.   Ima   da   pišuvaš seminarska.*
    has.not-impers running.away.   has-impers PRT   write.2SG paper
    Taka e spored   pravilnikot.
    thus is according regulation.the
    'There is no way out. You will/shall write the paper. This is according to the rules.'

Inflected *ima*-constructions have a deontic meaning of obligation imposed by some external force: circumstances, social norms, etc. The speaker informs the addressee about this obligation without insistence or emotional involvement, most often in order to remind, explain, make an excuse, etc., as in (7). Therefore, inflected *ima*-constructions can be considered as exponents of circumstantial modality.

(7) *Da te   potsetam,   imaš   da   pišuvaš seminarska.*
    PRT you-ACC remind.1SG have-2SG PRT write.2SG paper
    'Let me remind you, you have to write a paper.'

In comparison to the inflected variant, uninflected constructions cover a wider functional zone of deontic modality. They also express obligation directed to the addressee, but it is usually strongly imposed by the speaker, often with an emotional overtone of threat (8). The speaker, who has legitimate authority over the addressee, expects the addressee to fulfill his/her wish. The position of the speaker is rather different in the inflected constructions in which the speaker is an outside observer.

(8) *Ima   da   pišuvaš   seminarska i točka!*
    has-impers PRT write.2SG   paper   and full.stop
    'You will write a paper and write you will!'

This difference is noticeable even in contexts where the deontic source in the uninflected construction is not the speaker but some authority (6). With such utterances the speaker states that a future obligation exists, but at the same time s/he also expresses confidence in the subject's abiding by that obligation (e.g. pay the tax, do homework, etc). The same could refer to a third person in a kind of 'reported obligation' (9).

(9) Slušna   li za noviot zakon? Imal,   nemal
    heard.2SG Q for new-the law   have.PART have.not.PART
    televizor, site   ima   da   plaḱaat TV   taksa.
    TV   all   has-impers PRT   pay.3PL TV   tax
    'Have you heard about the new law? No matter whether you have or not a
    TV set, everybody has to/will pay the TV tax.'

The examples show that the semantic difference between the two variants stems from the type of the deontic source: in the inflected constructions the speaker feels that the subject has an obligation imposed by some social norms (therefore *Imam da rabotam* 'I have to work' but not *Imam da spijam* 'I have to sleep'). In the uninflected constructions the deontic source is the speaker who wants his/her wish to be fulfilled (in the commissive use the speaker and the addressee coincide).

Our main hypothesis is that the pragmatic difference between the two variants is based on performativity: the uninflected constructions belong to performative speech acts. In the 1st person the construction is used in a commissive speech act (the speaker imposes an obligation on him/herself), while in the 2nd person it is a directive. The inflected construction cannot express an order; *Imaš da pišuvaš seminarska* 'You have to write a paper' is an assertive speech act, a statement that reminds the addressee of a duty, while the uninflected *Ima da pišuvaš seminarska* 'You will write a paper' constitutes a sharp order.[9]

When a speech act with the uninflected *ima* is directed to a third person, the modality of deontic necessity shades into epistemic necessity. The speaker, via a declarative sentence, makes a speech act in order to achieve a certain communicative goal, namely to persuade the listener in the inevitability of a future situation.[10] The uninflected *ima* here is a modal that "causes the utterance of a declarative sentence to perform a speech act in addition to or instead of the act of assertion" (Portner 2009: 137). With the *ima*-construction the confident speaker performs a speech act of persuasive prediction. The speaker's confidence stems from the knowledge of facts that "force" him/her to strongly believe that a certain situation is bound to happen. It means that the predictive meaning of *ima* is subjective as it reflects high degree of speaker's confidence: the speaker logically infers the necessity of realization of some future situation in the light of what s/he knows. But at the same time, in uttering the prediction, the speaker tries

---

9 Polish and Czech allow the performative use of this construction (only inflected variant): *Masz to zrobić!* (Pol) and *Máš to udělat!* (Cz) are translatable as 'You shall do that!'
10 The term 'situation' refers to a state of affairs (SoA), which does not have any reference in the world.

to persuade the addressee that there is epistemic necessity for the realization of this future situation. Following Bybee et al. (1994: 247), we call this meaning 'epistemic certainty' because such markers[11] epistemically qualify the future, but a certain deontic component is also present in the "predictive" *ima* due to the underlying relation of logical necessity. The meaning of epistemic certainty in categorical predictions seems to be the most grammaticalized meaning of the uninflected *ima*. It is semantically related to the deontic meaning of strong obligation: in directives the speaker makes "the world fit the words" (Yule 1996: 55), in predictions s/he insists that "the fit" is imminent.

It can be deduced from the previous discussion that the three speech acts coded by the uninflected *ima*-constructions belong to "directive situations" (Mauri and Sanso 2012: 156) because of their manipulative force: they are aimed at changing the behavior of the addressee in compliance with the wishes of the speaker. Operating in manipulative directive situations these meanings belong to both deontic and epistemic modality, but the ratio between them depends on the type of speech act. Drawing on Mauri and Sanso (2012: 162), we think that the identity of person (1st, 2nd or 3rd person) plays a crucial role in determining the type of directive speech act since "in directive situations person is not an epiphenomenon, but rather a functional factor." It means that the identity of the performer determines the type of directive speech act conveyed by the uninflected *ima*-construction, as shown in Table 1.

Table 1: Mapping of construction types and speech act types.

Construction type	INFLECTED circumstantial modality	UNINFLECTED deontic/epistemic modality
1st person	assertive	commissive/ prediction
2nd person	assertive (reminder)	directive/persuasive prediction
3rd person	assertive	persuasive prediction

The meaning of the uninflected *ima*-constructions depends on the person. In each person one of the three pragmatic components of directive situations is foregrounded: speaker's wish, appeal or expectation for the desired situation to be brought about in the future (cf. Mauri and Sanso 2012: 156). In commissives the speaker expresses a resolve to carry out his/her wish, in directives he/she appeals

---

[11] Crosslinguistic support for existence of markers that indicate speaker's confidence in the realization of a future event is found in Bybee et al. (1994: 247–248). Both Bybee et al. (1994: 248) and van der Auwera and Plungian (1998: 68) consider certainty as part of epistemic modality.

to the addressee, and in predictions the speaker convinces the addressee in his/her high expectation that a future situation is imminent.

This discussion leads to an affirmative answer to the question whether the formal distinction between inflected and uninflected constructions in Macedonian was pragmatically motivated. The tendency for iconicity of form and function in Macedonian may have caused the formal delimitation of the two deontic meanings within the system of *ima da*-constructions according to their discourse function: the inflected constructions serve as neutral judgments, whereas the uninflected constructions are used in manipulative speech acts.

3 Historical considerations

The development of modal *ima* can be better understood if one takes into consideration the wide semantic range and the syntactic flexibility of the source verb *iměti* 'have' in Old Church Slavonic (Grković-Major 2011). Replicating the Greek model, it occurred with abstract nouns, complex constructions with non-finite forms and even underwent auxiliation. Given that the constructions with *have* and *be* "form the kernel of syntax" (Isačenko 1974: 44), South Slavic languages belong to the 'have' type, although historical sources suggest that Common Slavic was a 'be' language.[12]

The precursor of the modal *habere*-construction (*habere* + infinitive) in Balkan Latin and Church Slavonic was used to translate futurity in biblical Greek (Asenova 2002: 205–211), but later it was replaced by the devolitive *velle* + infinitive construction. The use of the two constructions (with *habere* and with *velle*) expressing future is also a Balkan feature. But what really contributes to the Balkan status of these constructions is their parallel evolutional history in all Balkan languages (cf. Asenova 2002: 201) and the interrelation between them. Modeled after the Greek pattern with a devolitive verb, the new periphrastic future form proceeded along the regular steps of language change in all Balkan languages (14th–16th centuries), though not at the same speed, nor with the same intensity. The grammaticalization of *velle* into a future tense marker was facilitated by the loss of the infinitive; the form of the resultant future marker reflects a dialectal variation. By

---

[12] European languages, according to Isačenko (1974: 44), can be typologically divided into 'have' and 'be' types depending which verb is used in the most elementary patterns. In 'have' languages, the verb *have* tends to grammaticalize (ibid., 69). All Slavic languages except Russian (partly Ukrainian and Belorussian) adopted *have* in their grammatical systems due to contact with Germanic, Romance and Greek languages.

the 18th century, *velle*-constructions replaced positive future *ima*-constructions, but the negated *ima*-constructions survived the sweeping change[13] only to further grammaticalize into an indeclinable future marker (*nema* in Macedonian, *njama* in Bulgarian).[14] It is possible that the grammaticalization of *ne* + *ima* into a particle *nema/njama* in this construction has triggered the analogical rise of its positive formal counterpart, the uninflected *ima*-construction.

The entrenchment of the *velle*-future at the expense of *habere*-future took place on the whole Balkan linguistic territory except its periphery, leaving *habere*-constructions as the only means of expressing futurity in Albanian Gheg, Italo-Albanian, and Italo-Greek dialects (Asenova 2002: 216).[15] In other Balkan languages and dialects, where both future forms co-existed, *habere*-constructions withdrew from the tense system and became a complementary means for expressing modality.

What makes this construction interesting is the blend of modal and futural semantics. The semantic complexity derives from implicatures of obligation and futurity created in the construction: the subject "possesses" an unactualized (imposed or desired) situation.[16] Which semantic component was prevalent in the source construction is not very clear: Benveniste (1960/1966) suggests that in the development of this construction the meaning of predestination played a crucial role, while Cyhun (1981: 160) thinks that there is no evidence that *habere*-constructions expressed pure futurity and were not "unburdened" by modal meanings. This position is shared by Večerka (1996: 82) who, relying on diachronic evidence, argues that in Old Church Slavonic (OCS) the construction *iměti* + infinitive was indeterminate between obligative and predictive meanings. Isačenko (1974: 50) emphasizes the imported character of the constructions with *iměti* noting that: "The numerous translations with *iměti* which are found in OCS texts are without exception loan translations from the Greek constructions with *exein*."

---

13 This is attributed to the close affinity between negation and modality (Cyhun 1981: 145). According to Cyhun (1981: 172), this functional and semantic asymmetry between the positive and negative future forms can be explained by the strength of the modality of negation.
14 Kramer (1998: 412) argues that they are even more frequent in Bulgarian: "When we look at the negative constructions, the invariant *njama da* has almost totally displaced *ne šte*. We do not see competition between the forms as we did in Macedonian."
15 Daco-Romanian uses *habere*-future as opposed to *velle*-future in Romanian and Aromanian. However, the *habere* form is used for obligations known as '*futurum necessitates*' (Ilievski 1988: 215–217).
16 As in the case with other possessive sources, for instance English *have to* (Brinton 1991), the grammaticalization of *ima* 'have' was triggered by the immediate proximity of the subjunctive *da*-clause. Also see Bybee et al. (1994: 184) who say: "The obligation sense in *have got to* derives from the sense imparted by the infinitive verb form...".

More recently, other authors underline the ambivalent constructional semantics of *iměti*: McAnallen (2011: 168) notes that in the Late Proto-Slavic period, the constructions with this verb were the most frequent, though "the semantics and pragmatics of *iměti* 'have' in Slavic are harder to pin down". Referring to *iměti* + infinitive constructions in OCS translations, Danylenko (2011: 163) argues that: "the modality of Slavic *iměti* ... was difficult to distinguish from the temporal meaning proper in most of the contexts" as in *to kako imatъ razuměti* '[and] how have-I to-understand (that)'. Moreover, Danylenko claims that *iměti* was seldom used to render the Greek sigmatic future[17] except for a few cases with future time reference. He illustrates this claim with "a well known example" (ibid, 162) from the *Ostromir Gospel* of 1056–57 (Lk 18: 22, Mt 19: 21), given here in (10).

(10) vъsa jeliko imaaši   prodaždь i   razdai   ništiimъ
     all much   have.2sg sell.IMP and give.IMP   poor.DAT.PL
     iměti   *imaaši*   sъkrovišče   na   nebese
     have.INF have.to.2SG treasure.ACC in   heaven.LOC
     'Sell all that thou hast, and distribute unto the poor, and thou shalt have treasure in heaven.'

But even in this example *iměti* + infinitive is used for prediction, not future reference. In other examples that we have found in early OCS texts (13th–14th centuries) *iměti* has the same predictive function, as in the following example from the *Radomir Gospel* (141v 14–18).[18]

---

17 In OCS another means of expressing futurity was a perfective stem of the verb, and two periphrastic constructions: with the future form of *esse* and with the verb *begin* followed by an imperfective verb (Ilievski 1988).

18 The following examples confirm this conclusion:
(i) *aželi ... plъti živete   imate   oumrěti* (Karpin Gospel, 199/31; 8,13)
    if   flesh live.2PL have.2PL die.INF
    'If you live by the flesh you shall die.'
(ii) *Pravo glagolǫ vamъ   iže   ašte   ne priimetъ   carstvie božie jako otrok ne*
     truly say.1SG you.DAT who these not receive.3SG kingdom divine like child NEG
     imatъ   vъniti
     have.3SG enter.INF
     'Truly I say to you, whoever does not receive the kingdom of god like a child will not enter (into it).' (Radomir Gospel, 110 8/21–25. L 18, 17)
(iii) *i reče   Ahazъ ne imamъ   vъsprositi niže   imamъ   iskousiti gospoda*
      and said.3SG Ahaz   not have.1SG ask.INF   not.and   have.1SG   test.INF lord
      'But Ahaz said, I will not ask; I will not put the Lord to the test.'
                                            (Grigorovič's Paremeinik 27/25–26)

(11) i otvěštavъ reče: glagolǫ vamъ jako ašte si oumlъčatъ:
and replying said.3SG speak/.1SG you.DAT if these REFL be.silent.3PL
kamenie vъzopiti imatъ
stones cry.out.INF have.3PL
'and he replied: I am telling you, if these fall silent, the stones will cry out.'

In all these examples the *iměti*-construction is used as a means to translate modally marked futurity in Greek[19] in speech acts of solemn predictions. The fusion of modal and futural meanings in the construction is based on the inference of necessity: some event is bound to occur in the future, "especially if the source is God's authority" (Traugott and Dasher 2002: 128).

It is reasonable to assume, then, that the dominant meaning in the source construction in OCS was epistemic necessity rather than futurity. When these semantically underspecified future markers were faced with the advancing *velle*-future constructions in Balkan Slavic, the modal meaning of *habere*-constructions became salient in performative uses. Compared with the fate of Romance *habere*-constructions, in which *habere* was grammaticalized into a future tense marker (Isačenko 1974: 71), South Slavic *habere*-constructions were affected by a regressive process of language change. Namely, under the pressure of a contact-induced rival form[20] they developed in the opposite direction: from future tense markers to modal constructions of necessity (deontic and epistemic in the uninflected *ima*). Both the deontic modality and the future tense refer to non-factual, projected situations,[21] which may explain why the semantic derivation goes in both directions: future markers may develop modal meanings, and modal markers may develop future meanings (Palmer 1998: 216–218).

The paucity of reliable historical data allows only speculations about possible pathways of the semantic change of the inflected *ima*-construction. Given the present functional distribution of the two types of constructions we presume that the development of uninflected from inflected *ima* in Balkan Slavic occurred subsequently, driven by the need for formal differentiation between non-performative (agent-oriented) and performative (speaker-oriented) types of modality. The

---

[19] Those are: sigmatic future, periphrastic future with *mellein*, and subjunctive future under negation.

[20] The semantic change of *ima*-constructions raises the question whether it should be treated as an external or contact-induced internally-motivated change. Joseph (2000) argues that it is important how a borrowed syntactic construction "takes hold in a language" and thinks that "the spread of a pattern into a language" is language-internal.

[21] Although the primary function of future markers is temporal reference (Nuyts 2001: 173), it is questionable whether futurity is a purely temporal concept (see Lyons 1995: 319).

formal separation between these modal categories was enabled by the existence of an available form: the uninflected *ima* for existential meaning.

However, more historical support is needed for the verification of this hypothesis. In the late 18th century a single inflected *ima*-construction for expressing prediction is recorded in Daniel's *Lexicon Tetraglosson: imaš da se pretiliš* 'you will become fat' (literally "you-have to self you-exaggerate"; Ilievski 1988: 223), although all the other future forms are formed with the devolitive particle *ḱe*. In the dialectal texts collected by Verkoviḱ (see Verkoviḱ 1985) in the mid-19th century,[22] we found the inflected variants mostly in non-performative uses, but one example (12) might be considered as a directive speech act.

(12) *Ta otide   kaj carot,   mu   veli: Oh caru, imaš   da mi*
     he went.3SG to king.DEF him.DAT said O king   have.2SG PRT me.DAT
     davaš! – Od   što   sinko imam   da ti   davam?
     give.2SG from what son   have.1SG PRT you.DAT give.1SG
     'He went to the king and said: – O king, you have to give me (the gold)!
                                –What do I have, my son, to give you?' (Verkoviḱ 1985: 178)

Similar inflected constructions expressing circumstantial obligation are quite common in mid-19th century folk tales (Cepenkov 1989),[23] but a future certainty uninflected construction is also attested (13).

(13) *Dve ḱerki   omaživ   i   mnogu stoka po niv   dadov*
     two daughters gave.in.marriage.1SG and much cattle   for them gave-1SG
     i   za drugata   ḱerka   što ja   imam   ima   da davam   i
     and for other.the daughter that her have.1SG has-impers PRT give.1SG and
     mnogu pari   po nea.   (Cepenkov 1989: 64)
     much money for her
     'I have given two daughters away in marriage and I have given lots of cattle for them and for the other daughter that I have I am to give lots of money for her.'

In view of the fact that these constructions belong to spoken language, diachronic evidence is extremely hard to find. We hypothesize that in Macedonian the uninflected *ima*-constructions must have developed from the inflected, reflecting the principle of transparency between form and function, but it is impossible to

---

22 From Lagadin region near Thessaloniki characterized by an intense Slavo-Greek contact at that time (Joseph 2000).
23 The tales were written in central dialect (from Prilep, Republic of Macedonia).

locate when exactly it happened. This change was aided by several factors: the tendency of modal verbs to become impersonal, the presence of the existential impersonal *ima* and the wide distribution of negated invariable future *nema*-constructions (fused negative marker *ne* + *ima*).[24] Being formally symmetrical with uninflected *ima*-constructions these negative future tense markers stand in a converse relation with *ima*-constructions, both often interpreted as more categorical (Topolinjska 2009: 38). Under the pressure of these factors, the inflected *ima* has grammaticalized into an indeclinable particle *ima* expressing speaker's discourse intentions towards the addressee. These intentions involve speaker's manipulation of the addressee (including persuasion) and his/her subjective stance: resolve and close interpersonal distance.

4 Research results and analysis

In order to achieve the goal of our investigation, we compared the functional zone of this isomorphic *habere*-construction in five Balkan languages. For this purpose we designed a questionnaire containing 14 situations, each one prompting the use either of an inflected or uninflected *ima da*-construction. The questionnaire, translated into Bulgarian, Serbian (southern variant), Albanian (spoken in the Republic of Macedonia) and Greek, was administered to native speakers of each analyzed language.[25] The answers were fed into a data base and used for a quantitative analysis. The initial hypothesis, based on our knowledge of these languages, was that only in Macedonian is the distinction into two formal variants maintained regularly and that this distinction reflects a speech act orientation of the more grammaticalized uninflected form.

The analysis was conducted in several stages: first we looked at the form of the modal verb in this construction in all languages, then we analyzed the data we got for the three sentences that represent the Macedonian inflected *ima*-constructions (circumstantial obligation), and next we analyzed the sentences representing the uninflected *ima*-constructions in Macedonian (both deontic and epistemic meanings). In the end we compared the results which enabled us to

---

[24] The construction *nema* + *da*-clause is extensively used as a negative future marker in Macedonian alongside the less frequent strategy involving the invariable future marker *ḱe* 'will' (*ne ḱe odam* vs. *nema da odam*).

[25] The informants were of various ages, but predominantly university students between 20 and 30 years of age. The Macedonian sample was the largest (128 informants), while those from the other languages were considerably lower: 68 for Albanian, 48 for Serbian, 38 for Bulgarian, and 30 for Greek.

draw relevant conclusions about the functional distribution of the modal *habere*-construction in these languages.

4.1 Differentiation in form

Table 2 shows the overall results of the distribution of inflected and uninflected forms in all languages in the two modal *habere*-constructions we identified in Macedonian. The results confirm the existence of a formal division between the two types of these constructions in Balkan Slavic languages. In 'circumstantial obligation' all Slavic language speakers chose predominantly the inflected form, when they considered the *habere*-construction possible. The few uses of the non-inflected form in Macedonian were most probably due to reanalysis. However, the inflected/uninflected division is not so sharp in Bulgarian and in Serbian regarding the 'future certainty' construction: 28.66% of the Bulgarian informants and almost 11% of the Serbian informants chose inflected forms in situations where future certainty was expressed.

Table 2: Overall distribution of inflected and uninflected forms in questionnaire results.

	Circumstantial obligation		Epistemic certainty	
	inflected (%)	uninfl. (%)	inflected (%)	uninfl. (%)
Macedonian	91.43	8.57	3.06	96.68
Bulgarian	96.15	3.85	28.66	71.33
Serbian	96.2	2.38	10.97	89.03
Albanian	98.46	1.54	93.92	6.08
Greek	100.00	0	100	0

We find little information about the form and function of modal *habere* in Serbian and in Bulgarian against which to check our results. In the Academy Syntax of the Serbian language, Piper (2005a: 662) mentions the construction with the verb *imati* as a means of issuing an order. The example he cites, *Ima(š) da ćutiš*! 'Shut up!', indicates that both the inflected and uninflected form is possible, but the difference in meaning is not discussed.[26] Hansen (2001: 133–140) distinguishes

---

[26] In the chapter on predication, Piper (2005b: 325) notes that "infinitive is common in constructions with the verbs *imati* and *nemati* in modal use" (*Naređenje se ima odmah izvršiti.* 'The order shall be carried out immediately.'), but no further explanation is given.

two deontic functions of *imati* in *imati* + *infinitive/da-clause* in Serbian/Croatian: 'obligation' and 'fatalistic future', but stops short of mentioning any difference in form. However, our collected examples suggest that the existence of two variants (inflected and uninflected) in Serbian could be linked to some meaning differentiation. This is confirmed by Predrag Piper in his comments to the questionnaire situation given in (14): "both the inflected and uninflected form is possible, but the function is not the same, *ima* has a more categorical deontic meaning, while *imaš* softens the deonticity".[27]

(14) *Sada ću govoriti o onima koji treba da postanu sveštenici.*
_____ *(ima, imaš) da učiš grčka slova, kako bi znao da pročitaš i rastumačiš Sveto Evanđelje. Tada ćeš, brate moj, postati sveštenik.*
'Now I will talk about those who are to become priests. You_____ (*have*-uninflected, *have*-2SG) to learn Greek letters, so as to read and interpret the Gospel. Only then, my brother, will you become a priest.'

Some regular form-function alliance is also not clearly explained in accounts on Bulgarian *imam* 'have'. Asenova (2002: 206), pointing out the lack of semantic differentiation between the two variants in native grammars, notes that both verbs are used in colloquial speech to express a future activity with shades of obligation and necessity. Krapova (1999: 86) argues that "in the case of *imam*, the impersonal construction *ima da* is still competing with the personal one", but mentions no difference in meaning, even though her examples seem to be distinct (despite the fact that it is hard to determine for lack of wider context): the inflected one in (15) expresses circumstantial obligation, while the uninflected one (16) is more likely to code future certainty, even though the English translation does not indicate the difference.

(15) *Ivan ima da piše pisma.*
Ivan has PRT write.3SG letters
'Ivan has to write letters.' (from Krapova 1999: 81)

(16) *Az ima mnogo da uča.*
I have-impers much PRT study.1SG
'I have to study a lot.' (from Krapova 1999: 86)

---

[27] It is not clear if the distinction between more/less categorical deontic meaning corresponds to the distinction directive/circumstantial obligation. It seems that in Serbian the inflected *imati* can be used for less categorical directives as well, but this matter requires further investigation.

It is obvious, then, that both in Serbian and Bulgarian the form of the modal *habere* is not subject to free variation, but correlates with functional differentiation. However, according to the questionnaire results, the inflected form in these two languages is found in functions in which Macedonian uses only the uninflected *ima*. This fluctuation between the two forms supports our hypothesis that the uninflected *habere* is more grammaticalized in Macedonian than in the other two languages and that its association with particular types of meaning is stronger.

Albanian and Greek speakers, as expected, did not make the distinction in form in situations where *habere*-construction was used: in all modal meanings where it was accepted the *habere*-verb is inflected. Albanian speakers showed a small degree of indeterminacy, especially in the 'epistemic certainty' meanings, probably due to influence from Macedonian, while Greek speakers invariably used the inflected forms. The distribution of functions is discussed later in 4.3.

4.2 Analysis of the results for the inflected forms

In our previous research (Bužarovska and Mitkovska 2011) we argued that the Macedonian inflected construction syntactically and semantically exhibits the properties of a less grammaticalized construction: the possessive meaning is still felt (more or less), the modal meaning varies between possibility, volition and obligation; the *ima*-construction is sensitive to transitivity and allows a small number of verbs. Thus, we hypothesized that the transitive constructions such as (17), from the questionnaire, are more readily accepted than the low transitive (18) and the intransitive (19) ones, also from the questionnaire.

(17) *Nedelno popladne, tatkoto saka da im dade zadača na decata da ja izmijat kolata. Majkata veli: Ne gi angažiraj decata, mnogu se zafateni. _____ (ima, imaat) da pišuvaat domašno za utre.*
 'Sunday afternoon, the father wants to give a chore to the children to wash the car. The mother says: Don't engage the children, they are busy. They _____ (*have*-uninflected, *have*.1SG) to do the homework for tomorrow.'

(18) *Vašata prijatelka vi se javuva na Fejsbuk. Vie odgovarate: Posle k'e ti se javam. Sega nemam vreme. Prvo _____ (ima, imam) da odgovoram na nekolku imejli. Itno e.*
 'Your friend contacts you on Facebook. You answer: I'll write to you later. I don't have time now. First I _____ (*have*-uninflected, *have*.1SG) to reply to some e-mails. It's urgent.'

(19) *Vašite prijateli ve kanat da odite na zabava. Vie velite: Izvinete, ne možam, utre _____ (ima, imam) da stanam rano. Avionot mi trgnuva vo pet.*
'Your friends invite you to a party. You say: Sorry, I can't, tomorrow I _____ (*have*-uninflected, *have*.1SG) to get up early. The plane takes off at five.'

One of our aims in designing the questionnaire was also to test this hypothesis and to check the degree of acceptance of the *habere*-construction for 'circumstantial obligation' in all examined languages. The results of our research are presented in Table 3. Albanian and Greek speakers exhibit the highest degree of acceptability for all three situations, and, as expected, used only the inflected form. This was not the case with the three Balkan Slavic languages, where the inflected form also dominates, but the degree of its acceptability varies from language to language.

Table 3: Frequency of inflected constructions in 'circumstantial obligation'.

	Sent.	inflected (%)	uninflected (%)	other (%)
Macedonian	1	59.37	3.12	37.50
	2	36.16	0.80	64.06
	3	4.69	5.47	89.84
Bulgarian	1	89.47	0	10.53
	2	57.89	2.63	39.47
	3	50.00	2.63	47.37
Serbian	1	52.08	0	47.92
	2	29.17	0	70.83
	3	4.17	2.08	93.75
Albanian	1	95.59	2.94	1.47
	2	91.18	1.47	7.35
	3	95.59	0	4.41
Greek	1	96.30	0	3.70
	2	96.30	0	3.70
	3	96.30	0	3.70

The percentages for 'other' indicate non-acceptability of the sentence with the verb *ima*, be it inflected or uninflected. The informants suggested some other modal verb instead, mainly *treba* 'should' or *mora* 'must, have to'. The results confirmed our initial hypothesis that the degree of grammaticalization of the *habere*-construction in Balkan Slavic depends on the transitivity of the verb. In all three languages, the *ima* modal is judged most acceptable in the transitive situation, less so in the low transitive situation and the least in the intransitive situation. On the whole, Bulgarian speakers demonstrate the highest degree of acceptability, the intransitive situation being accepted by 50% of the informants, which suggests that the modal *imam* for circumstantial obligation is quite well established in the language. Serbian speakers accepted *imati* in transitive constructions with 52%, and rejected it in the intransitive situation, suggesting the use of some other modal verb. However, such uses are found in Serbian, as illustrated in (20), though they may be characterized by a certain regional or stylistic flavor.

(20) *Žurim,   imam   da   idem na razna   mesta,*[28]...
Hurry.1SG have.1SG PRT go.1SG to different places
'I'm in a hurry, I've got to go to a number of places, ...'

The acceptability judgments by the Macedonian speakers are lower than expected. The high percentage of rejection of *ima* in the intransitive sentence is surprising: though not very common, such constructions are attested in everyday communication (21).

(21) *Sega brzam   da ne mi   zatvorat, imam   da*
now hurry.1SG PRT not me.DAT close.3PL have.1SG PRT
odam do prodavnica, ... da   kupam   nekoi raboti
go.1SG to shop,   ... PRT buy.1SG some things
'I must hurry now or the shops will close, I have to go to the shop, ... to buy some things.'

Regarding the status of the *habere*-verb expressing 'circumstantial obligation' we can conclude that in this function the verb *ima* is not fully grammaticalized in Balkan Slavic, unlike in Albanian and Greek.

4.3 Analysis for the results of the uninflected forms

As explained above, 'epistemic certainty' covers a cluster of contiguous meanings of the Macedonian uninflected *ima*-construction. These meanings are defined in the ensuing analysis according to the speech act orientation of the

---

[28] Attested.

construction: commissive, directive, reported obligation and predictive. We included nine situations expressing 'epistemic certainty' in the analysis (two commissive, two reported obligation, one directive and four predictions). Two situations that featured in the questionnaire were not considered since one turned out to be rather ambiguous between circumstantial and directive, and the other construction verges on idiomaticity. The questionnaire results for *habere*-constructions expressing 'epistemic certainty' (based on the use of the uninflected *ima* 'in Macedonian) are shown in Table 4.

In this part of the analysis we examine two issues: (a) the form of the *habere*-construction – inflected or uninflected in each given situation in Balkan Slavic languages[29]; and (b) the acceptability judgements of examples with *habere*-construction expressing 'epistemic certainty' in each language. The goal is to determine the scope of use of deontic and epistemic meanings of this construction in all examined languages.

Table 4: Frequency of uninflected constructions in 'epistemic certainty'.

	Type of modal function	inflected (%)	uninflected (%)	other (%)
Macedonian	Commissive 1sg	0.78	89.84	9.37
	Reported obligation 2/3pl	4.29	73.04	22.65
	Directive 2sg	2.34	77.34	20.31
	Strong prediction 2sg & 1/3pl	2.73	79.10	16.01
	Total	**2.53**	**79.83**	**17.07**
Bulgarian	Commissive 1sg	9.21	40.79	50.00
	Reported obligation 2/3pl	2.63	31.58	65.79
	Directive 2sg	31.58	2.65	65.79
	Strong prediction 2sg & 1/3pl	10.53	59.21	30.26
	Total	**13.49**	**33.59**	**52.96**
Serbian	Commissive 1sg	5.21	79.17	15.62
	Reported obligation 2/3pl	13.54	38.54	47.92
	Directive 2sg	8.33	54.17	37.50
	Strong prediction 2sg & 1/3pl	6.77	75.52	17.71
	Total	**8.10**	**65.74**	**26.16**

---

[29] The discrepancy in percentages received for the inflected form in the epistemic certainty subclass (Table 4) compared to those in Table 2 is due to the fact that the data in Table 2 refer only to the sentences deemed acceptable with *habere* by the subjects, while in Table 4 the percentage is calculated on the basis of all items, considering also those where the category of 'other' was chosen.

Table 4 (continued)

	Type of modal function	inflected (%)	uninflected (%)	other (%)
Albanian	Commissive 1sg	91.91	5.15	2.94
	Reported obligation 2/3pl	94.12	2.21	3.68
	Directive 2sg	85.29	14.70	0
	Strong prediction 2sg & 1/3pl	93.38	5.12	1.47
	Total	91.18	6.80	2.02
Greek	Commissive 1sg	7.40	0	95.60
	Reported obligation 2/3pl	7.40	0	95.60
	Directive 2sg	22.22	0	77.78
	Strong prediction 2sg & 1/3pl	26.86	0	73.14
	Total	15.97	0	84.03

As expected, Macedonian speakers chose predominantly uninflected forms. The percentage of the inflected forms was slightly higher in 'reported obligation' probably because of some association with the meaning of circumstantial obligation characteristic of the inflected variant. Without marked intonation and contextual support the intended meaning of epistemic certainty may not be available. Regarding the acceptability judgement, a considerable percentage (17.07%) of 'other' was obtained in Macedonian, which may indicate that speakers did not think that the verb *ima* was felicitously used in these situations. This was unexpected, since the examples had been taken predominantly from Macedonian sources (only one from Serbian and Bulgarian, respectively). The reactions we got from the interviewed informants suggest that some speakers considered the *ima*-construction unusual in written form: without the strong stress and intonation corresponding to the situation the *ima*-construction alone did not evoke the intended meaning. In personal communication some speakers explained that they felt that *ima*-constructions were too forceful and thus not preferred, although possible.

In Bulgarian and Serbian there is some variation in respect to both form and meaning. Regarding the form of the accepted *habere*-constructions, despite the predominance of uninflected constructions, speakers of these languages chose a slightly higher percentage of inflected forms than Macedonian speakers. This may be attributable to several reasons: the Macedonian sample was much bigger, the situations had a more familiar ring for Macedonian speakers and/or the division between the two *habere*-constructions in the other two languages is less clear. The percentage of the inflected forms is higher in Bulgarian (13.49% compared to 8.10% in Serbian), but it seems that the score was affected by the choice in one particular sentence employed in a directive situation (22), from the questionnaire, in which Bulgarian speakers either chose the inflected variant or rejected it, suggesting *trjabva* 'should' instead. Only a small fraction of subjects (2.65%) chose the uninflected *ima*.

(22) *Vašijat naematel ne si go platil naema za njakolko meseca. Vie ste mnogo sărdit i kazvate:*
_____ *(ima, imaš) da go platiš naema ili šte te izhvărlja.*
'Your tenant has not paid his rent for several months. You are very angry and tell him:
_____ (*have*-uninflected, *have*.2SG) pay the rent or I will throw you out!'

The obtained questionnaire data show that there is variation between the inflected and uninflected forms in Bulgarian and that the distinction regarding 'circumstantial obligation' could be blurred as in (23) and (24), if subjectivity is not clearly indicated in (23) by the intonation and pragmatic strengtheners (*daže, baja*). Still, very few examples with uninflected *ima da* in directive function were found.

(23) ...*to daže ne e London, ami baja ima   da platiš dokato se*
it even not is London, but a.lot has-impers PRT pay.2SG until REFL
dobereš do Ljutăn...[30]
get.2SG to Luton
... 'but it's not in London, so you will/have to pay a lot until you get to Luton.'

(24) *Zaštoto sled tova imaš   da platiš i   montaž, balans i*
because after that have.2SG PRT pay.2SG and mounting balancing and
stave   debelo...[31]
becomes thick
'Because after that you will have to pay both mounting and balancing, and it amounts to a lot ...'

In Serbian, the use of uninflected *ima*-constructions seems to be similar to that in Macedonian, but more Serbian speakers (13.54%) chose the inflected variant for 'reported obligation'. We assume that the inflected form was probably chosen for two reasons: (a) lack of expressivity characteristic of written language, so for some subjects it did not carry enough force and emotional involvement; (b) some situations may have been understood as less forceful and hence interpreted as 'circumstantial obligation'. This has to do with speaker's degree of confidence about the realization of a future event. The assertoric force of uninflected constructions

---

30 http://forum.investor.bg/forum/макроикономика-управление-и-реформи/4193-скандално-отношение-на-wizzair/page3
31 http://www.opelclub.bg/index.php?showtopic=85761

expressing 'reported obligation' is based either on personal conviction in the inevitability of a future event or on knowledge of the strength of the given circumstantial obligation. It is this second meaning that overlaps with circumstantial obligation coded by inflected constructions, where the speaker expresses an objective view, devoid of subjectivity. Nuyts (2001: 180) uses the term 'merger', when "it is immaterial for the understanding of an utterance which of the readings is actually meant, because they are not mutually exclusive." In the situation presented in (25), from the questionnaire, the inflected variant is interpreted as circumstantial obligation (you have the duty), while the uninflected variant predicts the realization of this obligation. While in Macedonian strong prediction is pragmatically understood, in Serbian it might be more open to subjective interpretation.

(25) *Jesi li čuo što su rekli na vestima? Imao – nemao televizor, svi _____ (ima/ imaju) da plaćaju televizijsku taksu.*
'Have you heard what they said on TV? No matter whether you have or not a TV set, all (*have*-uninflected, *have*.3PL) pay the TV tax.'

The acceptability of *habere*-constructions in the given situations is a more complex issue and the results we received from this questionnaire should be judged with caution. We mentioned above some possible reasons why Macedonian speakers chose 'other' rather than the *ima*-construction. This may apply to the Serbian and Bulgarian speakers, but the percentages suggest other reasons as well. The total acceptability of the uninflected *ima*-construction expressed by Serbian speakers was slightly lower than that of Macedonian speakers, but twice as high as that of Bulgarian speakers (65.74% compared to 33.59%), which may lead to the conclusion that this construction is not very common in Bulgarian. However, this runs counter to our observations. The sample of collected examples contains a number of Bulgarian uninflected *ima*-constructions with modal meanings similar to those in Macedonian. The results suggest that there may be considerable differences, which warrant further investigation. It seems that Bulgarian uninflected *ima* is more strictly limited to prediction, expressing strong speaker conviction in the fulfillment of the event (26). These forms seldom code external obligation (threats, prohibitions, etc) as well as speaker commitment. Indeed, we found no deontic examples in our Bulgarian corpus.

(26) *Ta ...ako si mălčiš ... ima da te motat.*[32]
So if REFL keep.silent.2SG ... has-impers PRT you.ACC cheat.3PL
'If you don't say anything they will cheat you.'

---

[32] https://vukajlija.com/ima-da-te/149195

Unlike Bulgarian, it is not uncommon in Serbian to employ uninflected constructions for speaker-oriented obligation, as illustrated in examples (27) and (28).

(27) *Gos'n Macola – ima   da te   složim ko metar drva!!!*[33]
Mr. Matsola – has-impers PRT you.ACC put.1SG as meter wood
'Mr. Matsola, I am going to stack you as a pile of wood!'

(28) *Dok te   ja hranim ima   da me   slušaš!*[34]
until you.ACC it feed.1SG has-impers PRT me.ACC listen.2SG
'Until I provide for you, you will obey me!'

It seems that the Bulgarian uninflected *ima*-construction is also subject to more structural restrictions,[35] especially in respect to verbal aspect: imperfective verbs tend to co-occur with *ima*, while perfective ones match with *šte*. It has been pointed out by questionnaire informants that the replacement of perfective verb stems with imperfective ones increases the acceptability of the *ima*-construction. Additionally, stative verbs do not seem to be paired with the modal *ima*. This may account for the fact that Bulgarian speakers rejected a high percentage of 'epistemic certainty' *ima* in the questionnaire situations.

As pointed out earlier, in both Albanian and Greek the standard variant is the inflected *habere*-construction, but it turns out that there is difference in the distribution of meanings. Albanian speakers accepted its use in all sub-meanings of 'epistemic certainty' with a high percentage (91.18%), using the inflected *habere*-construction (which is the norm). The slight intrusion of the uninflected construction could be attributed to influence from Macedonian, which is most pronounced in directive uses (29). Greek speakers, on the other hand, accepted the *habere*-construction for 'epistemic certainty' marginally, explaining that it was obsolete and had a dialectal ring to it. It was accepted only as a second choice for strong prediction, as in (30).

(29) *Qiraxhiu juaj nuk e ka paguar qiranë disa muaj. Ju jeni shumë i hidhëruar dhe thoni: _____ _____ (ka, ke) për ta paguar qiranë ose do të përjashtoj.*
'Your tenant has not paid his rent for several months. You are very angry and tell him: _____ (*have*-uninflected, *have*-2sg) pay the rent or I will throw you out!'

---

[33] From *Brašno u venama* by Igor Štiks.
[34] www.vaseljenska.com
[35] We are grateful to Iliyana Krapova, Ivelina Tchizmarova, Marina Džonova for their insightful comments that have led to these conclusions.

(30) *Bravo ayori mu! Me tetio talento* _____ *(exi/exis) na jinis ðevteros Paganini!*
'Well done, my child! With such talent you _____ (*have*-uninflected/
have.2SG) become a second Paganini!'

Even though the modal uninflected *habere*-construction is used on a dialectal level in Greek (Asenova 2002: 203), it has become an unproductive, obsolete pattern. In order to trigger the use of uninflected *habere* in predictions, Greek speakers mark the utterance as subjective by expressive intonation and emotionally charged vocabulary. For instance, the neutral prediction of imminent rain when seeing a flash of lightning is coded with a future marker *θa* in *θa vreksi* 'It will rain', but a strong prediction is conveyed by the *habere*-construction[36] in the idiomatic expression *Exi na riksi vroxi me touloumi!* 'It will be pouring with rain!' (literally "has.3SG PRT throw.3SG rain with sack")

5 Conclusion

The results of this investigation confirmed our initial hypothesis that Macedonian adheres strictly to the semantic-pragmatic distinction between the two formal variants of *ima*-constructions. The formal distinction between performative and non-performative uses of these constructions reflects the tendency of Macedonian for a more transparent form-function correlation. This distinction overlaps with another pragmatic opposition: objective vs. subjective. Performative uses are characterized by speaker's subjective attitude stemming from his/her authority over the subject. Consequently, high subjectivity is associated with issuing orders (in uninflected) as opposed to stating obligations (in inflected).

However, other expectations related to the scope of distribution of this construction in each analyzed language were not entirely confirmed. Although it was confirmed that the non-Slavic languages (Albanian and Greek) have only the inflected variant we did not expect them to be so different with respect to

---

[36] It is possible that an additional reason why modal *habere*-constructions have a rather limited distribution in Greek is the presence of a formally identical but non-modal construction with negated perfect meaning: that the subject has not performed the activity in the subjunctive clause for a certain period of time, as in *Exo na ton do ðio xronia* 'I haven't seen him for two years' (literally "have.1SG PRT him see.1SG two years"). Another reason for the limited range of this construction may involve the pressure from the standard norm.

distribution: in Albanian this construction seems to be very common as the informants accepted it in all functions, while in Greek it mainly codes circumstantial obligation, being almost obliterated in 'epistemic certainty' meanings.

In Balkan Slavic, the three languages exhibit gradient distribution regarding the use of both inflected and uninflected construction. In Bulgarian and Serbian the pragmatically-driven division into two formal types is not maintained so regularly as in Macedonian. In Bulgarian, expressing obligation is more likely to be coded with an inflected than with an uninflected *habere*-construction, both directive and circumstantial, but for the former other types of constructions seem to be preferred. In Serbian, on the other hand, the distinction between inflected and uninflected *imati* with an obligation function is subject to intensity of the illocutionary force and/or to stylistic considerations. According to the frequency distribution of the inflected constructions in the questionnaire, they seem to be most grammaticalized in Bulgarian and the least in Serbian.

Uninflected *habere*-constructions in Macedonian are equally used in deontic and epistemic uses brought together under the category of 'epistemic certainty'. In Serbian they are used in much the same way (though some affinity for deontic uses is noted), while in Bulgarian they exhibit a robust preference for coding strong prediction. Moreover, the acceptability of uninflected constructions in Bulgarian is subject to more restrictions than in the other two languages. This suggests that the less grammaticalized Bulgarian *ima*-construction has a restricted functional zone (similarly to Greek, where the *habere*-construction is marginalized) mainly confined to predictive functions, as opposed to Macedonian and Serbian which have developed directive as well as predictive functions.

The typological significance of our findings is that all Balkan Slavic languages have undergone grammaticalization of *habere*-constructions but not to the same degree.[37] In Macedonian the formal division between the two variants strictly coincides with the discourse function of non-performative assertive speech acts vs. performative non-assertive speech acts. In the other two Slavic languages this division is somewhat obscured. In these languages the modal *habere*-construction came to be marked (via morphological loss) for illocutionary force and for subjectivity. The analysis of the examples shows that the use of the uninflected *ima* requires subjective discourse with a high involvement of the speaker, or else *ima* can be replaced with a modal verb or a future marker. This fact gives us ground to consider the uninflected *ima*-constructions as markers of

---

[37] Compare Joseph's opinion about language change in the Balkans: "the Balkans differ from other areas or other individual languages in which change has occurred not in the kind of change that has occurred or the mechanisms of change that have occurred, but really only in the degree to which the changes have been involved with language contact..." (Joseph 2000: 147).

subjectivity in the Balkan Slavic systems of modal verbs. The formal marking of uninflected *ima*-constructions represents an example of grammaticalization of discourse functions, which served as "entry points for the development of structural change" (Friedman 2000: 1349).[38]

In view of the fact that *habere*-constructions have unjustifiably been neglected in the majority of academic work on Balkan languages we hope that the hypotheses and conclusions set forth in this paper will encourage further research of these constructions. What is needed is a systematic investigation of the functional distribution of (inflected and uninflected) *habere*-constructions in each individual language in the Balkans. Establishing the place of the modal *habere* with respect to other modal and future markers in each language may reveal whether its pragmatization and speech act orientation is a common typological development or just a feature of Balkan Slavic.

References

Aronson, Howard I. 2007. *The Balkan Linguistic League, "Orientalism," and Linguistic Typology*. Ann Arbor / NY: Beech Stave Press.
Asenova, Petya. 2002. *Balkansko ezikoznanie: Osnovni problem na balkanskija ezikov săjuz* [Balkan Linguistics: Fundamental problems of the Balkan Linguistic Union]. V. Tărnovo: Faber.
Benveniste, Émile. 1960/1966. 'Être' et 'avoir' dans leurs fonctions linguistiques. In *Problèmes de linguistique générale*, Émile Benveniste (ed.), 187–207. Paris: Gallimard.
Brinton, Laurel J. 1991. The origin and development of quasimodal *have to* in English. Paper presented at the 10th International Conference on Historical Linguistics, Amsterdam 1991. <http://faculty.arts.ubc.ca/lbrinton/> (15.02.2012).
Bužarovska, Eleni and Liljana Mitkovska. 2011. Lični te *ima da*-konstrukcii vo makedonskiot jazik [Personal *ima da*-constructions in Macedonian]. *Makedonski jazik* LVII, 120–133.
Bybee, Joan, Revere Perkins, and William Pagliuca. 1994. *The evolution of grammar: tense, aspect, and modality in the languages of the world*. Chicago: University of Chicago Press.
Čašule, Ilija. 1989. Modalnite glagoli vo makedonskiot jazik [Modal verbs in Macedonian]. *Prilozi* 14/2, 89–117. Skopje: MANU.
Cepenkov, Marko. 1989. *Narodni prikazni*. Kniga 5. Realistični prikazni. Skopje: Makedonska kniga.
Cyhun, Gennadij A. 1981. *Tipologicheskie problemy balkanoslavyanskogo yazykovogo areala* [The typological problems of Balkan Slavic Sprachbund]. Minsk: Nauka i tehnika.
Dahl, Östen. 2000. The Grammar of Future Time Reference in European Languages. In *Tense and Aspect in the Languages of Europe*, Östen Dahl (ed.), 309–328. Berlin: Mouton de Gruyter.
Danylenko, Andrii. 2011. Is there any inflectional future in East Slavic? A case of Ukrainian against Romance reopened. In *Grammaticalization in Slavic Language. From Areal and Typological Perspectives*, Motoki Nomachi (ed.), 147–177. Sapporo: Slavic Research Center.

---

[38] Friedman (2000: 1349) argues that "The grammaticalization of discourse functions tends to occur in those regions where multilingualism is most complex."

Grković-Major, Jasminka. 2011. The development of predicative possession in Slavic languages, in: *The Grammar of Possessivity in South Slavic Languages: Synchronic and Diachronic Perspectives*, Motoki Nomachi (ed.), 35–54. Sapporo: Slavic Research Center.

Givón, Talmy 1990. *Syntax: functional introduction*. Vol. II. Amsterdam: Benjamins.

Hansen, Björn. 2001. *Das slavische Modalauxiliar: Semantik und Grammatikalisierung im Russischen, Polnischen, Serbischen/Kroatischen und Altkirchenslavischen*. München: Otto Sagner.

Friedman, Victor A. 1977. *The grammatical categories of the Macedonian indicative*. Columbus: Slavica.

Friedman, Victor A. 2000. Pragmatics and Contact in Macedonian. *Južnoslovenski filolog* 56, 1343–1351. (http://home.uchicago.edu/~vfriedm/Articles/155Friedman00.pdf.)

Ilievski, Petar H. 1988. *Balkanološki lingvistički studii* [Balkan Linguistic Studies]. Skopje: IMJ.

Isačenko, Alexander V. 1974. On 'have' and 'be' languages. In *Slavic forum. Essays in linguistics and literature*, Michael Flier (ed.), 43–77. The Hague: Mouton.

Joseph, Brian D. 1983. *The Synchrony and Diachrony of the Balkan Infinitive: A Study in Areal, General and Historical Linguistics*. Cambridge: Cambridge University Press.

Joseph, Brian D. 1990. When Verbs Collide. In *Papers from the Ohio State Mini-Conference on Serial Verbs*, Brian Joseph and Arnold Zwicky (eds.), 77–90. *Ohio State Working Papers in Linguistics* 39.

Joseph, Brian D. 2000. Processes of Spread for Syntactic Constructions in the Balkans. In *Balkan Linguistik: Synchronie und Diachronie*, Christos Tzitzilis and Christos Symeonidis (eds.), 139–150. Thessaloniki: University of Thessaloniki.

Koneski, Kiril. 2000. *Makedonski jazik za stranci: sreden kurs* [Macedonian Language for Foreigners: intermediate course]. Skopje: UKIM.

Kramer, Christina E. 1986. *Analytic modality in Macedonian*. München: Verlag Otto Sagner.

Kramer, Christina E. 1998. Negation and Grammaticalization of Have and Want Futures in Bulgarian and Macedonian. *Canadian Slavonic Papers*, Vol. 29/ 3–4, 407–416.

Krapova, Iliyana. 1999. The system of auxiliaries in Bulgarian. In *Topics in South Slavic syntax and semantics*, Mila Dimitrova-Vulchanova and Lars Hellan (eds.), 59–89. Amsterdam: Benjamins.

Lindstedt, Jouko. 2000. The perfect – aspectual, temporal and evidential. In *Tense and aspect in the languages of Europe*, Östen Dahl (ed.), 366–383. Berlin: Mouton de Gruyter.

Lyons, John. 1995. *Linguistic semantics: an introduction*. Cambridge: Cambridge University Press.

Mauri, Caterina and Andrea Sanso. 2012. The reality status of directives and its coding across languages. *Language Sciences* 34, 147–170.

McAnallen, Julia. 2011. Predicative Possession in Old Church Bible Translation. *Indo-European syntax and pragmatics: contrastive approaches*, Oslo Studies in Language 3(3), 155–172.

Mitkovska, Liljana and Eleni Bužarovska. 2012. Tipovi modalnost vo nemenlivite *ima da*-konstrukcii. [Types of modality in indeclinable *ima da*-constructions]. *Makedonski jazik* LXIII, 83–103.

Mitkovska, Liljana and Eleni Bužarovska. 2014. Deontic or epistemic? *Habēre* as a modal marker of future certainty in Macedonian. In *Modes of Modality. Modality, Typology, and Universal Grammar*, Elisabeth Leiss and Werner Abraham (eds.), 193–217. Amsterdam: Benjamins.

Narrog, Heiko. 2012. *Modality, Subjectivity and Semantic Change. A Cross-Linguistic Perspective*. Oxford: Oxford University Press.

Nuyts, Jan. 2001. *Epistemic modality, language and conceptualization.* Amsterdam: Benjamins.
Palmer, Frank R. 1998. *Mood and modality.* Cambridge: Cambridge University Press.
Piper, Predrag. 2005a. Modalnost. In *Sintaksa savremenoga srpskog jezika – prosta rečenica*, Milka Ivić (ed.), 636–649. Beograd/Novi Sad: SANU.
Piper, Predrag. 2005b. Predikat. In *Sintaksa savremenoga srpskog jezika – prosta rečenica*, Milka Ivić (ed.), 301–345. Beograd/Novi Sad: SANU.
Portner, Paul. 2009. *Modality.* Oxford: Oxford University Press.
Searle, John R. 1975. A Taxonomy of Illocutionary Acts. In *Language, Mind, and Knowledge*, vol. 7, K. Günderson (ed.), 344–369. Minneapolis: University of Minnesota Press.
Topolińska, Zuzanna. 1995a. Convergent Evolution, Creolization and Referentiality. In *Prague Linguistic Circle Papers*, vol.1, Eva Hajičová, Miroslav Červenka, Oldřich Leška, and Peter Sgall (eds.), 239–247.
Topolinjska, Zuzana. 1995b. *Makedonskite dijalekti vo Egejska Makedonija. Sintaksa.* Tom I. [Macedonian Dialects in Aegean Macedonia, Syntax. Vol.1]. Skopje: MANU.
Topolinjska, Zuzana. 2000. *Polski-makedonski: gramatička konfrontacija. Studii od morfosintaksata* [Polish-Macedonian: grammatical confrontation. Studies in morphosyntax]. Skopje: MANU.
Topolińska, Zuzanna. 2008. O pewnych niedocenianyh bałkanizmach w systemie werbalnym języka serbskogo [On some understudied balkanisms in Serbian verbal system]. *Južnoslovenski filolog* 64, 509–515.
Topolinjska, Zuzana. 2009. *Polski-makedonski: gramatička konfrontacija. Negacija.* Vol. 9 [Polish-Macedonian: grammatical confrontation. Negation. Vol. 9]. Skopje: MANU.
Traugott, Elizabeth C. and Richard B. Dasher. 2002. *Regularity in semantic change.* Cambridge: Cambridge University Press.
van der Auwera, Johan and Vladimir Plungian. 1998. Modality's semantic map. *Linguistic Typology* 2: 79–124.
Večerka, Radoslav. 1996. *Altkirchenslavische (Altbulgarische) Syntax. Die innere Satzstruktur Die innere Satzstruktur.* Vol. 2. Freiburg: U.W.Weiher.
Verkoviḱ, Stefan I. 1985. *South Macedonian Folk Tales.* Skopje: Makedonska kniga.
Yule, George. 1996. *Pragmatics.* Oxford: Oxford University Press.

Gabriela Bîlbîie and Alexandru Mardale
The Romanian subjunctive from a Balkan perspective

Abstract: This paper deals with the distribution and the interpretation of the subjunctive in Romanian, focusing on its morpho-syntactic pattern and its use in main interrogative clauses, where it displays Balkan Sprachbund properties. First, we provide evidence for the impact of the Balkan pattern by demonstrating an affixal status for the Romanian subjunctive marker *să*, an analysis that could be extended to the Bulgarian particle *da* and to the Greek particle *na*. Second, we argue that main interrogative clauses with subjunctive verbs are root clauses, not elliptical constructions. We then propose a typology of the subjunctive uses in main interrogatives, by using two discursive strategies (i.e. Question / Assertion pair, and Question / Question pair) and two distribution tests (i.e. free-context uses and dialogical uses). We propose an analysis that takes into account both the pragmatic and the semantic level. Crucially, subjunctive interrogatives involve a weak call-on-addressee and implicit modality arising from the intrinsic properties of the subjunctive itself. Our study shows a richer semantic and pragmatic potential of the subjunctive mood in Romanian interrogatives compared to other Romance languages. We finally provide a historical overview of the subjunctive use in Romanian, aiming to show that there is no evidence for language contact with respect to the emergence of the subjunctive in Romanian.

Keywords: subjunctive, modal markers, interrogatives, Balkan Sprachbund, Romanian

---

Note: This research was supported by the LabEx EFL project, strand 2 *Experimental syntax* (operation SA2) and by the strategic grant POSDRU/159/1.5/S/140863, Project ID 140863 (2014), co-financed by the European Social Fund within the Sectorial Operational Program Human Resources Development 2007 – 2013. We wish to thank Larisa Avram, Donka Farkas, Danièle Godard, Virginia Hill and Jean-Marie Marandin for their comments and suggestions, as well as the editors of the present volume and the audience of the Workshop *Balancing the Universal and the Particular in Balkan Morpho-Syntax Convergence* of the SLE 2013. All errors or misunderstandings are ours.

Gabriela Bîlbîie, University of Bucharest & Laboratoire de Linguistique Formelle – UMR 7110 CNRS, gabriela.bilbiie@gmail.com
Alexandru Mardale, INaLCO & SeDyL – UMR 8202 CNRS, alexandru.mardale@inalco.fr

https://doi.org/10.1515/9783110375930-012

1 Introduction

As Joseph (1999) suggests, Romanian is very well situated to allow for very interesting comparisons from both the genetic and the geographic point of view, with Romance and Balkan languages, respectively. It is well known that Romanian is a language displaying both Romance and Balkan features, which can be seen either in its lexicon or in its morpho-syntax. One of the linguistic phenomena showing this double relatedness of Romanian is the subjunctive mood. Romance similarities have been discussed by Farkas (1992), in particular for Romanian and French, with respect to the distribution of the subjunctive and indicative moods in finite complement clauses (see also Godard 2012). Less attention was paid to Balkan similarities with respect to the subjunctive mood. An important Balkan Sprachbund property (cf. Tomić 2006) is that subjunctive verbal forms follow a similar pattern, that is a particle precedes an indicative verb form. Another Balkan Sprachbund property, only generally considered before to the best of our knowledge (though see Ammann and van der Auwera 2004), concerns the high frequency of the subjunctive in main interrogative clauses, distinguishing Romanian from other Romance languages.

We are interested here in these two aspects related to the distribution and the interpretation of the subjunctive in Romanian, a phenomenon that mainly illustrates areal influences. First, we take a closer look at the morpho-syntactic status of the subjunctive, in particular the status of the subjunctive marker (Section 2). Second, we examine the distribution of the Romanian subjunctive in main clauses, in particular in main interrogatives (Section 3). Before we conclude, we briefly provide a historical explanation for the high frequency of the subjunctive (Section 4).

2 Morpho-syntactic aspects related to the subjunctive mood

Two issues are adressed here: on the one hand, the status of the subjunctive mood, by looking at the verbal inflection, and on the other hand, the morpho-syntactic status of the subjunctive markers in Balkan languages, with a focus on Romanian *să*.

Let us first recall the inflectional paradigm of the Romanian subjunctive, which displays two tenses, present and perfect. Both of them involve the particle *să* (cf. Lat. *si* 'if/whether') and a more or less specified verbal form. In present subjunctives, most verbal forms are the same as for the present indicative, except for the 3rd person singular and plural, where there is an alternation between these two moods, as shown in Table 1 below for the verb *a cânta* 'to sing'. Note that the only verb having a specific subjunctive paradigm for all persons is *a fi* 'to be' (e.g. *să fiu* 'be.SUBJ.1SG' vs. *sunt* 'be.IND.1SG', *să fii* 'be.SUBJ.2SG' vs. *ești* 'be.IND.2SG', *să fie* 'be.SUBJ.3SG' vs. *este* 'be.IND.3SG').

Table 1: Present subjunctive of the verb *a cânta* 'to sing'.

Person	Present subjunctive	Present indicative
1 sg	să cânt	cânt
2 sg	să cânți	cânți
3 sg	**să cânte**	**cântă**
1 pl	să cântăm	cântăm
2 pl	să cântați	cântați
3 pl	**să cânte**	**cântă**

In perfect subjunctives, there is only one (analytical) form for all persons, that is the verb *fi* 'be' followed by the past participle of the respective verb, as illustrated in Table 2 for the verb *a cânta* 'to sing':

Table 2: Perfect subjunctive of the verb *a cânta* 'to sing'.

Person	Perfect subjunctive
1–3 sg/pl	să fi cântat

2.1 The status of the subjunctive mood

One general question that arises when we take a closer look at the Balkan subjunctive is whether it is a mood by itself or only a variant of the indicative. The traditional answer is that for languages like Bulgarian and Greek, which have the same verbal exponent for both the indicative and the subjunctive, the subjunctive is a variant of the indicative and has no autonomous status, since it lacks specific inflection (see a.o. Feuillet 2012). However, one can find some evidence showing the specificity of the subjunctive in the Balkan area. Thus, for Greek, there is a crucial morpho-aspectual difference between the subjunctive and other moods: the Perfective Non-Past, e.g. 3sg *milisi* 'speak', can only appear as a dependent form in subjunctive uses (Mackridge 1985, Holton, Mackridge &

Philippaki-Warburton 1997) as illustrated in (1d), and is never found in the indicative (1b), unless preceded by *tha*, the marker of the future and conditional.[1]

(1) a. *Milai*   *yalika*.
       speak.NON-PERF.NON-PAST.3SG French
       'S/he speaks French.'
   b. **Milisi*   *yalika*.
       speak.PERF.NON-PAST.3SG French
   c. *Kseri* **na** *milai*   *yalika*.
       know   SUBJ.MRK speak.NON-PERF.NON-PAST.3SG French
       'S/he knows how to speak French.'
   d. *Kseri* **na** *milisi*   *galika*.
       know   SUBJ.MRK   speak.PERF.NON-PAST.3SG French

Concerning the subjunctive inflection in Romanian, it displays some specific forms and a specific and exclusive subjunctive marker *să*. More precisely, the subjunctive in Romanian has specific verbal forms for the 3rd person singular and plural of all verbs (as shown previously in Table 1) and a specific full paradigm for the verb *a fi* 'to be'. Those are indeed enough arguments to consider that the Romanian subjunctive is a mood by itself and not a variant of the indicative.

As for other Balkan languages which do not have enough pervasive evidence for the individuality of the subjunctive mood, we follow Asenova (2002: 152) who assumes that, whatever the category under which the constructions with *da* are described for Bulgarian, they have the same uses as their counterparts in the other Balkan languages, namely they have a subjunctive value. Moreover, we conclude with the Feuillet (2012: 117)'s words: "il existe un subjonctif typiquement balkanique constitué d'un marquant qui a la particularité d'être en même temps un subordonnant spécifique" [there is a typical Balkan subjunctive displaying a particle which has the peculiarity to be simultaneously a specific subordinating marker (our translation)].

2.2 The status of the subjunctive markers

A common Balkan issue concerns the subjunctive markers, i.e. Romanian, like Bulgarian and Greek, displays a specific marker for this mood, namely *să* (cf. Bulg.

---

[1] We thank Dimitra Kolliakou for pointing it out to us.

da, Grk. *na*). The common etymological issue is that this particle is intrinsically a conditional marker (see Hill 2013 a.o.) and functioned as such up to the 17th century in Romanian. After this date, it suffered a semantic attrition (i.e. bleaching), being re-analysed as a mood marker, while its Bulgarian and Greek counterparts continue to be used with this genuine conditional meaning. Notice also that Romanian *să* was initially underspecified with respect to the mood selection.

In certain specific contexts (more precisely in main imperative clauses, with the 3rd person singular and plural, which are clearly non-ambiguous subjunctive contexts), Romanian subjunctive may occur 'bare' (without the marker *să*), as in (2).[2]

(2) a. **Fie** *două drepte paralele.*
 'Consider two parallel lines.'
 b. **Facă**-*se voia Ta.*
 'Your will be done.'
 c. **Ducă**-*se pe pustii!*
 '(Let him) go to hell!'

2.2.1 An areal problem

By looking at the particles *să* in Romanian, *da* in Bulgarian and *na* in Greek occurring with the subjunctive in these languages, a common controversial question in the Balkan area arises, namely what is the grammatical status of these markers occurring with what is called the subjunctive. They are to be categorized either syntactically as complementizers (like their counterparts introducing the indicative) or morphologically as morphemes (i.e. affixes). Some researchers analyze them as having a simultaneous double role (cf. Dobrovie-Sorin 1994 for Romanian, Giannakidou 2009 for Greek, etc.).

2.2.2 Evidence for affixal status for the Romanian marker *să*

Traditional grammars list the subjunctive markers in the complementizer category, along with their 'that'-counterparts introducing the indicative clauses:

---

[2] According to Hill (2013), these 'bare' subjunctives are attested very early in Romanian (being the traces of the Latin present subjunctive), before the emergence of the subjunctive with the marker *să* in the 16th century.

Romanian *să* vs. *că*, Bulgarian *da* vs. *če*, Greek *na* vs. *oti*, because of possible permutations, like the one illustrated in (3).

(3) *Sper* **{*că* / *să*}** *îl citeşti azi.*
hope.1SG {that.IND / SUBJ.MRK} CL.3SG.MASC read.2SG today
'I hope you will read it today.'

However, a more detailed description shows that, for example in Romanian, the particle *să* marking the subjunctive and the complementizer *că* occurring with the indicative mood don't have the same syntactic distribution. Unlike *că*, which systematically occurs at the left edge of the clause, *să* cannot be separated from its verbal host by a constituent like *azi* 'today' in (4a), but only by affixes, such as the pronominal clitic *îl* 'it'. Moreover, *să* can be co-occurrent with initial introductors, e.g. the complementizer *ca* in (4b), if there is some preverbal constituent. *Să* may be co-occurrent with other complementizers such as *dacă* 'if' in (4c) or relative introductors such as the relative pronoun *care* 'who' in (4d).

(4) a. *Sper* **{*că* / *să}** <u>*azi*</u> *îl citeşti.*
hope.1SG {that.IND / SUBJ.MRK} today CL.3SG.MASC.ACC read.2SG
'I hope you will read it today.'
b. *Sper* *(*ca*) <u>*azi*</u> **să**-*l citeşti.*[3]
hope.1SG that today SUBJ.MRK-CL.3SG.MASC.ACC read.2SG
'I hope that today you will read it.'
c. *Mă întreb* **dacă să** *vin.*
REFL wonder.1SG if SUBJ.MRK come.1SG
'I wonder whether I should come.'
d. *Caut o secretară* **care să** *ştie limba română.*
look.1SG a secretary who SUBJ.MRK know.3SG language.DEF Romanian
'I'm looking for a secretary who speaks Romanian.'

The particle *să* displays a number of affix-like properties, following some of the main diagnostic criteria for affixal status (Zwicky and Pullum 1983, Miller 1992). As illustrated before in (4), it has a rigid ordering, being strictly adjacent to the verb; only the insertion of other clitics – pronominal or adverbial items – is allowed (5a). *Să* has a high degree of selection with respect to its host, being compatible only with verbs in subjunctive moods. Furthermore, we observe that, unlike *că*, the particle *să* cannot have wide scope over coordination (5b), its repetition on

---

[3] The pronominal clitic *îl* 'it' may occur under a reduced form –*l* (compare (3) and (4b)), cf. the discussion further.

each coordinated host being obligatory. Finally, as a morphophonological idiosyncrasy, we mention the fact that *să* can be the phonological host of pronominal clitics (5c), which in the presence of *să* can occur under a reduced form.

(5) a. ***să***   *i-o*   *mai*   *cânte*
      SUBJ.MRK CL.3SG.DAT-CL.3SG.FEM.ACC CL.ADV sing.3SG
      'that he still sing it to her'
   b. *Sper*   *să*   *plece*   *el*   *şi*   *(*să*)   *rămână ea.*
      hope.1SG SUBJ.MRK leave.SUBJ he and SUBJ.MRK stay.SUBJ she
      'I hope for him to leave and for her to remain.'
   c. {*să*-mi   / *să*   îmi}   *spună*
      {SUBJ.MRK-CL.1SG.DAT / SUBJ.MRK CL.1SG.DAT} tell.3.SUBJ
      'Let him tell me.'

Consequently, we consider (*contra* GALR 2005) that the particle *să* is not a complementizer, but rather a morphological affix of the subjunctive mood (cf. Barbu 1999).

2.2.3 Extension to other Balkan markers

The same analysis could be extended to the other two particles (cf. data from Avgustinova 1997, Asenova 2002, Alexopoulou and Kolliakou 2002, Monachesi 2005), even though a continuum is observed across these three languages, as schematized in Table 3 (and see also Sims and Joseph (This volume, Sections 3.1 and 3.2) regarding Greek *na* and the Albanian counterpart *të*).

Table 3: A comparative view on Balkan subjunctive markers.

Affixal property	Rom. *să*	Bulg. *da*	Grk. *na*
Rigid ordering	+	+	+
Narrow scope in coordination	+	+	+
High degree of selection	+	±	–
Co-occurrence with a complementizer	+	?	?

All these particles have a rigid ordering in the verbal complex and a strict adjacency to the verb, to be interrupted only by pronominal or adverbial clitics (see Romanian data in (4a) above, Bulgarian data in (6) and Greek data in (7)),[4] and

---

4 We thank our native informants, Snejana Gadjeva for Bulgarian and Dimitra Kolliakou for Greek.

must be repeated with each coordinated verb (cf. Romanian (5b) above, Bulgarian (8) and Greek (9)). As for the degree of selection with respect to their host, Romanian *să* selects only subjunctive verbs; Bulgarian *da* selects verbs in both perfective and imperfective contexts (10), while Greek *na* can be found in more general contexts, with or without verbs (in the last case, followed, for example, by a Noun Phrase (11a) or nothing (11b)).[5] Data are less clear for Bulgarian and Greek, when it comes to the co-occurrence of the subjunctive marker with a complementizer.

(6) a. *Njama   az   da   xodja   tam.*   (Bulg)
    NEG.FUT I   SUBJ.MRK go.1SG there
    'It's not me who will go there.'
  b. **Njama   da   az xodja   tam.*
    NEG.FUT SUBJ.MRK I   go.1SG there

(7) a. *Zitise   na   tu   to   dosi   simera i Zoi.* (Grk)
    ask.PAST.3SG SUBJ.MRK 3.MASC 3.NEUT give.PRES.2SG today the Zoi.NOM
    'S/he asked that Zoe give it to him today.'
  b. **Zitise   na   {simera / i Zoi}   tu   to   dosi.*
    ask.PAST.3SG SUBJ.MRK {today / the Zoi.NOM} 3.MASC 3.NEUT give.PRES.2SG

(8) *Nadjavam   se   da   svărši̇š   bărzo   rabota*
    hope.1SG REFL SUBJ.MRK finish.2SG quickly work
    i   *(da)   dojdeš   s   nas na kino.   (Bulg)
    and SUBJ.MRK come.2SG with us to cinema
    'I hope that you will quickly finish work and come with us to the cinema.'

(9) *... na   agorasi   ke   *(na)   pulisi   metohes.*   (Grk)
    SUBJ.MRK buy.3SG and SUBJ.MRK sell.3SG shares
    '... that s/he buy and sell shares.'

(10) a. *Da   ti   ja   davam   li?*   (Bulg)
     SUBJ.MRK CL.DAT.2SG CL.ACC.3SG.FEM give.IMPERF.1SG INTERR
     'Should I give it to you?'
   b. *Da   ti   ja   dam   li?*
     SUBJ.MRK CL.DAT.2SG CL.ACC.3SG.FEM give.PERF.1SG INTERR

---

5 In this regard, we adopt a position different from that of Joseph (1981), but similar to that of Christidis (1991). Joseph (1981) considers the subjunctive *na* and the deictic *ná* in Modern Greek to be synchronically (and also diachronically) distinct.

(11) a. **Na** to spiti mas! (Grk)
 SUBJ.MRK the house our
 'This is our house!'
 b. **Na!**
 'Here you are!'

From a historical point of view, we note that the first uses of *să* in Old Romanian get much closer to other Balkan subjunctive particles than *să* in Modern Romanian. According to Hill (2013), *să* was underspecified for the mood selection (indicative (12a), subjunctive (12b), infinitive (12c), conditional (12d), cf. attested examples given by Hill 2013) and, even more, it was no strictly adjacent to the verb, the insertion of lexical items between *să* and the verb being allowed (13).

(12) a. ***să*** *veți fi îmblîndu...*
 if will.2PL be following
 'if you will be going alone...'
 (Hill 2013, (36a))
 b. *... **să** fie fost...*
 if be.SUBJ.3SG been
 '... if there were...'
 (Hill 2013, (36b))
 c. ***să*** *greșire ție fratele tău...*
 if wrong.INF you.DAT brother.DEF your
 'if your brother wrongs you...'
 (Hill 2013, (36c))
 d. *... **să** are zice voao cineva*
 if would.COND say.3SG you.DAT somebody
 '... if somebody says to you'
 (Hill 2013, (36d))

(13) ***să*** <u>inimile noastre</u> *nu se întăritare noao...*
 if hearts.DEF our not REFL agitate.INF us.DAT
 'if our hearts will not get angered...'
 (Hill 2013, (37a))

To conclude this section, the evidence for the affixal status of these particles is most pervasive in Romanian and least pervasive in Greek.

3 The subjunctive in main clauses: the case of interrogatives

As mentioned in the introduction of this paper, a very interesting fact, underestimated in the literature, concerns the high frequency of the subjunctive in main interrogative clauses in Romanian, as in other Balkan languages, which sets Romanian apart from other Romance languages. Before focusing on this aspect, we provide a short overview of the subjunctive uses in embedded vs. main clauses, showing the alternations which are available between the subjunctive and other moods.

3.1 Mood alternations in embedded vs. main clauses

Romanian subjunctives may occur both in embedded and root clauses. According to the syntactic context in which they occur, Frâncu (2010) distinguishes between *dependent* and *independent* subjunctive. The dependent subjunctive appears in embedded clauses, where it is selected by some predicate in the main clause, and it does not contribute any specific meaning. On the other hand, the independent subjunctive appears in main clauses, where no explicit higher predicate triggers its occurrence. In these cases, it carries various specific semantic and prosodic effects, which Frâncu (2010) defines in terms of expressivity and special intonation.

In most of the previous works, much attention was paid to the subordinate contexts which are considered to be crucial for the syntax of subjunctives. In embedded clauses, the subjunctive can occur in various contexts, involving two alternations with other moods: an alternation with the infinitive on the one hand, and an alternation with the indicative on the other hand. We are not going into details about these 'embedded' subjunctives, we only list and illustrate them. The alternation between the subjunctive and the infinitive, the most studied (Jordan 2009, Frâncu 2010, Cotfas 2011, Hill 2013, Nedelcu 2013, etc.), may occur in control (14a) and aspectual (14b) structures, where the infinitive loses ground to the subjunctive, but also in 'absolute' circumstantial adjuncts (15a), relative clauses with no antecedent (15b), subject or predicative clauses (15c), etc., in all these contexts the alternation being rather free. Concerning the alternation between the subjunctive and the indicative, one observes two sub-types, according to the complementizer realization in the indicative clause: (i) subjunctive clauses may occur in alternation with indicative clauses introduced by *de* (16a), an alternation which was more visible at the dawn of Modern Romanian than nowadays (cf. Frâncu 2010, Sava 2012, Hill 2013), and (ii) subjunctive clauses may alternate with indicative clauses introduced by the complementizer *că* (mostly in complement clauses (16b) and relative adjuncts (16c)). The latter received more attention in the Romance space (see Farkas 1992 and 2003, Godard 2012).

(14) a. *Vreau {să* **scriu** */ a* **scrie**}.
 want.1SG SUBJ.MRK write.1SG / INF.MRK write
 'I want to write.'
 b. *Incepe {să* **ningă** */ a* **ninge**}.
 start.3SG SUBJ.MRK snow.3SG / INF.MRK snow
 'It starts snowing.'

(15) a. *A venit fără {să mă* **anunţe** */ a mă*
 has come without SUBJ.MRK me.ACC warn.3SG / INF.MRK me.ACC
 anunţa}.
 warn
 'He came without warning me.'
 b. *N-are ce {să* **facă** */* **face**}.
 not-have.3SG what SUBJ.MRK do.3SG / do.INF
 'There's nothing he can do.' (literally : 'He has nothing to do.')
 c. *{Să* **pleci** */ a* **pleca**} *de acasă nu e uşor.*
 SUBJ.MRK leave.2SG / INF.MRK leave from home not is easy
 'Leaving home is not an easy thing.'

(16) a. *Au venit {să* **mănânce** */ de au* **mâncat**}.
 have.3PL come SUBJ.MRK eat.3PL COMP have.3PL eaten
 'They came to eat.'
 b. *Sper {să* **reuşească** */ că va* **reuşi**}.
 hope.1SG SUBJ.MRK succeed.3SG / that will.3SG succeed.INF
 'I hope he will succeed.'
 c. *Nu sunt un om căruia {să-i* **placă** */ îi*
 not am a person who.DAT SUBJ.MRK-him.DAT like.3SG / him.DAT
 place} *minciuna.*
 like.3SG lying.DEF
 'I am not a person who likes lying.'

Concerning the subjunctive in main clauses (i.e. the so-called 'independent' subjunctive), we observe that it can occur in imperative, interrogative and, marginally, declarative clauses, in alternation with various other moods. In imperative clauses, there are two alternations: (i) subjunctive/imperative (for the 2nd person singular and plural, as in (17a)), conveying a directive illocutionary force, which ranges from commands to suggestions, the directive force being attenuated in subjunctive contexts compared to their imperative counterparts;[6] and (ii) subjunctive/conditional (in imprecation and affective formulae, as in (17b)). In interrogative clauses, the subjunctive may alternate with presumptive or indicative mood, as shown in (18). We mention here a special use of the subjunctive in main declarative clauses (19), where one observes the same tripartite alternation subjunctive/presumptive/indicative mood, the subjunctive and presumptive moods being used as epistemic-evidential markers in order to express the non-commitment to the truth of the information transmitted (i.e. marking an approximation).

(17) a. *{Să faci / Fă}* ce ți-am zis!
SUBJ.MRK do.2SG / do.IMP what you.DAT-have.1SG told
'Do what I told you!'
b. *{Să-l ia / Lua-l-ar}* dracu'!
SUBJ.MRK-him.ACC take.3SG / take-him.ACC-would hell
'Let him go to hell!'

(18) *{Să fie / O fi / E}* ora 9?
SUBJ.MRK be.3SG / PRESUMP.3SG be / is hour.DEF 9
'Would it be 9 o'clock?'

(19) *{Să fie / Or fi / Sunt}* vreo 3 ani de-atunci.
SUBJ.MRK be.3 / PRESUMP.3PL be / are.3PL some 3 years from-then
'It must be 3 years since that time.'

As mentioned above, if we compare previous work on both embedded and main distributions, we note an unexpected discrepancy between the amount of work devoted to the analysis of subjunctives in embedded clauses compared to its uses in main clauses, as if the subjunctive would be the mood of subordination par excellence (see Avram 2015). The 'independent' subjunctive is most of the time just mentioned in the literature (except for Frâncu 2010, Zafiu 2011), more attention being paid to the subjunctive in imperative clauses compared to the interrogative ones (according to Frâncu 2010 and Zafiu 2011, most of 'independent' subjunctive uses would be in imperative clauses [90%]).

---

[6] An additional tripartite alternation would be between the subjunctive, imperative and infinitive in contexts of advices and warnings:

(i) *{Să nu se consume / Nu consuma(ți) / A nu se consuma}* alcool!
'Do not consume alcohol!'

In this section, we focus on the understudied aspect of the 'independent' subjunctive by looking at interrogative clauses. It matters for two reasons. First, from an empirical point of view, there is no exhaustive description of subjunctive uses in interrogatives, which are more frequent than assumed. Second, from a comparative perspective, previous works miss a typological generalization: By looking especially at the subjunctive in imperative clauses, Romanian is considered to behave like other Romance languages with respect to the 'independent' subjunctive (Frâncu 2010). By paying more attention to interrogatives, we observe that Romanian shares striking similarities with the Balkan languages, which a priori increases the domain of the Balkan Sprachbund properties. Thus, one observes that the subjunctive can occur in main interrogative clauses in other Balkan languages too.

(20) a. *Unde* **să** **merg**? (Rom)
    where SUBJ.MRK go.1SG
    'Where should I go?'
 b. *Kăde* **da** **otida**? (Bulg)
    where SUBJ.MRK go.1SG
    'Where should I go?'
 c. *Pu* **na** **pao**? (Grk)
    where SUBJ.MRK go.1SG
    'Where should I go?'

Other Romance languages, such as French, don't allow the subjunctive in interrogative clauses (21a). Instead, they use the infinitive (21b) or the conditional (21c) mood:

(21) a. **Où* **que j'aille**? / **Où* **puissé-je** *aller*? (French)
    where that I go.SUBJ.1SG where can.SUBJ-I go.INF
    'Where should I go?'
 b. *Où* **aller**?
    where go.INF
    'Where to go?'
 c. *Où* **puis**-*je aller*? / *Où* **pourrais**-*je aller*?
    where can-I go.INF where could-I go.INF
    'Where can I go ? / Where could I go ?'

3.2 Independent subjunctive or elliptical clauses?

Before describing the various contexts with subjunctive in main interrogative clauses, we must answer a theoretical question related to the syntactic status of a main clause with a subjunctive: is it a true independent clause or rather an embbeded subjunctive in a clause with an elliptical main verb?

Avram (2015) argues in favour of the elliptical account, by considering the subjunctive embedded under a covert modal verb. She distinguishes between three covert modals in three different constructions:

(i) the surrogate imperative subjunctive (22a) – analyzed as an embedded clause under a covert deontic modal of necessity *trebuie* 'must';
(ii) the interrogative-dubitative subjunctive (22b) – an embedded clause under a covert epistemic modal of possibility *se poate / e posibil* 'could';
(iii) the 'mirativity' subjunctive (22c) – an embedded clause under a covert subject-oriented modal of possibility *poate* 'can'.

(22) a. *(Trebuie)* **să   pleci!**
       must   SUBJ.MRK leave.2SG
       'You must leave.'
   b. *(Se   poate   / E posibil)* **să   fie**   oare   acasă?
       REFL can.3SG / is possible SUBJ.MRK be.3SG maybe at-home
       'Could (s)he be at home?'
   c. Crin *(poate)* **să   danseze?!**
       Crin can.3SG SUBJ.MRK dance.3SG
       'Can Crin dance?'

According to Avram (2015), all 'root' subjunctives are embedded clauses in disguise, sharing the same syntactic structure but not the same covert matrix modal. Such an analysis is of interest if and only if: (a) one can reconstruct a modal matrix verb from any 'independent' subjunctive in a regular fashion, and (b) the semantic and discursive properties of 'elliptical' occurrences are the same as that of full clauses. We observe that these conditions are not always verified.

The modal value is not necessarily linked to a subjunctive construction-type. We observe several ambiguous/underspecified 'independent' subjunctives, where it is the context that disambiguates, specifying the modality of the subjunctive clause. For each of the examples in (23), several modal verbs can be reconstructed.

(23) a. *Cum (e posibil/   poți)   să   slăbești   fără   efort?*
       how is possible / can.2SG SUBJ.MRK lose.weight.2SG without effort
       'How is it possible to lose weight effortlessly?' /'How can one lose weight without effort?'
   b. *Ce   (trebuie / pot)   să   fac   în asemenea situații?*
       what should / can.1SG SUBJ.MRK do.1SG in such situations
       'What should/could I do in such a situation?'

c. *Când (e posibil / trebuia / putea)* **să** **fi plecat?**
      when is possible / should / can.IPFV.3SG SUBJ.MRK be left
      'When can/should/could she have left?'

In some cases, it is very difficult (or even impossible) to reconstruct any modal verb. This is the case in the so-called '*wh*-imperatives', where one makes a suggestion by using an interrogative clause, as in (24a). In this case, one cannot reconstruct any indicative modal verb (epistemic (24b), deontic (24c) or subject-oriented modal (24d)); in order to save this analysis, the only possibility would be to reconstruct a subject-oriented modal verb such as *a putea* 'can' under its subjunctive form, as in (24e), which leads to a subjunctive recursivity problem on the one hand, and to semantic divergences on the other hand ((24a) and (24e) obviously have neither the same syntactic structure, e.g. the verb *a începe* 'to begin' changed its mood in (24e), nor the same interpretation).

(24) a. *De ce* **să** **nu începem** *cu tăria?*
        from what SUBJ.MRK not start.1PL with booze.DEF
        'Why not start with the booze?'
     b. #*De ce e posibil să* **nu începem** *cu tăria?*
        from what is possible SUBJ.MRK not start.1PL with booze.DEF
        'Why can we not start with the booze?'
     c. #*De ce trebuie să* **nu începem** *cu tăria?*
        from what should SUBJ.MRK not start.1PL with booze.DEF
        'Why must we not start with the booze?'
     d. #*De ce putem să* **nu începem** *cu tăria?*
        from what can.1PL SUBJ.MRK not start.1PL with booze.DEF
        'Why may we not start with the booze?'
     e. *De ce să* **nu putem începe** *cu tăria?*
        from what SUBJ.MRK not can.1PL start.INF with booze.DEF
        'Why couldn't we start with the booze?'

The same observation could be made concerning various conventionalized patterns, as in (25), where the reconstruction of a modal verb in these specific contexts looses the pragmatic effects at work in its counterpart.

(25) A: *Știi că Maria e din nou însărcinată?*
        know.2SG that Maria is from new pregnant
     B: *Ei, ce (#pot) să-ți spun? Mare brânză!*
        eh what can.1SG SUBJ.MRK-you.DAT say.1SG big cheese
     A: 'Do you know that Maria is pregnant again?' B: 'Well, what can I say? Big deal!'

If a reconstruction mechanism has to be assumed, besides the modal verbs presented above, there are other verbal candidates too, as in (26a) or (26b), so it is difficult to come with an exhaustive list or a regular mechanism involved in the presumed reconstruction. Since it is ad-hoc and dispensable, the syntactic reconstruction of a (modal) verb must be abandoned.

(26) a. *(Vrei / fac bine)* **Să-ți spun?**
 want.2SG do.1SG well SUBJ.MRK-you.DAT say.1SG
 'Do you want me to tell you?' / 'Should I tell you?'
 b. Cu cine *era* **să-mi** las părinții? Sora
 with whom was SUBJ.MRK-me.DAT leave.1SG parents.DEF sister.DEF
 mea e plecată în Italia, eu am rămas singurul lor sprijin.
 my is left in Italy I have.1SG remained sole.DEF their support
 'Who could I have entrusted my parents to? My sister is away in Italy, I am their sole support.'

Furthermore, the semantic and pragmatic contribution of the elliptical clause is not the same as that of the one in full modal clause, the later being more restricted in its interpretation. The 'independent' subjunctive, due to its discursive underspecification, triggers more pragmatic and dialogical effects than its modal counterpart. Reducing all these occurrences to a 'dependent' subjunctive deprives the subjunctive of its rich pragmatic potential, especially in interrogative contexts.

For all these reasons, we consider that there is no ellipsis in these contexts and that 'independent' subjunctive clauses are indeed root subjunctives, a proposal in accordance with *Simpler Syntax Hypothesis* of Culicover and Jackendoff (2005 : 5): "The most explanatory syntactic theory is one that imputes the minimum structure necessary to mediate between phonology and meaning". This analysis brings us to consider the subjunctive as an underspecified mood, compatible a priori with both embedded and non-embedded contexts.

3.3 The subjunctive in main interrogative clauses

We now come back to our target, as presented in Section 3.1 above. Since the subjunctives in main interrogatives are related to several discursive strategies, we briefly present, first, the theoretical background on interrogatives. Then, we proceed to a detailed description of the subjunctive uses in main interrogative clauses, and finish with some concluding remarks.

3.3.1 Descriptive and theoretical background on interrogatives

Before presenting each subjunctive interrogative construction, we present the descriptive and theoretical tools that help us describe the discursive strategies used in these constructions.

First, concerning the question of taxonomy (Krifka 2001), we observe that the independent subjunctive may occur with all major types of questions, that is:
(i)   polarity questions (*yes/no* questions), as in (27a);
(ii) *wh*-questions (27b), including multiple *wh*-questions (both matching questions and conjoined questions)[7] as in (27c);
(iii) alternative questions (explicitly marking disjunction), such as (27d).

(27) a. *Oare așa să   fie?*
        really so SUBJ.MRK be.3SG
        'Could that be so?'
     b. *Cine să   fi venit?*
        who SUBJ.MRK be come
        'Who could have come?'
     c. *Cine (și) ce   să   facă?*
        who and what SUBJ.MRK do.3SG
        'Who could do what?'
     d. *Să   plec   sau să   nu plec?*
        SUBJ.MRK leave.1SG or SUBJ.MRK not leave.1SG
        'Should I leave or not?'

Second, concerning the illocutionary force of an interrogative clause, we observe that, besides ordinary interrogatives which require an explicit response from the addressee, there are many instances of rhetorical questions with a subjunctive verb. We agree with Caponigro and Sprouse (2007) who consider that rhetorical questions behave syntactically and semantically as regular questions, but differ from them at the pragmatic level, i.e. they involve no call-on-addressee, since the answer is explicited by the context. Thus, if the answer of an ordinary question is not known to the speaker and can only come from the addressee, in rhetorical questions the addressee is not expected to answer, since the information requested is already provided in the background. In more formal terms, rhetorical questions are interrogatives conveying a biased question whose answer is Common Ground (i.e. predictable or known by both the speaker and the addressee) and whose

---

[7] For more details about multiple questions in Romanian, see Bîlbîie and Gazdik (2012).

dialogue impact requires the activation of such a content (Marandin 2008). The bias in a rhetorical question can be made explicit by a fragment such as *parcă n-ai şti* 'you know it very well', as in (28). In this sense, rhetorical questions are considered redundant and uninformative interrogatives (Rohde 2006, Caponigro and Sprouse 2007). Unlike ordinary questions, rhetorical questions are not asked to trigger an increase in the amount of Common Ground, but their goal is rather to highlight a proposition in the Common Ground, as the starting point of a discourse or its natural 'obvious' conclusion ('emphatic statements', cf. Egg 2007).[8]

(28) A : *Ce   face Ion?* B : *Ce   **să**   **facă?** Parcă n-ai   şti,*
          what does Ion   what SUBJ.MRK do.3SG as.if not-would.2SG know
         pierde timpul!
         loses time.DEF
    A : 'How is Ion?' B : 'How could he be? As if you didn't know, he is wasting his time.'

Third, concerning the interactive stance itself, we can distinguish (cf. Ginzburg 2012) between dialogues (i.e. an interaction between two or more speakers, where one speaker asks a question or makes an assertion and the other speaker reacts to it) and monologues (self-answering/self-querying: the speaker can address the issue herself vs. contexts with two successive questions utterred by a single speaker, where the second question influences the first).

3.3.2 Different discursive strategies in subjunctive interrogatives

Romanian, like other Balkan languages (as shown in (20) above), systematically displays the subjunctive in main interrogatives in order to express various pragmatic and dialogical functions. As Farkas (1985, 1992), Villalta (2007, 2008), Godard (2012) a.o. showed, the subjunctive mood is motivated in contexts where the interpretation requires taking into account alternative situations. The interrogative domain creates such an environment. The interrogative domain is generally a phenomenon of interlocution (mainly dialogue), where the speaker is in focus (s/he doubts, doesn't believe, hesitates, etc.).

Before presenting the main discursive strategies observed with subjunctive interrogatives, we have to note a general tendency we observe with respect to

---

[8] For a typology of rhetorical questions, see Lee-Goldman (2006): assert-the-opposite (containing implicit negation), question-for-response (having an obvious answer), specific-answer (answer relevant to the surrounding context), and wrong-opinion.

the licensing of the subjunctive in interrogative clauses, namely that the subjunctive is generally not used with ordinary information seeking questions; it cannot appear in completely neutral situations, quiz questions or pure into-seeking questions such as in (29), where only the indicative is allowed. The subjunctive is thus not freely licensed in interrogatives. There is something special about it at both the semantic and the pragmatic level.

(29) a. [*A police officer asking a driver to legitimate himself:*]
Cum {vă **cheamă** / #să vă **cheme**}?
how you.PL.ACC call.IND.3/ MRK.SUBJ you.PL.ACC call.3
'What's your name?'

b. [*A teacher asking her students a quiz question:*]
Cât {**fac** /#să **facă**} trei plus patru?
how-much make.IND.3PL /SUBJ.MRK make.3PL three plus four
'How much equals three plus four?'

c. [*John wants to know when his friend will finish his own house:*]
Când {**vei termina** / #să **termini**} casa?
when will.2SG finish / SUBJ.MRK finish.2SG house.DEF
'When will you finish the house?'

d. [*John asking Mary if she wants to join the group:*]
{**Vii** /#să **vii**} cu noi?
come.IND.2SG / SUBJ.MRK come.2SG with us
'Are you coming with us?'

We observe two main discursive strategies at work with independent subjunctives in Romanian interrogatives:

(i) The first discursive strategy displays a regular *Question*/Assertion pair. In the first part of the pair, we have an interrogative clause using the subjunctive, while in the second part, the assertion (usually associated with a declarative clause) makes explicit an answer response ('A is about Q' in Ginzburg 2012's terms). Subjunctive interrogatives of this type have generally free-context values in the sense that they can be uttered 'out-of-the-blue' (cf. Section 3.3.2.1). If a dialogue is involved, they occur in its first turn.

(ii) On the other hand, the second discursive strategy displays a Question/ *Question* pair. Interestingly, in the second part of the pair, instead of having an answer response to a query, one has a query response using the subjunctive (in other terms, a query Q1 is answered with a query Q2, and Q2 influences Q1, cf. Ginzburg 2012). Subjunctive interrogatives of this type have dialogical values (i.e. context-dependent values), the query responses being in this case reactive utterances (i.e. they involve a reaction to a previously raised issue). They are frequently rhetorical questions (cf. Section 3.3.2.2).

We now provide further details about the subtypes occurring with each of these two strategies.

3.3.2.1 Free-context uses of the subjunctive in interrogatives

As mentioned above, the subjunctive can be used in an interrogative clause uttered 'out-of-the-blue' and yielding some specific pragmatic effects in Romanian.

First, it can be used to express doubt and uncertainty with respect to hypotheses or suppositions based on present situations (30) or past situations (31) either in polar or in *wh*-interrogatives. This subjunctive use corresponds to what Zafiu (2011) calls 'epistemic subjunctive'. It occurs especially with state and non-intensional verbs, and it is not felicitous under embedding (32). Here, the subjunctive is in competition with the presumptive mood (e.g. *o fi* instead of the subjunctive *să fie*), with the same values. In all these examples, the subjunctive contributes a dubitative-epistemic modality and, in many cases, an additional mirativity effect is observed (see the continuation of examples (30b) and (30c)).

(30) a. *Televizorul – aparent inofensiv. Oare așa* **să** **fie**?
television.DEF apparently harmless really so SUBJ.MRK be.3SG
'The TV – apparently harmless. Could it be so?'
b. **Să** **fie** *ora 9? M-aș mira.*
SUBJ.MRK be.3SG hour 9 me.REFL.ACC-would.1SG surprise.INF
'Could it be 9 o'clock? I'd be surprised.'
c. *Ce* **să** **fie** *în neregulă cu calculatorul, de nu mai pornește?*
what SUBJ.MRK be.3SG in wrong with computer.DEF from not yet start.3SG
Nu pot să-mi închipui care ar fi problema.
not can.1SG SUBJ.MRK-me.DAT imagine.1SG what would.3SG be problem.DEF
'What can be wrong with the computer, (since) it won't start? I can't imagine what the problem could be.'

(31) a. *Să* *fi plecat trenul?*
SUBJ.MRK be left train.DEF
'Could the train have left?'
b. *Cine să* *fi venit?*
who SUBJ.MRK be come
'Who could have come?'

(32) ??*Mă întreb [dacă **să** **fie** ora 9].*
me.ACC ask.1SG if SUBJ.MRK be.3SG hour.DEF 9
'I'm wondering if it's 9 o'clock.'

A second subclass of subjunctive uses concerns the contexts in which one requests advice by means of an alternative question (33a), a polar question (33b) or a *wh*-question (34). The advice may have to do with an intention (in this case, additionnaly expressing the speaker's dilemma) or an obligation. These uses correspond to the 'deliberative subjunctive' (cf. Frâncu 2010) or the 'deontic subjunctive' (cf. Zafiu 2011), and mostly occur with action and intensional verbs. Unlike the first subclass, the subjunctives of the second subclass are felicitous under embedding (35). All these examples illustrate the deontic modality[9] contributed by the subjunctive.

(33) a. ***Să** plec sau **să** nu plec?*
SUBJ.MRK leave.1SG or SUBJ.MRK not leave.1SG
'Should I leave or not?'
b. ***Să** vină mâine, domnule doctor?*
SUBJ.MRK come.3SG tomorrow, Mr. Doctor
'Should s/he come tomorrow, Doctor?'

(34) a. *Ce **să** **fac** acum?*
what SUBJ.MRK do.1SG now
'What should I do now?'
b. *Când **să** **vină**, domnule doctor?*
when SUBJ.MRK come.3SG, Mr. Doctor
'When should s/he come, Doctor?'

(35) *Te întreb {dacă **să** **plec** / ce **să** **fac** acum}.*
you.ACC ask.1SG whether SUBJ.MRK go.1SG / what SUBJ.MRK do.1SG now
'I ask you {whether I should go / what I should do now}.'

With the same modal flavour the subjunctive is massively used for title-making in instructions. These are mostly *wh*-questions (36) and have a generic

---

9 'Deontic' is here understood in a very general sense, i.e. in consonance with certain laws, conventions, obligations or other such normative options, including also someone's desires or goals (see Portner 2009 for a fine-grained distinction of modalities).

reading (cf. the use of the 2nd person singular with a generic flavour in (36a) and (36c)):

(36) a. *Cum să   slăbeşti   fără   efort?*
    how SUBJ.MRK lose-weight.2SG without effort
    'How to lose weight without effort?'
  b. *Ce să   facem când ne   doare   stomacul?*
    what SUBJ.MRK do.1PL when usACC hurt.3SG stomach.DEF
    'What should we do in case of stomach cramps?'
  c. *Când să   faci   primul   test de sarcină?*
    when SUBJ.MRK do.2SG first.DEF test of pregnancy
    'When should one do the first pregnancy test?'

Our data seem to favour an analysis in which the subjunctive mood plays the role of a modal element itself, providing good grounds for establishing a connection between grammatical mood and semantic modality. In the above examples, there is an implicit (epistemic or deontic) modality at work, carried by the subjunctive itself in most of the cases. It is thus plausible to assume that the subjunctive mood in these cases has the meaning of a modal element.

3.3.2.2 Rhetorical uses of the subjunctive in interrogatives

There are also several subclasses of subjunctives in dialogical rhetorical questions. We first look at *wh*-interrogatives, then at polar interrogatives and finally at some lexicalized interrogatives using this mood.

First, *wh*-rhetorical questions, unlike ordinary *wh*-questions, ask to reconsider (or even to strongly or less strongly negate) the presupposition triggered by the first question (37). They are traditionally analyzed as biased assertions or "queclaratives" (Sadock 1971), containing implicit negation (i.e. assert-the-opposite rhetorical question). The subjunctive use in these contexts is thus biased for negative answers.

(37) a. A: *Maria a fost invitată la petrecere?* B: *Cine să   o   cheme?*
       Maria has been invited to party   who SUBJ.MRK her.ACC call.3
       A: 'Has Maria been invited to the party?' B: 'Who could have asked her?'
  b. A: *Ai   candidat pentru postul   de asistent?*
       have.2SG applied for   position.DEF of assistant
     B: *De unde să   ştiu   că era un post?*
       of where SUBJ.MRK know.1SG that was a position
     A: 'Did you apply for the assistant position?' B: 'How could I have known about this?'

A second subclass of *wh*-rhetorical questions concerns contexts in which the subjunctive interrogative marks the obviousness of the answer. This is usually done by repeating the same verbal lexeme (38). The answer to the question asked by the first speaker seems very obvious to the second speaker, who treats it rather as a 'non-receivable question'.

(38) a. A: *Ce <u>face</u> Ion?* B: *Ce **să facă**?*
what does Ion   what SUBJ.MRK do.3SG
Parcă n-ai   şti,   pierde timpul!
as.if not-would.2SG know loses time.DEF
A: 'How is Ion?' B: 'How could he be? As if you didn't know, he is wasting his time.'
b. A: *Unde <u>te   duci</u> în vacanţă?*
where you.ACC go.2SG in vacation
B: *Unde **să   mă   duc**? La casa   de la ţară,*
where SUBJ.MRK me.ACC go.1SG at home.DEF of in country
că în altă parte, n-am   bani.
that in other part   not-have.1SG money
A: 'Where are you going on holiday?' B: 'Where could I go? At the house in the countryside, since I don't have money to go elsewhere.'
c. A: *Cum <u>e să   fii</u> însurat, Mitică?* B: *Cum **să   fie**?*
how is SUBJ.MRK be.2SG married Mitica   how SUBJ.MRK be.3SG
A: 'What is it like to be married, Mitică?' B: 'How could it be like?'

In the same subclass we include *wh*-interrogatives generally introduced by *cum* 'how' (and often preceded by the discursive particle *păi*) in positive or negative contexts (39). This kind of questions draws on the properties of the two rhetorical subcases mentioned above: they negate the presupposition triggered by the preceding context, creating a biased answer with reversed polarity, and simultaneously mark the obviousness of the answer, by giving explicit evidence for it.

(39) a. *Păi cum **să   trăiască** oamenii   cu   300 sau 400 de ron*
PRT how SUBJ.MRK live.3PL people.DEF with 300 or   400 of RON
pe lună, când mâncarea este scumpă?
per month when food.DEF is   expensive
'How on earth can people live on 300 or 400 RON a month when food is so expensive?'
b. *Păi cum **să   primeşti** tu 7 milioane*
PRT how SUBJ.MRK   receive.2SG you 7 millions

     pe ea   dacă a   mea este identică   și valorează   5 milioane?
     for it.FEM if POSS.FEM mine is   identical and worth.3SG 5 millions
     'How can you get 7 million for yours if mine is identical and is worth 5 million?'

c. *Mănânci toată ziua, cum **să**   **nu te**   **îngrași**?*
   eat.2SG all day how SUBJ.MRK not you.ACC fatten.2SG
   'You eat all day long, how can you not get fat?'

d. *Păi cum **să**   **nu fii**   mândră cu o așa frumusețe?*
   PRT how SUBJ.MRK not be.2SG proud with a so beauty
   'Well, how can you not be proud of such a beauty?'

e. *Cine **să**   **vină**   dacă nu Maria?*
   who SUBJ.MRK come.3SG if   not Maria
   'Who is there to come if not Maria?'

More generally, other reactive *wh*-rhetorical questions may use subjunctive in order to reject the assumption derived from the previous utterance (40a) or to express the speaker's disagreement with or objection to the current proposal/suggestion (40b), and also to allow for additional pragmatic effects, such as sarcasm, irony (40c) or pity (40d).

(40) a. *Întrebat de presă dacă are vreun regret, Băsescu a răspuns:*
      asked by press if   has some regret Băsescu has answered
      « *De ce   **să**   **fiu** supărat, omule?* »
        of what SUBJ.MRK be.1SG upset   man.VOC
      'When asked by reporters whether he had any regrets, Băsescu answered: « Why would I be upset, man? »'

b. *De ce **să**   **facem** cum a zis el?*
   of what SUBJ.MRK do.1PL how has said he
   'Why would we do as he said?'

c. *Cum **să**   **stea**   el pe un pat de spital   românesc?*
   how SUBJ.MRK stay.3SG he on a bed of hospital Romanian
   'How can he ever lie on a Romanian hospital bed?'

d. *Cum **să**   **stea**   sărăcuțu' în frig atâta   timp?*
   how SUBJ.MRK stay.3SG poor.DEF in cold so.much time
   'How can/would the poor soul stay out in the cold for such a long time?'

Finally, the subjunctive can be used in *wh*-interrogatives introduced by the *wh*-phrase *de ce* 'why' usually with a negative verbal form (cf. the particle *nu* 'not') as in (41a-b), in order to make a suggestion (so-called '*wh*-imperatives'). The same applies with illocutionary verbs such as *a spune* 'to tell' (41c) or *a recunoaște* 'to admit' (41d) in parenthetical contexts.

(41) a. *De ce să   nu începem cu   tăria?*
       from what SUBJ.MRK not start.1PL with booze.DEF
       'Why not start (~ let's start) with the booze?'
   b. *De ce să   nu facem cum a   zis el?*
       of what SUBJ.MRK not do.1PL how has said he
       'Why not do (~ let's do) as he says?'
   c. *De ce să   n-o   spun pe-aia   dreaptă,*
       of what SUBJ.MRK not-it.FEM.ACC say.1SG DOM-DEM.FEM right
       nu-mi   place   deloc de el.
       not-me.DAT please.3SG at-all of him
       'Why wouldn't I say what is right, I don't like him at all.'
   d. *De ce să   nu recunosc,   sunt îndrăgostită lulea.*
       of what SUBJ.MRK not recognize.1SG am in.love   deeply
       'Why not admit it (~ to tell the truth), I'm deeply in love.'

Moving now to polar interrogatives, we start with polar interrogatives with a 'mirativity subjunctive', such as (42a), described in details in Avram (2015). These constructions[10] are labeled 'Mad Magazine sentences' in Akmajian (1984), or 'Incredulity Response Construction' in Lambrecht (1990), and have a special intonation contour (progressive raising contour, plus prosodic stress), that captures the speaker's surprise in regards to the preceding context.[11] Mirativity is related here to new information that is not easily assimilated by the speaker (Peterson 2013). The surprise can be made explicit by an initial interrogative pronoun of type *ce* 'what' (42b) or *cum* 'how' (42c). The incredulity flavour comes from an overt 'negative' coda (e.g. *nu pot să cred* 'I don't believe that'), which disconfirms or casts doubt on any alternative introduced

---

10 The Romanian mirativity subjunctive construction is similar, as in other cases, to root infinitives in other languages, such as Spanish, German, English (see Grohmann 2000 for examples).
11 The fact that mirativity constructions can be verbless (and compatible with the coordinating conjunction *și* 'and' as in (i)) shows that speaker's incredulous response does not concern the time at which the situation or event described in the preceding context takes place, but rather the abstract predicate-argument structure of that context (Lambrecht 1990).

(i) *Crin (și) (să   fie)   mulțumit?!*
    Crin (and) (SUBJ.MRK be.3SG) pleased
    'Crin pleased?!'

by the subjunctive clause. The cancellation of the mirative meaning, as in (42d), leads to a contradiction (or at least to infelicity). All these examples minimally contain an argument (typically the subject) and its predicate. Note also the presence of a complex punctuation, i.e. question-exclamation marks, correlated with a specific intonation contour.

(42) a. *Crin* **să** **învețe** *sintaxă?! Nu apucăm noi ziua aia!*
Crin SUBJ.MRK learn.3SG syntax not get.1PL we day.DEF that
'Crin learn syntax?! We won't live to see that day!'
(Avram 2015, (1))

b. *(Ce?) Victoraș al nostru* **să** **plagieze?!** *Imposibil!*
(what?) Victoraș POSS.MASC our SUBJ.MRK plagiarize.3SG impossible
'Our Victoraș plagiarize?! Impossible!'

c. *(Cum?) Tocmai tu* **să-mi** **faci** *una ca asta?! Nu pot să cred.*
(how?) exactly you SUBJ.MRK-me.DAT do.2SG one like this not can.1SG
SUBJ.MRK believe.1SG
'What? You behaving like this to me?! I can't believe it.'

d. *Ion* **să** **ia** *examenul de sintaxă?! #Nu mă surprinde deloc.*
Ion SUBJ.MRK take.3SG exam.DEF of syntax not me.ACC
surprise.3SG at-all
'Ion passing the syntax exam?! It doesn't surprise me at all.'

Related to these mirative contexts are the examples in (43), which follow the same syntactic pattern as in (42), but yield additional pragmatic effects: indignation, protest.

(43) a. A: *Ți-ai făcut temele?* B: *Eu* **să** **nu-mi** **fac** *temele?!*
you.DAT-have.2SG done homework.DEF I SUBJ.MRK not-me.DAT do.1SG homework.DEF
A: 'Have you done your homework?' B: 'Me, not do my homework?'

b. A: *Ar fi bine să-ți ceri scuze de la Maria.*
would.3SG be well SUBJ.MRK-you.DAT ask.2SG apologies of to Maria
B: *(Tot) eu să-mi* **cer** *iertare?*
still I SUBJ.MRK-me.DAT ask.1SG forgiveness
A: 'You should apologize to Maria.' B: 'Should I be the one to apologize?'

c. A: *Du-te și spală vasele.*
go.IMP-you.ACC and wash.IMP dishes.DEF

B: *Numai eu să   fac   treabă mereu?!*
     only I   SUBJ.MRK do.1SG work always
  A: 'Go wash the dishes.' B: 'Why should I be the only one around to do the house chores?'

Most of these rhetorical subjunctive interrogatives are reactive utterances, limiting the answer to a fixed set of possibilities, e.g. negative answers.

Finally, there are some lexicalized interrogatives using the subjunctive to convey irony (44a), refutation (44b), hesitation (= delay answering) in (44c), surprise (= put on hold) in (45) or low-value judgments (46). These are *wh*-interrogatives with *ce* 'what' followed by the verbs *a spune, a zice* 'to say' in (44), *a vedea* 'to see' (45) and *a face* 'to do' (46).

(44) a. A: *Ştii   că Maria e din   nou însărcinată?*
            know.2SG that Maria is from new pregnant
         B: *Ei, ce să-ţi   spun? Mare brânză!*
            eh what SUBJ.MRK-you.DAT say.1SG big cheese
         A: 'Do you know that Maria is expecting her second baby?' B: 'Well, what can I say? Big deal!'
     b. *Ei, ce   să   zici   şi tu acum, ca   să   ieşi*
        eh what SUBJ.MRK say.2SG too you now that SUBJ.MRK get.out.2SG
        cu faţa   curată?
        with face.DEF clean
        'Well, what can you say now to get away with it?'
     c. *Despre fată, ce   să   spun? Are 30 de ani şi nu e*
        about girl what SUBJ.MRK say.1SG has 30 of years and not is
        măritată.
        married
        'As for the girl, what can I say? She is 30 and not yet married.'

(45) a. *Dau   să   intru   în casă... Când colo, ce   să*
        give.1SG SUBJ.MRK enter.1SG in house when there what SUBJ.MRK
        vezi? Uşa   era descuiată!
        see.2SG door.DEF was unlocked
        'I was about to go in... When - what do you know - the door was unlocked!'
     b. *Câţiva mafioţi, care încercau   să   recupereze nişte bani,*
        several mobsters who tried.IMPERF.3PL SUBJ.MRK recover.3PL some money

> *au   vrut   să-l*
> have.3PL wanted SUBJ.MRK-him.ACC
> *răpească   pe   băiatul datornicilor.*
> kidnap.3PL DOM son.DEF debtors.GEN
> *Când colo, ce   să   vezi? Din greșeală,*
> when there what SUBJ.MRK see.2SG from error
> *au   furat un alt   copil.*
> have.3PL stolen an other child
> 'Several mobsters, who were trying to get some money back, intended to kidnap the debtors'son. When - what do you know - they kidnapped another child by mistake.'

(46) a. *Lucrează ca portar.   Ce   să   facă   și el,*
       work.3SG as doorman what SUBJ.MRK do.3SG too he
       dacă altceva   mai bun nu găsește?
       if   something.else more good not find.3SG
       'He works as a doorman. What can he do, if he can't find a better job?'
   b. *Ce   să   fac   și eu, ca să   nu pic   în depresie,*
       what SUBJ.MRK do.1SG too I   that SUBJ.MRK not fall.1SG in depression
       m-am   înscris la călărie.
       me.ACC-have.1SG enrolled to riding
       'What can I do to avoid feeling depressed, I took up horse-riding.'

As a peripheral fact, we want to mention a 'dialogical ellipsis' strategy, using the subjunctive marker *să* without a verb. In dialogical contexts, a very specific verbless *wh*-interrogative, having the form *cum să nu* (the *wh*-word *cum* 'how' followed by the subjunctive marker *să* and by the negation marker *nu*) can be used as a polarity particle response in Romanian, in exactly the same way as polarity particles *da* 'yes' and *ba da* 'yes' are used, and sometimes it can even co-occur with one of these two polarity particles. Its antecedent can be either a regular polar interrogative (47a) or a declarative (47b), both having either affirmative (response by *da* in (47a)) or negative (response by *ba da* in (47b)) verbal forms.

(47) a. A: *Mă   poți   ajuta?* B: *(Da,) cum să   nu.*
        me.ACC can.2SG help.INF   yes   how SUBJ.MRK not
        A: 'Can you help me?' B: '(Yes), of course.'
   b. A: [*talking about the quality of shoes*] *Auziți,   dar asta nu e piele.*
                                              hear.IMP.PL but this not is leather

B: *(Ba da,)* **cum să** **nu,** *uitați-vă* *pe etichetă.*
REV.PRT yes how SUBJ.MRK not look.IMP.PL-you.ACC at label
A: 'Excuse me, this can't be leather.' B: '(Yes it is), how could it not be, have a look at the label.'

3.3.3 Concluding remarks on subjunctive interrogatives

In the light of the empirical data presented in the previous section, two main issues can be identified at the semantic and the pragmatic levels, respectively. First, we observed that free-context uses of the subjunctive in interrogatives involve an implicit modality, i.e. syntactically there is no covert modal involved, but semantically there is an implicit – epistemic or deontic – modality contributed by the subjunctive itself. Moreover, Romanian data in (30)-(31) show that the modality potential of the subjunctive interrogatives is richer than the modality potential of infinitival counterparts in English, assumed to be limited to only deontic/bouletic modality (Bhatt 2000). Second, we observed various uses of the subjunctive in rhetorical questions, with no call-on-addressee (no obligation exerted on the addressee). Our hypothesis is that there is an overlap between these two aspects: some rhetorical questions may involve an implicit modality too, and many free-context uses are less directly addressed than in those interrogatives using the indicative mood, so they involve a weak call-on-addressee, as shown by the acceptability of the special interrogative marker *oare* in these contexts (see (27a) or (30a) above). According to Farkas (2010), the particle *oare* cannot be used with pure information seeking questions; when it occurs, it signals the optionality of the answer (i.e. it removes the obligation from the addressee to answer that question). The division of labour between these two semantic and pragmatic effects remains to be investigated in more details in a further research. Additionally, the subjunctive interrogatives have very rich pragmatic effects which are activated in the dialogue.

After drawing up the inventory of main subjunctive uses in interrogatives in both free and rhetorical contexts, we have to add that many of the subjunctive interrogatives are a priori ambiguous between two or more readings. Thus, the 'out-of-the-blue' example in (48a) can be used either with a deontic modality in title-making instructions as in (48b), or as a rhetorical question as in (48c). These cases show the importance of the context in evaluating the discursive use and the additional pragmatic effects which are at work.

(48) a. *Cum **să** slăbești?*
 how SUBJ.MRK lose-weight.2SG
 'How can you lose weight?'
 b. *Cum **să** slăbești rapid, dar sănătos?*
 how SUBJ.MRK lose-weight.2SG quickly but healthily
 'How can you lose weight quickly, but healthily?'
 c. *Cum **să** slăbești când mănânci numai lucruri nesănătoase?*
 how SUBJ.MRK lose-weight.2SG when eat.2SG only stuff unhealthy
 'How can you lose weight if you eat only unhealthy stuff?'

All these empirical facts show the rich semantic and pragmatic potential of the subjunctive mood in the interrogative domain in Romanian, compared to other Romance languages, where the discursive effects presented above are covered by several moods (indicative, conditional, infinitive, imperative). Our hypothesis is that the subjunctive has similar potential in other Balkan languages,[12] such as Bulgarian or Greek, as shown by examples mentioned in (20) above and in (49–50). This calls for further research.

(49) a. *Ti **da** ne si poet-ăt?* (Bulg)
 you SUBJ.MRK not be.2SG poet.DEF
 'You wouldn't be the poet, would you?'
 b. *Dali **da** se otkaža ot zaminavane-to si*
 INTERR SUBJ.MRK REFL.CL give-up.1SG from departure.DEF POSS.REFL
 za Varna?
 for Varna
 'Should I cancel my trip to Varna?

(50) a. *Pu **na** pao?* (Grk)
 Where SUBJ.MRK go.1SG
 'Where should I go?'
 b. ***Na** zi kanis i **na** mi zi?*
 SUBJ.MRK live.3SG someone or SUBJ.MRK not live.3SG
 'To be or not to be?'

From a theoretical perspective, this study challenges the traditional one-to-one mapping (e.g. Sadock and Zwicky 1985) between syntactic clausal types and

---

[12] This hypothesis is a priori supported by the data, as mentioned by native speakers (Dimitra Kolliakou for Greek, and Snejana Gadjeva for Bulgarian).

illocutionary forces (or speech acts) and supports the polyfunctionality of clausal types (Gazdar 1981, Ginzburg and Sag 2000, Beyssade and Marandin 2006). A syntactic clausal type (here, the interrogative clause) can be used to carry out more than one pragmatic function; in particular, main interrogative clauses displaying the subjunctive can be associated with (self)-questioning, requesting/commanding or asserting. According to Ammann and van der Auwera (2004), the polyfunctionality of a verbal mood covering optative, imperative and hortative uses is a Balkan peculiarity. This study also supports the two dimensions of a speech act: speaker's commitment (i.e. speaker's dialogical attitude towards the content of his occurrence) and speaker's call-on-addressee (i.e. obligation exerted on the addressee); this double import for the speech act is visible, for example, in the rhetorical questions studied above, where the speaker is committed to the propositional abstract (i.e. question) on the one hand and, on the other hand, the addressee is called to take up the utterance as a proposition (Beyssade and Marandin 2009) or as an 'emphatic statement' (Egg 2007).

4 A historical explanation for the high frequency of subjunctives

According to Tomić (2004, 2006), one of the strongest Balkan features is the fact that the emergence of the subjunctive coincides with the weakening of the infinitive, the latter mood being either reduced in its uses or completely eliminated from the verbal modality. This progressive weakening of the infinitive distinguishes Romanian from other Romance languages and puts it closer to Balkan languages such as Greek, Bulgarian, Albanian, Macedonian and partially Serbo-Croatian.[13] Most of the Balkan languages such as Bulgarian and Greek show an infinitive loss as a one-step process, i.e. infinitive forms are replaced with subjunctive forms. According to Hill (2013), infinitive attrition in Romanian has taken place in a two-step process: first, the replacement of long infinitives with short *a*-infinitives[14] and simultaneously with *de*-indicative clauses (in pre-Early Modern Romanian); second, the emergence of subjunctive forms (starting around the 16th century) together with the re-analysis of the conditional conjunction *să* as a subjunctive

---

13 We have to note that this also occurs in some Southern Italian dialects.
14 The suffix *-re* of the long infinitives disappears and a pre-verbal mood marker (i.e. *a* from the Latin preposition *ad*) is created. Thus, the long infinitive *cântare* 'to sing' is progressively replaced by a short infinitive form *a cânta* 'to sing' (Hill 2013 notices that the pre-verbal *a* co-occurred with the long infinitive in litterary texts until the 18th century).

mood marker. The steps of the emergence of the subjunctive in Romanian are illustrated in (51) and (52) below.

(51) a. *au dzis că-i "pre lesne **a** **plini** măria*
has said that-is too easy INF.MRK fulfill.INF majesty
ta giurămîntul".
your oath.DEF
'He said that is too easy for your Majesty to fulfill the oath.'
(Hill 2013, (19))
b. *au poruncitŭ **de** **au** **făcut** un sicreiu.*
has ordered COMP have.3PL made a coffin
'He has ordered (them) to make a coffin.'
(Hill 2013, (11b))
c. *A poruncit **să** **facă** un sicriu.*
has ordered SUBJ.MRK make.3PL a coffin
'He has ordered (them) to make a coffin.'

(52) a. *Merg **a** **lucra**.*
go.1SG INF.MRK work.INF
'I go to work.'
b. *Merg **de** **lucrez**.*
go.1SG COMP work.1SG
c. *Merg **de** **să** **lucrez**.*
go.1SG COMP SUBJ.MRK work.1SG
d. *Merg **să** **lucrez**.*
go.1SG SUBJ.MRK work.1SG

However, as Frâncu (2010) and Hill (2013) argue, there is no evidence for language contact with respect to the emergence of the subjunctive in Romanian (*contra* Sandfeld 1930, Joseph 1983), the context in which this mood emerged in Romanian being fundamentally different from what happened in other Balkan languages. These authors consider that language internal triggers are at work. According to Hill (2013), in Greek the loss of the infinitive starts in the 7th century and closes by the 15th century (see also Joseph 1980, Tomić 2006). On the other side, in Romanian, the attrition process is still incipient in the 16th century (because of the productivity of short infinitives and *de*-indicatives), and there is no evidence for language contact around the 15th-16th centuries. The subjunctive emerges in Romanian much later than in other Balkan languages, because, unlike other Balkan languages, Romanian had an infinitive form still available in the verbal paradigm along with a *de*-indicative form. If a language contact has to be involved in Romanian, that would concern rather *de*-indicatives in Early Modern Romanian, an innovation which is chronologically concomitant with the emergence of the subjunctive in other Balkan languages and which formally mimics the replacement of infinitives in these languages (cf. Hill 2013), since it displays a desemanticized particle (i.e. *de*) followed systematically by an indicative form, as the particle *da* in Bulgarian and the particle *na* in Greek.

Both Frâncu (2010) and Hill (2013) put the emergence of the subjunctive in Romanian down to language internal changes in the list of complementizers: the elimination or specialization of *de* (cf. Hill 2013), the fixation (and desemantization) of the conditional conjunction *să* as a subjunctive mood marker. Frâncu (2010) mentions an other linguistic factor playing a significant role, namely the Romanian preference for personal constructions (cf. the synthetic character of Romanian, preferring to express the person of the verb by synthetic means).

The concept of Sprachbund is therefore questionable with respect to the emergence of the subjunctive along with the attrition of the infinitive in Romanian. This serves as a lesson in analyzing a similar phenomenon in a linguistic area: despite the ressemblances a phenomenon shares in the same linguistic area, it may involve independent triggers and different justifications. This seems to be the case for the emergence of the subjunctive in Romanian and this could be the case for other linguistic phenomena too, such as the future with the verb *volo* followed by the infinitive (cf. Frâncu 2010).

5 Conclusions and perspectives

This paper addresses a property of Romanian grammar, namely, the use of subjunctives in interrogative clauses, which singles it out within the Romance family, but is unsurprising in the Balkan Sprachbund context. Previous studies (in particular, Frâncu 2010's monograph) have failed to observe the impact of the 'independent' subjunctive because of the wrong quantitative evaluation: i.e. the subjunctive 'directives' were considered much more frequent. Two aspects distinguish Romanian from other Romance languages and bring it closer to Balkan languages: (i) the availability of a specific subjunctive particle, which has been argued here to have an affixal status, and (ii) the routine occurrence of the subjunctive in main interrogative clauses. Concerning the latter point, we have shown that main interrogatives with subjunctive verbs cannot involve a syntactically covert modal. Subjunctive interrogatives involve on the one hand an implicit – epistemic or deontic – modality at the semantic level, and on the other hand, a weak call-on-addressee at the pragmatic level, visible especially in rhetorical questions. The division of labour of these two levels needs further investigation.

Much remains to be done. For example, a comparative study is needed for subjunctive modality according to the distribution of the subjunctive verbs in various clausal types (main interrogatives (53a), selected clauses (53b) and relatives (53c)). The intuition is that semantically the subjunctive triggers the same modality effects, namely, epistemic or deontic readings.

(53) a. *[Ce să fac]? Nu-mi trece răceala deloc.*
what SUBJ.MRK do.1SG not-me.DAT pass.3SG cold.DEF at.all
'What can I do? This cold won't go away.'
b. *Nu știu [ce să fac]. Nu-mi trece răceala deloc.*
Not know.1SG what SUBJ.MRK do.1SG not-me.DAT pass.3SG cold.DEF at.all
'I have no idea what to do. This cold won't go away.'
c. *Nu sunt genul de om [care să facă figuri].*
not am kind.DEF of man who SUBJ.MRK do.3SG figures
'I am not the kind of man who shows off.'

Moreover, after finding more evidence for the weak call-on-addressee in subjunctive interrogatives, we have to offer a theoretical analysis of Romanian subjunctives in interrogatives. Finally, cross-linguistically one needs to consider more data from Bulgarian, Greek and other Balkan languages in order to obtain a fine-grained typology of interrogatives using the subjunctive marker. Therefore, this paper is only the beginning of a more comprehensive investigation of the subjunctive mood in interrogative clauses, which is an understudied phenomenon at this time.

References

Akmajian, Adrian. 1984. Sentence Types and the Form-Function Fit. *Natural Language and Linguistic Theory* 2(1). 1–23.
Alexopoulou, Theodora and Dimitra Kolliakou. 2002. On Linkhood and Clitic Left Dislocation. *Journal of Linguistics* 38(2). 193–245.
Ammann, Andreas and Johan van der Auwera. 2004. Complementizer-headed main clauses for volitional moods in the languages of South-Eastern Europe: A Balkanism. In Olga Mišeska Tomić (ed.), *Balkan Syntax and Semantics*, 293–314. Amsterdam/Philadelphia: John Benjamins.
Asenova, Petya. 2002. *Balkansko ezikosnanie. Osnovni problemi na balkanskija ezikov săjuz.* Sofia: Faber.

Avgustinova, Tania. 1997. *Word Order and Clitics in Bulgarian*. Saarbrücken dissertations in Computational Linguistics and Language Technology. Vol. 5.
Avram, Larisa. 2015. A Mirativity Subjunctive in Romanian. In Ionuț Pavian (coord.), *Inspre și dinspre Cluj. Contribuții lingvistice. Omagiu profesorului G.G. Neamțu la 70 de ani*. Cluj: Editura Scriptor - Argonaut.
Barbu, Ana-Maria. 1999. Complexul verbal. *Studii și cercetări lingvistice* 1. 39–84.
Beyssade, Claire and Jean-Marie Marandin. 2006. The Speech Act Assignment Problem Revisited: Disentangling Speaker's Commitment from Speaker's Call on Addressee. In Olivier Bonami and Patricia Cabredo-Hofherr (eds.), *Empirical Studies in Syntax and Semantics* 6, 37–68.
Beyssade, Claire and Jean-Marie Marandin. 2009. Commitment: une attitude dialogique. *Langue française* 162. 89–108.
Bhatt, Rajesh. 2000. Covert Modality in Non-Finite Contexts. Technical Report No. IRCS-00–01, University of Pennsylvania Institute for Research in Cognitive Science.
Bîlbîie, Gabriela and Anna Gazdik. 2012. Wh-coordination in Hungarian and Romanian multiple questions. In Chris Piñón (ed.), *Empirical Issues in Syntax and Semantics*, 19–36. http://www.cssp.cnrs.fr/eiss9/.
Caponigro, Ivano and Jon Sprouse. 2007. Rhetorical questions as questions. In Estela Puig Waldmüller (ed.), *Proceedings of Sinn und Bedeutung* 11, 121–133. Barcelona: Universat Pompeu Fabra.
Christidis, Anastasios. 1991. On the categorical status of particles: The case for holophrasis. *Lingua* 82. 53–82.
Cotfas, Maria Aurelia. 2011. *On the syntax of the Romanian subjunctive: control and obviation*. University of Bucharest doctoral dissertation.
Culicover, Peter and Ray Jackendoff. 2005. *Simpler Syntax*. Oxford University Press.
Dobrovie-Sorin, Carmen. 1994. *The Syntax of Romanian. Comparative Studies in Romance* [Studies in Generative Grammar 40]. Mouton de Gruyter.
Egg, Markus. 2007. Meaning and use of rhetorical questions. In Maria Aloni, Paul Dekker and Floris Roelofsen (eds.), *Proceedings of the 16th Amsterdam Colloquium*, 73–78. New York: Academic Press.
Farkas, Donka. 1985. *Intensional descriptions and the Romance subjunctive mood*. New York: Garland.
Farkas, Donka. 1992. On the Semantics of Subjunctive Complements. In Paul Hirschbühler and Konrad Koerner (eds.), *Romance Languages and Modern Linguistic Theory. Papers from the 20th Linguistic Symposium on Romance Languages (LSRL XX)*, 69–104. Amsterdam/Philadelphia: John Benjamins.
Farkas, Donka. 2003. Assertion, belief and mood choice. Paper presented at the Workshop on conditional and unconditional modality, ESSLLI, Vienna.
Farkas, Donka. 2010. The grammar of polarity particles in Romanian. In Anna Maria Di Sciullo and Virginia Hill (eds.), *Edges, Heads, and Projections: Interface properties* [Linguistik Aktuell / Linguistics Today 156], 87–124. John Benjamins.
Feuillet, Jack. 2012. *Linguistique comparée des langues balkaniques*. Paris: Institut d'Études Slaves.
Frâncu, Constantin. 2010. *Conjunctivul românesc și raporturile lui cu alte moduri*. Iași: Casa Editorială Demiurg.
Gazdar, Gerald. 1981. Speech act assignment. In A. Joshi, Bruce Weber and Ivan Sag (eds.), *Elements of Discourse Understanding*, 64–83. Cambridge University Press.

GALR: Guțu-Romalo (coord.). 2005. *Gramatica limbii române*. Bucharest: Editura Academiei Române.

Giannakidou, Anastasia. 2009. The dependency of the subjunctive revisited: Temporal semantics and polarity. *Lingua* 119(12). 1883–1908.

Ginzburg, Jonathan. 2012. *The Interactive Stance: Meaning for Conversation*. Oxford University Press.

Ginzburg, Jonathan and Ivan Sag. 2000. *Interrogative Investigations: the form, meaning and use of English interrogatives*. Stanford: CSLI Publications.

Godard, Danièle. 2012. Indicative and subjunctive mood in complement clauses: from formal semantics to grammar writing. In Chris Piñón (ed.), *Empirical Issues in Syntax and Semantics*, 129–148. http://www.cssp.cnrs.fr/eiss9/.

Grohmann, Kleanthes. 2000. Null Modals in Germanic (and Romance): Infinitival Exclamatives. *The Belgian Journal of Linguistics* 14. 43–61.

Hill, Virginia. 2013. The emergence of the Romanian subjunctive. *The Linguistic Review* 30(4). 547–583.

Holton, David, Peter Mackridge and Irene Philippaki-Warburton. 1997. *Greek: A comprehensive Grammar of the Modern Language*. London and New York: Routledge.

Jordan, Maria. 2009. *Loss of Infinitival Complementation in Romanian Diachronic Syntax*. University of Florida doctoral dissertation.

Joseph, Brian. 1980. A New Convergence involving the Balkan Loss of the Infinitive. *Indogermanische Forschungen* 85. 176–187.

Joseph, Brian. 1981. On the Synchrony and Diachrony of Modern Greek *na*. *Byzantine and Modern Greek Studies* 7. 139–154.

Joseph, Brian. 1983. *The Synchrony and Diachrony of the Balkan Infinitive: A Study in Areal, General and Historical Linguistics*. Cambridge University Press.

Joseph, Brian. 1999. Romanian and the Balkans: Some Comparative Perspectives. In Sheila Embleton, John Joseph and Hans-Josef Niederehe (eds.), *The Emergence of the Modern Language Sciences. Studies on the Transition from Historical-Comparative to Structural Linguistics in Honour of E.F.K. Koerner*. Vol. 2: *Methodological perspectives and Applications*, 218–235. Amsterdam/Philadelphia: John Benjamins.

Krifka, Manfred. 2001. For a structured meaning account of questions and answers. In Caroline Fery and Wolfgang Sternefeld (eds.), *Audiatur Vox Sapientia. A Festschrift for Arnim von Stechow*, 287–319. Berlin: Akademie Verlag.

Lambrecht, Knud. 1990. What, me worry? 'Mad Magazine sentences' Revisited. *Proceedings of the Sixteenth Annual Meeting of the Berkeley Linguistics Society*, 215–228.

Lee-Goldman, Russell. 2006. A typology of rhetorical questions. Presentation at the Syntax and Semantics Circle. http://www1.icsi.berkeley.edu/~rleegold/ling/syntaxcircle-rqpresent.pdf

Mackridge, Peter. 1985. *The Modern Greek Language*. Oxford University Press.

Marandin, Jean-Marie. 2008. The Exclamative Clause Type in French. In Stefan Müller (ed.), *Proceedings of the HPSG'08 Conference*, 436–456. Stanford: CSLI Publications.

Miller, Philip. 1992. *Clitics and Constituents in Phrase Structure Grammar*. New York: Garland.

Monachesi, Paola. 2005. *The verbal complex in Romance: a case study in grammatica interfaces*. Oxford University Press.

Nedelcu, Isabela. 2013. *Particularități sintactice ale limbii române în context romanic: Infinitivul*. Bucharest: Editura Muzeului Național al Literaturii Române.

Peterson, Tyler. 2013. *Rethinking Mirativity: The Expression and Implication of Surprise*. Manuscript, University of Arizona.

Portner, Paul. 2009. *Modality*. Oxford University Press.
Rohde, Hannah. 2006. Rhetorical questions as redundant interrogatives. *San Diego Linguistics Papers* 2. 134–168.
Sadock, Jerrold. 1971. Queclaratives. In Douglas Adams, Mary Ann Campbell, Victor Cohen, Julie Lovins, Edward Maxwell, Carolyn Nygren and John Reighard (eds.), *Papers from the 7th Regional Meeting of the Chicago Linguistics Society*, 223–232. Chicago Linguistics Society.
Sadock, Jerrold and Arnold Zwicky. 1985. Speech Acts Distinctions in Syntax. In Timothy Shopen (ed.), *Language Typology and Syntactic Description*, 155–196. Cambridge University Press.
Sandfeld, Kristian. 1930. *Linguistique balkanique: problèmes et résultats*. Paris: Champion.
Sava, Cristinel Silviu. 2012. *Complementizatorii în limba română veche*. University of Bucharest doctoral dissertation.
Sims, Andrea and Brian D. Joseph. This volume. Morphology versus Syntax in the Balkan Verbal Complex.
Tomić, Olga Mišeska (ed.). 2004. *Balkan Syntax and Semantics*. Amsterdam/Philadelphia: John Benjamins.
Tomić, Olga Mišeska. 2006. *Balkan Sprachbund Morpho-syntactic Features* [Studies in Natural Language and Linguistic Theory 67]. Dordrecht: Springer.
Villalta, Elisabeth. 2007. *Context Dependence in the Interpretation of Questions and Subjunctives*. University of Tübingen doctoral dissertation.
Villalta, Elisabeth. 2008. Mood and gradability: an investigation of the subjunctive mood in Spanish. *Linguistics and Philosophy* 31(4). 467–522.
Zafiu, Rodica. 2011. Observații asupra semanticii conjunctivului românesc. In Rodica Zafiu, Camelia Ușurelu and Helga Bogdan-Oprea (eds.), *Limba română. Ipostaze ale variației lingvistice*, 163–171. Bucharest: Editura Universității din București.
Zwicky, Arnold and Geoffrey Pullum. 1983. Cliticization vs. Inflection: English N'T. *Language* 59(3). 502–513.

Tomislav Sočanac
Subjunctive complements in Balkan languages: Problems of distribution

Abstract: This paper deals with the subject of Balkan subjunctive mood (BlkS), specifically the distribution of subjunctive complements across different Balkan languages (e.g.: Greek, Romanian, Bulgarian). These languages exhibit unusual distributional patterns in this context, because they introduce subjunctive complements under a wide range of predicates (both control and non-control verbs), which are more lexically diverse than the subjunctive-selecting verbs in non-Balkan languages. As a result, BlkS as such is associated with a diverse range of meanings, which cannot be subsumed under any of the cross-linguistic semantic definitions of the subjunctive that were previously proposed in the literature (e.g. irrealis, non-veridicality, intensionality). Nevertheless, the analysis proposed in this paper, which looks at BlkS through the prism of the syntax-semantics interface (as defined in Chomsky 1995), reaches a coherent theoretical account of BlkS distribution. All BlkS complements are subsumed under the same syntactic clause type, whereas the formal and semantic contrasts that they exhibit are analyzed as a result of different syntactic derivations observed with complements belonging to the subjunctive clause type, which can produce different structural outputs at the syntax-semantics interface, resulting in different types of interpretations.

Keywords: Mood, Balkan subjunctive, subjunctive distribution, syntax-semantics interface, structural truncation

1 Introduction

The issue of subjunctive distribution has always posed a number of theoretical problems for authors studying mood, both intra- and cross-linguistically. Most of the generalizing definitions that were proposed in the literature in order to account for the nature of the subjunctive fell short when it came to subsuming the full distributional range of clauses associated with this mood.[1] The primary reason

---

[1] Some of the more influential definitions of the subjunctive that one could mention in this context are those based on notions such as non-assertivity (Hopper 1975), non-veridicality

Tomislav Sočanac, Ca' Foscari University, Venice, tomislav.socanac@unige.ch

for this is the fact that, in addition to some of the more typical cross-linguistic contexts of subjunctive use, such as those exemplified in (1–2), where subjunctive complements appear under desiderative or directive predicates and are associated with irrealis-type meanings, there is also a number of atypical cases of subjunctive distribution, such as in complements to factive-emotive (3) or control predicates (4), which are much more difficult to include under any global definition of the subjunctive:

(1) *Ordenó   que   vengas.* (Spanish)
    ordered-3SG that come-2SG-SUBJ
    'He ordered you to come.'

(2) *Thelo   na   odhiji.* (Greek)
    want-1SG SUBJ drive-3SG
    'I want him to drive.'

(3) *Je regrette qu'il soit   parti.* (French)
    I regret that he has-SUBJ left
    'I regret that he left.'

(4) a. *Arxizo   na   grafo.* (Greek)
       begin-1SG SUBJ write-1SG
       'I begin to write.'
       (Roussou 2009: 1815)
    b. *Ion a   reușit   să   vină.* (Romanian)
       John has managed SUBJ come-3SG
       'John managed to come.'

This paper primarily deals with the problems posed by the type of subjunctives we observe in (4), because they are more specific to Balkan languages. As for the subjunctive complements to factive emotive predicates such as those in (3), they are not studied here because they feature much less prominently in Balkan than they do in Romance languages. If we look at some of the Balkan counterparts of the French example in (3), we can observe that a factive emotive verb such as *regret* introduces the indicative, not the subjunctive complement in Balkan languages:

(Giannakidou 1998) or intensionality (Farkas 1992). Like most others, they face problems in light of subjunctives such as those in (3) and (4).

(5) O   Pavlos lipate pu   efije   i   Roxani.   (Grk)
    the Paul is-sad that-IND left-3SG the Roxanne
    'Paul regrets that Roxanne left.'
    (Giannakidou 2009: 1886)

(6) *Sažaljavam   če   Ivan ne dojde.*   (Bulgarian)
    regret-1SG that-IND Ivan not came-3SG
    'I regret that Ivan didn't come.'
    (Krapova 2002: 110)

In Sočanac (2017), I address some of the reasons for the differences in the cross-linguistic distribution of the subjunctive in such contexts, but I am unable to go into them here due to space constraints.[2] The primary focus of this paper is those cases of subjunctive distribution that are characteristic of Balkan languages, involving complements such as the ones in (2) and (4).

In Section 2, I approach the issues related to Balkan subjunctive (BlkS from now on) from a more descriptive point of view, first briefly addressing its morpho-syntactic realization, which is different from the one we typically observe across languages, and then outlining its distribution, which will be the central issue of concern here. In Section 3, I propose a theoretical account of BlkS distribution that subsumes a broad range of subjunctive clauses under a common syntactic analysis. To be a bit more precise, all BlkS complements that we look at are analyzed as syntactically selected under the same type of CP, whereas the formal and semantic differences that they exhibit are seen as a result of the different syntactic derivations that they undergo post-selection, which may alter the basic structural make-up associated with the subjunctive CP-clause type, and produce different structural outputs at the syntax-semantic interface.[3] Finally, in Section 4, I recap my findings and conclude the paper.

---

[2] See fn. 9 for a bit more detail on this point, though.
[3] In this context I adopt a standard minimalist view of language (i.e. the T-model of grammar), whereby the syntactic derivation is assumed to feed the semantic, interpretative component (see Chomsky 1995).

2 BlkS realization and distribution

2.1 Realization

While subjunctive mood is typically marked through dedicated subjunctive verb forms cross-linguistically, Balkan languages exhibit a different type of marking in this context. BlkS is marked through a separate syntactic item, typically appearing at the beginning of the subjunctive clause, which is morphologically distinct from the comp(lementizer)s used to introduce indicative-type clauses, as we can observe through the examples of Romanian (7) and Greek (8) below[4]:

(7) a. *Maria crede **că** Ion a plecat.* (Rom)
  Mary believes that-IND John has left
  'Mary believe John left.'
 b. *Maria vrea **să** plece Ion.*
  Mary wants SUBJ leave-3SG John
  'Mary wants John to leave.'

(8) a. *Nomizo **oti** efije.* (Grk)
  think-1SG that-IND left-3SG
  'I think he left.'
 b. *Tu ipa **na** fiji.*
  him ordered-1SG SUBJ leave-3SG
  'I ordered him to leave.'
  (Roussou 2009: 1814)

The subjunctive markers in (7–8b) have received a lot of attention in the Balkan literature, with some authors defining them as comps inserted in C (e.g. Dobrovie-Sorin 1994; Krapova 1998) and others as particles inserted in some lower structural position (e.g. Giannakidou 1998; Rivero 1994; Terzi 1992). Even though the syntactic realization of BlkS per se is not a major focus of this paper, I assume an approach that is closer to the one defended by the latter group of authors, for reasons that are internal to the argument I put forward in Section 3 (see fn. 22 in particular).

---

[4] The only slight exception in this context out of the Balkan languages I study here is Serbian, because the latter typically introduces both indicative and subjunctive complements through the item *da*. Nevertheless, various authors have demonstrated that the indicative *da* and subjunctive *da* are actually different syntactic items, with different properties (e.g. Sočanac 2011; Todorović 2012).

2.2 Distribution

BlkS complements also exhibit some unusual patterns when it comes to their distribution: in addition to the more typical cases of subjunctive subordination, such as those exemplified in (7–8b), which involve complements referred to as *intensional subjunctives* (as in Farkas 1992), one can observe BlkS in a whole range of additional syntactic contexts, which are more idiosyncratic to Balkan languages (a small sample of such contexts is exemplified below).[5]

(9) *Ivan trjabva da dojde.* (Bulg)
    John must SUBJ come-3SG
    'John must come.'

(10) *O Kostas bori na odhiji.* (Grk)
     the Kostas can SUBJ drive-3SG
     'Kostas can drive.'
     (Roussou 2009: 1815)

(11) *Ivan je uspeo da stigne na vreme.* (Serbian)
     John has managed SUBJ arrive-3SG on time
     'John managed to arrive on time.'

(12) *Ion începe să scrie.* (Rom)
     John begins SUBJ write-3SG
     'John begins to write.'

Complements such as those in (9–12) are unusual in the context of the crosslinguistic properties of the subjunctive mood both when it comes to their syntactic and when it comes to their semantic properties.

---

[5] I should briefly note that some of the subjunctive-selecting predicates in Balkan languages can be described as "dual mood choice verbs", in the sense that they can introduce both the indicative and the subjunctive mood in their embedded complement. This is the case, for instance, with verbs of saying, which acquire a directive dimension when associated with the subjunctive, or cognitive verbs such as *know*, which acquires a dynamic modal reading when it introduces the subjunctive (Roussou 2009; Sočanac 2017). In Sočanac (2017), I argue that the optionality in such cases is only apparent, because we actually have two separate, homophonous lexical entries, one selecting the indicative and one the subjunctive complement, as shown by the fact that the two items are associated with different lexical semantic properties, and their complements with different clausal properties. I leave this issue aside in the present paper, and only focus on the subjunctive-selecting variants.

They are unusual syntactically because they exhibit obligatory subject control (manifested through the mechanism of agreement sharing between the matrix and the embedded predicate). In contrast, subjunctive complements cross-linguistically tend to appear in non-subject-control environments - in fact, they are often associated with the anti-control property of *subject obviation* (more on that in Section 3). The fact that Balkan languages employ the subjunctive in control contexts is related to one of the phenomena subsumed under the term *Balkan Sprachbund*,[6] specifically the infinitive loss: most languages of the Balkan region have, to a greater or lesser degree, replaced their infinitives with finite control complements associated with subjunctive morphology, such as those in (9–12), which explains why BlkS, on the whole, distributes much more widely than most of its cross-linguistic counterparts (see Joseph 1983, for instance).[7] I refer to the latter type of complements from now on as *control subjunctives* (borrowing the label from Landau 2004).

Control subjunctives also exhibit some unusual properties from a semantic point of view, which further compound the problems related to the cross-linguistic semantic analysis of the subjunctive mood as such: even though some of these complements (such as the one in [9]) are associated with similar irrealis modal interpretations that one observes with the subjunctive cross-linguistically, others (as in [11–12]) are associated with entirely realis, indicative-type meaning and no discernable modality at all. As a result, the latter type of complements pose problems for most of the semantic definitions of the subjunctive that have

---

[6] The term *Balkan Sprachbund* refers to the linguistic phenomenon whereby Balkan languages, despite belonging to several different families, nonetheless share certain common properties in different areas of their grammar (see Mišeska Tomić [2006] and the references therein for a more detailed account of this phenomenon). Given the unifying linguistic tendencies in the context of Balkan Sprachbund, most of the data related to BlkS discussed in this paper, e.g., control or tense properties of different types of subjunctives, are equally observed across all languages that I am interested in here (I avoid using more intricate language-specific data given the broad focus of the article, as well as limitations of space).

[7] The phenomenon of infinitive loss is subject to some regional variation (see also Krapova and Cinque, this volume). On the whole, languages more to the South-East of the Balkan region (e.g. Greek, Albanian, Bulgarian) have lost their infinitive in greater degree than those situated more to the North (e.g. Romanian) or to the West (e.g. Croatian) (Joseph 1983). Here I abstract away from these regional variations and only focus on those varieties that have replaced their infinitives with subjunctives. Thus, for instance, when it comes to a language such as BCMS (Bosnian, Croatian, Montenegrin, Serbian), or Serbo-Croatian, under the older labeling, I refer to it here as Serbian because the Serbian variety employs control subjunctives more productively than, for instance, Croatian, whose speakers tend to employ the infinitive in such contexts (although this too is subject to some regional variation).

been proposed by various authors. For instance, they are problematic for the theoretical approach that defines the subjunctive in terms of non-veridicality, which has been particularly influential in the literature on mood (Giannakidou 1998, Giannakidou 2009). According to this perspective, subjunctive is selected by predicates that are defined as non-veridical, in the sense that they do not entail any truth commitment on the part of the speaker or the matrix subject towards the proposition denoted by the embedded complement. However, predicates such as those in (11–12) presuppose a truth commitment on the part of the speaker, and should hence be defined as veridical. As such, they would be expected to introduce the indicative mood in their embedded complement, which is contrary to facts.

Even though the problems posed by this type of complements are difficult to resolve if one analyzes BlkS from a purely semantic point of view, the approach that I develop in the following section, which looks at BlkS through the prism of the syntax-semantics interface, allows me to coherently subsume the atypical cases of BlkS distribution (as in [11–12]) and the more typical intensional subjunctives (such as those in [7–8b]) under the same formal analysis. All these BlkS complements are analyzed as constituting the same clausal mood category, syntactically associated with the same CP clause type, whereas the formal and semantic differences that they exhibit will be explained as the result of the different types of syntactic derivations that they undergo, whereby they may alter the basic structure associated with the subjunctive CP clause-type, and thus produce different structural outputs at the syntax-semantics interface, resulting in different interpretations.

3 BlkS clause type: Common CP, different derivations

The analysis that I put forward here provides a common explanatory framework that accounts for the formal and semantic diversity associated with BlkS distribution. The most important observation to be made in this context is that BlkS complements which are more atypical from a semantic point of view (e.g. 11–12) are also syntactically more anaphoric. This correlation can be accounted for through the mechanism of structural truncation: those complements that are more anaphoric are analyzed as associated with more truncated structures, which implies that they send less featural specifications associated with the subjunctive CP-clause structure to the interface with semantics, explaining why they are further removed from the typical subjunctive meaning. In order to introduce this argument, I first begin by outlining my formal analysis of the subjunctive clause type itself.

3.1 Subjunctive CP clause structure

As regards the basic clausal structure associated with BlkS, I assume a fairly simple syntactic representation which has been relatively standard in Balkan literature (Rivero 1994; Roussou 2000; Terzi 1992), as represented in (13):

(13) [CP [ModP [TP [vP]]]]

I thus analyze BlkS complements as associated with the clause-typing CP-projection, an additional modal projection situated between CP and TP,[8] and then the lower tense and verbal projections below it (the latter is of less interest here). The only part of the structure in (13) which I formalize here in more detail, because it becomes relevant for the argument below, is the subjunctive CP projection itself.

First of all, I argue that the subjunctive CP should be analyzed as the embedded instance of the matrix imperative CP. The primary motivation for this analysis is the fact that typical intensional subjunctive complements, exemplified in BlkS contexts in (7–8b), were shown to closely pattern with imperatives in a number of properties that they exhibit (Han 1998; Kempchinsky 2009; Portner 1997; Sočanac 2017).[9] For instance, Portner (1997) noted that

---

8 The modal projection ModP (sometimes labeled as MoodP or ModalP, depending on the authors) has often been seen as the host for BlkS mood markers, at least by those authors that analyzed the latter as particles as opposed to comps (e.g. Rivero 1994; Terzi 1992). Even though I maintain ModP as the locus of clausal modality in the context of BlkS complements, I do not see it as the place of insertion of BlkS particles, primarily because the latter can appear in some complements that are not semantically associated with any modality, e.g. those in (11–12). See fn. 22 for more detail on this point.
9 Note that this syntactic analysis applies in the context of intensional subjunctives, as well as Balkan control subjunctives, as I show in Sections 3.2 and 3.3. It does not, however, apply to some other types of subjunctives, such as those introduced under factive-emotive predicates of the type we observed earlier on in (3). The latter pattern with indicative/declarative clauses when it comes to the properties listed above, not with imperatives, which is why I analyze them in Sočanac (2017) as being syntactically associated with the indicative CP, and not the subjunctive/imperative CP. The same analysis is then also used to explain some variations in the cross-linguistic distribution of this type of subjunctives, specifically the fact that they are less extant in Balkan (or Slavic) than they are in Romance languages, as we already observed earlier on: given that the

the two types of clauses pattern in terms of their propositional content (unlike indicatives/declaratives, which denote propositions that can be judged as true or false, subjunctives and imperatives denote propositions that cannot); Kempchinsky (2009) observed that subjunctives and imperatives exhibit common properties in the area of (anti)control (more on that point in Section 3.2); Sočanac (2017) showed that they pattern when it comes to their temporal properties; Han (1998) or Jary and Kissine (2014), among others, noted that the two types of clauses exhibit a number of distributional overlaps across languages. I do not develop these arguments in further detail, but take them as sufficient grounds for the claim that imperatives and embedded subjunctives should be analyzed as syntactically introduced under the same type of CP. This is not a particularly new claim in the context of intensional subjunctives (it has already been proposed by authors such as Han [1998] or Kempchinsky [2009], among others), but here I propose to apply the same type of analysis to control subjunctives as well.[10]

Before I move on to a closer syntactic analysis of BlkS, I first focus on the underlying feature make-up of the subjunctive/imperative CP. In Sočanac (2017), I analyzed this CP as containing a feature cluster consisting of two features organized in a hierarchical configuration- an analysis partly based on Han (1998). The feature cluster in question consists of the higher Dir(ective) feature, which denotes clause type,[11] and the lower Mod(al) feature, which denotes intensional world-anchoring in the sense of Farkas (1992), i.e., the type of world-anchoring whereby the proposition in question is not anchored to any particular world but

---

former groups of languages morphologically mark their subjunctive closer to the CP domain (as opposed to using verbal morphology), the introduction of subjunctive markers under an indicative-type CP produces a clash with the selectional requirements of the matrix predicate, and is hence avoided.

10 An anonymous reviewer has suggested a different possible analysis of the subjunctive-imperative link, based on the approach put forward in Huntley (1984). Huntley argued that imperatives can be analyzed as subordinate clauses, whose matrix instances contain an additional modal operator. So, under this approach, instead of analyzing subjunctives as embedded instances of matrix imperatives, the reverse would obtain, i.e. imperatives could be analyzed as matrix instances of embedded subjunctives. Even though teasing out the differences between these two types of approaches in greater detail is outside the scope of this paper, I note that Huntley's approach does not contradict the general outlines of the analysis defended here, and is compatible with the claim that subjunctives and imperatives are syntactically closely related categories, associated with the same type of CP (whether this CP is used by default in matrix or in embedded types of syntactic environments is of less central concern here).

11 Directivity is usually seen as the prototypical function associated with the imperative mood (see Jary and Kissine [2014], and the references therein), which is why I relate the imperative/subjunctive clause type to the clause-typing Dir-feature.

to a set of possible worlds, which is a semantic property associated with both matrix imperatives and embedded intensional subjunctives.

The full structural description associated with the subjunctive CP clause type, which I use as the basis for my analysis of BlkS distribution, is therefore the one in (14):

(14) [CP $_{\text{Dir>Mod}}$ [ModP [TP [vP]]]]

All BlkS complements of the types observed in (7–12) are assumed to be introduced under this same type of CP at the point of selection, but then different complements are claimed to undergo different syntactic derivations post-selection, whereby they end up truncating varying chunks of the basic subjunctive CP structure in (14) before they reach the interface with semantics. In Section 3.2, I explain how this syntactic truncation analysis can account for some of the formal contrasts that one observes between different BlkS complements, whereas in Section 3.3, I look at the semantic implications of this analysis.

3.2 Subjunctive CP and structural truncation

Various authors have already noted that different types of BlkS complements exhibit different syntactic properties, with some being more deficient than others in this sense. More specifically, control subjunctives (C subjunctives from now on) were shown to exhibit more anaphoric properties than non-control (NC) subjunctives.[12] For instance, Varlokosta (1993) noted in the context of Greek that, whereas NC subjunctives involve two separate clausal domains, C subjunctives involve syntactic clause union and semantic event unification between the matrix and the embedded clause. Krapova (1998) went on to provide additional evidence for a similar analysis in the context of Bulgarian subjunctive, focusing in particular on the area of clausal tense. She showed that NC subjunctives can introduce embedded tense markers that conflict with the matrix tense (15), whereas C subjunctives cannot (16), which was once again explained as a result of the anaphoric nature of the latter type of complements.

---

[12] The label NC subjunctive subsumes all BlkS complements that do not exhibit obligatory subject control, so it also applies to those complements (e.g. complements to desiderative verbs) that may optionally involve a control reading depending on context. In this sense, the NC label I use here is similar to the "Free subjunctive" (FS) label used in Landau (2004). Nevertheless, while I adopt Landau's labeling in the context of C subjunctives, I do not use his FS label, because not all NC complements can be shown to exhibit free subject reference. See (17), for instance.

(15) *Iskah   da   dojdeš   utre.*
   wanted-1SG SUBJ come-2SG tomorrow
   'I wanted you to come tomorrow.'

(16) * *Ne možah   da   kupja   knigata   utre.*
   not could-1SG SUBJ buy-1SG book-the tomorrow
   'I could not buy the book tomorrow.'
   (Krapova 1998: 83)

Krapova argued that the grammaticality contrast in (15–16) showed that, in the case of C subjunctives, the embedded and the matrix clause form a single time frame, whereas with NC subjunctives, matrix and embedded clauses denote two separate time frames. Landau (2004) then went on to apply Krapova's tense observations in the context of a wider analysis of BlkS in control and non-control environments.

While both Krapova and Landau provided a lexicalist-type explanation for the different degree of anaphoricity that one can observe between NC and C BlkS complements in the context of tense, referring to the difference in the featural make-up of the embedded T-head (or I-head, under Landau's labeling), I provide a different theoretical account of this contrast, which is more structure-based. Specifically, I claim that NC subjunctives maintain the embedded subjunctive CP under which they were selected by the matrix predicate, whereas C subjunctives truncate it during the derivation. A similar analysis was already proposed by some authors in order to account for the differences between finite non-control structures and non-finite control structures across languages, the former being viewed as associated with a CP projection and the latter with a smaller IP/TP structure (e.g. Kempchinsky 1986; Watanabe 1993). Here I argue that the same type of analysis can be applied to BlkS as well, despite the fact that the latter is associated with finite complementation in both control and non-control syntactic environments.

Before I focus more closely on the differences between NC and C subjunctives in this context, I first look at some finer contrasts that can be observed between NC subjunctives themselves. This group contains BlkS complements that are more typical cross-linguistically (i.e. complements such as those in [7–8b]) because they are selected by intensional predicates and denote irrealis-type meanings. Nevertheless, one can observe some nuance formal and semantic differences between these complements as well, which can be explained in light of the featural analysis of the subjunctive CP I proposed earlier on. The relevant distinction in this context is the one between complements that maintain the Dir-feature in their CP and those that strip it, which is syntactically manifested through the difference in control properties exhibited by these complements.

The most important formal property associated with Dir, according to the argument I put forward in Sočanac (2017), is linked to anti-control and the phenomenon of *subject obviation*- i.e. the ban on co-reference between the matrix and the embedded subject.[13] Even though this phenomenon is not as widely observed in the context of BlkS as it is in (non-Balkan) Romance or Slavic languages, where it is exhibited by intensional subjunctives more generally, one can nonetheless observe subject obviation with a more restricted group of BlkS complements as well, namely complements to directive predicates, which can be semantically described as embedded imperatives.[14]

(17) a. *Marija$_i$ je naredila da ode* $_{*i/j}$. (Srb)
Mary has ordered SUBJ leave-3SG
'Mary ordered *(him/her) to leave.'
b. *Ion$_i$ a ordonat să vină* $_{*i/j}$. (Rom)
John has ordered SUBJ come-3SG
'John ordered *(him/her) to come.'

On the other hand, the same anti-control effect is not observed in intensional-type BlkS complements when they are selected by verbs other than directives. For instance, BlkS complements to desiderative predicates, unlike their counterparts in languages such as French, Spanish or Russian, do not exhibit subject obviation[15]:

(18) a. *O Kostas$_i$ theli na odhiji$_{i/j}$.* (Grk)
the Kostas wants SUBJ drive-3SG
'Kostas wants (him/her) to drive.'
(Roussou 2009: 1812)

---

[13] For more on the notion of subject obviation, see Kempchinsky (1998), Picallo (1985), Raposo (1985), or Schlenker (2005), among others.

[14] In Sočanac (2017), I argue that the subject obviation effect associated with the Dir-feature in subjunctives is related to a similar anti-control effect one observes in simple imperatives, where Dir bans subject-speaker co-reference, which explains why we do not observe imperatives in first person singular. This analysis is based on the one put forward in Kempchinsky (2009), the difference being that Kempchinsky associated the anti-control effect observed in these two types of clauses with an imperative-related operator, as opposed to a feature.

[15] This contrast can be explained in light of the Balkan-Sprachbund-related phenomenon of infinitive loss, which resulted in the absence of the so-called 'subjunctive-infinitive competition' in BlkS complements such as those in (18), responsible for the ban on control reading in their (non-Balkan) Romance and Slavic counterparts (see Bouchard [1984] or Schlenker [2005] for more on the notion of subjunctive-infinitive competition). Of course, subject control per se is not banned in Romance or Slavic complements to desiderative verbs, but it is restricted to non-finite complementation.

b. *Ivan$_i$ iska da dojde$_{i/j}$.* (Bulg)
John wants SUBJ come-3SG
'John wants (him/her) to come.'

In fact, the preferred reading in complements such as those in (18) is the one involving subject control, whereas the non-control reading is more contextually marked.

Given the analysis that views the anti-control effect observed in (17) as a function of the Dir-feature, the conclusion is that BlkS NC complements should be divided in two groups based on the underlying formal properties of their CP: on the one hand, we have complements to directive predicates that maintain Dir, whose CP corresponds to the representation in (19); on the other hand, we have complements to other intensional predicates, such as desideratives in (18), which correspond to the representation in (20):

(19) [CP $_{\text{Dir>Mod}}$]

(20) [CP $_{\cancel{\text{Dir}}\text{>Mod}}$]

The CP-structure in (20) thus represents the first example of the structural truncation that one observes in the context of BlkS clause type. In what follows, we observe some further applications of this mechanism, which can account for some of the more important differences that can be observed between NC subjunctives, on the one side, and C subjunctives, on the other.

The most obvious formal difference that C subjunctives exhibit with respect to their NC counterparts is related to the referential properties of the embedded subject:

(21) a. **O Kostas bori na odhiyo.* (Grk)
    the Kostas can SUBJ drive-1SG
  b. *O Kostas$_i$ bori na odhiji$_{i/*j}$.*
    the Kostas can SUBJ drive-3SG
    'Kostas can drive.'
    (Roussou 2009: 1815)

(22) a. * *Ivan počinje da studiram.* (Srb)
    John begins SUBJ study-1SG
  b. *Ivan$_i$ počinje da studira$_{i/*j}$.*
    John begins SUBJ study-3SG
    'John begins to study.'

The examples in (21–22) illustrate the obligatory control property in the context of BlkS: matrix and embedded predicates must share common φ-features, and the subjects of two clauses must be co-indexed. I argue that this property is best explained through the CP-truncation analysis of C subjunctives.

First of all, the claim that C subjunctives lack an embedded CP allows to straightforwardly incorporate BlkS control data within some broader syntactic theories. For instance, it is in line with the contemporary phasal approach to syntax, proposed in Chomsky (2001). According to this perspective, CP-clauses constitute phases, which are seen as syntactically opaque domains that are impenetrable to syntactic operations outside of that domain.[16] Thus, given that obligatory subject control involves a syntactic binding relationship between the subjects of the matrix and the embedded clauses, the phasal view of syntax would predict that there should be no CP-phase boundary between the two clauses in such cases, which is in accordance with my own analysis in the context of C BlkS complements.[17]

This analysis is further reinforced if we appeal to the more traditional, Government and Binding (GB) perspective on syntax and, more specifically, the condition A governing the binding of anaphors (Chomsky 1981):

(23) Condition A: An anaphor must have an antecedent within its own binding domain.

Given that the empty anaphoric subject in C BlkS complements (which can be called PRO to simplify the analysis[18]) is bound by the matrix subject, this means that the matrix and the embedded clauses must be part of the same binding

---

16 To be a bit more precise, the Phase Impenetrability Condition (PIC) states that in phase HP, the "domain of H is not accessible to operations outside HP; only H and its *edge* are accessible to such operations" (Chomsky 2001: 13). Nevertheless, the simplified version of PIC as presented in the text above is sufficient in the context of the present discussion on subject control, because the empty anaphoric subject is generally not seen as associated with CP-phase edges according to the more standard control analyses, and hence the obligatory control reading associated with a given clause may be seen as indicative of its non-phasal status.

17 When it comes to BlkS complements associated with optional control, such as those selected by desiderative predicates in (18), I argue in Sočanac (2017) that their control properties are not determined syntactically, but rather on a semantico-pragmatic basis, which is why the control reading in such cases is context-dependent. Given that PIC only applies to syntactic binding relationships, the control reading in such cases does not violate it, even if such complements maintain the embedded CP.

18 I should note that there is some disagreement in BlkS literature as to the exact formal properties of the embedded anaphoric subject in different Balkan languages. Some authors analyze the latter as PRO (e.g. Iatridou 1988; Krapova 1998). Others analyze it as obligatorily co-referential *pro* (e.g. Farkas 1985; Philippaki-Warburton 1987). Given that control per se is not my main concern here, I assume a more standard PRO analysis.

domain. This requirement is, once again, satisfied under the current analysis, because the embedded CP truncation with C subjunctives implies that the embedded clause is incorporated within the matrix CP domain. As a result, the embedded PRO subject can enter into a control relationship with the matrix subject within the same binding domain, which is in accordance with the condition A.

Finally, the syntactic analysis of C subjunctives in terms of CP-truncation can also account for the differences between NC and C subjunctives that we observed here earlier on, for instance the temporal contrasts that were noted in this context by Krapova (1998) or Landau (2004). Recall the examples in (15–16), where we observed that, unlike NC complements, C subjunctives cannot introduce embedded temporal markers that conflict with the matrix tense, which was seen as indicative of the fact that the two clauses in such cases constitute a single time frame. A similar analysis was also proposed in Varlokosta (1993), where it was claimed that C subjunctives involve semantic event unification between the matrix and the embedded clause. All these conclusions naturally follow from the CP-truncation analysis, which views the embedded clause as incorporated into the matrix CP domain, explaining why the two clauses are semantically interpreted as a single event with a single time frame.

A range of additional syntactic data is available in further support of the analysis just presented,[19] but discussing them is beyond the scope of the present paper. I turn instead to a consideration of some of the semantic implications of the syntactic account of BlkS I just developed. This further reinforces the present analysis, because the syntactic differences between various BlkS complements as analyzed under the current approach systematically correlate with the semantic differences that they exhibit as well, particularly with regard to the type of modal interpretation that a given complement is associated with.

3.3 Structural truncation at the syntax-semantics interface

At this point, I use the structural truncation analysis of Section 3.2 to account for some broader semantic distinctions that can be observed in the context of BlkS distribution. The most important semantic differences between various BlkS complements can be explained by claiming that different complements send

---

[19] There is a large series of data, most of which are more language-specific, which further reinforce the syntactic analysis of the C vs. NC subjunctive distinction via the CP-truncation account. One could mention, for instance, the contrasts between the two types of clauses in terms of pronoun vs anaphor binding, NPI-binding, negation scope, or the availability of complementizers and other CP-related items, among others (Sočanac 2017).

different types of structural outputs associated with the basic subjunctive CP clause structure (reproduced below) to the syntax-semantics interface, resulting in different interpretations.

(24) [CP $_{Dir>Mod}$ [ModP [TP [vP]]]]

In this context, I assume a strict syntax-semantics mapping perspective, which views each aspect of meaning (particularly as it pertains to mood and modality) as encoded through some type of feature that is passed on from the syntactic derivation to the semantic component.[20]

Recall that the first structural distinction observed in the context of (24) was related to NC complements: on the one hand, there were those that contained Dir and exhibited subject obviation (17) while on the other, there were those that stripped Dir and exhibited subject free reference (18). Here I focus on the semantic implications of this formal distinction. Even though all NC BlkS complements are associated with similar, intensional-type semantics and, as such, they are closer to the typical cross-linguistic meaning related to the subjunctive mood than most other BlkS complements, there is nonetheless a finer semantic difference that can be observed between these NC complements as well, which can be explained by reverting to the truncation analysis from the previous section.

The difference in question can be viewed in terms of semantic specificity: complements to directive verbs, which contain Dir, are more specified with regards to their meaning, and closer to simple imperatives in this sense, than is the case with other NC intensional subjunctives, which do not contain Dir. Given that they denote reported directive speech acts, complements such as those in (17) are the only ones that can be directly related to the prototypical function associated with the imperative mood in matrix contexts (i.e. directive illocutionary

---

20 This theoretical perspective is compatible with, and partly based on, the cartographic approach to syntax, defended by authors such as Rizzi (1997) or Cinque (1999), among many others. One of the basic ideas behind cartography is that the semantic interpretation of a given clause is determined by features that project their own functional projections in syntax. The theoretical consequence of this idea is the proliferation of atomic, functionally very specified XP projections within the syntactic structure. Thus, for instance, CP or ModP would not be analyzed as single XPs under this approach, but as more articulated syntactic layers consisting of several smaller atomic projections, each encoding a different aspect of meaning associated with a given clause. Even though a more detailed application of the cartographic approach to syntax in the context of BlkS is outside the scope of this paper, the semantic analysis of BlkS distribution proposed here (specifically the idea that various different BlkS complements can be analyzed in terms of semantic feature superset-subset relations, based on the size of their structure) is perfectly compatible with the theoretical assumptions behind cartography.

force – see fn. 11), which is why they are the only group of subjunctives that can be described as embedded imperatives. Other NC subjunctives, while still exhibiting the intensional world-anchoring that one observes with simple and embedded imperatives, also denote a broader spectrum of irrealis-type meanings (see [26], for instance).

The difference between the two types of NC complements in this context can be analyzed in terms of a semantic feature superset-subset relationship: complements corresponding to the CP structure in (26) can denote a broad range of intensional interpretations because they only contain the semantic Mod-feature that encodes this type of meaning (having stripped the higher Dir), whereas those corresponding to the CP structure in (25) can only denote a certain type of intensional meaning (i.e. directive), because they also contain the hierarchically superior Dir-feature, which further specifies their interpretation:

(25) [CP $_{Dir>Mod}$ [ModP [TP [vP]]]]

    a. *Marija$_i$ je naredila da ode $*_{i/j}$.* (Srb)
       Mary has ordered SUBJ leave-3SG
       'Mary ordered *(him/her) to leave.'

(26) [CP $_{\cancel{Dir}>Mod}$ [ModP [TP [vP]]]]

    a. *O Kostas$_i$ theli na odhiji$_{i/j}$.* (Grk)
       the Kostas wants SUBJ drive-3SG
       'Kostas wants (him/her) to drive.'
    b. *Ion$_i$ se așteaptă să vină$_{i/j}$ mâine.* (Rom)
       John expects SUBJ come-3SG tomorrow
       'John expects (him/her) to come tomorrow.'
    c. *Ivan$_i$ prihvaća da dođe$_{i/j}$ sutra.* (Srb)
       John accepts SUBJ come-3SG tomorrow
       'John accepts (for him/her) to come tomorrow.'

Nevertheless, once again, given that all NC complements in (25–26) still preserve the subjunctive CP upon reaching the interface with semantics, they all denote a range of meanings that is more typical of the subjunctive mood cross-linguistically.

On the other hand, when it comes to those BlkS complements that are claimed to truncate their CP, i.e., C subjunctives, they can denote a more diverse range of interpretations: some C subjunctives (specifically complements to deontic modals, such as the one in [9]) exhibit a similar type of irrealis modal meaning as the ones we observe with NC subjunctives; other C complements have a more realis interpretation but can still be associated with a type of modality (e.g., complements to dynamic modals, as in [10]); others yet cannot be associated with any modality (for instance, complements to implicative [11] or aspectual predicates [12]). The semantic diversity associated with C subjunctives can, once again, be explained in the light of the syntactic analysis given in Section 3.2 and its implications in the context of feature superset-subset relations and semantic specificity: given that complements such as those in (9–12) truncate the subjunctive CP, which means that they also remove the featural specifications contained within this CP, the syntactic output that they send to the syntax-semantic interface allows for a broader range of interpretations. This is why C subjunctives, on the whole, exhibit a much greater degree of semantic diversity than is the case with NC subjunctives. In what follows, I apply the syntactic truncation analysis in the context of C subjunctives in a bit more detail, in order to explain some semantic contrasts that can be observed between various C subjunctives themselves.

The most important semantic distinction that can be observed in the context of C subjunctives is the one between complements that denote some type of modality (e.g. 9–10) and those that are not associated with any modality (e.g. 11–12). This difference can also be explained in light of the basic subjunctive clause structure in (24) and the different degrees of truncation it may undergo. Even though a more detailed syntactic analysis that would demonstrate some more fine-grained differences in the left-periphery structure between complements such as those in (9–10) and those in (11–12) is outside the scope of this paper, the semantic distinction in terms of (non)modality that can be observed between them is best explained (especially in the light of the strict syntax-semantics mapping perspective I assume here) through the analysis that views ModP, i.e., the locus of clausal modality, as present in the former group of complements and absent in the latter, which is why the latter group of complements does not denote any modality in the semantic component.

Thus, if we look at BlkS distribution in terms of a structural continuum, then the group of complements that follow the more typical NC subjunctives are those selected by different types of modal verbs (a couple of which are reproduced below). These are the complements that truncate their CP but maintain their ModP, and thus correspond to the structure in (27). Once again, this explains why they still denote different types of modal meanings once they reach the interface with semantics.

(27) [CP ~~Dir>Mod~~ [ModP [TP [vP]]]]

    a. *Ivan trjabva da dojde.*   (Bulg)
       John must SUBJ come-3SG
       'John must come.'

b. *O Kostas bori na odhiji.* (Grk)
the Kostas can SUBJ drive-3SG
'Kostas can drive.'

C subjunctives such as the one in (27a) denote deontic modality, similar to the one we observe in NC subjunctives, whereas those such as the one in (27b) denote dynamic modality related to notions such as ability or capacity.²¹

The remaining BlkS C complements that we will be dealing with here, i.e. those selected by predicates such as aspectuals or implicatives, are not associated with any type of modality. Given the syntax-semantics mapping perspective adopted here, their lack of modal meaning is best explained through further structural truncation. Complements of this type should thus be seen as associated with the most truncated structure of all Balkan subjunctives, stripping not only the subjunctive CP but also ModP, as represented below²²:

(28) [CP~~Dir>Mod~~ [ModP~~ [TP [vP]]]]

a. *Ivan je uspeo da stigne na vreme.* (Srb)
John has managed SUBJ arrive-3SG on time
'John managed to arrive on time.'

b. *Ion începe să scrie.* (Rom)
John begins SUBJ write-3SG
'John begins to write.'

---

21 If one viewed BlkS distribution in terms of a hierarchical semantic scale of related meanings, which is the theoretical implication of the strict syntax-semantics mapping perspective I assume here, then the fact that complements to deontic modals such as the one in (27a) are semantically closer to intensional NC subjunctives than is the case with complements to dynamic modals (as in [27b]) should also be formally accounted for through feature superset-subset relations, either by postulating a hierarchical feature cluster within ModP as well, or by expanding ModP into a more articulated, hierarchical modality layer, similar to Cinque (1999, 2001) and thus in accordance with the cartographic approach to syntax (see fn. 20). I propose the latter type of analysis in Sočanac (2017).
22 At this point, I need to return to the issue of the syntactic realization of BlkS mood markers such as *na* or *să* in (28a-b) briefly addressed in Section 2.1. Even though most authors that analyzed such items as mood particles have viewed them as inserted under a Mod-type projection, my claim has been that they should be seen as inserted under the lower T-head (Sočanac 2012, Sočanac 2017). This analysis was primarily motivated by the data exemplified in (28) – i.e. the fact that these items can appear in complements that do not exhibit any modality. But there are also other reasons in favor of the T-insertion analysis of BlkS markers. For instance, several authors have noted the temporal properties associated with such elements (Giannakidou 2009; Sočanac 2011; Todorović 2012).

Complements such as those in (28a-b), which have always posed particular problems for the analysis of BlkS because they introduce subjunctive morphology even though they are associated with non-modalized, indicative-type meanings, can thus be straightforwardly accounted for in light of the current analysis: they strip the entire left periphery associated with the subjunctive CP clause structure, which is the clausal area where meaning related to mood and modality is encoded in the context of BlkS, and only maintain the lower part of the structure containing TP and vP, which is not essentially different from the same part of structure we observe in indicatives (at least not when it comes to semantically mapping the types of meaning that are most relevant to mood distinctions). Thus, the atypical, realis meaning that such complements exhibit should be seen as merely an additional manifestation of their syntactic anaphoricity.

4 Conclusion

This paper has dealt with the issue of subjunctive distribution in the languages of the Balkan Sprachbund, which exhibit some specific patterns in this context because a number of them have replaced their infinitives with subjunctives (to a greater or lesser degree). As a result, BlkS is more widely distributed than most of its cross-linguistic counterparts, which also means that it is more semantically diverse, thus further compounding the theoretical difficulties related to reaching any type of cross-linguistic semantic definition of the subjunctive mood as such. Nevertheless, the analysis put forward here, looking at BlkS from the syntax-semantics interface prism, has been able to subsume BlkS complements associated with very diverse formal and semantic properties under the same clause-type analysis. The contrasts that were observed between these complements – both syntactic contrasts in terms of anaphoricity and semantic contrasts in terms of specificity – are all explained through the mechanism of structural truncation, whereby different complements end up sending varying chunks of the basic subjunctive CP clause structure to the interface with semantics.

References

Bouchard, Denis. 1984. *On the content of empty categories*. Dordrecht: Foris.
Chomsky, Noam. 1981. *Lecture on government and binding*. Dordrecht: Foris.
Chomsky, Noam. 1995. *The minimalist program*. Cambridge: MIT Press.

Chomsky, Noam. 2001. Derivation by phase. In Michael Kenstowicz (ed.), *Ken Hale: A life in language*, 1–52. Cambridge, MA: MIT Press.
Cinque, Guglielmo. 1999. *Adverbs and functional heads: A cross-linguistic perspective*. Oxford: Oxford University Press.
Cinque, Guglielmo. 2001. Restructuring and the order of root modal heads. In Guglielmo Cinque & Giampaolo Salvi (eds.), *Current studies in Italian syntax: Essays offered to Lorenzo Renzi*, 137–155. Amsterdam: Elsevier.
Dobrovie-Sorin, Carmen. 1994. *The syntax of Romanian*. Berlin: Mouton de Gruyter.
Farkas, Donka. 1985. Obligatorily controlled subjects in Romanian. *Papers from the 21st annual meeting of the Chicago Linguistic Society*, 90–100. University of Chicago.
Farkas, Donka. 1992. On the semantics of subjunctive complements. In Paul Hirschbühler & Konrad Koerner (eds.), *Romance languages and the modern linguistic theory*, 69–104. Amsterdam: John Benjamins.
Giannakidou, Anastasia. 1998. *Polarity sensitivity as (non)veridical dependency*. Amsterdam: John Benjamins.
Giannakidou, Anastasia. 2009. The dependency of the subjunctive revisited: Temporal semantics and polarity. *Lingua* 119. 1883–1908.
Han, Chung-Hye. 1998. *The structure and interpretation of imperatives: Mood and force in universal grammar*. Philadelphia: University of Pennsylvania PhD dissertation.
Hopper, Joan B. 1975. On assertive predicates. In John P. Kimball (ed.), *Syntax and semantics*, 91–124. London: Academic Press.
Huntley, Martin. 1984. The semantics of English imperatives. *Linguistics and philosophy* 7. 103–134.
Iatridou, Sabine. 1988. On nominative case assignment and a few related things. Ms. MIT.
Jary, Mark & Kissine, Mikhail. 2014. *Imperatives*. Cambridge: Cambridge University Press.
Joseph, Brian D. 1983. *The synchrony and diachrony of the Balkan infinitive: A study in areal, general and historical linguistics*. Cambridge: Cambridge University Press.
Kempchinsky, Paula. 1986. *Romance subjunctive clauses and Logical Form*. Los Angeles: UCLA dissertation.
Kempchinsky, Paula. 1998. Mood phrase, case checking and obviation. *Selected papers from the 27th Linguistic symposium on Romance languages*, 143–154. Amsterdam: John Benjamins.
Kempchinsky, Paula. 2009. What can the subjunctive disjoint reference effect tell us about the subjunctive?. *Lingua* 119. 1788–1810.
Krapova, Iliyana. 1998. Subjunctive complements, null subjects and case checking in Bulgarian. *University of Venice working papers in linguistics*. 8(2). 73–93.
Krapova, Iliyana. 2002. On the left periphery of the Bulgarian sentence. *University of Venice working papers in linguistics*. 12. 107–128.
Krapova, Iliyana and Guglielmo Cinque. This volume. Universal constraints on Balkanisms. A Case study: the absence of Clitic Climbing.
Landau, Idan. 2004. The scale of finiteness and the calculus of control. *Natural language and linguistic theory* 22. 811–877.
Mišeska Tomić, Olga. 2006. *Balkan Sprachbund: Morphosyntactic Features*. Dordrecht: Springer.
Philippaki-Warburton, Irene. 1987. The theory of empty categories and the pro-drop parameter in Modern Greek. *Journal of linguistics* 23. 289–318.
Picallo, Carmen. 1985. *Opaque domains*. New York: CUNY PhD dissertation.

Portner, Paul. 1997. The semantics of mood, complementation and conversational force. *Natural language semantics* 5(2). 167–212.
Raposo, Eduardo. 1985. Some asymmetries in the binding theory of Romance. *The linguistic review* 5. 75–110.
Rivero, Maria-Luisa. 1994. Clause structure and V-movement in the languages of the Balkans. *Natural language and linguistic theory* 12. 63–120.
Rizzi, Luigi. 1997. The fine structure of the left periphery. In Liliane Haegeman (ed.), *Elements of grammar*, 281–337. Berkeley: Kluwer.
Roussou, Anna. 2000. On the left periphery: Modal particles and complementizers. *Journal of Greek linguistics* 1. 65–94.
Roussou, Anna. 2009. In the mood for control. *Lingua* 119. 1811–1836.
Schlenker, Philippe. 2005. The lazy Frenchman's approach to the subjunctive (Speculations on reference to worlds, presuppositions, and semantic defaults in the analysis of mood). In Twan Geerts, Ivo van Ginneken & Haike Jakobs (eds.), *Romance languages and linguistics theory 2003: Selected papers from "Going Romance"*, 269–310. Amsterdam: John Benjamins.
Sočanac, Tomislav. 2011. Subjunctive in Serbian/Croatian. *Generative grammar in Geneva* 7. 49–71.
Sočanac, Tomislav. 2012. Subjunctive complements in Serbian/Croatian: Distributional issues. *Generative grammar in Geneva* 8. 1–23.
Sočanac, Tomislav. 2017. *Subjunctive complements in Slavic languages: A syntax-semantics interface approach*. Geneva: University of Geneva dissertation.
Terzi, Arhonto. 1992. *PRO in finite clauses: A study of the inflectional heads of the Balkan languages*. New York: CUNY PhD dissertation.
Todorović, Nataša. 2012. *The subjunctive and indicative da-complements in Serbian: A syntactic-semantic approach*. Chicago: University of Illinois PhD dissertation.
Varlokosta, Spyridoula. 1993. Control complements in Modern Greek. *University of Maryland working papers in linguistics* 1. 144–163.
Watanabe, Akira. 1993. *AGR-based theory of grammar*. Cambridge: MIT PhD dissertation.

Language Index

Akan 219
Albanian
– Arbëresh 178
– Gheg 177, 258
– Southern Albanian 21, 178
– Tosk 177
Armenian 22
Aromanian
– Ohrid 75
– South Aromanian 60
– Turia 60
Austronesian 219, 236

Balkan Romance 6, 7, 19, 50, 71, 76–79, 102, 114, 139, 176, 177
Balkan Romani 19, 37–47
Balkan Slavic 6, 19, 43, 50, 53, 54, 64, 71, 76, 78, 79, 80, 137, 139, 142, 152, 181, 192, 230, 249–275. See also BlkS
Balto-Slavic 16
Bantu 208, 234
BCMS 320
BCS 152, 168, 179, 184. See also BCMS; Bosnian-Croatian-Serbian; Montenegrin
Belorussian, 257
BlkS 317–334. See also Balkan Slavic
Bosnian 45, 92, 152, 320
Bosnian-Croatian-Serbian 37, 152
Bulgarian
– Early Modern Bulgarian 171
– Gabrovo 173
– Gela 184
– Gora 30
– Middle Bulgarian 170, 172, 174
– Moesian 173
– Pirdop 173
– Rhodope 180, 184
– Sliven 42, 47
Buru 219

Catalan 151, 194
Church Slavonic 79, 82, 250, 257
Croatian. See also BCS; BCMS; Serbo-Croatian

– Čakavian 89, 90, 94
– Kajkavian 93
Czech 96, 152, 227, 230, 232, 239–242, 255

Dacoromanian 50
D(r)ehu 239
Dutch 20, 222, 235, 236

East South Slavic 99
English
– Irish English 87

Finno-Ugric 16, 220
French 18, 19, 82, 110, 113, 157, 219, 279, 290, 316, 326

Georgian 20
German 18, 203, 233, 302
Germanic 16, 22, 207, 219, 220, 222, 223, 230, 232, 233, 236, 241, 243, 257
Grecanico 175, 186
Greek
– Biblical Greek 250, 257
– Medieval Greek 168, 174, 175, 181
– Modern Greek 115, 157, 159–162, 165, 174, 175, 219, 224, 225, 226, 230, 285
– New Testament Greek 171, 195, 250
– Northern Greek 21, 30, 50, 52
– Southern Italy Greek 186
Griko 175

Hopi 14
Hungarian 194, 208–211, 214

Illyrian 13, 52
Indic 6, 7
Indo-European 6–7, 14, 15, 22, 23, 51, 77, 177
Iranian 22–23
Istroromanian 50
Italian 151, 153, 155–157, 166, 181, 182, 183, 219, 238, 308
Italo-Albanian 258. See also Albanian, Arbëresh
Italo-Greek 258. See also Grecanico; Griko

Kazakh 46
Kirghiz 46
Klallam 236, 241
Koromfe 237, 241
Koyra Chiini 239

Lakota 239
Lithuanian 23, 128

Macedonian
– Ohrid 75, 77
Mandarin 219
Meglenoromanian 50
Montenegrin 37, 320

Niger-Congo 219, 237

Ostyak 194, 211

Pama-Nyungan 107
Persian 105, 113
Polish 152, 226, 227, 230, 232, 239, 241, 242, 255
Portuguese 151

Romance
– Bova 186
Romani
– Arli 3, 40–42, 47
– Barutči 40, 42, 47
– Finnish Romani 75
– Kriva Palanka 40, 41, 46, 47
– Sliven 42–43, 46, 47
Romanian
– Muntenia-Oltenia 30, 31
Russian 1, 227, 228, 230, 239–243, 257, 326

Salentino 181, 184
Salish 236

Serbian. *See also* BCS; BCMS; Serbo-Croatian
– Kamenitsa 180
– Old Serbian 179
Serbo-Croatian. *See also* BCS; BCMS; Serbian
– South-Eastern 178
– Štokavian 92
– Torlak 178
Shona 208
Slavic
– East Slavic 223
– South Slavic 53, 107, 120, 250, 257, 260
– West Slavic 223
Slovene 93, 94, 96
Slovenian 152
Spanish 80, 107, 144, 151, 152, 195, 196, 197, 302, 326

Tahitian 236, 241
Tajik 23
Tatar 37, 46
Thracian 13, 52
Turkic 7, 37, 38, 46, 47, 51
Turkish
– Cypriot Turkish 186

Ukrainian 257
Uzbek 46

Venetian 89, 90, 94
Vulgar Latin 195, 207

Wallachian 79, 102, 170
Warumungu 107
Welsh 105, 109, 126, 144, 239

Yiddish 223
Yucatec Mayan 239

Subject Index

Accent 41, 197, 205
Adjective 19, 25, 40, 55, 60, 61, 73, 145, 161, 233
Admirative 39, 43–47. *See also* Mirative
Adverb 25, 29, 117, 225, 229
Adverbial 24, 25, 29, 57, 58, 172, 205, 283, 284
Affix 17, 50, 74, 104–107, 110, 114, 115, 120, 126, 128, 132, 134, 137, 145, 158, 205, 282–284
Agent 58, 89, 135, 253, 260
Agglutination 21, 24
Analytic 3, 20, 21–22, 27, 50, 58, 70–82, 100, 144, 174, 250
Analytism 3, 6, 54, 74–78, 80
Anaphoric 156, 171, 210, 321, 324, 328
Animacy 64, 196–198, 206, 211, 213
Antecedent 159, 165, 167, 168, 210, 287, 305, 328
Anti-Balkanism 3, 49, 63
Aorist 24, 25, 40, 42, 55, 58, 61, 132
Areal typology 14, 19, 49–65
Argument structure 76, 77, 88, 99, 117, 158, 192, 211, 302
Article
 – definite 23, 24–27, 37, 72, 208, 233, 236–238, 241, 243
 – indefinite 18, 57–59
Aspect
 – imperfective 25
 – perfective 24
Auxiliary 21, 40, 41, 75, 77, 104, 105, 108, 109, 112, 113, 120, 122, 123, 125–127, 129, 131, 133–137, 139, 152, 156, 170–174, 178, 179, 227

Balkanism 1, 2, 3, 14, 15, 19, 20–24, 27, 34, 42, 50–52, 54, 63, 71–74, 77, 79–82, 123, 151–186, 250–252
Balkanization
 – degrees of 19
Balkan Linguistic Union (BLU) 14, 15, 18–20, 23, 24, 25, 27, 30, 64
Biclausal (Bi-clausal) 4, 154, 157, 158, 159, 164–167, 169, 179
Bilingualism 29–34, 56, 63, 76–79, 81, 82

Borrowability 3, 49, 63–64
Borrowing 1, 3, 6, 50–52, 60–63, 74–76, 80, 102, 138, 140–143, 320

Calque 1, 60, 62, 63, 74, 96
Cartographic 51, 219, 221, 330, 333
Case 1, 3, 4, 7, 30, 39, 40–47, 50, 51, 54, 56, 57, 59, 60, 62, 71, 73, 76–78, 81, 88, 89, 91, 92, 96, 109, 113, 117, 128, 138, 140, 141, 145, 151–186, 193, 196–202, 204, 206, 211–214, 218, 221, 266, 287–308, 310, 325, 330, 332
Case Theory 96, 196
Category 29, 33, 52, 55, 57, 64, 73, 76, 78, 107, 109, 170, 196, 198, 206, 213, 233, 268, 274, 281, 282, 321
Change 6, 34, 38, 50, 51, 53, 64, 71, 73–75, 119, 151, 172, 174, 193, 207, 208, 229, 260, 262, 274, 275
Clause union 154, 324. *See also* Restructuring
Clitic
 – climbing 170–176, 177–179, 180–182
 – doubling 5, 72, 73, 77, 78, 144, 192–214 (*see also* Object doubling; Object reduplication)
Communicative 38, 39, 54, 72, 255
Comparative 3, 5, 7, 15, 19, 20, 23, 57, 60, 65, 96, 193, 284, 290, 311
Complementizer 5, 6, 44, 77, 121, 122, 162, 163, 166, 172, 175, 180, 183, 184, 219–229, 240, 243, 282–285, 287, 288, 310, 329
Complexification 3, 70, 71–73, 76, 82
Conditional 20–21, 46, 122, 135, 225, 250, 281, 282, 286, 289, 290, 307, 308, 310
Confirmativity 39, 40
Constituent 21, 55, 106, 108, 136, 159, 175, 233, 234, 238, 283
Construction 1, 4, 5, 16, 19, 23, 26, 27, 29, 32, 50, 51, 56, 57, 59, 62, 74, 75, 88–90, 94, 96, 97, 103, 105, 106, 109–116, 118, 121, 122, 126–128, 132–134, 136–138, 143, 144, 151–154, 156, 157, 158, 163, 164, 166, 167, 169–174, 176, 179, 180, 193, 206, 208, 226, 239, 249–275, 281, 291, 294, 302, 310

https://doi.org/10.1515/9783110375930-015

Contact 1–4, 7, 8, 13–82, 87–97, 100–102, 122, 134, 137–143, 185, 193, 195, 207, 249, 250, 252, 257, 260, 261, 265, 274, 309
Contact linguistics 1–3, 38, 60, 77
Containment 218–243
Control 4, 157–162, 164–169, 193, 287, 316, 320, 323–329
Converb 46, 57
Convergence 15, 19, 23–29, 34, 51, 63, 71, 74, 76–78, 100, 101, 138, 140, 142, 192, 207, 278
Creolization 23, 72, 250, 251

D-hierarchy 5, 192, 194, 197, 198, 201, 206, 211, 213, 214
Dative 16, 20, 23, 26, 37, 62, 76, 77, 110, 125, 129, 154, 171, 196, 199–201, 205–207, 211, 213, 218
Declarative 3, 27, 42, 45, 220, 223, 225, 228, 252, 255, 288, 289, 296, 305, 322, 323
Definiteness 24, 53, 55, 64, 197, 198, 204, 206, 209, 213, 236, 242
Degree of comparison 20–22
Deictic tense 156, 158
Deletion 116, 119, 183, 184
Demonstrative 5, 62, 208, 218–220, 222, 227, 228, 229, 232–243
Determiner 108, 109, 201, 208, 210
Dialect 30, 33, 40, 42, 44, 47, 50, 52, 55, 60, 61, 63, 89, 90, 92, 93, 94, 122, 180, 181, 184, 185, 186, 261
Differential object marking (DOM) 5, 194, 197, 199, 201, 213
Divergence 33
DP 109, 163, 196, 197, 202, 205, 209, 213, 241–243
Dubitative 27, 28, 39–42, 45–47, 291, 297

Emphatic 44, 45, 47, 124, 132, 133, 163, 295, 308
Enclitic 62, 71, 73, 108, 123, 125, 127, 129, 172
Epistemic 154, 155, 224, 253, 255, 256, 260, 262, 263, 265, 267, 268, 269, 272, 274, 289, 291, 292, 297, 299, 306, 310, 311
Eurolinguistics 13–14, 15, 19

European Linguistic Union 2, 14
Europeanism 2, 14, 15, 19, 20–23
Evidential
– confirmative 40
– non-confirmative 39
Exponence 107, 109, 110, 112, 127

Factivity 203, 223
Finiteness 128, 157, 162
Functional 2–5, 23–29, 62, 63, 77, 105, 108, 109, 110, 126, 134, 142, 152, 154–159, 162, 163, 171, 173, 179, 180, 185, 198, 211, 219, 221, 222, 231, 233, 243, 251, 253–256, 258, 260, 262, 263, 265, 274, 275, 330
Future 20, 21, 23, 51, 64, 111, 112, 113, 141, 185, 250, 252, 257, 260, 262

Gender 33, 34, 41, 55, 60, 110, 145, 201
Generic 90, 207, 298, 299
Geographic 51, 53, 138, 279
Geography 8, 51, 52, 57, 76, 140
Gerund 57, 58
Grammaticalization 1, 5, 21, 74, 138, 142, 198, 204, 207, 251, 257, 258, 266, 274, 275

Hierarchy 2, 3, 5, 14, 23, 34, 65, 154, 155, 162, 179, 180, 192, 194, 197, 198, 201, 206, 211, 213, 214, 221, 222

Illocutionary 44–46, 252, 253, 274, 288, 294, 302, 308, 330
Imperative 27, 29, 50, 117, 118, 123, 125, 173, 282, 288–291, 307, 308, 322, 323, 326, 330
Imperfect (tense) 21, 25, 28, 37, 40, 42, 43, 61, 132
Impersonal 4, 87–97, 135, 145, 262, 264
Indicative 27, 41, 104, 118, 137, 166, 174, 184, 279–283, 286–289, 292, 296, 306, 307, 310, 316, 318–323, 328, 329, 334
Infinitive 4, 15, 20–24, 27–28, 55, 72, 73, 77, 141, 142, 152, 157, 158, 162, 164, 167–180, 185, 186, 250, 257–259, 263, 264, 286, 287, 289, 290, 307–310, 320, 326

Inflection 53, 71, 77, 105–107, 113, 134, 239, 279–281
Information structure 211
Intensional 298, 316, 319, 321–327, 330, 331, 333
Interface 1, 5, 6, 102, 103, 107, 114, 133, 317, 321, 324, 329–334
Interrogative 3, 6, 32–33, 37, 42–47, 62, 130, 182, 185, 219, 220, 222, 225, 226, 229, 279, 287–311
Intertranslatability 3, 77, 78, 82
Intransitive 37, 88, 89, 117, 265, 267
Inverse Agreement Constraint 210, 211, 214
Irrealis 20–21, 135, 154, 164, 171, 226, 227, 316, 320, 325, 331
Isomorph 57, 60, 102, 250, 262
Isosemantism 76, 77

Kayne's Generalization 193, 194, 196, 198, 199, 202

L1 6, 78–81
L2 6, 78–81
Language contact 1, 2, 3, 4, 8, 15, 30, 53, 64, 73, 87–88, 96, 97, 101, 102, 138, 141, 142, 249, 274, 309
Language shift 52, 53, 63, 79, 80, 82
Lexeme 29, 50, 60, 61, 63, 102, 103, 106, 110, 132, 300
Linguistic geography 51, 57, 76

Merger 20, 23, 30–32, 73, 141, 271
Mirative 39, 154, 303. *See also* Admirative
Modal
– verb 174–176, 253, 262, 266, 267, 274, 291–293
– particle 37, 152, 157, 182–184
Monoclausal 4, 154, 156, 157, 158, 160, 169
Mood 5, 23, 28, 132, 154, 162, 224, 225, 250, 279–284, 286, 287–290, 292, 293, 295, 297, 299, 306–311, 315, 318–323, 330, 331, 333, 334
Morphologization 4, 21, 101–103, 120, 121, 127, 128, 132, 134, 137, 138, 142, 143, 146
Morphology 2, 4, 5, 27, 34, 74, 87, 99–146, 158, 162, 180, 181, 186, 233, 320, 323, 334

Morpho-syntax 1, 2, 6, 193, 278, 279
Multilingualism 3, 8, 80, 82, 122, 140

Nanosyntactic 219, 220, 232, 233, 243
Nanosyntax 5, 219, 221, 243
Negation 16, 18, 19, 54, 116, 118, 122, 124, 135, 173, 203, 258, 260, 295, 299, 305, 329. *See also* Negator; Negative
Negative 16, 18, 19, 37, 46, 57, 61, 62, 96, 118, 122, 128, 129, 130, 173, 185, 258, 262, 299, 300, 301, 302, 304, 305. *See also* Negator; Negation
Negator 115, 124, 129, 130, 135. *See also* Negation; Negative
Noun 29, 46, 53, 57, 58, 62, 71, 103, 108, 113, 143, 145, 201, 208, 221, 222, 233, 234, 243, 257
Noun phrase 33, 62, 109, 196, 285
NP 108, 109, 233, 241, 242

Object doubling 143–146, 212. *See also* Clitic, doubling; Object reduplication
Object reduplication 144, 252. *See also* Clitic, doubling; Object doubling
Optative 27, 28, 37, 46, 308

Paradigm 27, 73, 74, 102, 103, 104, 110–114, 126, 127, 132–134, 137, 202, 208, 220, 231, 237, 279–281, 309
Paradigm Function Morphology 102, 110, 126, 133
Parallel 20, 21, 24, 37–47, 101, 119, 120, 127, 131, 138, 140, 142, 177, 185, 207, 257
Parameter 4, 87, 88, 94, 97, 241
Parameter theory 4, 87–88, 91
Participle 24, 37, 40, 43, 47, 54, 55, 58, 59, 61, 75, 77, 110, 125, 133, 177, 178, 250, 280
Particle 3, 4, 21, 32, 37, 42, 44, 45, 47, 55, 62, 77, 105, 123, 125, 127, 130, 135, 152, 157, 162, 169, 170, 178, 181–184, 224, 226, 250, 258, 261, 262, 279, 281–284, 300, 301, 305, 306, 310
Passive 16, 40, 55, 64, 88, 90, 92, 93, 96, 110, 111, 135
Past tense 15, 20, 21, 75, 77, 112

PCC 5, 194, 205, 206, 211–214. *See also* Person Case Constraint
Perfect
– 'be'-perfect 18
– 'have'-perfect 16, 18
Performativity 252, 255
Periphrases 21, 111–113, 133, 134. *See also* Periphrasis; Periphrastic
Periphrasis 103, 107, 110–114, 134, 156, 171, 174, 175. *See also* Periphrases; Periphrastic
Periphrastic 74–77, 92, 110–114, 127, 133, 134, 138, 153, 156, 171, 174, 177, 178, 257, 259, 260. *See also* Periphrases; Periphrasis
Person Case Constraint 5, 194. *See also* PCC
Phonology 50, 117–119, 138, 293
Pivot 19, 89, 90, 92, 93, 94, 96
Pluperfect 28, 42, 75, 123, 132
Possession 26, 62, 250
Possessor 16, 26, 62, 73, 76
Pragmatization 275
Pro-Drop 2, 87, 200
Predicate 91, 92, 154, 156, 157, 161, 165, 176, 178, 183, 227, 287, 302, 303, 320, 323, 325
Prefix 55, 128, 135, 232–234, 238, 243
Preposition 24, 30, 31, 57, 61, 62, 77, 144, 177, 196, 197, 308
Prestige 40, 45, 79, 80, 81, 82, 250
Proclitic 114, 123, 124, 129, 172, 250
Prominence 5, 197, 205
Pronoun 19, 50, 61, 62, 88, 92, 104, 109, 115, 116, 117, 118, 120, 138, 144, 146, 163, 171, 172, 177, 197, 209, 212, 219, 222–227, 229, 283, 302, 329
Prosodic 54, 109, 116, 123–125, 127, 129, 130, 131, 133, 134, 136, 137, 172, 222, 287, 302

Raising 4, 97, 154, 158–164, 179, 302
Reduction 4, 73, 139, 157
Redundancy 54–56, 62, 72, 73
Reduplication 144, 252. *See also* Repetition
Reflexive 14, 17, 88, 89, 90, 91, 94, 96, 97, 110, 128, 135, 171, 206, 208–210
Repetition 29, 63, 283. *See also* Reduplication

Restructuring 4, 33, 34, 151, 152, 154, 156, 157, 158–166, 168, 169, 171–173, 175–180, 182, 249. *See also* Clause union

Semantics 1, 5, 6, 21, 24, 29, 117, 118, 158, 164, 207, 258, 259, 321, 324, 329–334
Simplification 3, 15, 23, 30, 71–73, 81, 82, 250
Sociolinguistics 3, 14, 23, 38, 70–73, 78, 80–82
Specificity 5, 82, 113, 197, 280, 330, 332, 334
Speech act 252, 255–257, 260–262, 267, 274, 275, 308, 330
Sprachbund 1–6, 8, 14, 18, 51, 53, 57, 64, 65, 71, 79, 80, 82, 94, 97, 100–102, 134, 137–143, 151, 152, 157, 168, 193, 196–198, 206–211, 249–275, 278–311, 315–334
Standard 58, 65, 79, 92, 121, 122, 141, 226, 272, 322, 328
Standard Average European 14, 16, 18, 20
Stress 124, 129–131, 134, 269, 302
Subject 14, 15, 50, 57–60, 72, 73, 88, 89, 92, 105, 108, 131, 136, 138, 158, 159, 161, 164–168, 180, 183, 184, 195, 196, 198, 203, 208, 211, 227, 249, 255, 258, 265, 272, 287, 320, 321, 326–330
Subjectivity 252, 270, 271, 273–275
Subjunctive 4, 5, 6, 22, 27, 28, 41, 114, 118–120, 122, 129, 141, 157–169, 184, 225, 227, 250, 252, 253, 258, 260, 273, 278–311, 315–334
Subordinate 27, 65, 87, 133, 136, 156, 287, 323
Subordinator 119, 180, 183
Substratum 15, 54, 87
Suffix 128, 227, 236, 238, 308
Suppletion 22, 55
Surface 3, 25, 100, 101–104, 121, 122, 129, 131, 135, 140, 141, 146, 156
Surface structure 140, 141
Syncretism 5, 19, 200, 201, 202, 218–243
Syntax
– convergent 49, 193
Synthesis 64, 103, 106, 113, 118, 120, 134, 137, 140, 142, 143, 145

Taxis 56–60
Tense. *See* Aorist; Deictic tense; Future; Past; Perfect
Theta Theory 96
Topic 5, 44, 101, 194, 197, 198, 202, 204, 205, 206, 207, 211, 213, 225, 250
Topicality 5, 146, 197
Transfer 1, 4, 6, 29, 32, 72, 80, 96, 97, 140
Transparency 76, 154, 251, 261
Typological 3, 5, 7, 13–34, 37, 38, 46, 47, 56, 57, 59, 60, 65, 73, 119, 144, 192–214, 251, 253, 274, 275, 290
Typology 1–3, 5, 6, 14, 15, 19, 38, 49–65, 72, 295, 311

Unaccusative 88, 90–94, 96
Unergative 89, 90

Universal Grammar 1, 4, 5, 91, 151, 182, 185, 198, 213, 214
Universals 1, 2, 6–8, 22, 87, 90, 198, 207, 208

Verb 21, 42, 43, 45–47, 50, 57, 59, 64, 71–73, 75–77, 88–90, 99, 108, 110, 112, 113, 115–121, 123–138, 141, 142, 144, 145, 152, 153, 155–162, 164, 165, 167, 172, 174, 176, 179–181, 203, 210, 219, 224, 228, 250, 253, 257, 259, 262, 263, 265–267, 269, 272, 274, 279, 280, 281, 283–286, 291–294, 305, 310, 316, 318
Verbal complex 4, 99–146, 154, 168, 284
VP 108, 122, 130, 162, 202, 334

WH-phrase 182, 301
WH-word 101, 172, 224, 305
Word order 2, 33–34, 59, 61, 73, 100, 121, 172

www.ingramcontent.com/pod-product-compliance
Lightning Source LLC
Chambersburg PA
CBHW031754220426

43662CB00007B/403

Narratologia

Contributions to Narrative Theory

Edited by
Fotis Jannidis, Matías Martínez, John Pier,
Wolf Schmid (executive editor)

Editorial Board
Catherine Emmott, Monika Fludernik, José Ángel García Landa, Inke Gunia,
Peter Hühn, Manfred Jahn, Markus Kuhn, Uri Margolin, Jan Christoph Meister,
Ansgar Nünning, Marie-Laure Ryan, Jean-Marie Schaeffer, Michael Scheffel,
Sabine Schlickers

Band 64